International Health Care Reform

Concerns about the quality and costs of health care are ubiquitous in developed countries. A key challenge in the twenty-first century will be how to efficiently ensure justice in the distribution of health care resources. Since the 1980s reform has focused on harnessing competition to more efficiently achieve social justice ends.

International Health Care Reform analyzes the new wave of health care reform, comparing internal market reform and managed competition reform and looking at what role managed care plays in each of these. These models are examined in the context of their implementation in the UK, New Zealand, the US and the Netherlands. The ability of these new reform models to ensure the accountability of decision-makers is compared, as is their flexibility to allow the most efficient supply-side configuration, their response to the problem of monopoly on the supply side, and their response to the problems of monitoring and measuring quality.

For those new to the area of health policy and health care reform, this book clearly explains: the arguments in economics and justice for government intervention; the structure and dynamics of health care systems; and the new competition-oriented reform models. For more advanced scholars, this book brings a unique and fresh perspective, drawing on the disciplines of law, economics and political science, to tackle intractable issues in the design of a health care system. This book will assist all those concerned with how best to strike a balance between individual needs and societal interests and more generally between equity and efficiency in a health care system.

International Health Care Reform provides an interdisciplinary perspective on the latest trends in health reform and will be welcomed by students and researchers of health economics, health law and health and social policy.

Colleen M. Flood is Assistant Professor, Faculty of Law, University of Toronto, Canada. She was previously Associate Director of the Health Law Institute, Dalhousie University.

Routledge Studies in the Modern World Economy

International Health Care Reform

A legal, economic and political analysis

Colleen M. Flood

London and New York

First published 2000
by Routledge
11 New Fetter Lane, London EC4P 4EE

Simultaneously published in the USA and Canada
by Routledge
29 West 35th Street, New York, NY 10001

Routledge is an imprint of the Taylor & Francis Group

Typeset in Baskerville by
HWA Text and Data Management, Tunbridge Wells
Printed and bound in Great Britain by
TJ International Ltd, Padstow, Cornwall

British Library Cataloguing in Publication Data
A catalogue record for this book is available from the British Library

Library of Congress Cataloging in Publication Data
A catalog record for this book has been requested

ISBN 0-415-20844-0

Contents

Figures

Tables

Abbreviations

ACC	Accident Compensation Corporation
AIDS	acquired immune deficiency syndrome
BMA	British Medical Association
CHEs	Crown Health Enterprises
CON	Certificate of Need
DRGs	Diagnosis Related Groups
ENT	ear, nose and throat
ERISA	Employee Retirement Income and Security Act
ESRD	End Stage Renal Disease
GDP	gross domestic product
GP	general practitioner
HIPAA	Health Insurance Portability and Accountability Act
HIV	human immunodeficiency virus
HMOs	Health Maintenance Organizations
IHC	Intellectual Handicapped Society
IPAs	Independent Practice Associations
NHS	National Health Service
OECD	Organization for Economic Co-operation and Development
PCGs	Primary Care Groups
POS	Point of Service
PPOs	Preferred Provider Organizations
PPS	Prospective Payment System
QALYs	quality adjusted life years
RAWP	Resource Allocation Working Party
RHAs	Regional Health Authorities

Acknowledgements

Thanks must go to many people but first and foremost to Michael Trebilcock, Faculty of Law, University of Toronto. He has been unflagging in his encouragement of me, both in this work, and in all my academic and professional efforts. His intellect, his visionary scholarship, and his kindness have enriched my life.

Thanks also to Andreja Zivkovic and Alison Kirk at Routledge and John Hodgson at HWA Text and Data Management for their work in getting this manuscript into final shape.

Thank you to the many people who helped me obtain information regarding the systems under study or who discussed issues with me, particularly John Luhrs, Toni Ashton, Erik Schut, Lynn McKenzie, and Pauline Allen. Thanks also to Peter Coyte, Bernard Dickens, Hudson Janisch, Julia Hall, and Margo Hall, all at the University of Toronto, for the help they gave me with different aspects of this project. Many thanks also to the organizations that provided funding for my studies, particularly the Faculty of Law and the School of Graduate Studies in the University of Toronto, the John F. Olin Fund, Massey College, the New Zealand Federation of University Women, and the Spencer Mason Trust.

Thank you to my former colleagues at the Faculty of Law and in the Health Law Institute, Dalhousie University for their encouragement, particularly Jocelyn Downie, Fiona Bergin, and Barbara Carter. Thank you also to Brad Abernethy for proofreading some chapters and to my wonderful research assistants, James MacDonald and Martina Munden, for checking citations, formatting, and proofreading.

Thank you to my friends Nicole and Cathie and to all my loyal New Zealand friends – Helen, Sue, Ibby, Jim, and Johnny – for all their support. To the magnificent and unsurpassable Rebecca – thank you for all the letters, presents, recipes, and all your magical optimism. To my family in New Zealand, especially Wayne, Kath, Camea, Diane, Ronnie, Sharon, Murray, Chloe, and Joan, all of whom I miss so very much; thank you for your encouragement.

And finally, thank you to my dear friend and partner, Andreas Warburton. His Swiss efficiency has been great for helping with proofreading, his British sense of humor has helped make writing fun, and his Canadian generosity and tolerance have helped me through to finishing this book.

1 Introduction

Why reform?

Since the middle of the 1980s, health care reform has been one of the top policy initiatives of most Western industrialized states. A new wave of reform has emerged that focuses on harnessing competition to more efficiently achieve social justice ends. This book analyzes this wave of health care reform and compares two types of competition-oriented reform models – internal market reform and managed competition reform. These models are looked at in the context of their implementation in the UK, New Zealand, the US, and the Netherlands. This book tries to determine which reform model best solves the complex optimization problem of how to strike a balance between individual needs and societal interests and more generally between equity and efficiency.

Managed competition reform and internal market reform models represent an important change from the traditional approach to health care reform. This traditional approach focuses on reducing the resources available to a health care system (e.g. the hospital beds, nursing services, technology, etc.). This traditional approach assumes that physicians, when faced with restricted resources, will allocate resources optimally amongst various medical needs. By contrast, the new reform models require purchasers – government-appointed authorities, private insurers, or risk-bearing groups of health providers – to proactively manage and allocate resources amongst different health care needs. Purchasers are expected to manage treatment decision-making by physicians and other health providers. Managed competition and internal market reform combine elements of both government planning and market approaches. Managed care, another concept that is often referred to in the context of health care reform, is the mechanism through which managed competition proposals seek to obtain cost savings, but as described further below, can be employed in any health care system.

Before describing the competition-oriented reform models, a preliminary question must be addressed: why is health care reform needed? A number of factors have converged creating strong pressures for health care reform in developed countries. These factors include:

- concerns over increases in total spending on health care services;
- concerns over rapidly increasing government spending;
- access and rationing concerns; and
- concerns over the cost-effectiveness and, indeed, effectiveness of many services supplied.

Let us look more closely at the forces contributing to reform throughout the 1980s and 1990s, beginning first with the concern over growth in total health care spending. Throughout the 1970s there were significant increases in the proportion of gross domestic product (GDP) (the total value of all goods and services produced by a country) absorbed by health care spending. Between 1972 and 1982 there was a 36-percent, 30-percent, 26-percent and 25-percent increase, respectively, in the percentage of GDP spent on health care in the US, New Zealand, UK, and the Netherlands. Between 1982 and 1992 there was only a 2-percent increase in the Netherlands, but the US, New Zealand, and the UK still saw increases, respectively, of 36 percent, 12 percent, and 20 percent.[1] These increases were partly due to the after-effects of the oil-shocks and to recessionary periods that slowed the growth of GDP within these countries. However, there was a concern that even if growth rates in GDP improved it would not be enough to keep pace with the aging of the baby boomers and their demands for high quality medical care and the best medical technology available.

Although increasing costs are often cited as a justification for health care reform, it is far from clear what is "too much" in terms of total expenditures on health services. Why are we not similarly concerned that we are spending increasing amounts on telecommunications services, cable television, computer products, or novelty toys? The concern over rising total health care expenditures is, in fact, rooted in two separate issues – concern over government spending and concern over inefficiency.

In most Organization for Economic Cooperation and Development (OECD) countries, government pays for the majority of health care expenditures. Even in the US, government expenditures account for over 44 percent of total health care spending. Moreover, in most countries, health care is the most significant component of total government expenditures. Thus, increased concern over public sector deficits has been a strong impetus for health care reform.

It is often difficult to disentangle fiscal realities from ideological pursuits, but a further factor contributing to calls for health care reform has likely been a rise in ideology, questioning the legitimacy and role of government in all sectors. This new ideology has not been the sole domain of neo-conservatives; governments of many political stripes have privatized and deregulated formerly government-owned industries, e.g., telecommunications, electricity, gas, broadcasting, airlines. In a number of countries, the final stages of reinventing government are resulting in re-engineering and/or partial privatization of social service systems such as education and health.

A further factor driving health care reform is concern over inefficiency. Despite mushrooming health care expenditure, there have not been significant improvements in health outcomes. So the question arises: are we getting value for money? Health economists have led the charge in this critique, emphasizing the lack of evidence for the cost-effectiveness or even effectiveness of many health care services. The economists' critique is explored further in Chapter 2 but, in a nutshell, economists view this problem as resulting from leaving allocation decisions in physicians' hands. Physicians are portrayed as being resistant to outside scrutiny of their decision-making processes and as having little or no incentive to be sensitive to the costs and benefits of the services they supply or recommend. Wide variations have been recorded in the kinds of health care services delivered to people with similar health needs. Thus, the concern has arisen that the present allocation of resources across health needs and between health services utilized to meet those needs reflects what is optimal from the medical profession's perspective rather than what is optimal from society's perspective.

Why have allocation decisions been left to physicians? Historically, both public and private insurers have been passive "indemnity insurers," paying physicians a fee for every service they decided to provide (this is called a "fee-for-service" payment). As discussed in Chapter 3, both public and private insurers in the four countries under study have failed to scrutinize the services that physicians supply and the recommendations that physicians make with regard to drugs, hospitalization, referrals, etc. Thus, there has been relatively little pressure brought to bear on physicians to supply and recommend cost-effective care by those responsible for paying for health care services. There has also been little effective management to ensure the optimal allocation of resources between different health needs, as well as the choice of the most cost-effective service in response to each particular need.

To a lesser degree, health care reform has also been initiated in response to concerns by patients and citizens over their ability to access services and over the quality of services provided. Starting in the late 1970s, single-payer systems (relying to a large degree on government funding) reduced growth in spending by closing hospitals and reducing the numbers of hospital beds. The consequent increases in waiting lists and times resulted in widespread public concern and a sense that health care systems were not responding to patient and societal needs.[2] Citizens and patients have traditionally had very few direct mechanisms through which to ensure the accountability of health care decision-makers, leaving them feeling disenfranchised and frustrated. In systems that relied to a greater degree on private finance, such as the US and the Netherlands, there were concerns over access to insurance coverage for high-risk individuals who were facing increasingly higher premiums or excluded altogether from private insurance markets.

Concerns over government spending, inefficiency, reduced access and quality, and a general policy shift towards rethinking government's role and government programs, have combined to create a strong force for health care reform.

Managed competition and internal market reform are both reform models that seek to harness competition to achieve distributive goals and to change the incentive structure for decision-makers within a health care system.

The reform models

The language of health care reform can often be confusing and there seems to be a small cottage industry in inventing phrases and acronyms for the various new emerging arrangements between governments, private insurers, purchasers, providers and patients. This makes it very important to clarify at the outset of this book what is meant by the terms "internal market reform," "managed competition reform" and "managed care." As there is no one acknowledged theory of the internal market, I describe this model by reference to its implementation in the UK and New Zealand. With regard to managed competition, I describe the key features of the model originally designed by Enthoven and as proposed and implemented in the Netherlands. With regard to managed care, I describe this as a feature that could be adopted in many kinds of systems but is now most associated with the US system, given the huge growth in managed care that has occurred since the failure of President Clinton's 1993 managed competition proposals.

Internal market reform and the purchaser/provider split

Over the course of the decade, the UK and New Zealand have each sought to create what is known as an "internal market." Proposals for reform of the UK's National Health Service (NHS) were first announced in 1989. Subsequently, the reforms were implemented through the National Health Service and Community Care Act 1990, (UK), (1990), c. 19. On 8 December 1997, the UK government published a policy paper (known as a White Paper) detailing further reform of the UK internal market.[3] Enabling legislation was passed on 30 June 1999 in the form of the Health Act 1999, (UK), (1999), c. 8. In New Zealand, the then Minister of Health released his proposals for internal market reform in 1991.[4] Subsequently, many of the reforms were implemented pursuant to the Health and Disability Services Act 1993, (NZ), 1993, No. 22, but, as in the UK, there have been a number of significant changes made to the original reform plan.

The original goal of internal market reform in the UK and New Zealand was to split the purchaser and provider roles of regional or area health authorities. This was in order to eliminate what was viewed, in both jurisdictions, as a conflict of interest, as the old health authorities had been responsible both for purchasing hospital and community services and for managing and providing public hospital services. The reformers' perception was that the old public hospitals were not performing as efficiently as they could, because they could always rely on getting extra funding from their own coffers.

Internal market reform requires government-appointed purchasers (100 Health Authorities in the UK and one Health Authority in New Zealand) to bargain and enter into contracts with competing public and private health service providers. Initially, it was intended that the new Health Authorities would be the sole purchasers (known in economic terms as monopsonies) of publicly-funded health services in their region and would buy a comprehensive range of health services on behalf of the people living in their regions. A split was created between the purchasing and provision of hospital and other health services: in both the UK and New Zealand, the Health Authorities are not permitted to provide health services directly. On the other side of the split are public hospitals, which in both countries are now managed by crown corporations. In the UK these are called "NHS Trusts" and in New Zealand they are called "Crown Health Enterprises." In both systems these new enterprises are meant to act much more like private firms and compete with each other and private providers for supply contracts with the new Health Authorities. Thus the term "internal market" is something of a misnomer as the market created is not intended to be completely internal to the public sector, although in reality it continues to be largely so.

Exceptions to the purchaser/provider split in the UK's internal market were "GP Fundholders." Fundholding was originally an "add-on" to internal market reform but rapidly assumed increasing importance. GP Fundholders were groups of general practitioners (family doctors), serving at least 5,000 patients. Prior to 1 April 1999, over 3,500 Fundholders received public funding, in the form of capitated budgets, with which to buy drugs, diagnostic tests and x-rays, outpatient services and approximately 20 percent of hospital and community services, on behalf of the patients enrolled with them. Within Fundholders, the purchaser and provider roles were combined in one enterprise to the extent that a physician was able to substitute the supply of his/her own services instead of buying services from other providers. The New Labour reforms of December 1997 called for the abolition of GP Fundholders as of 1 April 1999. They are to be replaced by new organizations called "Primary Care Trusts." These Trusts are to be much larger groups of general practitioners and community nurses that will receive capitated budgets from the government with which to purchase a full range of publicly-funded health care services from public hospitals and other health providers. In New Zealand "Independent Practice Associations" (IPAs) have been established and these too are exceptions to the purchaser/provider split that characterizes the bulk of the internal market. There has been a change of terminology such that now IPAs are referred to as Budget-holders. Budget-holders are physician groups of varying size paid on a capitated basis by the Health Authority to cover the cost of specified services for their patients such as drugs, diagnostic texts, x-rays etc. Fundholders, Primary Care Trusts, IPAs, and Budget-holders are all examples of "managed care," which is described further below.

Figure 2 in Chapter 3 depicts the structure of the NHS internal market prior to the New Labour Reforms of December 1997. Figure 3 depicts the New Labour Reforms. Figure 1 depicts New Zealand's internal market in 1996.

Managed competition reform

In an internal market citizens have no choice but to rely upon a government-appointed purchaser (generally a Health Authority) to purchase on their behalf publicly-financed health services. They cannot indicate their dissatisfaction with a purchaser's performance by shifting a share of public funding to another purchaser. This is in contrast to managed competition reform. Managed competition requires private insurers to compete for customer allegiance within a regulated system that is progressively financed.

Enthoven is often considered to be the creator of the managed competition model and his writing on this subject commenced in the late 1970s.[5] Since then he has advocated many different versions of managed competition reform. In the Netherlands, what became known as the Dekker Committee (named after its chair Dr W. Dekker) produced a report in March 1987 which proposed managed competition reform of the Dutch health care system.[6] The reform plan has been changed several times since 1987 and implementation has been incremental and still continues today.[7] President Clinton also proposed a version of managed competition reform in 1993 for the US system.[8] This proposal was ultimately unsuccessful but the prospect of significant reform sparked a huge growth in managed care arrangements and the dynamics of the US system have changed significantly since the 1993 proposals.

A managed competition system is designed to ensure that competition occurs between insurers on the basis of cost and quality rather than risk avoidance. Insurers would have a different function (purchasing and management functions would be as important as the insurance function) and behave quite differently from present private insurers. To reflect both the purchasing and risk bearing functions of private insurers in the context of managed competition reform I refer to them as "insurer/purchasers."

A managed competition system is financed largely progressively with there being little or no connection between individual contributions and entitlements to health insurance and/or services. Managed competition might be perceived as US-style reform but it would in fact result in a very different system from that currently seen in the US. Managed competition models, unlike the present US system which leaves over 43 million people without insurance, seek to ensure universal coverage of citizens for a range of health care services. What range of health care services is covered is something that must be determined, but it is generally referred to as a "core" or a "comprehensive" range of services. Thus allocation decisions with regard to the core or comprehensive range of services are determined on the basis of need and not ability to pay.

In a managed competition system insurer/purchasers would not receive premiums directly except for a small percentage. Instead, a "sponsor" (probably a government-appointed body or a government department) would obtain funds from general taxation revenues or income-adjusted premium payments from individual citizens. Each individual in the system would periodically (probably annually or biannually) choose their particular insurer/purchaser. The sponsor would facilitate this process, making sure that competition occurs only on cost

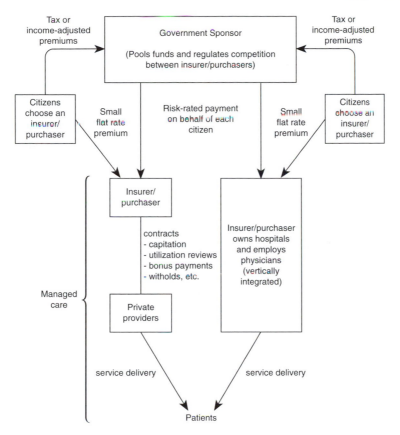

Figure 1.1 The managed competition model.

and quality dimensions. The sponsor would pay on behalf of each individual a risk-adjusted sum to their chosen insurer/purchaser. Each individual would also pay to each chosen insurer a small flat fee, which must be the same fee for every individual enrolled with that insurer, although the amount of the flat fee could differ from insurer to insurer. As a consequence, insurer/purchasers will have incentives to be cost-effective and to compete on the quality of services provided and the flat premium fee in order to attract enrollees. The incentive to compete on cost, price, and quality will lead them to enter into various forms of managed care relationships with health care providers. In fact, Enthoven has said that he now refers to his model for managed competition as "managed care-managed competition" to emphasize that what are meant to compete are integrated delivery systems supplying comprehensive care.[9]

Figure 1.1 depicts the structure of a managed competition system. What is shown is a simplification of possible managed care arrangements, for it shows insurer/purchasers either being vertically integrated (i.e. owning hospitals and employing physicians) or contracting out with hospitals, physicians, and other health care providers. In fact, insurer/purchasers could choose to be vertically integrated for some health service markets and contract out in others.

Managed care

Managed care may form part of *any* health care system but it is a vital component of managed competition reform and has assumed increasing importance in internal market reform. In the wake of the failure of President Clinton's proposals for national health care reform in the US, there has been nothing less than a managed care revolution as private insurers and employers are seeking to shift market power from health care providers to themselves.

In a nutshell, managed care is where an insurer/purchaser (who may be the government, a private insurer, an employer or a consortium of hospitals and/or physicians) attempts to influence the cost, volume, and quality of health services supplied and/or recommended by health care providers.[10] Enthoven notes that managed care arrangements (which are sometimes now referred to by the new buzzwords of "integrated financing and delivery systems") come in a variety of types.[11] Although there are many different approaches to managed care, all are characterized by a refusal to passively reimburse hospitals and physicians for every service they provide. In managed care arrangements, insurer/purchasers monitor and review the delivery of services and physicians' recommendations. A managed care arrangement may have the following features:

- an insurer/purchaser may limit patients' choice of providers to those it has elected to contract with and impose a surcharge on patients who choose providers outside of those listed;
- an insurer/purchaser may seek to contract with or employ physicians whose practices are likely to promote primary and preventive care;
- an insurer/purchaser may pay physicians or groups of physicians and/or other health care providers on a capitation basis, i.e. a fixed sum per enrollee for a fixed time period (generally per month or per annum).[12]

Unlike internal market reform, managed care does not mandate a "purchaser/provider split." An insurer/purchaser may choose to own the hospitals and employ the physicians it needs to deliver health care (in economic terms known as "vertical integration") as opposed to contracting with them on an arm's length basis. The three main types of managed care organizations in the US, Health Maintenance Organizations (HMOs), Preferred Provider Organizations (PPOs) and Point of Service Networks (POS Networks), are described in Chapter 3.

Managed competition and managed care are concepts that are often confused. Managed competition is a reform model for an entire system where the ultimate goal is to ensure coverage for all, on the basis of needs as opposed to ability to pay, for a core or comprehensive range of health care services. Managed care is an important feature of a managed competition system but also may be a feature of other systems that do not aspire to ensure coverage for all. In the US, managed care developments are ad hoc and are not part of a planned and integrated health system. The system leaves 43.2 million people without insurance, more than 10.6 million of whom are under the age of 19.[13] There is no specific government regulation at the federal level to ensure competition between managed care plans on the basis of cost and quality. In fact, as a result of competition between insurers *on risk avoidance*, the number of managed care plans that community-rate (i.e. cross-subsidize premiums from low-risk to high-risk individuals) has declined.[14] Present developments in the US can be distinguished from a managed competition system. In the latter there would be coverage for all citizens, it would be progressively funded apart from a small fixed premium payment, and explicit mechanisms would be in place to stimulate competition on cost and quality dimensions rather than risk avoidance.

The chosen health care allocation systems

A number of countries are seeking to reform their health systems by either introducing more competition into what were publicly-operated delivery systems or reconfiguring public and private roles in pluralist, insurance-based systems.[15] Examples include Finland, Sweden, countries comprising the former USSR, Germany, and Israel. This book focuses on competition-oriented reform in the US, the Netherlands, the UK, and New Zealand for several reasons. First, these four countries have either proposed or implemented internal market and managed competition models and all are seeing shifts towards managed care either by government design or as a market response. Thus it is possible to use these countries to compare internal market and managed competition reform models and to analyze the role of managed care within these models. Second, there is the radical nature of the reforms proposed in all four countries. The Netherlands, the UK, and New Zealand were some of the first countries in the world to implement competition-oriented reform and it is possible to assess the impact of reform over the course of several years. Moreover, the reform models actually implemented have been a pale shadow of those originally proposed. Thus, there is scope to discuss the political and other impediments to sweeping reform. Finally, lessons may be able to be drawn from the experiences of these four countries by a country like Canada that has a relatively similar socio-economic and legal structure, as it contemplates the prospects for health care reform in the next century.

The need for an interdisciplinary approach

In this book I strive to take an interdisciplinary approach which is necessary in order to fully analyze an institutional design. The disciplines of law, economics, and political science all provide valuable analytical tools.

A traditional legal scholar might initially ask what law has got to do with health care reform. In fact the law is integral to the success or failure of an institutional design. Both international and domestic law may prescribe individual entitlements to health care services and protect the interests of minorities and vulnerable groups. Determinations made with regard to which health services are publicly-funded and which are not may be subject to judicial review. Legislation is passed to create new institutional arrangements and prescribes the powers, responsibilities, and rights of health care providers, insurers, suppliers, purchasers, patients, interest groups and citizens. Departments, agencies or tribunals may be given regulatory powers to ensure the quality of health services, medical equipment and goods and to oversee hospitals and other institutions. Legal liability imposed through the common law (particularly tort law) on health care providers, purchasers, and patients may affect their behavior and impact on both the costs and distribution of health services in society. Supply contracts are a vital element of competition-oriented reform models and the question arises of whether existing laws are effective in this special milieu. Competition or anti-trust law is important, as competition-oriented reform often requires the consolidation of market power on the demand side of the market but the response of providers may be to attempt to consolidate market power on the supply side.

From an economist's perspective, one must inquire as to which reform proposals will result in institutional arrangements that are more efficient than alternatives. There are three measures of efficiency to be concerned with. The first, allocative efficiency, is essentially concerned with the appropriate allocation of scarce resources within an economy to satisfy all our varied wants and needs. This measure of efficiency strives to ensure that we do not spend more on goods and services we want than their true underlying cost to society. The second measure of efficiency, technical efficiency, focuses on ensuring that a particular good or service is produced with the least expenditure of resources.[16] One can also talk about the technical efficiency of a particular regulatory regime in terms of how effective it is in achieving its economic, social or political objectives. Finally, dynamic efficiency looks at the long-term picture and whether an industry or firm or regulatory structure is flexible and dynamic enough to respond to changes to ensure on-going technical efficiency.

Political science is important for it assists in understanding what weight governments will give to the sometimes competing considerations of efficiency, equity, and government cost control. The discipline also aids in understanding what incentives are needed to ensure that government, insurers, purchasers, and health service providers are accountable for their decisions to the patients and/or policyholders and/or citizens they represent. It also assists in estimating the difficulties with implementation of any particular theoretical model and therefore in predicting the type of reform that is most likely to be successfully implemented.

This book begins in the next chapter by considering from first principles the rationale for government intervention in health care systems on economic and distributive justice grounds. Before analyzing reform it is vital that there is a clear understanding of what the objectives of reform should be. It is in fact impossible to measure the merit of a regulatory structure without identifying what its objectives are or should be. This chapter does not analyze what governments' objectives are but rather what distributive and economic objectives are justified from a theoretical perspective. Evans questions the wisdom of exploring whether or not government has to intervene directly to structure and regulate a health system, given the accumulation of international experience that direct intervention is necessary.[17] However, international experience has not yet revealed the optimal design in terms of public and private roles. Examining efficiency and equity arguments for government intervention will help to provide a better understanding of which roles and decisions are best performed and made by whom.

An examination of the need for government intervention on the grounds of distributive justice and market failure does not result in a prescription for how to design a health care system. Chapter 3 discusses the different approaches taken in the four countries under study. The systems that existed in the US, the UK, New Zealand and the Netherlands prior to reform proposals in the late 1980s and early 1990s are discussed in some detail. Here also is a description of the implementation of internal market and managed competition reform in the UK, the Netherlands and New Zealand and, in the case of the US, the failure of President Clinton's managed competition reform proposal and the managed care revolution that was sparked.

Ensuring accountability of decision-makers for the decisions they make in the long and short term is fundamental to the success and sustainability of a health care system. A system must balance the interests of individual patients with larger societal interests. However, most systems are characterized by a paucity of measures designed to ensure the accountability of decision-makers in this regard and instead are characterized by efforts to shift the cost of bad and inappropriate decisions to others. Chapter 4 analyzes and compares mechanisms to ensure accountability of government-appointed purchasers in internal markets with the accountability of competing private insurer/ purchasers in a managed competition system. I utilize Hirschman's concepts of "voice," "exit" and "loyalty" to classify different sorts of political and market incentives that may be deployed to ensure accountability.

The rapid development in the importance of GP Fundholders in the UK and IPAs and Budget-holding in New Zealand suggests that internal market reform may in fact be a transitional arrangement on the road towards some variation of managed care/managed competition contracting. In Chapter 5, I consider the merits of the purchaser/provider split as the underlying rationale of the internal market model and compare this with the more flexible managed competition model which allows insurer/purchasers to be either vertically integrated or to contract out.

An impediment to consumer choice of competing insurer/purchasers in a managed competition system is where, due to economies of scale or historic government policy, there is a monopoly provider in a particular market. In Chapter 6, I consider the problem of monopoly on the supply side and the need for regulation of natural monopolies in order that competing insurer/purchasers are able to offer their plans to all residents of a particular area. One must also consider the likely response of providers to reform, namely to consolidate to increase market power. Neither the managed competition nor internal market models specifically deals with this problem. Financial integration of providers into systems may in fact be a preferred policy option as it would allow co-ordination in service delivery and minimize opportunities for cost-shifting. I discuss how competition law must be in place that will allow health providers to form financially integrated mini systems but yet prohibit arrangements where health providers are simply seeking to improve their negotiating power with insurer/purchasers.

Quality of care is generally thought of in terms of skill in diagnosis and treatment. At some point in every health care system a trade-off must be made between increased cost and increased quality. Is an increase in quality in terms of extra years or days of life gained, diminishment of pain, minimization of side-effects etc. worth the extra costs? In Chapter 7, I argue that there are three paradigms of quality that a system must strive for. The first is technical or production quality – skill in providing a particular treatment or service. The second is quality in terms of choosing the most cost-effective service for a particular need. The third paradigm is quality in terms of prioritization of health needs. Health care systems have historically focused exclusively on technical quality, largely ignoring the second and third paradigms of quality in a system. I discuss incentives to ensure quality within various payment methods, including salaries, fee-for-service, and capitation. I also look at the extent to which ethical codes, professional self-regulation, and the threat of malpractice actions will ensure the quality of services delivered. The competition approach emphasizes measuring quality of care in terms of health outcomes; however, measuring quality care is more complicated than in many other markets and cannot always be assessed in terms of health outcomes. I explore the need for continued government regulation, self-regulation by health care professionals, and other measures to ensure the quality of care that is not readily measurable in terms of outcomes.

It has been said that the key issue in considering alternative forms of health care reform is "what kinds of decisions are best made by whom?"[18] This book goes a step further and questions how to ensure that decision-makers are exercising their discretion in the best interests of both patients and society at large. The key optimization problem in any health care system is how to ensure that decision-makers make good decisions that balance the needs of society with the needs of particular individuals and, more generally, balance equity and efficiency. This book compares the relative prospects of managed competition and internal market reform in solving this optimization problem. The approach of this book thus draws on the work of Coase to the extent that it responds to his plea to study how alternative economic arrangements actually work in practice – the comparative institutional approach.[19]

Notes

1 Organization for Economic Cooperation and Development, *The Reform of Health Care Systems: A Review of Seventeen OECD Countries* (Paris: OECD, 1994) p. 37, Table 4.1.

2 R.V. Saltman and C. Von Otter, *Planned Markets and Public Competition: Strategic Reform in Northern European Health Systems* (Buckingham: Open University Press, 1992) p. 13 identifies public resistance to continued rationing by queue of certain elective surgical procedures, particularly for the elderly, as a force that has contributed to health care reform initiatives.

3 See *The New NHS: Modern, Dependable*, A White Paper, Cm 3807, 8 December 1997. Online. Available HTTP: http://www.official-documents.co.uk/document/doh/newnhs/contents.htm (accessed 15 March 1999).

4 S. Upton, *Your Health and the Public Health: A Statement of Government Health Policy* (Wellington: Minister of Health, July 1991) pp. 11–19.

5 For a fuller description of managed competition/managed care contracting, see A. C. Enthoven, 'Consumer-Choice Health Plan (First of Two Parts): Inflation and Inequity in Health Care Today: Alternatives for Cost Control and an Analysis of Proposals for National Health Insurance', (1978) 298(12) *New Eng. J. of Medicine* 650, and A. C. Enthoven, 'Consumer-Choice Health Plan (Second of Two Parts): A National-Health-Insurance Proposal Based on Regulated Competition in the Private Sector', (1978) 298(13) *New Eng. J. of Medicine* 709. More recently, see A. C. Enthoven, 'The History and Principles of Managed Competition', (1993) 12 *Health Affairs* (Supp.) 24. See, however, U. E. Reinhardt, 'Lineage of Managed Competition', (1994) 2 *Health Affairs* 290, who traces the managed competition idea back to H. M. and A. R. Somers at a presentation in 1971.

6 Adview van de Commissie Structuur en Financiering Gezondheidszorg (Commission on the Structure and Financing of Health Care), *Bereidheid tot Verandering* (Willingness To Change), ('s Gravenhage: Distributiecentrum Overheidspublikaties, 1987).

7 J. Hurst, *The Reform of Health Care: A Comparative Analysis of Seven OECD Countries,* OECD Health Policy Studies No. 2 (Paris: OECD, 1992) p. 97 and *Health Care Reform in the Netherlands* (Ministry of Welfare, Health and Cultural Affairs, Fact Sheet V-5–E, 1993) p. 5.

8 See White House Domestic Policy Council, *The Clinton Blueprint: The President's Health Security Plan* (New York: Times Books, 1993).

9 As quoted by P. Newman, 'Interview With Alain Enthoven: Is There Convergence Between Britain and the United States in the Organization of Health Services?', (1995) 310(6995) *BMJ* 1652.

10 See generally D. Mechanic, 'Opinion Managed Care: Rhetoric and Realities', (1994) 31(2) *Inquiry* 124, and R. J. Arnould *et al.*, 'The Role of Managed Care in Competitive Policy Reforms', in R. J. Arnould, R. F. Rich and W. D. White (eds), *Competitive Approaches to Health Care Reform*, (Washington, DC: Urban Institute Press, 1993).

11 A. C. Enthoven, 'On the Ideal Market Structure for Third-Party Purchasing of Health Care', (1994) 39(10) *Soc. Sci. Med.* 1413 at p. 1414.

12 See J. K. Iglehart, 'Physicians and the Growth of Managed Care', (1994) 331(17) *New Eng. J. of Med.* 1167.

13 Physicians for a National Health Program, press release, 'Number of Americans Without Health Insurance Jumps to 43.2 Million'. Online. Available HTTP: http://www.pnhp.org/press998.html (accessed 17 March 1999).

14 J. Gabel, 'Ten Ways HMOs Have Changed During the 1990s', (1997) 16(3) *Health Affairs* 134.

15 Saltman and Von Otter, *op. cit.*, at pp. 15–16, and W. P. M. M. van de Ven, R. T. Schut and F. F. H. Rutten, 'Editorial: Forming and Reforming the Market for Third-Party Purchasing of Health Care', (1994) 39(10) *Soc. Sci. Med.* 1405.

16 Technical or productive efficiency occurs when the instruments in place achieve the realization of any given policy objective at the lowest possible cost in terms of the economic resources deployed – M. J. Trebilcock, *The Prospects for Reinventing Government*, (Toronto: C. D. Howe Institute, 1994) at p. 7.

17 R. G. Evans, 'Going for the Gold: The Redistributive Agenda Behind Market-Based Health Care Reform', (1998) 22(2) *J. Health Polit. Policy Law* 427 at p. 448.

18 The Health Care Study Group , 'Understanding the Choices in Health Care Reform', (1994) 19(3) *J. Health Polit. Policy Law* 499 at p. 508.

19 R. H. Coase, 'The Problem of Social Cost', (1960) 3 *Economica* 1.

2 Arguments in economics and justice for government intervention in health insurance and health service markets

In this chapter, I examine sources of market failure in both health insurance markets and health care service markets so as to be clear as to where government intervention is necessary from the perspective of efficiency. I also explore the extent to which government intervention in health insurance and health care services markets is required on the grounds of a theory of distributive justice. Going back to first principles at this juncture will assist in analyzing reform proposals in subsequent chapters. It is impossible to evaluate the benefits and costs of health care reform without first identifying what the objectives of the health care system are or should be.

Commencing with an economic analysis of the sources of market failure can be criticized as importing the implicit assumption that less government is, all other things being equal, better than more and that distributional concerns are of less consequence than efficiency considerations. This criticism has validity and by commencing with an economic analysis I do not wish to discount distributive and other non-economic goals. I strive to document distributional considerations throughout the economic analysis. There is a need to understand the source of market failures in a system to better predict what will be the systemic effects of measures designed to achieve distributional goals. Moreover, although economics has relatively little value in terms of formulating social objectives, it has greater legitimacy as a tool of design. In other words, it makes sense to try to achieve social objectives in the most efficient way possible. This is because the fewer resources deployed to realize a particular social or non-economic objective the more resources there are available to achieve other valued objectives. It is possible that efficient regulatory solutions may be rejected as contrary to other values we have, e.g. the use of vouchers may be criticized as diminishing the dignity and autonomy of recipients. However, generating models that should efficiently achieve social justice goals will, at a minimum, help in selecting the best regulatory design balancing all these considerations.

Market failure in the health care insurance and service supply markets

Sources of market failure in health care insurance and supply markets are discussed below under the headings of externalities, adverse selection, minimization of administration and transaction costs, moral hazard, information asymmetry, and economies of scale.

Externalities

Externalities are a source of failure in health care markets, as they represent unsatisfied demand. For example, externalities arise where a society wishes to have the benefits of medical research that private enterprise is unwilling to undertake. Government may intervene to meet this unsatisfied demand in society by directly subsidizing research and/or developing trademark or patent law to encourage private investment in research. Externalities also arise where we are prepared to pay for the consumption of health care services by others living in our community. For example, it is of benefit that the whole community is immunized against contagious disease as this reduces each individual's risk of infection. There are, however, impossibly high costs associated with each citizen attempting to identify and contract with those individuals who either cannot afford, or are reluctant, to be immunized. There is also a free-rider problem, as many citizens may not contribute in the expectation that others will pay or do the work from which they can benefit. Government may intervene to correct this market failure and to fulfil unsatisfied demand. In a developed country, the intervention required, although very important, is not significant relative to total health care expenditures, as the risk of contagious disease has substantially declined in the twentieth century.

Demand for immunizations and other public health services is due to each individual's desire to protect and maximize his/her own standard of health. However, many individuals in society are also prepared to pay for the consumption of health care services by others who cannot afford them on moral grounds. Culyer has advanced the theory of a "caring" externality in health care justifying government intervention.[1] The concept of a caring externality relates to the notion of social or distributive justice (discussed below) although the two concepts are different as the former focuses on the entire society as opposed to individual rights. Evans argues that health care services are what are known as "merit goods," as society in general considers that individuals in particular circumstances should consume them.[2] He notes that society's attitude is paternalistic, rather than altruistic, as collectively society is not prepared to pay for frivolous or unnecessary services but only what is perceived as being effective and essential care. Evans' analysis, however, seriously discounts the "caring" in the so-called "caring externality." The care and comfort of the terminally ill or disabled may not meet Evans' criteria of effectiveness in terms of measurable health improvements, yet many if not most individuals in society want to ensure these kinds of needs are met and may even value them over certain curative services.

Refusing to supply basic care to a patient who cannot afford it may well result in significant extra costs subsequently being incurred if the patient's condition seriously deteriorates. This will not be a problem if a society is prepared to allow those in need of care to suffer or die without medical assistance. The existence of a caring externality suggests this will not be the case. Physicians find it difficult to refuse to treat the impecunious when faced directly with an individual who is at risk of serious harm or loss of life, but rather than bearing the costs of treatment themselves may seek to pass these on to other insured patients. Thus, even those in society not prepared to pay for health care services for those in need may have these costs imposed upon them by others as a component of their own cost of health care. This appears to be the case in the US.[3]

Western industrialized societies all seem to accept that some level of subsidy should be made available to the poor to allow them to participate in health insurance markets (and thereby health service markets). What is much less clear is who should be defined as poor and for what range and quality of health care services the poor should receive a subsidy. There is also the issue of whether it is effective to provide the poor with a subsidy or a voucher to purchase health insurance given the economic problems of adverse selection, moral hazard and information asymmetry (all discussed below).

Adverse selection

Health insurance markets are closely related to and impact on demand and supply in health service markets. The analysis that follows demonstrates that the demand for and existence of health care insurance in an unregulated market contributes to and compounds market failures in health care service markets.

Apart from preventive health care services, our demand for health care services is frequently contingent on developing an illness or suffering an injury and we may not be able to predict the likelihood that this will happen. Consequently, we are often unable accurately to predict our own future demand for health care services and cannot always save for the cost of health care services needed in the future. This uncertainty coupled with the high cost of treating some diseases and afflictions means that in the absence of insurance even the most prudent individual could face financial ruin in the event of serious illness or injury. Serious illness or injury can be a financial disaster not only because of the cost of care but because an individual's income-earning stream is interrupted or eroded permanently. Consequently, all other things being equal, there will be a demand for insurance to cover the risk of needing high-cost services like hospital services[4] and even to cover the risk of needing relatively low-cost services over an extended period in the case of a chronic illness.

The problem of adverse selection occurs in private insurance markets when high-risk individuals choose to buy the most comprehensive insurance policy available. The difficulty is that insurers are unable to distinguish between high-risk individuals (to whom they would charge higher premiums) and those individuals that are simply risk-averse and want to purchase comprehensive coverage. This problem is rooted, as are many problems in the health insurance and health service markets, in a lack of accurate information.[5]

If a private insurer assesses premiums on the basis of the average risk for a whole community (a practice known as community rating), then low-risk individuals will subsidize high-risk individuals. An insurer may attempt to use risk proxies like employment, age, gender and historical utilization of services to assess individual or group risk. However, there still may be individuals within groups classified by insurance companies as high-risk who, because of a variety of factors peculiar to that person, are not high-risk. Adverse selection occurs as these individuals would purchase full coverage for a premium reflecting their actuarial risk, but are unable to do so because insurers do not have sufficient information with which to distinguish these individuals from *truly* high-risk individuals.[6] Those individuals who assess themselves as low-risk may elect to bear the risk of ill health or injury individually and stop purchasing insurance (self-insure). The departure of these low-risk individuals from the insurance pool will raise the average cost of premiums for the remaining policyholders and cause further departures by low-risk individuals.[7]

It is very difficult to estimate the magnitude of the adverse selection problem. Its potential seriousness is demonstrated by the fact that prior to the introduction of Medicare in 1965–6, 50 percent of Americans over the age of 65 were completely uninsured against the cost of illness and only half of those with health insurance had adequate coverage for hospitalization expenses.[8] Undoubtedly some of the uninsured elderly would have been prepared to pay a premium price that reflected their real risk but were unable to obtain coverage from insurers who could not or would not distinguish very high-risk elderly people from others. The fact that 5 percent of all the aged entitled to the government's Medicare program account for over 50 percent its total costs and that 36 percent of those covered do not make any claims[9] suggests that there are significant differences in risk between elderly individuals.

One must distinguish the problem of adverse selection from the problem of high premiums for high-risk individuals. The operation of an unregulated private insurance market, where insurers compete on the basis of risk selection, will result in very high premiums or, perhaps, no coverage at all for the chronically sick and aged. A relatively small fraction of the population requires most of the health care services. Health care expenditures for the disabled are five times more than those for the non-disabled, the old use far more medical services than the young, and medical costs rise very sharply shortly before death.[10] In the US, about 72 percent of annual national health expenditures are spent on 10 percent of the population.[11] If an insurer can exclude individuals who are likely to frequently utilize expensive services then it can significantly reduce its operating costs. Thus, unlike sellers of most other goods and services, sellers of insurance have good reason to be concerned about who buys their services.[12]

The irony is that the unregulated operation of a health insurance market will result in those who objectively are in the most need of health care services being unable to obtain them because of the high cost of insurance or because of exclusionary policies. However, failure to provide affordable health insurance to those who most need it is not a source of market failure. Neo-classical economic theory is rooted in utilitarianism and the goal of an efficient market is to maximize overall benefits to a society given available resources. The efficiency of the market is not undermined, in economic theory, by distributional inequities. This view seems particularly impoverished with respect to health care.

Minimization of administration and transactions costs

Administration or loading costs increase as insurance companies seek to compete by assessing the risks of certain groups or individuals and these costs have to be included in the cost of health insurance premiums. Generally it is assumed that the total amount of health insurance demanded in an economy will diminish as administration or loading costs increase.[13] However, Fuchs and Vladeck argue that demand for health insurance does not taper off substantially as premiums rise.[14] As they explain, this is because demand for health insurance is relatively "inelastic." What this means is that the demand for services is relatively unresponsive to changes in price and prices can increase significantly without the volume of services demanded declining to the same degree. Demand for health insurance is inelastic and people will continue to buy it even when it is very expensive, as people are risk adverse and gain utility from freeing themselves from cost considerations in the period of emotional strain associated with illness, disease or injury.

Possibly there are some economies of scale associated with the supply of health insurance. In economic terms, economies of scale are said to occur where long-run average costs decline. Economies of scale usually occur in industries where there are high capital investments required before even one unit of service or good can be produced. Thus, the higher the volume of services or goods supplied the lower the average cost of producing each service or good. Those who argue that there are economies of scale in administration rely on the low administrative costs recorded in "single-payer" systems like Canada, the UK, and New Zealand (where government pays for 70 percent or more of health expenditures) compared to multi-payer systems like the US (over 1,500 private insurers).[15] For example, in the US in 1991, administration costs amounted to 5.84 percent of total (public and private) health expenditures and 8.49 percent of private expenditures.[16] In addition to the recorded administration costs in the US are the costs associated with health care providers dealing with numerous insurers and complying with their various requirements before obtaining reimbursement.[17] By comparison, in Canada, administration costs in 1990 comprised just 1.28 percent of total public and private health expenditures.[18]

Administrative costs are reduced in single-payer systems but in truth these savings do not predominantly arise from economies of scale; rather, they are due to the fact that single-payer systems do not engage in risk-selection and risk-rating of premiums. Administration costs are lower, as the government does not devote its energies to the avoidance of high-risk individuals in the way unregulated private insurers in the US do.

It is very important to note that simply because a system has higher administrative or transactions cost does not mean that it is less efficient overall. One has to weigh additional administrative costs against any additional benefits of such a system, say in terms of better health outcomes, a more responsive system, etc. For example, in 1991 the Netherlands recorded administrative costs of 5.12 percent of total health care expenditures which is significantly higher than that incurred in Canada. On the other hand, the Netherlands still spent less on health as a percentage of GDP than Canada[19] and arguably has at least as good if not better health outcomes. Moreover, although incurring higher administrative costs and higher costs overall, the Netherlands performs better on most health outcome indicators than either the UK and New Zealand and does not have a problem with waiting lists and times for general medical services. As we will see in subsequent chapters, a paucity of good management characterizes many health care systems. Good management, however, has a cost but the cost should be more than offset by improvements in efficiency and equity.

Moral hazard

Moral hazard has been the focus of much academic attention and is often portrayed as the primary cause of cost escalation in health insurance and service markets. As Pauly describes it, generally moral hazard arises "whenever an individual's behavior that affects the expected loss is altered by the quantity of insurance he obtains."[20] There are two forms of moral hazard. First, insured people may take fewer preventive steps than they would in the absence of insurance to lessen their own risk of requiring health care services in the future e.g. engaging in known high-risk activities like smoking, mountain climbing, or unsafe sex (*ex ante* moral hazard).[21] Second, moral hazard is said to arise when patients demand more (or more expensive) health care services than they would if they had to pay for those services out of their own pockets (*ex post* moral hazard). This chapter focuses on the second form of moral hazard as it has generated the most concern in the economic literature. It should be noted that although the usual focus of moral hazard is upon the patients' behavior, moral hazard is also a problem in insurance markets. Moral hazard occurs in this sense when insurers take excessive financial risks with premiums that are paid at the beginning of a coverage period.[22] Government will generally regulate insurers to prevent this and often require the establishment of a guarantee fund.

The *ex post* moral hazard problem focuses on the patient who, at the point of delivery, is consuming more resources than they ought. Pauly argues that moral hazard costs "represent the consumption of units of medical care whose value to the consumer is less than their cost, because the insurance coverage reduces the user price below cost."[23] The problem with how the moral hazard problem is depicted in this statement is that it assumes that patients in general want to consume more health care services just as they may want to consume more ice-cream cones or cars. Given the generally unpleasant (or at least not pleasurable) nature of tests, procedures, operations, and medicines, this is a highly debatable assumption. The degree to which moral hazard is a problem depends on the nature of the health care service. For example, I may happily consume additional massage therapy services or homemaking services but, assuming that I am not masochist, I am unlikely to want more surgery than I really need.

The important moral hazard problem is not the consumption of more services than is needed but being indifferent to the price of the different services available to satisfy a health need. The *very* point of purchasing health insurance is that policy-holders want to ensure that they have enough resources to purchase health care services that doctors may tell them they need in the future. Therefore it is not rocket science to predict that at the time patients are told they need particular services, they will consume more services than they would have in the absence of insurance. Without insurance they may not have been able to afford the care they are told they need. Thus, the moral hazard problem is better characterized as the problem of fully insured patients lacking any incentive to discriminate between health providers or health care services *on the basis of cost*. This is well demonstrated by the fact that compared to other OECD countries the US has low per capita utilization rates of health care services.[24] What distinguishes the US from other countries is not high per capita utilization of hospital or physician service but the high prices charged for those health care services.[25] It is also important to note that in most systems patients cannot access most health care services without their general practitioner's referral or prescription.[26] General practitioners are the gatekeepers to the consumption of more expensive services and they tell patients what services they need. Thus, the true moral hazard problem is not so much patients being indifferent to the costs of different services and treatments but their advising physicians being indifferent to these costs.

The traditional economic response to the problem of *ex post* moral hazard is for insurers to impose user charges at point of service so that patients become more price-sensitive. However, unless the charges imposed reflect the underlying cost differentials of services and providers there is still no incentive to select appropriately between different services and different providers. Moreover, imposing charges on patients does not respond to the problem that patients cannot access many services (nor would they want to) without the advice and recommendation of their general practitioner.

In response to the imposition of user charges many individuals may demand further insurance to cover the cost thereof (known as "gap" or "supplementary" insurance). The existence of gap insurance mutes the degree to which user charges are likely to succeed in enhancing the price-sensitivity of patients.

User charges will potentially only impact on the demand of those individuals who cannot afford gap insurance. Government could possibly intervene in health markets by limiting or prohibiting the purchase of gap insurance to make patients at all income levels more price-sensitive.[27]

User charges may also discourage poorer patients from seeing their doctors in the first place. Stoddart *et al.* also note that in the face of user charges individuals are just as likely to forego those services they really need as opposed to those they may forego without harm.[28] This again relates to a problem of a lack of accurate information, as patients may not know which health needs they really must seek help for and rely on their doctor to act as a filter. If patients forego essential treatment this can lead to more downstream costs for themselves and for the health care system overall. A large experiment conducted in the US by the RAND corporation on the effect of patient user charges found user charges reduced utilization without adversely affecting health outcomes, except for low-income individuals with hypertension, vision or dental problems.[29] However, the results of this study must be read with caution. As mentioned above, the problem of cost in the US does not appear to stem from over-utilization of health care services but due to high and rising prices for health care services. Thus, the fact that user charges result in declining utilization is not necessarily a positive feature, for what it should be intended to do is to make patients shop around for cheaper health care services rather than reduce service consumption. The results of the RAND experiment study must also be viewed with extreme caution as the study excluded the elderly and the chronically ill – two sectors of the population that consume a significant proportion of health care services. It also should be noted that despite the RAND experiment's findings that ultimate health outcomes were not adversely affected by user charges, the experiment did find that patients would be equally deterred from using services that were considered necessary and unnecessary.[30] Whether the rationing of necessary services will have an adverse effect on ultimate health outcomes is something that, if able to be measured at all, may only be able to be measured in the long term. In this regard it is of note that some of the services that were found to be more sensitive to price were preventive services and mental health care services. It also appears clear from the RAND experiment that if user charges were not targeted at the income of the patient in question then user charges would disproportionately affect lower income patients.[31]

User charges could be targeted at various income levels so as not to discourage the purchase of health care services by poorer patients; however, the administrative costs of targeting and collecting user charges may outweigh any resulting efficiency gains.[32] There are other possible mechanisms apart from user charges available to counter moral hazard (or at least the effects of moral hazard), each with advantages and disadvantages. These include price regulation, nationalization of health insurance and the use of monopsony (single buyer) bargaining power to control health expenditures, managed care, and changing from a fee-for-service method of reimbursement. These mechanisms and others are discussed in subsequent chapters.

Information asymmetry

There are two equally important components to a patient's contract with a physician. First, a physician makes a diagnosis and tells a patient what his or her medical needs are. Then the physician advises the patient what health care services he or she requires for those medical needs. In advising what services a patient needs, a physician may advise a patient to consume services provided by the physician herself or an associated provider.

An information asymmetry problem arises between a physician and patient as many patients will not know what their health needs are nor the costs and benefits of particular treatments available to meet those needs. Given the cost and difficulties of acquiring information regarding the quality and appropriateness of services, patients are encouraged to rely on their physician's professional skill. A patient's physical or emotional distress and/or haste may contribute to a patient's unquestioning reliance on his/her physician.[33] It is often not only difficult for a patient to judge the quality of services before consumption but afterwards as well. Except in very obvious cases of poor-quality service when things go radically wrong, we often accept our physician's own assessment of his/her performance and of the short- and long-term consequences for our health.[34]

The moral hazard problem means that patients are unlikely to question the cost-effectiveness of a physician's recommendations for treatment. Where physicians and other health providers are paid on a fee-for-service basis, they will have a prima facie financial incentive to recommend that their patients consume more of their own services than is cost-effective.[35] The existence of an information asymmetry between physicians and patients allows physicians to act upon that incentive. Thus the combination of moral hazard, information asymmetry and fee-for-service payments creates a strong recipe for increasing health expenditures and inefficiency. The information asymmetry problem not only exists between physicians and patients but also between physicians and potential regulators/managers. This means that physicians are well placed to game any system designed to counteract the effects of moral hazard, information asymmetry, and fee-for-service. For example, physicians may respond to price caps or a fall in demand by some patients as a result of the imposition of user charges by recommending increased utilization by patients whose demand for health care services is inelastic because of the fact they have gap insurance or are wealthy.[36]

To what extent is it likely that physicians will actually take advantage of the information imbalance existing between themselves and most patients? Arrow notes that the ethical indoctrination of physicians becomes important in establishing a trust relationship between physicians and patients.[37] An internalized ethical code means that a physician is more likely to act in a patient's best interest than in his/her own naked self-interest thus reducing agency costs. The medical profession self-governs its own behavior to minimize opportunities for individual physicians to undermine patients' confidence in the medical profession in general. Entry into the profession is restricted and members are required to operate according to ethical codes that are determined by the profession. Thus, physicians' moral and ethical codes will mean they are highly unlikely to knowingly recommend treatments without any clinical benefit. Physicians will also wish to ensure their continued reputation in order to ensure patients make return visits to them, and to avoid medical malpractice actions (although, as discussed in Chapter 7, relatively few cases of negligence result in suits for medical malpractice). However, even within these parameters, physicians have a wide discretion to advocate the consumption of services that are not cost-effective. For example, physicians can advocate the consumption of services that, while not harmful, are of small marginal benefit or more costly services than are necessary to satisfy a particular health need. This problem of provider-induced demand is aggravated by the moral hazard problem as neither patients nor physicians are sensitive to the cost of services. It is also arguably aggravated by the desire of patients to have something "done" when they visit a doctor and the desire of patients to shift responsibility for vital decisions to skilled professionals.[38]

Although one can intuitively appreciate the *potential* for providers being able to influence demand for their own services, the empirical evidence for this is not clear-cut. On the one hand, there are many studies that conclude physicians and health service providers are influencing demand for their own services.[39] On the other hand, there are commentators that argue that the proposition that fee-for-service reimbursement leads to practitioners supplying more health care services than is cost-effective is unproven.[40] Clearly, there are variations in the ways that providers respond to financial incentives and that the reasons for provider behavior are multi-factorial.[41] Factors influencing behavior may include education and training, the practice of colleagues and peers, and absorption of ethical norms. Trade-offs may also be made by physicians between working longer hours and generating a higher income by providing more services.[42]

The argument over whether or not in a fee-for-service system physicians influence demand *for their own services* clouds what is the more important issue, namely that physicians are insensitive to the cost of *all* services that they recommend. Physicians prescribe drugs, diagnostic tests, the use of various technologies, and admit and discharge patients from hospital yet have no incentive to be sensitive to the cost-effectiveness of the various services they recommend. Stoddart *et al.* note that the estimates of the cost of physician-generated inappropriate use of health care services vary but are sometimes as large as 30–40 percent of all services including hospital services and drugs.[43] All sorts of factors may influence a physician in how she uses her discretion in making recommendations to the patient and there have traditionally been very few checks on this decision-making process. For example, a recent study showed that US cardiologists are 60 percent less likely to refer a black woman for a common procedure to test the heart's blood vessels than her white counterpart.[44]

The information asymmetry problem can also aggravate costs if providers seek to compete with each other on the basis of perceived quality (by physicians who admit patients to hospitals and by patients themselves) rather than price. The moral hazard problem of third-party insurance in an unregulated fee-for-service system means that hospitals often do not have to compete for custom on the basis of price, but will seek to attract patients with the promise of high-quality care. Quality of health care may, however, be very difficult to measure because of information problems. Hospitals will therefore tend to compete with each other on the basis of what Donabedian describes as "structural" measures as surrogate indicators of quality, e.g. the actual buildings and beds, technology, and skilled labor employed.[45] Hospitals will attract the allegiance of physicians (who refer or admit patients to the hospital) by providing the type of technology demanded by them in that region and amenities such as adjacent offices. Thomson notes that this type of competition increases hospitals' costs as physicians like hospitals to have spare capacity to suit their needs and prefer the latest technological equipment and highly-trained support staff.[46] A hospital that displays a high number of qualitative indicators does not, however, necessarily supply higher quality care or result in better patient outcomes. Therefore in areas where there are many competitors, contrary to what neo-classical economic theory would predict, prices may increase rather than fall in an unregulated fee-for-service market.

In response to the information asymmetry problem a government may intervene to control costs by restricting the number of inputs into the health system. This has been a common reform initiative in single-payer systems like Canada where the government has reduced the numbers of hospital beds, nursing staff, and technology in the hope that physicians, when faced with limited resources, will appropriately prioritize health needs and respond with the most cost-effective services possible. A government may attempt to change the financial incentives that physicians have to exploit their market power deriving from information asymmetries. This might involve the use of annual prospective global budgets for hospitals, managed care, and changing the fee-for-service payment system for physicians. These changes may be achieved by direct regulation and/or through contracts (as per the internal market model). Alternatively, government could delegate responsibility for micro-managing the supply side to private institutions and require these institutions to compete on price and quality dimensions (as per the managed competition model). All potential solutions have costs and benefits and are discussed in subsequent chapters.

Economies of scale

Depending on the particular health service market in question there may be economies of scale on the supply side. As mentioned above, economies of scale occur in a market when long-run average costs decline over time and are generally associated with industries or sectors where there are high start-up costs before even one good or service can be produced. For example, because of the high capital costs involved in hospital construction it is likely that in rural areas it would be inefficient to have more than one hospital, as to do so would duplicate high fixed costs. This would be a waste of society's scarce resources and thus allocatively inefficient. If government intervenes to prevent more than one hospital in a region then the problem arises that the hospital is a monopoly. From an economic perspective the problem with a monopoly is that it generally prefers to produce at a higher price and at lower output than in a competitive market.[47] The result is economic inefficiency if consumers substitute away from the monopolist's higher priced services to other services that are of a relatively cheaper price but in real terms cost more to produce (allocative inefficiency). There are also significant distributional consequences flowing from allowing an unregulated monopoly as there is a wealth transfer from consumers to the monopoly owners. A large wealth transfer means that consumers have not reduced their consumption in the face of price increases either by abstinence or through the consumption of substitutes (i.e. demand is inelastic). This will be so in the case of many hospital services as demand is likely to be highly inelastic and there are few realistic substitutes.

In response to the monopoly problem a government could regulate the price a monopolist charges to eliminate supra-normal (excessive) profits, and regulate and monitor the quality of services produced by the monopoly. Regulatory costs may be high, however, given that hospitals will have much better information than a regulator about their own costs and the quality of the services they supply. Some commentators believe that regulatory costs will outweigh any inefficiencies resulting from unregulated monopoly and recommend instead reliance upon "competition for the market" or a "contestable market."[48] In other words, provided there is the threat that a new entrant could supplant the incumbent monopoly, the monopoly will supply services at a price and quantity that is closer to what would occur in a competitive market.[49] At the other end of the regulatory spectrum, in response to the monopoly problem and the high costs of regulation, a government may choose to nationalize (i.e. own and operate) the hospitals themselves. In the UK and New Zealand government finances, owns, and operates the majority of hospitals, and not just those that would, in the absence of government intervention, hold a monopoly position. The problem of monopoly supply and the costs and benefits of possible regulatory solutions to it are discussed further in Chapter 6.

Distributive justice

In an unregulated health insurance market those who are most likely to be in need of health care may be priced out of the market as insurers look to avoid high-risk enrollees. Although there are significant instances of market failure justifying government intervention in health insurance and health service markets, most agree that the paramount justification for government intervention rests in a theory of distributive justice.

What is a theory of distributive justice? Beauchamp and Childress describe any such theory as "an attempt to establish a connection between the properties or characteristics of persons and the morally correct distribution of burdens and benefits in society. The connection may be found, for example, in desert, in effort, or in misfortune."[50]

There are four theories of justice often discussed with respect to allocating health care services. These theories are libertarian, utilitarian, egalitarian, and communitarian. A full discussion of these theories is beyond the scope of this work and what follows is an abbreviated summary. Libertarians view individual free choice as central to justice and strongly oppose governments taking resources from one set of individuals, through taxes or otherwise, to benefit another set of individuals. Libertarians are not opposed to distribution other than through market processes provided it is the free choice of each member of the group. Utilitarians support redistribution where such redistribution would result in the "greatest possible balance of value over disvalue"[51] or, to put it another way, redistribution would maximize the greatest good. Egalitarian theories of justice require that there be redistribution to ensure that individuals are given an equal share of at least some goods and services. Generally, egalitarian theories do not advocate equal distribution of all resources but rather sufficient redistribution to ensure some basic human functions. John Rawls' egalitarian theory of justice is probably the best known. He argues that vital economic goods and services should be distributed equally, unless an unequal distribution would work to everyone's advantage.[52] Communitarians too are concerned with redistribution to ensure an equal share of resources, but this is part of a larger concern of equal membership and participation in a community.[53]

Most Western industrialized states seem to prefer an egalitarian theory of distributive justice in allocating health care resources. It is usually stated that access to health care services should occur on the basis of *need* as opposed to ability to pay; however, not all potentially beneficial health care services are provided. Even the most generous of systems has explicit limits on care provided, e.g., not covering the full cost of prescription drugs, cosmetic surgery, or private rooms. Moreover, most publicly-funded systems have implicit limits by limiting the resources available to the health care system and leaving physicians to allocate resources between different needs. The UK government ensures access for all individuals to physician and hospital services without payment although it does impose small charges for drugs needed outside of hospitals. The New Zealand government ensures access for all individuals to hospital and specialist services without payment although it only partially subsidizes general practitioner services and drugs. The Dutch government ensures access for all its citizens for emergency and long-term care services and ensures access for the poorer 60 percent of the population to hospital and physician services. Contributions to the Dutch insurance schemes are linked to income and not on how many services a person uses. A survey of nine European countries by

Wagstaff *et al.* show policy-makers to be in broad agreement as to what constitutes equity in the allocation of health care. The consensus was that financial
contributions should be related to ability to pay, that all citizens should have
access to health care, and that access to and receipt of health care should
depend on need rather than ability to pay.[54]

The requirement that health care resources be allocated on the basis of
need as opposed to ability to pay essentially turns the usual market assumptions
on their head. Normally the more people are willing and able to pay, the more
or higher quality goods and services they receive. Justice, however, dictates
that health care resources be distributed on the basis of need. Those people in
society who are in greater need should get the care they need and this should
be funded by those in society who are able to pay. This means in general that
the wealthy should subsidize the poor and that the healthy should subsidize
the costs of caring for the sick. In the US, where most people have to purchase
private insurance to finance their health care, the financing system is highly
regressive.[55] What is meant by this is that poor people contribute a much greater
share of their incomes towards health care than richer people as poverty and
ill-health are often closely correlated. Wagstaff *et al.* found that systems that
rely extensively on user charges like the US and New Zealand (for general
practitioner care) are also regressive. Thus, the means by which a health care
system is financed is crucial from the perspective of satisfying the principle of
ensuring access on the basis of need as opposed to ability to pay.

What is it that makes health care different from other goods and services
such that governments feel they must intervene to redistribute resources? Health
certainly has the characteristics of one of Rawls' "primary goods" (although,
interestingly, not so characterized by Rawls), being something that a rational
person would want irrespective of what else she would want, all other things
being equal.[56] Treatment of disease can stop, prevent, or ameliorate physical
deterioration, pain, and premature death. Health is of overriding importance
to most of us as without good health our ability to participate in democratic,
economic, and social life is severely limited. Daniels grounds a right to health
care services in the idea of fair opportunity: "[p]roperties distributed by the
lottery of social and biological life are not grounds for morally acceptable
discrimination if they are not the sorts of properties that people have a fair
chance to acquire or overcome."[57] Health is fundamental to our feelings of
well being, security, comfort, and ultimately happiness. We care very deeply
not only about our own good health but that of our family and friends and to
a lesser but still significant extent of the health of others in our community. We
also know that as we grow older ultimately our health must deteriorate and
this can either be very quickly, for example, in the case of a fatal heart attack,
or a slow deterioration, through cancer or a chronic disease. Generally, we do
not know what our own life-path holds in store for us in terms of illnesses,
disabilities, and the way that we will die. This uncertainty characterizes each
and every one of our lives. The high cost of many health care interventions
coupled with the uncertainty of what our health care needs will be makes it
difficult to save funds to pay for services when they are needed.

One must, however, not mistakenly assume that access to health care services will ensure a fair allocation of health. The endless utilization of health care services will not necessarily result in better health. Other determinants of health besides access to health care services include biological factors, physical environment, lifestyle, and social environment.[58] Access to social welfare services, education, and socioeconomic status may have as great an impact (although more indirect and long term) on health as the consumption of health care services.[59] Equity in the context of health is, however, generally characterized as achieving a fair distribution of health care services rather than achieving a fair distribution of health, as the latter goal is viewed as too problematic.[60] Thus, fair access to medical and health care services is used as a very rough proxy for access to health. This explains why, even in countries that attempt to provide universal access to a very broad range of health care services, the poor and otherwise vulnerable populations are in significantly poorer health relative to other people within the country in question.[61] Notwithstanding the strong appeal of the arguments in favor of equal access for equal need, there are some that find the concept illogical.[62] This is because it seems contradictory to ensure an individual access to the latest medical technology such as heart and liver transplants yet not to ensure her adequate shelter, nutrition, income, and education. The irony is even greater when one acknowledges that, in the long run, these factors are as likely to influence one's health as access to health care services. However, it is somewhat nihilistic to argue that unfairness in the distribution of most resources can be used to justify unfairness in the area of health care allocation. There is surely an argument that individuals that are restored to or are maintained in as good health as is possible through the utilization of health care services have much better prospects for providing for themselves with respect to shelter, income, education, and nutrition.[63] Moreover, most Western industrialized countries do in fact ensure that their citizens have a minimum level of social security and access to education, at least up to the tertiary level.

As socioeconomic status is closely associated with poor health it may be just as rational to focus on targeting and improving the welfare of low-income groups as it is to finance a universal health care program. However, putting in place wealth redistribution programs cannot be the sole solution. Even in relatively healthy societies people still get injured, get sick, and eventually die. It is at these key moments of vulnerability that we want health care services and we have the most empathy for those in need of health care services. Many in society, I believe, would place less value on living an extra year of life at the end of a long life than on having medical and nursing care to alleviate the pain and other effects of the illness that finally kills them. Thus, access to health care services is so fundamental to life, our quality of life, and how we eventually die that people should have access to them even if they cannot afford to pay for them.

Having reached the conclusion that most Western industrialized nations do (and should) aspire to ensure access to health care services on the basis of need as opposed to ability to pay, one could stop there and move quickly on with designing a system that efficiently achieves this goal. This is tempting because of the difficulty, slipperiness, and subjectiveness inherent in determining what values should determine the allocation of health care resources. However, we must resist the temptation and wrestle on with this topic. The general egalitarian principle of access on the basis of need as opposed to ability to pay leaves a great deal unspoken. In particular, should all beneficial care be provided and, if not, what range and quality of health care services should be available to meet health needs? Who determines what health care needs are and prioritizes those needs? Also, as can be seen from the discussion above, even though an egalitarian theory of distributive justice seems to be paramount in most health care systems in Western industrialized countries, in fact, different health care systems reflect a mixture of libertarian, communitarian, egalitarian, and utilitarian theories of distributive justice.

Let us first deal with the problem that health care systems actually reflect a variety of distributive justice principles. The US system is something of an aberration amongst developed countries as it gives more weight to libertarian values than to egalitarian, utilitarian, or communitarian values. The US system does not guarantee everyone even emergency care. However, egalitarian values have some relevance as evident from the Medicaid and Medicare programs (respectively for the poor and the elderly) although, as discussed in Chapter 3, even these programs have a significant component of user charges. More important are polls showing that Americans would prefer a health care system that ensured access for everyone to health care. Libertarian values are important in other systems as well. For example, there seem to be continual battles in most systems as to whether user charges should be levied (rationing through price) so that there is at least some incentive for patients to consider the costs and benefits of the services consumed. More important, Americans are not alone in accepting a two-tier system where people are able to use their own money to buy "higher system medical care (e.g. more convenience, amenities, attention from the doctor)."[64] All systems (Canada being the notable exception for hospital and physician) allow their citizens to purchase faster care in the private sector. Privately purchased care may or may not be objectively of higher quality but certainly can be accessed without waiting and generally has better amenities in terms of hotel-like accommodation. There is also a cost in terms of lost market signals in shifting from a system that allocates according to the ability to pay (the libertarian preference) to one of need (the egalitarian/communitarian preference). For example, if people are prepared to pay a lot for life-saving technology this sends a clear signal to the manufacturers of this technology that it is highly valued and to produce more. If a government usurps this process, ratcheting down the price, less of the technology will be supplied in subsequent years.

Utilitarian values are becoming of increasing importance in many health care systems. Many systems are focusing more on the production of health and population health rather than health care for individuals. Once a government intervenes to create a publicly-funded system, the system takes on its own internal logic. For example, once it is decided that everyone who needs it should have access to hospital care (an egalitarian perspective), then it is easy to shift to arguing that the system should also cover basic primary and preventive care in order to stop people getting ill in the first place (a utilitarian perspective). An economic analysis is based in utilitarianism as it focuses on producing the maximum good irrespective of the distribution of benefits. Economists argue that the performance of publicly funded health care systems should be measured by their ability to generate "health" rather than equal access to health care services. For example, some economists argue that new technology should be assessed on its ability to produce "quality adjusted life years" (QALYs). Such an approach, geared as it is to maximizing the health of the population, can have a discriminatory impact on the elderly, disabled, chronically and terminally ill.[65] Once one is working within the concept of a publicly-funded system it is easy to abstract away from the egalitarian principles justifying the system in the first place, and shift to a utilitarian principle of trying to maximize "health." A system must, however, balance individual needs for health care services with what is in the best interest of society in general in terms of maximizing health outcomes.

Communitarian values are present in different health care systems to a greater or lesser degree. Communitarians argue strongly in favor of the concept of equal access for equal need and argue against allowing individuals to buy higher-quality services over and above that provided by a publicly-funded system. The argument is that inequities in access to health care services are unacceptable due to the special nature of health. Dougherty argues: "...there is something more repugnant about unequal treatment in matters as intimate as life, death, and the quality of life than in the general arena of consumer goods and services."[66] He contrasts our general acceptance of first-class seating on airplanes with our general reluctance to accept that a poor father must pass through a first-class neo-natal unit to visit his own new-born child who is not receiving the same standard of care even though the care may be adequate.[67] Walzer argues that the provision of medicine constitutes a separate sphere of justice within which equality should reign. Walzer notes:

> "were medical care a luxury these discrepancies [in access] would not matter much; but as soon as medical care becomes a socially recognized need, and as soon as the community invests in its provision, they matter a great deal . . . Doctors and hospitals have become such massively important features of contemporary life that to be cut off from the help they provide is not only dangerous but also degrading."[68]

Canada forces all of its citizens into its publicly-funded program covering hospital and physician services and effectively precludes the purchase of private supplementary insurance to buy these services more quickly in the public sector. Wealthy Canadians can, however, cross the border into the US to receive private care if they wish. Most countries do not force their citizens into a publicly-funded program and instead allow them to purchase private care with their own funds if they want quicker or better treatment than that offered by the public sector. However, in publicly-funded systems, such as the UK and New Zealand, the private sector generally only supplies non-emergency, non-acute care. When it comes to emergencies and the vast majority of acute care services, rich and poor alike are treated in the public sector. Thus, the communitarian ethic applies for the most dramatic, life-saving types of health care. Developments in potentially life-saving but expensive technology are putting pressure on the communitarian ethic of publicly-funded health care systems.[69]

The general principle that health care resources should be allocated on the basis of need as opposed to ability to pay does not address two important questions. First, who determines and prioritizes needs? Second, what range and quality of health care services should be available to meet those needs?

Given limited resources choices must be made regarding the circumstances in which we are prepared to provide medical services to individuals and what these services will include, given that these resources could also be deployed to some other use that might be equally as important to any particular individual. As Callahan notes, what is essential or adequate in terms of health care services cannot be defined independently of resources.[70] Thus, providing access to hip replacement operations in a country with severe food shortages is obviously inappropriate but will not be inappropriate in wealthier countries. Consequently, what will satisfy the demands of distributive justice with regard to health care in any particular country must depend on its particular social and economic circumstances and ultimately will have to involve political choices.[71]

Dworkin does not consider that issues of rationing are political alone. He argues that principles of justice allow the development of mechanisms for determining or rationing the health care services that should be available to everyone but which will not preclude wealthier individuals from buying more health care services if they so desire.[72] Dworkin utilizes a "veil of ignorance" (first developed in the work of John Rawls) to generate distribution principles. Essentially, the "veil of ignorance" is a thought experiment that requires us to imagine we are not yet born but, nonetheless, as members of a prospective community are able to discuss how we will order our community. We have information about the resources in our new society, and the costs and benefits of different health care services, but we have no knowledge or expectation about what our likely need for health care services will be over the course of our lives. In other words we do not know what our lot will be: whether rich or poor or whether we will suffer from cancer, heart disease, diabetes, asthma, etc. Dworkin believes that the resultant allocation decisions made by this notional society will, by necessary implication, be just. He argues that participants in this thought experiment would not elect to cover life-sustaining treatment for someone in a vegetable state. Nor would they elect to cover life-saving treatments for someone in the later stages of some irreversible form of dementia or agree to expensive treatments that are likely to extend life by very small amounts. However, the principles articulated by Dworkin do not take us far enough. To be of use, the members of the notional community would have to determine the values of a range of different health care needs/outcomes and which of these should be provided to everyone who needs them, given their cost. So, for example, would this potential society agree that everyone should have access to a life-saving operation with a 5 percent chance of success at a cost of $500,000.00? What Dworkin's analysis does clearly reveal is the need for public participation in the determination of the values placed upon the realization of health benefits/outcomes.

In publicly-funded systems, governments decide at a macro level how much public funding to devote to health care services relative to other needs, e.g., education, defense, etc. Governments also determine, in very general terms, the general categories of services to be publicly-funded, for example, hospital services, drugs, home care services, long-term care services, specialist services, etc. Beyond these broad categories, most publicly-funded systems leave the determination of who has a medical need, how to prioritize these needs, and the kind of service to be delivered within the hands of physicians. Governments of publicly-funded systems limit the resources to be made available to physicians who then must ration available resources between their various patients. This latter method of rationing has been the historical approach taken in many countries as there has been a reluctance to accept or acknowledge at a central level that health care resources have to be rationed. However, this approach may result in its own inequities. Studies suggest that physicians do not necessarily allocate resources according to objective criteria of clinical need. As mentioned earlier, there are wide variations in the supply of health care services that cannot be justified on differences in underlying clinical need. For example, in the UK, emergency readmissions to hospital are 70 percent higher in one area than in another, the proportion of women aged 25–64 screened for cervical cancer varies from 67 percent to 93 percent in different areas, and the number of hip replacements for those aged 65 and over varies from 10 to 51 per 10,000 of the population.[73] Physicians' decision-making processes are affected by their own financial self-interest, their peers, their particular medical education, when and where they received their medical education, and their own particular biases. Physicians make implicit decisions about the worth of people and the relative merit of their health needs on the basis of age, sex, health status, and visibility of the illness or disability. For example, a study released in 1999 shows that, even when fully insured, a US black person was 40 percent less likely than a white person with the same symptoms and risk factors to be recommended for catheterization, a common procedure to test the heart's blood vessels.[74] The fewer resources physicians have to work with, the more tragic the rationing decisions become. The rationing that occurs in physicians' offices on the grounds of age, health status, sex, etc. would probably not be tolerated if rationing decisions were more explicit and exposed to the sunlight of public scrutiny.

As countries are reforming their health care systems to be more competition-oriented, the process of determining total expenditures on health care services is shifting from an implicit to an explicit and more open form of rationing. In order to enable competition between groups of purchasers and/or providers, government-appointed bodies, such as New Zealand's Core Health Services Committee, struggle to determine what services to include in a package to be made available to everyone. Competition-oriented reform requires that explicit decisions be made about the range and minimum quality of services to be publicly-funded and this process is described in greater detail in Chapter 4.

If a government's goal is to ensure access on the basis of need as opposed to ability to pay, an economist might consider the appropriate response to be to subsidize the cost of private health insurance premiums (by a voucher) for the poor for a package of benefits considered just.[75] Let us set to one side for the moment the vexed question of what health care needs to cover and the market failure problems of adverse selection, moral hazard, administration costs and information asymmetries. With these problems aside, a subsidy for the poor immediately raises the prospect of individuals wishing for a free ride on the safety net designed for the poor.[76] For example, in the US, there is evidence of significant numbers of middle-class elderly people transferring their assets to their children in order to become eligible for Medicaid-covered nursing home care.[77] One can also envisage instances of people taking a risk they will not need health care services and, in the event that they do, seeking treatment as a charity case. Thus, it is arguably necessary to mandate that everyone purchase private insurance to cover the same benefits provided to the poor. There is also a problem that the services provided to the poor will be of low quality as the best providers may prefer the higher rates of reimbursement offered by private insurers.[78] As Weale notes, "[t]he principle that services for poor people are poor services is about as well attested an observation as we are likely to find in social affairs."[79] If a majority of the population do not have a vested interest in a publicly-financed health system then it may well deteriorate and eventually collapse through lack of voter support, thus jeopardizing access by the most vulnerable in society to needed health care services.

Conclusion

The unregulated operation of a health insurance market will perversely result in those who are most in need of health care services being priced out of or directly excluded from the market. Due to the importance of health to every individual's existence and dignity, an egalitarian theory of distributive justice seems to require governments to intervene to ensure a fairer distribution of resources. Justice cannot be discounted as a goal for a health allocation system and if ignored *will result in costs to the system in any event*. For example, the uninsured in the US may receive care if doctors feel unable to ignore their plight and the costs of this care will be borne to some degree by insured individuals. So either explicitly or implicitly a system has to absorb the costs of justice goals. Thus, the crucial task is not to design an efficient health allocation system per se but to design and implement a system that results in the optimal allocation of resources to the health sector and efficiently achieves the goal of satisfying justice concerns using these resources.

Justice, however, only seems to require of a government that it intervenes to ensure health care services for those people who cannot otherwise afford them. However, once having accepted the need to ensure access for people to services they would otherwise not be able to afford then the system itself takes on its own internal logic. It becomes possible to then justify a nationalized health insurance system covering all citizens or at least a majority of citizens for a comprehensive range of health care services on a mixture of justice, political, and economic reasons:

- to ensure that the quality of health care services supplied to those covered by the public system does not fall;
- to sustain continued political support for the public health system by capturing the middle-class and wealthy who are likely to have a greater influence on politicians;
- because the particular society in question rejects treating individuals in need (particularly of life-saving services) differently depending on their ability to pay (this is not, however, a conviction held by all societies);
- in order to reduce administrative or transactions costs;
- to avoid free-riding on a safety-net designed for the poor; that is, relatively wealthy people not buying insurance coverage in the expectation they will be able to play the system to receive coverage should it eventuate they do need health care services;
- to minimize opportunities for cost-shifting so that providers are not subsidizing the costs of care for people without health insurance from the prices charged to those with health insurance;
- to ensure comprehensiveness so as to minimize the ability or incentive of insurers and/or providers to shift costs to each other or on to society;
- to increase bargaining power on the demand side in order to deal with the problems of information asymmetry, moral hazard and monopoly supply.

The vexed question in all health care allocation systems, whether they simply provide vouchers for the poor or guarantee universal access, is what range and quality of health care services should be publicly-funded. In other words, what should comprise the "decent minimum", the "basic core" or "a comprehensive range?" This question will depend on the overall resources available to society and an appropriate balance must be struck between what is in the best interests of society and the best interests of particular individuals. Historically, governments have avoided explicit rationing of health care resources, preferring to set out in very broad terms the sorts of services to be covered and leaving further rationing decisions in the hands of physicians.

There are no obvious solutions as to what is the most appropriate form of government intervention in the financing and supply of health care services. That there is a role for government in determining the allocation of health care services is undisputed. That extensive government intervention can lead to problems of its own as exemplified in the command-and-control systems of New Zealand and the UK is also without doubt. Although there is support for nationalization of health insurance, there would not seem to be any justification for nationalization of hospitals and other health providers after reviewing the causes of market failure in health insurance and supply markets. The important question is how to achieve a balance between the benefits of competition (technical efficiency, dynamic efficiency, and responsiveness) and the benefits of government planning (equity and cost control). That there is a range of possible means by which to ensure access for every citizen to a range of health care services is amply demonstrated by the range of different health allocation systems in the world. The systems of New Zealand, the UK, the Netherlands, and the US reflect the continuum of health care allocation systems in terms of the public/private mix in financing health insurance and in the supply of health care services. Moreover, all these countries have, in recent times, proposed to reform their health care systems using generally what can be described as competition-oriented reform proposals. In the next chapter, we will examine the incentives operating in the different health care allocation systems in New Zealand, the UK, the US, and the Netherlands and their respective proposals for either managed competition or internal market reform. Chapter 3 provides the raw material for analysis in Chapters 4 to 7 of this book.

Notes

1   A. J. Culyer, 'The Nature of the Commodity Health Care and its Efficient Allocation', (1971) 23 *Oxford Economic Papers* 189.

2   R. G. Evans, *Strained Mercy: The Economics of Canadian Health Care* (Toronto: Butterworths and Co. [Canada], 1984) at p. 63 (hereinafter *Strained Mercy*).

3   Organization for Economic Cooperation and Development, *The Reform of Health Care Systems: A Review of Seventeen OECD Countries*, (Paris: OECD, 1994) (hereinafter OECD 1994 *Review of Seventeen Countries*) p. 317, notes those without insurance in the US sometimes receive care which is financed by charity and/or by shifting costs to other payers.

4   M. V. Pauly, 'Taxation, Health Insurance, and Market Failure in the Medical Economy', (1986) 24(2) *J. of Economic Literature* 629 at p. 639.

5   See generally M. Rothschild and J. E. Stiglitz, 'Equilibrium in Competitive Insurance Markets: An Essay on the Economics of Imperfect Information', (1976) 90(4) *Quart. J. of Econ.* 630.

6   *Strained Mercy, op. cit.*, p. 41.

7   See generally G. A. Akerlof, 'The Market for "Lemons": Quality Uncertainty and the Market Mechanism', (1970) 84(3) *Quart. J. of Econ.* 488.

8   P. A. Corning, *The Evolution of Medicare...From Idea to Law* (Washington, DC: Department of Health, Education, and Welfare, 1969) as cited by D. Blumenthal, 'Health Care Reform: Past and Future', (1995) 332(7) *New Eng. J. of Medicine* 465. The figures given are for 1962.

9   S. S. Wallack *et al.*, 'A Plan for Rewarding Efficient HMOs', (1988) 7(3) *Health Affairs* 80 at p. 84.

10 Organization for Economic Cooperation and Development, *US Health Care at the Crossroads* (Paris: OECD, 1992) at p. 35.

11 M. L. Berk and A. C. Monheit, 'The Concentration of Health Expenditures: An Update', (1992) 11(4) *Health Affairs* 145.

12 A. C. Enthoven and S. J. Singer, 'Market-Based Reform: What to Regulate and by Whom', (1995) 14(1) *Health Affairs* 105 at p. 106.

13 I. Erhlich and G. Becker, 'Market Insurance, Self Insurance, and Self Protection', (1972) 80(4) *J. Polit. Econ.* 623 at pp. 623–648 as cited by Pauly, 'Taxation, Health Insurance, and Market Failure in the Medical Economy', *op. cit.*, p. 639.

14 V. R. Fuchs, 'Economics, Health, and Post-industrial Society', (1979) 57(2) *Milbank Mem. Fund Quart.* 153, and B. C. Vladeck, 'The Market vs. Regulation: The Case for Regulation', (1981) 59(2) *Milbank Mem. Fund Quart.* 209, both cited *ibid.*, p. 639.

15 D. U. Himmelstein, S. Wolfe and S. Woolhandler, 'Cost Without Benefits: Administrative Waste in US Health Care', (1989) *New Eng. J. of Medicine* 441; S. Woolhandler and D. U. Himmelstein, 'The Deteriorating Administrative Efficiency of the US Health Care System', (1991) 324(18) *New Eng. J. of Medicine* 1253, and see S. Woolhandler and D. U. Himmelstein, 'Correction: The Deteriorating Administrative Efficiency of the US Health Care System', (1994) 331(5) *New Eng. J. of Medicine* 336. For a rebuttal of their arguments, see P. Danzon, 'The Hidden Costs of Budget-Constrained Health Insurance Systems', (paper presented at the American Enterprise Institute Conference, Washington, DC, 3 October 1991).

16 J.-P. Poullier, *OECD Health Systems: Facts and Trends 1960–1991* (Paris: OECD, 1993) at pp. 108–109 (hereinafter *OECD Health Systems: Facts and Trends*) lists total and public expenditures on health care for OECD countries and at pp. 112–113 lists total and public expenditures on health administration costs. In 1991, the US spent a total of $751,771 million with $329,960 million paid for by the public sector. In the same year the US spent $43,900 million on health administration costs, of which $8,100 million was attributable to the public sector.

17 *Strained Mercy, op. cit.*, p. 39.

18 *OECD Health Systems: Facts and Trends, op. cit.*, does not provide any 1991 figures for Canada, but records that Canada spent a total of $62,706 million (Canadian) on health care in 1990, $803 million of which was spent on health administration costs.

19 Calculated from figures provided in *OECD Health Systems: Facts and Trends, op. cit.*, at pp. 108–109 and at pp. 112–113.

20 M. V. Pauly, *op. cit.* at p. 630 referring to M. V. Pauly, 'The Economics of Moral Hazard: Comment', (1968) 58(3) *Amer. Econ. Rev.* 531.

21 For a discussion of why health care services should not be denied to those who engage in *ex ante* moral hazard, see R. L. Schwartz, 'Life Style, Health Status, and Distributive Justice', (1993) 3(1) *Health Matrix* 195 at p. 197.

22 F. A. Sloan, 'Does The Market Choose the Correct Incentives to Get to the Desired Outcomes? Market Failure Reexamined' in R. J. Arnould, R. F. Rich and W. D. White (eds), *Competitive Approaches to Health Care Reform* (Washington, DC: Urban Institute Press, 1993) at p. 264.

23 Pauly, 'Taxation, Health Insurance, and Market Failure in the Medical Economy', *op. cit.*, p. 640.

24 In 1991, the admission rate to US hospitals as a percentage of population was 13.7 compared to 10.9 in the Netherlands, 13.9 in New Zealand, 19.3 in the UK and an OECD average of 16.2. The average length of stay in a US hospital was 9.1 days compared to 33.8 in the Netherlands, 11.7 in New Zealand, 14 in the UK and an OECD average of 14.4 days. The number of physician contacts per capita in the US were 5.6 times per annum compared to 5.4 in the Netherlands, 3.8 in New Zealand, 5.7 in the UK and an OECD average of 6.1. Data from G. J. Schieber *et al.*, 'Health System Performance In OECD Countries, 1980–1992', (1994) 13(4) *Health Affairs* 100 at p. 106, Exhibit 4, from OECD data and their own estimates.

25 For example, W. P. Welch, D. Verrilli, S. J. Katz and E. Latimer, 'A Detailed Comparison of Physician Services for the Elderly in the United States and Canada', (1996) 275(18) *JAMA* 1410, found that the Canadian elderly receive a higher volume of physician services than the US elderly; however, Canada records overall lower expenditures per elderly person because the average price for physician services is much lower.

26 See G. L. Stoddart, M. L. Barer, R. G. Evans and V. Bhatia, *Why Not User Charges? The Real Issues: A Discussion Paper* (Ontario: The Premier's Council on Health, Well-being and Social Justice, September 1993) at p. 5. On the other hand, from a physician's perspective, it may be difficult to refuse requests by patients for services that are not cost-effective – see J. R. Williams and E. B. Beresford, 'Physicians, Ethics and the Allocation of Health Care Resources' in F. Baylis *et al.* (eds), *Health Care Ethics In Canada* (Toronto: Harcourt Brace, 1995) 121 at p. 124.

27 C. Donaldson and K. Gerard, *Economics of Health Care Financing: The Visible Hand* (London: Macmillan, 1992) at p. 46, note that in Australia, the government sets its own fee schedule and reimburses only 75 percent of this schedule for hospital care and 85 percent for general practitioner care. Doctors are free to charge patients fees higher than the government's fee schedule, but this extra amount cannot be privately insured.

28 For a discussion see Stoddart *et al., op. cit.,* pp. 5–7. See also J. Hurley and N. Johnson, 'The Effects of Co-payments Within Drug Reimbursement Programs', (1991) 18(34) *Canadian Public Policy* 473.

29 J. P. Newhouse and the Insurance Experiment Group, *Free For All? Lessons From The RAND Health Insurance Experiment.* (Cambridge, MA: Harvard University Press, 1994).

30 K. N. Lohr, *et al.,* 'Use of Medical Care in the RAND Health Insurance Experiment: Diagnosis- and Service-specific Analyses of a Randomized Controlled Trial', (1986) 25 (Supp.) *Medical Care* 531.

31 J. P. Newhouse *et al.,* 'Some Interim Results From A Controlled Trial of Cost Sharing in Health Insurance', (1981) 305(25) *New Eng. J. of Medicine* 1501 at p. 1505.

32 For example, the New Zealand government abandoned its $50 a night patient user charge for public hospitals partly because of a public outcry, but also partly because of the high administrative costs involved with collection. By the end of the first quarter (May 1992), after the introduction of user charges for public hospital services, outstanding debts fell in the range of 30–60 percent of total revenue from charges – 'Hospital Fees Unpaid Up To 63 percent', 18 June 1992, *New Zealand Herald,* as cited by T. Ashton, 'Charging for Health Services: Some Anecdotes from the Antipodes' in M. Malck *et al.* (eds), *Strategic Issues in Health Care Management* (Chichester/New York: John Wiley and Sons, 1993) at p. 16.

33 F. A. Sloan, *op cit.,* p. 260.

34 D. Reisman, *Market and Health* (New York: St. Martin's Press, 1993) at p. 8.

35 *Strained Mercy, op. cit.,* p. 71, C. Phelps, *Health Economics* (New York: Harper Collins, 1992) at p. 211, for a discussion of supplier-induced demand, and U. E. Reinhardt, 'The Theory of Physician-Induced Demand: Reflections After a Decade', (1985) 4 *Health Economics* 111.

36 Donaldson and Gerard, *op. cit.,* pp. 56–57.

37 K. J. Arrow, 'Uncertainty and the Welfare Economics of Medical Care', (1963) 53 *American Economic Review* 941 at p. 949.

38 G. Mooney and A. McGuire, 'Economics and Medical Ethics in Health Care: An Economic Viewpoint', in G. Mooney and A. McGuire (eds), *Medical Ethics and Economics in Health Care* (Oxford: Oxford University Press, 1988) at p. 14.

39 Increases in the volume of physicians' services in the US during the Medicare physician fee freeze over the period 1984 to 1986 were associated with a continuing rate of increase in per enrollee physician expenditures of 10 percent or more during each of the years that fees were frozen – J. Mitchell, G. Wedig and J. Cromwell, *Impact of the Medicare Fee Freeze on Physician Expenditures and Volume: Final Report* (Baltimore, MD: Health Care Financing Administration, 1988) as cited by K. M. Langwell and T. Menke, 'Controlling Costs of the US Health Care System: Trends and Prospects', in Arnould, Rich and White, *op. cit.,* p. 38. In the US, Fuchs has found that a 10-percent higher surgeon per capita ratio in any particular area will result in a 3 percent increase in the number of operations and an overall increase in price indicating that surgeons may be influencing demand for their own services – V. R. Fuchs, 'The Supply of Surgeons and the Demand for Operations' in V. R. Fuchs (ed.), *The Health Economy* (Cambridge, MA: Harvard University Press, 1986) p. 147; Evans argues that despite the historical increase in the number of physicians per capita in Canada and the US, physicians' average income and

workload have not fallen as market theory would normally predict, indicating that providers are able to influence demand for their own services – *Strained Mercy*, *op. cit.*, p. 87.

40 See, for example, J. Hurley and R. Labelle, 'Relative Fees and the Utilization of Physicians' Services in Canada', (1995) 4(6) *Health Economics* 419, and P. C. Coyte, 'Review of Physician Payment and Service Delivery Mechanisms', (1995 April) *Ontario Medical Review* 23.

41 See the discussion by C. E. Phelps and C. Mooney, 'Variations in Medical Practice Use: Causes and Consequences', in Arnould, Rich and White, *op. cit.*, pp. 171–172.

42 Hurley and Labelle, *op. cit.*

43 See Stoddart *et al.*, *op. cit.*, p. 6.

44 K. A. Schulman *et al.*, 'The Effect of Race and Sex on Physicians' Recommendations for Cardiac Catheterization', (1999) 340(8) *New Eng. J. Of Med.* 618.

45 A. Donabedian, 'Quality Assessment and Assurance: Unity of Purpose, Diversity of Means', (1988) 25(1) *Inquiry* 173.

46 R. B. Thomson, 'Competition Among Hospitals in the United States', (1994) 27(3) *Health Policy* 205.

47 See R. Posner, *Anti-trust Law: An Economic Perspective* (Chicago, IL: University of Chicago Press, 1976) at pp. 8–22.

48 See H. Demsetz, 'Why Regulate Monopoly?', (1968) *J. Law Econ* 55; W. Baumol, J. Panzer, and R. Willig, *Contestable Markets and the Theory of Industry Structure* (New York: Harcourt, Brace, Jovanovich, 1982), and W. Baumol, 'Contestable Markets: An Uprising in the Theory of Industry Structure', (1982) 72 *American Economic Review* 1.

49 The high sunk costs often attributed to establishing a hospital may render the threat of new entry and thus the prospect of contestable markets less viable. This problem may be alleviated to some degree in the future as advances in technology enable more outpatient and day-surgery and accordingly providers of secondary care can compete in markets without requiring as significant an infrastructure investment.

50 T. L. Beauchamp and J. F. Childress, *Principles of Biomedical Ethics*, 4th edn (New York: Oxford University Press, 1994) at p. 258.

51 T. L. Beauchamp and J. F. Childress, *Principles of Biomedical Ethics*, 3rd edn (New York: Oxford University Press, 1989) at p. 26.

52 J. Rawls, *A Theory of Justice* (Cambridge, MA: The Belknap Press of Harvard University Press, 1971).

53 C. J. Dougherty, 'An Axiology for National Health Insurance', (1992) 20(1–2) *Law Medicine and Health Care* 82 at p. 85.

54 A. Wagstaff *et al.*, 'Equity in the Finance of Health Care: Some International Comparisons', (1992) 11(4) *J. Health Econ.* 361 at p. 363, and see also J. W. Hurst, 'Reforming Health Care In Seven European Nations', (1991) 10(3) *Health Affairs* 7.

55 Wagstaff *et al.*, *ibid.* at p. 384.

56 J. Rawls, *op. cit.*, pp. 92–95, and see N. Daniels, *Just Health Care* (Cambridge: Cambridge University Press, 1985).

57 N. Daniels, *ibid.*, p. 271.

58 D. Ruwaard, P. G. N. Kramers, A. van den Berg Jeths and P. W. Achterberg (eds), *Public Health Status and Forecasts: The Health Status of the Dutch Population Over the Period 1950–2120* (The Hague: SDU Uitgeverij, 1994) at p. 27.

59 See generally R. G. Evans, M. L. Barer and T. R. Marmor (eds), *Why are Some People Healthy and Others Not?: The Determinants of Health of Populations* (New York: Aldine De Gruyter, 1994), and D. Vagero, 'Equity and Efficiency in Health Reform: A European View', (1994) 39(9) *Soc. Sci. Med.* 1203 at p. 1207.

60 G. Mooney, 'What Does Equity in Health Mean?', (1987) 40 *Wld. Hlth. Stat. Q.* 196 as cited by R. A. Carr-Hill, 'Efficiency and Equity Implications of the Health Care Reforms', (1994) 39(9) *Soc. Sci. Med.* 1189 at p. 1190.

61 See J. C. Hurowitz, 'Towards a Social Policy for Health', (1993) 329(2) *New Eng. J. of Med.* 130, and S. L. Ettner, 'New Evidence on the Relationship Between Income and Health', (1996) 15(1) *J. of Health Economics* 67 at p. 83.

62 See P. T. Menzel, 'Equality, Autonomy and Efficiency: What Health Care System Should we Have?', (1992) 17(1) *J. of Medicine and Philosophy* 33 at pp. 38–45.

63 See Daniels, *op. cit.*, pp. 26–28, arguing that health care should be provided to allow individuals to achieve 'species-typical normal functioning.'

64 A. C. Enthoven, 'On the Ideal Market Structure for Third-Party Purchasing of Health Care', (1994) 39(10) *Soc. Sci. Med.* 1413 at p. 1420.

65 For a discussion of the flexibility of QALYs see A. Williams, 'Cost-effectiveness Analysis: Is it Ethical?' (1992) 18 *Jnl. of Medical Ethics* 7. For a criticism of QALYs and an economic analysis of health issues generally see M. Loughlin 'Rationing, Barbarity and The Economist's Perspective' (1996) 14 *Health Care Analysis* 146.

66 Dougherty, *op. cit.*, p. 85.

67 *Ibid.*, p. 84.

68 M. Walzer, *Spheres of Justice: A Defense of Pluralism and Equality* (New York: Basic Books, 1983) at p. 89.

69 See for the example the case of *R v. Cambridge Health Authority, Ex Parle B* [1995] 1 F.L.R. 1055 (Q.B.). That case centered on B, a 10-year old girl diagnosed with non-Hodgkins lymphoma, who was denied public funding of further treatment at an estimated cost of £75,000 because of what was viewed as slim (10%) prospects for success.

70 D. Callahan, 'What is a Reasonable Demand on Health Care Resources: Designing a Basic Package of Benefit', (1992) 8 *J. of Contemporary Health Law and Policy* 1.

71 *Ibid.*

72 R. Dworkin, 'Justice in the Distribution of Health Care', (1993) 38(4) *McGill Law Journal* 883.

73 Statements from *The New NHS: Modern, Dependable*, a White Paper, Cm 3807, 8 December 1997 at section 2.22. Online. Available HTTP: http://www.official-documents.co.uk/document/doh/newnhs/contents.htm (accessed 30 March 1999).

74 See K. A. Schulman, 'The Effect of Race and Sex on Physicians' Recommendations for Cardiac Catheterization' (1999) 340(8) *New Eng. J. of Med.* 618.

75 *Strained Mercy*, *op. cit.*, p. 65.

76 D. Reisman, *Market and Health* (New York: St. Martin's Press, 1993) at p. 62, notes that a rational individual will evade the cost of private insurance to ride free on the public system where possible.

77 B. Burwell, *Middle-Class Welfare: Medicaid Estate Planning for Long-Term Care Coverage* (Lexington, MA: SysteMetrics/McGraw-Hill Inc., 1991) as cited by N. De Lew, G. Greenberg and K. Kinchen, 'A Layman's Guide to the US Health Care System', (1992) 14(1) *Health Care Financing Review* 151.

78 A. Weale, 'Equality, Social Solidarity and the Welfare State', (1992) 100 *Ethics* 473 at p. 474.

79 *Ibid.*

3 The reform of health care allocation systems in the US, the Netherlands, New Zealand, and the UK

This chapter provides an overview of the US, Netherlands, New Zealand, and UK health care systems. I discuss the four countries in a sequence that reflects a continuum in terms of levels of private funding and private delivery. At one end of the spectrum, the US relies to the greatest degree on private funding and private supply whereas at the other end, the UK relies to the greatest degree on public funding and provision. The Netherlands falls along this continuum closer towards the US, but there is a fundamental and crucial distinction with respect to access. Through regulation, the Netherlands ensures that the poorest 60 percent of the population are covered for comprehensive care, and that the entire population is covered for "exceptional" medical expenses. New Zealand falls closer on the continuum towards the UK, but what distinguishes New Zealand is its relatively high reliance on private financing (by patients themselves and by private insurance) for general practitioner services.

This chapter has four objectives:

- to discuss the cost and access problems that prompted reform in the late 1980s and early 1990s in all four countries (hence why some of the earlier figures discussed appear dated);
- to describe and discuss the reforms implemented or proposed in the early 1980s and 1990s;
- to briefly canvass progress and changes in the reform agendas since that time; and finally,
- to compare the structure and dynamics of the four health care systems in order to identify those key features of a system that will efficiently achieve access for all citizens to a comprehensive range of health care services on the basis of need as opposed to ability to pay.

The US health care system and the 1993 reform proposals

Problems in the system prior to reform proposals

The problems in the US system manifest themselves in cost escalation and lack of access to health care services for approximately 16 percent of the population.

Costs

In 1992 (a year before the Clinton reform proposals), the US spent 66 percent more on health care services as a percentage of GDP than the OECD average.[1] This figure is not as extreme as it first appears for in OECD countries there is a strong correlation between national wealth and national health care spending. The US is a very wealthy country but it still spends much more on health care services than the usual ratio of spending to national wealth. The US spends a one-third higher percentage of GDP than would be predicted from its real level of GDP.[2] Most OECD countries record a rising percentage of GDP being devoted to their respective health sectors over the last thirty years, but the US has experienced higher rates of growth than most countries.[3] The percentage of GDP devoted to health care rose from 5.3 percent in 1960 to 13.9 percent in 1993,[4] and in the early 1990s was predicted to reach 18.1 percent by the year 2000.[5] However, the managed care revolution, which has occurred since President Clinton's unsuccessful 1993 proposals for reform, has contributed to a significant reduction in the growth in health care spending. In 1996, 13.6 percent of GDP was spent on health care and it was predicted this figure would rise to 14.5 percent by 2001.[6]

Various factors are blamed for the growing costs of the US health system. These factors include high administrative costs (discussed in Chapter 2), the high costs of malpractice premiums and "defensive medicine."[7] An examination of the figures available suggests that these factors only contribute in a relatively small way to growing costs. For example, in 1990, the American Medical Association estimated that the cost of defensive medicine amounted to just 3 percent of total health spending.[8] As Table 3.1 demonstrates, the higher costs incurred in the US are not explained by a higher number of hospital beds in the system (column A) nor by people spending many more days in hospital once admitted (columns B and D).

Rather than higher utilization rates or numbers of hospital beds, higher costs in the US appear attributable to the intensity of care provided per episode of illness and higher payment rates for providers.[9] By "intensity of care" I refer to the number and types of tests, procedures, drugs, and professionals involved in servicing a particular medical need. For example, one study comparing treatment of patients with uncomplicated hypertension in the US and the UK found that physicians in the US ordered forty times more electrocardiograms, seven times more chest films, five times more blood counts,

Table 3.1 Hospital care measures

	A *In-patient care-beds per 1000 pop.*	B *In-patient care bed days per Capita*	C *In-patient occupancy rate (percent available beds)*	D *Average length of stay (days)*
Netherlands	11.4a / 11.2b	3.7a / 3.6b	88.7a / 88.7b	33.8a
New Zealand	7.6a / 6.8b	1.6a / 1.5b	57.3a	11.7a
UK	5.6a / 4.5b	2.0a / 1.7b	80.6d	14.0a
US	4.8a / 4.1b	1.2a / 1.1b	69.1a	9.1e

Key = a = 1991, b = 1996, c = 1981, d = 1986, e 1990

Source: This table includes data compiled by Schieber *et al.*, 'Health System Performance in OECD countries, 1980–1992', (1994) (Fall) 13(4) *Health Affairs* 100 at p. 106, Exhibit 4 and data from the *OECD Health Data 98: A Comparative Analysis of 29 Countries* (Electronic Database)

and four times more urinalyses than their British counterparts.[10] A recent study of physician services for the elderly in the US and Canada found that Canadians receive more basic care but 25 percent fewer surgical procedures such as cataract extractions and knee replacements.[11] Moreover, prices for health care services in the US are the highest of all OECD countries – 58 percent above the average.[12] Higher prices not only reflect higher profit margins for providers but also the use of greater technology and the provision of more intensive care per service.

Access and quality

Despite the government-sponsored programs of Medicaid (for the very poor) and Medicare (for the elderly); there are significant access problems. In 1993, 25 percent of the population lost health insurance coverage for some period during the following two years, 37 million Americans had no insurance, and a further 22 million lacked adequate coverage.[13] In 1997, the number of Americans without insurance climbed to 43.2 million, nearly 16 percent of the total population. Of these, 10.6 million were children.[14] Although the Medicare program provides insurance coverage for most of the elderly (over 65), the Medicaid program for the poor covers less than half of those below the federal poverty line.[15] The uninsured can sometimes get emergency hospital care supplied on a charitable basis, but there are wide variations in access to charity care across the country.[16]

Given the reliance of the US health system on employment-based insurance, it would seem logical that most of the uninsured will be unemployed. Surprisingly, 87 percent of families *without* health insurance have a member of the family engaged in part- or full-time work, and many are employed in small businesses. This may be due to the fact that small businesses face premiums that are 10–40 percent higher than those paid by large firms (because of the higher administration costs incurred for insuring a smaller population and the fact that risk cannot be pooled over a larger employee base.)[17] The high cost of health insurance also means that those who receive government income assistance and government subsidized health insurance are reluctant to take up employment because of the high cost of private insurance.[18] Also of concern is continuity of insurance coverage. Employees are unwilling to change jobs for fear of losing their existing entitlements as most insurers will not agree to insure pre-existing conditions.[19] Recent federal initiatives to address this particular problem are discussed below.

Even amongst the insured, there may be difficulty in accessing needed services because of high deductibles or user charges. Such a method of financing services is regressive as it imposes the greatest burdens on the poor and the ill. In the US, both private insurers and government insurers (Medicaid and Medicare) impose user charges and deductibles resulting in access to these services being determined on the basis of ability to pay. Medicaid recipients saw the proportion of their after-tax income devoted to user charges and deductibles increase from an average of 7.8 percent in 1972/3 to 11.5 percent in 1989. By comparison, the general population devoted, on average, below 5 percent of their after-tax income to user charges and deductibles.[20]

The US spends a significant amount on health care, but it is far from clear that value for money is received in terms of health improvements. Evidence in this regard is by nature speculative because of the difficulty of measuring linkages between the consumption of health care services and health outcomes, particularly over the longer term. Notwithstanding the difficulties with assessing performance using crude mortality and life expectancy indicators, it is hard to overlook infant mortality rates that are generally assumed to be sensitive to the quality of health care services available to the whole population.[21] Compared to other wealthy countries, the US performs poorly on infant mortality rates and with respect to the numbers of low birth-weight babies born. On the other hand, the US records the highest life expectancy at age eighty and over for men and the second highest for women amongst OECD countries.[22] This suggests that the US is allocating more resources to prolonging the life of the elderly as opposed to preventive and primary services that enable a basic standard of health care for the population as a whole. Living extra months or even years at the end of our lives may not, however, be what patients or society value. There have been anecdotal reports of physicians using invasive procedures to extend the life of a patient but disregarding the patient's resultant quality of life in terms of suffering, anguish, and pain.[23]

There are also enormous inequalities in health status.[24] The infant mortality rate for native Americans is 1.5 times the rate for Caucasians and the rate for Blacks is 2.1 times the rate for whites.[25] On average, a Black man in Harlem is less likely to reach his sixty-fifth birthday than a man living in Bangladesh.[26] Poverty, violence, and racism contribute to these outcomes. However, lack of initial access to primary and preventive health care services is presumably a contributing factor to the poor health outcomes for blacks although there has been remarkably little empirical research done with regard to demonstrating this.

Financing of health care services

Private health insurance

In the early part of the twentieth century, physicians and private hospitals established private health insurance plans, like Blue Cross and Blue Shield. Until relatively recently, the boards of insurance companies were dominated by physicians. As a result, Enthoven notes that health insurance policies have furthered the medical profession's interests by institutionalizing the "guild" principles of health care financing – fee-for-service billing, free choice of providers, solo practice, unconstrained choice of drugs by physicians, and the fiscal and clinical independence of physicians.[27]

Most states encouraged the proliferation of the non-profit physician-dominated Blue Cross and Blue Shield plans by granting these health insurers exemptions from financial requirements imposed on other commercial insurance companies and exemptions from property and income tax.[28] The percentage of the population with private health insurance grew from 9.1 percent in 1940[29] to 61.6 percent by 1991.[30] However, in the early 1990s private insurance only accounted for 33.5 percent of all health expenditures.[31] Clearly the burden of the costs of the highest users of care are borne by the government and patients themselves.

The earliest non-profit Blue Cross and Blue Shield plans did not engage in risk-selection; they calculated premiums on a community-wide basis. In other words, every person in a region paid the same premium irrespective of the relative risk of that person needing health care services. As competition between insurers grew, non-profit plans began to risk-rate premiums in order to remain competitive. This resulted in increased access problems as high-risk individuals, who are often poor, could not pay the increased premiums.

The growth of private health insurance was encouraged from the 1940s by tax exemptions whereby premiums paid by employers for employees were tax deductible expenses and premiums so paid were not taxed as employee income. As tax levels rose through the years this tax advantage became of increasingly greater value. Most commentators seem agreed that the historic tax treatment of health insurance premiums is both unjust and inefficient.[32] The tax exemption is unjust because it is a regressive means of financing health care where everyone, regardless of income, receives the same tax benefit (see the discussion in Chapter 2 for further clarification of this point.) In an otherwise progressive tax system, a tax exemption for health care costs favors higher income families disproportionately.[33] It is also unjust as the self-employed and individuals buying their own health insurance have not been granted similar tax benefits (although in 1996 the federal government enacted legislation to correct this problem.) It is inefficient as it results in employers and employees being less concerned about the price of insurance than they otherwise would be if they had to pay for the insurance with after-tax dollars. One study suggests that 80–100 percent of each dollar reduction in health care spending will translate into higher wages for employees.[34] Nonetheless, employees operate under the misapprehension that health premiums are a cost paid for by their employers and not by themselves.[35]

Employers have historically not been overly concerned with controlling health insurance costs given that premiums paid for employees are tax-deductible and that employers have been able to pass on rising costs in the form of reductions in the growth of the wages and salaries of employees. However, rising costs and growing foreign competition during the 1980s compelled employers to significantly lower operating costs, and at this time many employers began to examine ways by which to reduce health insurance costs for employees. One such measure was a move on the part of larger employers to self-insure rather than buying coverage for their employees from private insurers. The 1974 Employee Retirement Income and Security Act (ERISA) has had a profound effect on the rate of self-insurance by employers.[36] The ERISA legislation largely pre-empts state regulation of self-insuring employee benefit plans. As states have sought to regulate minimum benefit packages, this has encouraged the growth of self-insurance amongst larger employers anxious to avoid the cost of compliance with these regulations. Employers have also increasingly begun to purchase health care services from managed care plans, and this phenomenon is discussed further below.

The role of government

Over the years US governments (both federal and state) have played an increasing role in financing the health care system.[37] In 1960, the government only paid 25 percent of all health expenditures. By 1993 this had increased to 43.9 percent and in 1997 to 46.7 percent.[38] Numerous state health care initiatives have produced considerable variations between states in the design of their respective health care systems. The discussion below will focus primarily on the role of the federal government rather than the various state initiatives.

Unlike the UK, New Zealand and the Netherlands, the US failed to implement a national health insurance scheme in the 1930s and 40s. One possible explanation was the strong opposition of the American Medical Association; however, such opposition was not unique to the US and was overcome, albeit with difficulty, in other countries. Rothman argues that national insurance proposals failed because the physician-dominated Blues insurance plans worked hard to ensure access by the middle class to affordable coverage – and this tactic undermined political support for a national scheme.[39] In this endeavor the Blues plans largely succeeded, and the impetus for reform largely dissipated as it was widely considered that employment group insurance would grow to cover the entire population without government intervention.[40] This prediction, however, proved false.

By 1962, the need for reform had become pressing as 50 percent of Americans over the age of 65 were completely uninsured and only half of those with health insurance had adequate coverage for hospitalization expenses.[41] After the Democratic landslide of 1964, a federally funded Medicare program was implemented with the intention of providing coverage similar to that provided by the non-profit Blues insurers for those aged over 65.[42] Despite the strong opposition of the American Medical Association, there was significant public support for the Medicare proposals. Overnight, Medicare became the single largest health insurer in the country, covering 13 percent of the population.[43] Medicare not only covers those over 65 but also provides coverage for some non-elderly disabled people and those eligible under the End Stage Renal Disease (ESRD) Program (disabled and ESRD beneficiaries accounted for 12.6 percent of the Medicare population in 1996).[44]

Medicare is financed partly by premiums paid by those enrolled in the scheme but is topped up by social insurance taxes and general revenues. Under the Medicare plan, coverage is automatically provided for hospital care and related benefits under Part A. Medicare provides only very limited nursing home and other long-term care services. Additional premiums are required to be paid for enrolment in Part B of the Medicare plan, which covers physician and other ambulatory services, durable medical equipment, and certain other services. Medicare beneficiaries must pay deductibles and patient user charges for services under both Parts A and B. There is no cap on the total amount of user charges an individual may have to pay. Moreover, Medicare does not cover the cost of prescription drugs. In fact, the Medicare program pays for less than half of the medical expenses of its beneficiaries and consequently 70 percent of those enrolled in Medicare purchase supplementary private insurance.[45] In response to the proliferation of supplementary insurance plans and confusion on the part of elderly consumers, the federal government intervened in 1990 to limit the number of offered "Medigap" plans to ten standard plans.

In 1965, the Medicaid program was implemented. This plan provides for federal subsidies to be paid to those states that provide coverage for the very poor as defined by federal guidelines. Medicaid results in coverage for preventive, acute, and long-term care services for over 10 percent of the population. Notwithstanding, about half of those below the federal poverty line are not covered by Medicaid. Despite the existence of federal subsidies, few states opt to provide the maximum available coverage to Medicaid recipients allowed under federal regulation.[46]

Growing government expenditures on Medicare and Medicaid programs have caused concern.[47] In 1994, Medicare's board of trustees projected that its hospital insurance trust fund (Part A) would be bankrupt by 2001.[48] Recently, there have been a number of initiatives to control costs by introducing managed care into the Medicare and Medicaid plans.

The supply of health care services

Physicians

Unlike most other developed countries, the US has not historically relied on general practitioners as the gatekeepers to the access of patients to more expensive services such as specialists' services, hospital admission, etc. Until the recent rapid rise of managed care, insured patients could, for example, visit a specialist without a referral from a general practitioner. This increases the prospects for inappropriate matching of health care services with health needs: although a specialist can competently treat a minor complaint, it is much more cost-effective for a family doctor or nurse practitioner to do so. Perhaps because of the ability to access patients directly, the ratio of specialists to general practitioners is higher in the US than in other OECD countries.[49]

The average rate of compensation per US physician is much higher than in all other OECD countries – around 50 percent more than Canadian physicians and 300 percent more than UK physicians.[50] Physicians' real incomes in the US have remained fairly stable over the last thirty years even though the number of physicians per capita has risen substantially.[51] Between 1980 and 1989 there was an 80-percent increase in real spending per person on physician services despite the greater use of utilization controls.[52] This provides some support for the contention, discussed in Chapter 2, that physicians can influence demand for their own services in order to maintain their incomes.

Hospital-based physicians in many OECD countries are paid on a salary basis. By contrast, US hospital-based physicians have historically been paid on a fee-for-service basis and thus have had a financial incentive to recommend more profitable procedures to maintain or increase their incomes. Moreover, prior to recent reforms, there were few restrictions on practitioners having proprietary interests in the technology services they prescribe to their patients. A 1990 study of six imaging procedures found that physicians who self-referred (i.e. performed the procedure in their own offices) ordered more than four times as many imaging procedures per patient and charged more per procedure than physicians who referred patients to an independent radiologist.[53] Adding cost and extra utilization, total expenditures on imaging ranged between 4.4 and 7.5 times higher for self-referring than referring physicians. In more recent times, however, both federal and state legislation has been passed prohibiting referrals to services where the referring physician or a member of his family has a financial interest in the enterprise producing the service.[54]

Although most governmental efforts to contain expenditures have been directed at hospital expenditures, in 1989, Medicare adopted "Resource Based Relative Value Scales" to reform the way physicians are paid. This new method of payment involves the setting of prices based on the input resources required to produce each physician service. However, rather than calculating the real costs of production for individual physicians, the Medicare fee schedule estimates practice costs on the basis of historical charges. According to some critics this simply entrenched past inefficiencies and inequities, with specialists continuing to be over-compensated and generalists being under-compensated.[55]

Hospitals

The three different types of hospitals in the US are public, private not-for-profit, and private for-profit hospitals. The majority of hospitals are private not-for-profit organizations.[56] Historically, the three types of hospitals differed significantly in terms of the numbers of charity cases taken on and how revenues were raised. Now competitive pressures and the changing nature of financing are reducing these differences. Public hospitals are becoming increasingly dependent upon private insurers for revenues and private for-profit hospitals receive about half of their income from the government programs of Medicaid and Medicare.[57]

Hospital expenditures comprised 46.2 percent of total US health care expenditures in 1990. This is a somewhat smaller proportion than that spent by other countries on hospital care. Over the period 1980–9 there was a 64-percent increase in real spending per admission which more than offset the 13-percent drop in admissions.[58] This speaks again to the point made earlier that the growing costs of the US health care system are not due to increased utilization in terms of numbers of hospital days or higher admissions but high and rising costs incurred in treating each patient.

Although expenditures on medical technologies are growing in most countries, by international standards the population-adjusted supply of certain large-scale technologies in the US is extraordinarily high.[59] In other sectors such as telecommunications, technological advances have resulted in lower costs – so why has this not been the case in the health sector? An OECD report speculates that unlike other sectors, where consumers buy on the basis of cost-effectiveness, traditional insurance for health care has meant coverage for every non-experimental procedure that provides some benefit, regardless of its cost-effectiveness. Consequently, there are strong incentives within an unregulated system to produce, sell and buy high-cost technology that is only slightly more effective than low-cost options.[60]

Unlike most health care systems in developed countries, the US does not regulate the influx of physical capital.[61] However, in the 1980s the federal government did take steps to control Medicare and Medicaid expenditures on hospital services. Prior to the Omnibus Budget Reconciliation Act of 1981, states were required to pay hospitals for treatment of Medicaid and Medicare patients according to a reasonable cost methodology. The 1981 Act allowed states to pay hospitals for Medicaid patients an amount that would cover only the costs of efficiently operated hospitals. Consequently, the typical Medicaid hospital and physician payment is significantly lower than Medicare rates, resulting in 25 percent of physicians refusing to treat Medicaid patients.[62] In 1983, the federal government implemented the "Prospective Payment System" (PPS) for in-patient hospital services under Medicare. In place of retrospective fee-for-service reimbursement, hospitals are paid according to a schedule of rates based on the average costs of producing services nationwide for product lines defined by five hundred Diagnosis Related Groups (DRGs). Thus hospitals are not paid for the charges or costs actually incurred in a particular case. This was intended to provide an incentive for hospitals to operate more efficiently, as they are able to keep as profit any difference between their actual costs and the DRG payment. Some states took similar initiatives with respect to Medicaid payments. Under PPS the risk of the cost of treatment is shifted to hospitals and there is thus a strong incentive to contain costs. However, hospitals could still shift costs to other private insurers not utilizing PPS to cover the amounts lost or they could put more emphasis on out-patient care (which is not subjected to the same cost controls as in-patient care.)[63]

During the 1970s and 1980s, Maryland, New Jersey, New York and Massachusetts moved to impose global annual budgets on all hospitals and/or to regulate the prices that hospitals could charge all payers (and not just Medicare and Medicaid). This eliminates the ability of hospitals to cost-shift. Studies suggest that this regulation has been successful in containing costs, but despite its relative success this type of regulation has not been adopted by other states.[64]

The Clinton managed competition reform proposals

President Clinton's 1993 proposals for managed competition reform were motivated by a desire to provide all citizens with access to a comprehensive range of health care services (universal access) and to reduce costs without fundamentally changing the system of private insurance and private delivery. Subsequent to the release of the President's plan, several other proposals were introduced in Congress, but here I will focus only upon the President's plan.[65] The seven key points of the plan were as follows:

- universal access achieved largely by employer mandates;
- the creation of sponsors called "Regional Alliances" to consolidate market power on the demand side and to reduce information asymmetry problems;
- the stimulation of price competition between private insurance plans and the growth of managed care;
- global budgets to control overall expenditures;
- regulation to ensure quality;
- shifting resources from the training of specialists to the training of generalists;
- reforming medical malpractice law and anti-trust law.[66]

These key points are discussed further below.

Enthoven's managed competition model was the basis for President Clinton's 1993 reform proposals although, as we will see below, the plan was modified such that, ultimately, Enthoven did not support the Clinton initiatives.[67]

Universal access

The desire to ensure access to a comprehensive range of health care services for all US citizens was the Clinton Administration's primary goal. Responding to criticism of his proposals, President Clinton said:

> I have no special brief for any specific approach, even in our own bill, except this: if you send me legislation that does not guarantee every

American private health insurance that can never be taken away, you will force me to take this pen, veto the legislation, and we'll come right back here and start all over again.[68]

Clinton's proposal required that all employers pay for most of the cost of health insurance for all their employees and their employees' families, covering a comprehensive list of services including mental health care services, substance-abuse treatment, some dental services, and clinical preventive services. Employers would be required to pay 80 percent of the average cost of insurance covering a core package of health care services. The employee would be required to pay the balance between the employer's contribution and the premium price of the insurance plan he/she selected. The proposal also provided for government subsidies for low-wage firms and low-income individuals in order to assist in the purchase of health insurance. In addition, employer contributions would be capped at between 3.5 percent and 7.9 percent of payroll depending on the size of the firm and the level of salaries paid. The contribution of low-income individuals would be capped at 3.9 percent of their income.

Under the Clinton plan, health insurers could offer either low, high or combination cost-sharing arrangements. Under the high cost-sharing arrangements, deductibles for individuals could be up to $200 per episode of illness and for families, up to $400 per episode. The high cost-sharing plans could also impose user charges of up to 20 percent of the cost of the service in question; however, Clinton's proposal provided for an annual cap on out-of-pocket expenditures of $1,500 for individuals and $3,000 for families.

Regional alliances

Clinton's plan required government-appointed sponsors (referred to in the initial proposal as "Health Insurance Purchasing Cooperatives" and in subsequent amendments as "Regional Alliances") to act as intermediaries between consumers and insurers. Funding from government, employers, and consumers would be funneled through the Alliances and this would help consolidate the purchasing power of individual consumers and smaller employers. It was proposed that the Regional Alliances negotiate on behalf of everyone (except those on Medicare and employees in firms with over 5,000 employees) within a region for the purchase of health care insurance from private insurers.[69] States would be responsible for establishing Regional Alliances but would only be allowed to establish one Alliance in any particular region and would be required to ensure that each region encompassed a population large enough to ensure the Alliance controlled adequate market share to negotiate effectively with insurers. A state, if it wished, could have one Regional Alliance to serve its entire population.

Enthoven's original managed competition model provided that a sponsor (in Clinton's plan a Regional Health Alliance) would be able to select the health insurers that would be offered to consumers at enrolment time. This was not provided for in Clinton's reform plan for fear that Alliances would interfere with rather than enhance competition between insurers.[70] The Clinton proposal required Regional Alliances to offer a contract to every qualified health insurer in their region unless:

- the premium offered exceeded the average by 20 percent;
- the insurer discriminated on the basis of race, ethnicity, gender, income or health status;
- the quality of care offered was determined by the state (as opposed to the Alliance) to be unsatisfactory;
- the insurer failed to comply with contract requirements;
- the insurer offered a plan which allowed for fee-for-service reimbursement of providers and the Alliance already had contracts with three such insurers in the region.

Competition between health insurance plans and the growth of managed care

The Clinton proposal required that, annually, individuals would have the opportunity to choose new insurers if they wished. The Regional Alliance would oversee this selection process to ensure fair competition between insurers and in particular to ensure that insurers competed on price and quality dimensions rather than on their ability to avoid high-risk individuals. Information would be provided to citizens on each insurer's performance in terms of the satisfaction levels of their enrollees, how each insurer rated on nationally approved quality indicators, and any restrictions within their policy on choice of and access to providers.[71] Insurers would be prohibited from charging high-risk people higher premiums (risk-rating) except as expressly permitted by Regional Alliances. Insurers would be required to accept anybody who applied and would not be able to impose pre-existing condition exclusions or waiting periods. Insurers would also not be able to offer supplemental insurance covering the standard package of benefits required to be offered to everyone. This would make sure they had no incentive to reduce the quality of the standard package of benefits.

With respect to price competition, the Clinton plan provided that government subsidies and taxation benefits to smaller employers and poor individuals would be targeted at the average cost of all insurance premiums. It was proposed that if anyone wished to buy a plan that cost more than the average, then he or she (or the employer) should pay for this with after-tax dollars. Enthoven's model of managed competition required that government subsidies be targeted at the lowest-priced insurance plan to stimulate price competition. The Clinton Administration thought that targeting government subsidies at the lowest-priced plan would cause inequities, forcing the poor and near-poor individuals into the lowest priced plan.[72] Clinton was severely criticized by Enthoven and others for this particular initiative as it was considered to severely undermine the prospects for effective price competition.

As a result of competition between insurers on price and quality dimensions the Clinton proposal envisaged that HMOs and other forms of managed care plans would grow significantly. Private insurers would contract with various providers and offer consumers a variety of managed care plans. However, Regional Alliances would be required to ensure that a limited number of insurers continued to offer traditional coverage i.e., unrestricted choice of providers and paying providers on a fee-for-service basis. A positive characteristic of managed care plans (at least in theory) is that they put more emphasis on primary and preventive care rather than invasive and expensive hospital care. In other words they are more likely to construct a fence at the top of the cliff than to have several ambulances waiting at the bottom. In anticipation of this change in the emphasis of care the Clinton plan proposed shifting the balance in the graduate training of physicians from specialties to primary care, investing more in the training of nurse practitioners and physician assistants, and adjusting Medicare payment formulas to increase reimbursement for primary care.

To enhance the prospects of competition between insurers offering managed care plans, the Clinton plan proposed several amendments to competition law. These amendments included the publication of guidelines giving greater certainty to smaller hospitals as to what constitutes a legal merger, the specification of what joint ventures and arrangements are acceptable for both hospitals and physicians, and the repeal of exemptions from anti-trust laws enjoyed by health insurers. Other proposals, such as enabling health care providers to collectively negotiate fee schedules with Alliances, prima facie seem more directed at placating the medical profession than to furthering competition.

Global budgets

The Clinton proposal provided for a global budget to cap national expenditures on the comprehensive benefit package. It was proposed that caps be imposed on the average weighted premium for each Alliance so that the total of weighted averages for all Regional Alliances equaled the national per capita baseline target. The inflation factor allowed per annum was to be the increase in the Consumer Price Index; however, a "National Health Board" would be able to adjust the inflation factor for each alliance to reflect unusual changes in demographic and socioeconomic characteristics.

Economists in the Clinton Administration calculated that the costs of universal coverage and start-up costs would be offset by planned savings in Medicare, Medicaid, and other federal programs, and new revenues, such as an increase in tobacco taxes.[73] They estimated the new revenue plus savings would exceed the new costs over the period 1995-2000 by about $58 billion. Other commentators argued that the Clinton plan would result in a cost explosion and some estimated that the Clinton Administration underestimated the cost of premiums in the reformed system by 30 percent.[74] Another study calculated that the price of premiums would be 15.4 percent above that estimated by the Clinton Administration. Sheils and Lewin calculated that even if premiums were 15.4 percent above the Clinton estimate there would still be a cost saving of $25 billion if the Clinton plan was implemented.[75]

Regulation of quality

The Clinton reform plan provided for the creation of a National Health Board, consisting of seven members appointed by the President. The Board was to oversee the Regional Alliances, monitor quality standards, review the standard package of benefits to be made available to everyone, set a figure for a national global budget (i.e. covering all public and private expenditures on health care) and ensure this budget was not exceeded.

One of the ways that health care systems ensure the quality of care is through the threat of malpractice suits. The Clinton proposal provided for several amendments to medical malpractice law. It was proposed that patients must first attempt to resolve their malpractice claims through alternative dispute resolution before resorting to the general courts. Other proposals included that all actions include a specialist's affidavit attesting that malpractice had indeed occurred, that attorneys' fees for malpractice cases be limited to a maximum of 33.3 percent of the award, that a pilot program for national practice guidelines be developed with the idea that any physician showing compliance with these guidelines would be found to have met the required standard of care, that rules be established reducing the amount of the malpractice award by the level of compensation received from other sources, that provision be made for either the defendant or plaintiff to request that damages awarded be paid in installments to reflect the need for medical and other services, and that pilot projects be established to see whether malpractice liability would not be better shifted from individual doctors to insurers or managed care plans. These amendments may be justified as a means of trying to contain costs but in terms of ensuring quality care seem directed more at placating doctors and responding to their concerns over the increasing number and size of malpractice claims. It is understandable, of course, that part of the Clinton plan would be directed at appeasing vested interest groups and could be characterized as a necessary cost of enlisting support for the balance of the reform plan.

The failure of reform proposals

The need for reform of the health system in the US in order to ensure greater justice in the allocation of health care resources was (and still is) manifest. Despite a strong commitment on the part of the Clinton Administration, its attempts at effecting reform to ensure universal access proved unsuccessful.

The reasons for failure of the most recent attempt at establishing a national health insurance scheme in the US are many, but most are rooted in the political process and the power of interest groups. When President Clinton was first elected, there was strong public support for health care reform; Clinton was criticized for not making a reform proposal at that time.[76] The Clinton proposals were seen as very technical, incomprehensible, and thus likely to result in a bloated bureaucracy and cost increases. This prospect did not rest well with Americans who, in general, disapprove of big government.[77] In retrospect, the

Clinton Administration should have kept its initial proposals very simple and focused on selling the concept to the general public before fleshing out the technical details. However, Steinmo and Watts argue that the failure of health reform cannot be attributed to political missteps but rather to a failure of political institutions. In particular, they argue, the congressional system provides disaffected interest groups with "a multitude of wrenches and force to halt the entire legislative process."[78] Vested interests groups operating within the cash cow of the US system certainly had strong financial interests to use the political process to thwart the Clinton proposal. Physicians feared that government intervention would reduce their income earning potential and restrict their clinical autonomy. Insurance companies feared government intervention would restrict their profits. Employers, particularly small employers, were concerned about the extra costs that would be imposed on them to provide health insurance for employees and many were ideologically committed to the concept of self-help.[79] Many well-insured Americans could not be persuaded that ensuring universal access was possible without costs spiraling upwards or quality spiraling downwards. Although most Americans may be concerned over the unfairness of a system that leaves over 16 percent of the population uninsured[80] they may not be prepared to sacrifice personally any measure of the quality of health care services they receive. There also emerged a perception in 1994 that reform was not necessary to constrain costs as costs were being reined in through private managed care initiatives.[81]

The managed care revolution

In the US, as in many other countries, it was historically thought that "medical need" would place an upper limit on total health expenditures and so it was unnecessary and indeed harmful to put in place any measures to restrict the supply of health care services. However, as Bovbjerg *et al.* note, "need" is a subjective concept and almost any level of additional care will confer some benefit on a patient.[82] Passive insurers (whether public or private) coupled with health providers paid on a fee-for-service basis, results in incentives for providers to supply an ever-increasing number of services despite small or questionable benefits. More importantly, physicians have no incentive to be sensitive to the cost-effectiveness of the goods and services they recommend to their patients.

Although historically in the US most health providers were paid on a fee-for-service basis there were some significant exceptions. The first prepaid community-based health care plan was developed in Oklahoma in 1929 and similar organizations developed elsewhere through the 1930s.[83] In these plans people paid a fixed amount per year and in return they received a comprehensive range of health care services with few if any user charges. By contrast with traditional insurance plans people were restricted in the doctors and hospitals they could visit. These organizations were the precursors of what have come to be known as Health Maintenance Organizations (HMOs) that provide managed care. The federal Health Maintenance Act of 1973[84] was put in place to encourage the development of HMOs, the establishment of which may have otherwise been stymied by state laws that protected traditional insurers and fee-for-service medicine.

The three main types of managed care organizations presently in the US are HMOs, Preferred Provider Organizations (PPOs) and Point of Service Networks (POS Networks). HMOs employ physicians and own their own hospitals or instead contract with a limited number of independent institutions. Enrollees are entitled, in return for a fixed annual or monthly payment, to a comprehensive benefit package from health providers stipulated by the HMO. HMOs require their enrollees to use only the providers affiliated with them for all health care services except in the case of an emergency. HMOs usually impose no or low user charges. In PPOs, insurers selectively contract with health providers who agree to provide health care services on a discounted price schedule.[85] PPOs provide patients with a list of preferred providers and if a patient does not use one of the providers listed when seeking treatment then he/she must pay a higher user charge. POS Networks attempt to combine elements of HMO and PPO organizational arrangements. While historically patients (with sufficient insurance or financial resources) have been able to access the US health system at any level, POS Networks require enrollees to select a general practitioner who acts as a gatekeeper and coordinator of the delivery of care from a limited list of other providers. However, patients can elect to pay a higher user charge and obtain care from a provider who is not participating in the network. POS Networks are distinguishable from PPOs for in the former there is the element of coordinated care.[86]

The goal of managed care, as Mechanic describes it, is "to limit expensive care that is unnecessary without interfering with appropriate treatment."[87] Of course, the American Medical Association does not view managed care so positively. It sees managed care as

> the control of access to and limitation on physician and patient utilization of services by public or private payers or their agents through the use of prior and concurrent review for approval of or referral to service or site of service, and financial incentives or penalties.[88]

In general terms, managed care covers a variety of techniques whereby insurer/ purchasers (be they public or private) seek to make health care providers sensitive to the costs and benefits of the services they supply or recommend to their patients. It generally involves some degree of interference in a physician's decision to supply the best possible available care irrespective of cost or marginal benefit. It is this feature of managed care that physicians, naturally enough, generally do not like. Managed care may involve an insurer/purchaser requiring providers to obtain its authorization prior to admitting a patient to hospital or before a particular course of treatment is adopted. An insurer/purchaser may monitor in-patient service utilization rates and may actively manage the care of patients in need of potentially expensive care.[89] An insurer/purchaser may employ a high ratio of general practitioners to specialists in an attempt to create a culture within its organization directed more towards prevention than to cure. Managed care may also involve the use of financial incentives such as bonus payments for the realization of annual targets and capitation based payment structures. This latter initiative has caused particular concern for, depending on how the payment is structured, it may result in strong financial incentives to cut the quality of care supplied to patients.[90] Proponents of managed care claim that it will not only save costs but also be good for patients as it puts more emphasis on primary and preventive health care services. It is more cost-effective for the insurer/purchaser to keep their enrollee population healthy than to pay for acute-institutional care when people fall seriously ill. Chapter 7 discusses these claims more fully in the context of discussing how to ensure quality of care in a system.

In an ad hoc fashion, managed care has dramatically reformed the US health care system. The pace of change has been remarkable. In 1988, only 29 percent of full-time employees were enrolled in managed care plans. By 1993, this figure had climbed to 51 percent. By 1995, the percentage had jumped again to a staggering 73 percent and by 1997 to 85 percent.[91] In addition, the federal government has taken active steps to introduce managed care into Medicare and Medicare plans.[92] Between 1991 and 1996 the percentage of Medicaid beneficiaries enrolled in some form of managed care plan increased from 9.5 to 40.1 percent.[93] As at August 1998, 18.3 percent of Medicare beneficiaries were enrolled in an HMO plan.[94]

Significant growth in managed care in the private sector seems to have been sparked by the prospect of implementation of President Clinton's proposals and increased employer resistance to premium increases.[95] As mentioned earlier, exemption under ERISA from state regulation of employee insurance plans encouraged larger firms to self-insure. Thus, employers increasingly purchased coverage on behalf of their employees from managed care plans.

Research suggests that the shift from traditional fee-for-service insurance to managed care helped to control costs in the early 1990s.[96] The level of cost-savings made, however, seems to depend significantly upon the type of managed care organization. Each version of managed care results in a different mix of incentives for health providers and Mechanic notes that it should be no surprise in the US that there are large variations in practice, levels of performance, and physician and patient satisfaction.[97] At an aggregate level the significant growth in managed care has occurred at the same time as an unprecedented reduction in the growth in health care costs in the period 1990–5.[98] Slower price growth was the main reason for the deceleration in nominal health expenditures – insurers were securing contracts with health providers at discounted rates.[99] An important effect of the upsurge in managed care plans has been to put competitive pressure on traditional fee-for-service plans. The latter have taken steps to contain costs and the cost advantage of HMOs over fee-for-service insurers may eventually disappear. Premiums for traditional fee-for-service insurers are lower in regions where HMOs are highly concentrated.[100]

Recent data suggests that the downward trend in the rate of increase in health care costs has leveled out.[101] The important issue is whether the lower growth rate experienced in the early 1990s is a one-time response only to the introduction of managed care and whether once this effect has dissipated the growth rate in expenditures will increase once more. The best bets seem to be that managed care will have a significant one-time effect on costs with a small downward impact on long-term growth rates as managed care slows the rate of the diffusion and use of expensive technology.[102]

It is important to note that despite the reduced expenditure increases in the early 1990s, few of these benefits seem to have been passed on to consumers: premiums have continued to increase.[103] Moreover, there is no evidence that the managed care revolution has had any impact on improving justice in the allocation of health resources – at least in terms of increasing the proportion of the population with health insurance. In the absence of government intervention, managed care cannot result in a system that ensures every citizen has insurance coverage for a comprehensive range of services. By comparison, managed competition reform promises such a system. Reinhardt notes that

> the 'managed care revolution' in American health care will gain real momentum only if and when the government starts to rely on the power of genuine 'managed competition' that would force insurance companies and their rivals, provider-sponsored networks, to compete for enrollees openly and fairly on the basis of premiums and the quality of their products.[104]

Managed competition seeks to promote competition between insurer/purchasers on price and quality dimensions in order that insurers will have the incentive to purchase the most cost-efficient services on behalf of the people they represent. In doing so, it is assumed that insurer/purchasers will generally rely upon managed care techniques. Managed competition and managed care are complementary pieces to the puzzle of what constitutes a viable model for health care allocation.

Piecemeal reform in 1996 and 1997

Over the past decades, many states have passed legislation in an attempt to improve access to and the portability of health insurance. In particular, legislation was aimed at curbing the increasing risk-rating practices of private insurers and at limiting the economic impacts of people fearing to change their jobs in case they lose their existing coverage. However, there are significant variations in the extent of these reforms and, as a result of ERISA, self-funded employer group plans were exempt from these various state reforms.[105] Consequently, in 1996 the US federal government enacted the Health Insurance Portability and Accountability Act (HIPAA) in an effort to ameliorate some of the worst effects of risk-avoidance techniques on the part of insurers and to improve the portability of health insurance for the employed.[106] Although not directly tackling the problem of the uninsured in the system, the Act addresses public concerns over insurers, employers, and managed care plans dropping coverage for people once they become in need of expensive health care services. The Act amends the federal ERISA legislation which, as a result, now prohibits health insurers (including self-insuring employers and managed care plans) from limiting or denying coverage for pre-existing conditions for more than twelve months. After this waiting period of a year, coverage is portable to the extent that no new waiting period is allowed to be imposed if an employer switches insurers or if an employee changes jobs provided that the employee in question maintains coverage with a gap no longer than sixty-three days.[107] Employers are now prohibited from denying coverage to an employee or dropping an employee from coverage or charging a higher premium because of that person's or a dependant's health status or medical history. Other provisions of the Act prevent insurers and managed care plans denying coverage to small employee groups or to those individuals who at some point have had group insurance coverage for eighteen months or more and are ineligible for coverage from any other source.[108] Despite this federal initiative individuals are still experiencing significant problems in obtaining insurance if they lose group coverage for any reason. The General Accounting Office reports that "some carriers have discouraged individuals from applying for the coverage or charged them rates 140 to 600 percent of the standard premium...because they believe individuals who attempt to exercise HIPAA's individual market access guarantee will, on average, be in poorer health than others in the individual market."[109]

In 1997, in an effort to improve access by children to health insurance, the federal government implemented the Children's Health Insurance Program. This program, enacted as Title XXI of the Social Security Act, provides $24 billion in federal matching funds as block grants to states. The goal is to encourage states to offer affordable health insurance to working families that do not qualify for Medicaid but are below 200 percent of the federal poverty level. It is estimated that, when fully implemented, the program will result in over 2.3 million new children accessing health care coverage.[110]

The HIPAA legislation and the Children's Health Insurance Program are certainly important attempts to increase justice in the allocation of health care. However, ultimately, they are further piecemeal attempts at filling the fragmented patchwork of coverage that leaves 43.2 million people, many of them children, many of them poor, without basic health care insurance in the richest country in the world.

The rise of managed care in the US has injected cost consideration into clinical decision-making to the consternation of many. Thus, recently, the US legislature has turned its focus away from trying to provide coverage for the uninsured to protecting access to and the quality of health care for those with insurance coverage. In the Fall of 1999 several bills were before the House of Representatives seeking to ensure, for example, access to specialists and emergency care without prior approval. The main difference between the various bills put forward is the degree to which insured individuals will be able to sue insurers/managed care plans for denying or limiting benefits.[111]

The Netherlands' health care system and the 1987 reform proposals

From an international perspective the Dutch health care system merits close attention for its innovative managed competition reform proposals which were first proposed in 1987 and implemented on a piecemeal basis since 1992. The Dutch health care system merits particularly close attention by US policymakers as it is able to couple a high degree of reliance upon private insurance whilst still ensuring insurance coverage for nearly the whole population to a comprehensive range of care.

Problems in the system prior to reform proposals

Problems in the Dutch system prior to the 1987 proposals for managed competition reform can generally be characterized as cost and access problems.

Costs

The Dutch government recognized in the 1970s that fragmentation of funding between different insurers (Sickness Funds, private insurers, and the government) was contributing to increasing health expenditures.[112] Between the period 1970 and 1980, health care expenditures as a percentage of GDP increased from 6.0 percent to 8.2 percent.[113] Growth in expenditures was, however, successfully restrained through the 1980s due to a variety of government initiatives, and health expenditures as a percentage of GDP increased only from 8.2 percent in 1980 to 8.3 percent in 1989. The Netherlands' success in this regard suggests that it is not necessary to have a tax-financed single-payer system in order to be able to successfully contain costs and that cost-containment through regulation is possible. Nonetheless, throughout the 1980s, health expenditures were still above the level that would be predicted from the Netherlands' GDP relative to other OECD countries.[114] There was also concern that in the longer term expenditures would significantly increase because of the increasing percentage of individuals aged over 75.

Access and quality

Although there is no compulsory health insurance scheme covering all citizens for general medical expenses, the Dutch system still results in nearly 100 percent of its population having full insurance coverage. There are three important government-mandated insurance schemes. The first covers all citizens for "exceptional" medical expenses. The second ensures coverage for the poorer 60 percent of the population for general medical expenses. The third ensures coverage for all civil servants and their families (about 6 percent of the population) for general medical expenses. All these schemes are discussed further below. The government also regulates private insurers to prevent them risk-rating premiums in order to avoid the result of unaffordable premiums or no coverage at all for high-risk individuals.

As Table 3.2 demonstrates, in terms of access to "health" the Netherlands performs better than the US, the UK and New Zealand in terms of measures such as infant mortality and life expectancy.

Of course, as mentioned several times already, access to and the quality of health care services cannot be equated with health care outcomes because of all the other contributing factors to health (nutrition, employment, income, culture, etc.) It is, however, important to note that the reason for the better than average performance of the Netherlands cannot be attributed prima facie to lower rates of smoking, alcohol consumption, or unemployment.[115]

Notwithstanding a good performance with respect to health indicators, there are inequalities in health outcomes. In 1991, over 6 percent of the Dutch population either had foreign nationality or originated from one of the former Dutch colonies. Mortality rates for Surinamese and Antilleans are 20 percent higher than for the indigenous population. Mortality rates among Turkish and Moroccan children aged between 1 and 5 years is 2.5–3 times higher than that of the total population of the same age.[116] Despite these poorer health outcomes, qualitative and quantitative studies show, however, that Turks, Moroccans, and Surinamese are able with little impediment to access needed health care services.[117]

In terms of access by the general population to health care services there does not appear to be a significant concern regarding waiting lists and times; however, there are waiting lists for institutions caring for patients with chronic conditions such as psychiatric hospitals, nursing homes, and homes for the mentally handicapped.[118]

Table 3.2 Health status indicators

1995	Netherlands	US	UK	NZ
Infant Mortality (per 1000 live births)	5.5	8.0	6.0	7.0
Life expectancy for Females	80.4 yrs	79.2 yrs	79.7 yrs	79.5 yrs
Life expectancy for Males	74.6 yrs	72.5 yrs	74.3 yrs	74.2 yrs
No. of years of potential life lost	3261.6	4666.2	3616.0	4774.7

Source: *OECD Health Data 98: A Comparative Analysis of 29 Countries* (Electronic Database) (Created from Table A – note the figure for years of potential life lost for the US is from 1994)

Financing of health care services

The Dutch health care system has historically been financed from a number of public and private sources. In 1988, prior to managed competition reform proposals, compulsory health insurance premiums accounted for approximately 60 percent, general taxation for 14 percent, voluntary health insurance premiums for 16 percent, and patient user charges for approximately 11 percent of total health expenditures.[119] Plurality in financing has contributed to co-ordination and cost-shifting problems. For example, it has proved difficult for the government to transfer resources from secondary care to preventive and primary care as the former is heavily financed by the private sector while the latter is not. The Dutch government is not able to directly control health care expenditures like the UK and New Zealand governments (so-called "single-payer" systems financed predominantly from general taxation revenues). However, the publication of the government's annual health expenditure plan has effectively acted as an overall budget for both the public and private sector.[120]

Unlike New Zealand and the UK, where locally elected authorities have acted as both the purchaser and provider of hospital services, responsibility for the financing and delivery of all health care in the Netherlands has, historically, been split. Responsibility for financing the system has rested largely with private insurers and with Sickness Funds (private non-profit entities.) Historically, Sickness Funds have contracted on an arms-length basis with private health care providers to supply care to their enrollees. As in the US, private insurers in the Netherlands have historically reimbursed policy holders for all medical expenses incurred and have been reluctant to engage in direct contractual negotiations with doctors and hospitals.[121]

The role of government

Coalition governments have governed the Netherlands since the early part of this century. Historically, the Dutch political spectrum has been comprised of a social democratic party on the left, a conservative liberal party on the right, and, in the center, a Christian democratic party. This latter party has had a considerable influence on final government policy given its strategic position in the political center and has resulted in government policy being characterized by incremental rather than radical change.[122]

It is important to note that Dutch government does not have a significant role in direct financing of the health care system – only about 10 percent of total expenditures is derived from general taxation. However, indirectly it has a significant role on the financing of the system by requiring certain groups to buy certain types of insurance and by regulating private insurers. Prior to the 1987 proposals for managed competition reform there were two important pieces of government legislation in place with respect to financing health care services. These were the Sickness Funds Insurance Act 1964[123], that replaced the Sickness Funds Decree of 1941 (imposed during the German occupation), and the Exceptional Medical Expenses Act 1967.[124]

The Sickness Funds Insurance Act 1964 ensures coverage for about 60 percent of the population by requiring non-government employees, pensioners, and social security beneficiaries earning below a certain income level (56,000 guilders in 1994 and 64,300 guilders in 1999) to have an insurance policy with a Sickness Fund. The self-employed can acquire membership in a Sickness Fund on a voluntary basis. This plan covers most non-catastrophic health risks and ensures access to primary and secondary acute care, drugs, and transportation. The criterion used to judge whether a particular service is included in the basic benefit package has historically been whether or not the medical profession generally accepts the need for the service.[125] This general compulsory health insurance scheme was administered, prior to reform, by about forty independent non-profit Sickness Funds. By 1999 the number of Sickness Funds had fallen to twenty-five. The Sickness Funds have private origins in the guild tradition. They are organized on a regional basis and vary considerably in size, ranging from 4,000 to 250,000 members.[126] Sickness Funds are independent of government but they do rely on government financial support and are regulated in their activities. The Sickness Funds have historically not competed with each other and generally have held a monopoly in their respective geographic regions. Until recent reforms, they were required to contract with all willing providers in their respective regions.[127]

All of the Sickness Funds are members of the Society of Dutch Sickness Funds. The Society plays an important role in shaping health care policy in the Netherlands and is overseen by the Sickness Funds Council. This Council is comprised of representatives from employers, labor unions, patient advocacy groups, hospitals, physicians, the Sickness Funds themselves, and the government.

The Sickness Funds receive their revenues from the General Fund, which is administered by the Sickness Fund Council. Prior to reform each Sickness Fund was fully reimbursed retrospectively for the medical expenses it incurred, providing no incentives to ensure the delivery of cost-effective care. The premiums paid to the General Fund are set each year by regulation at a fixed percentage of employees' wages with a maximum upper limit. Dependants are covered at no extra charge. Premiums are paid jointly by the employer and the employee. In 1988, the employee and employer contributions combined were 5.1 percent of employees' gross wage.[128] A Dutch employee is directly responsible him or herself for a much greater proportion of the premium price than US employees are but the level of user charges at point-of-service has (at least until the advent of managed care in the US) been much lower for Dutch patients than American patients.[129] Elderly people below a certain income level have their premium payments subsidized by payments from the General Fund and by the government.

The Exceptional Medical Expenses Act 1967[130] requires that the entire population be insured for "exceptional expenses." This scheme was originally designed to cover long-stay patients of more than one year, the physically and/ or medically handicapped, and maternal and child health care services. Over time, it has expanded to cover less "extraordinary" expenses such as home care, drug, medical devices, etc. The premium is set at a percentage of employees' wages (4.55 percent with a real dollar ceiling) and is paid by the employer.[131] Administration of this compulsory insurance scheme is partly delegated to Sickness Funds and private insurers.[132]

All public employees of provincial and municipal governmental bodies and their dependants (around 6 percent of the population) are covered by a separate mandatory insurance scheme administered by twelve special private insurance arrangements. The premiums for these funds are adjusted for age and sex. The government pays for half of the premium price.[133]

Neither the Sickness Funds nor private insurers provide public health care services. Responsibility for communicable disease control, environmental health, and preventive programs such as vaccination and immunization has largely been left in the hands of elected local authorities. There has been little co-ordination between these elected authorities and Sickness Funds and private insurers.[134]

Private health insurance

Approximately 40 percent of the population were (and still are) free to purchase their own private insurance plan for all health care services except those covered under the Exceptional Medical Expenses Act. Despite the fact that the purchase of private insurance is not compulsory for the wealthier 40 percent of the population, in 1992 only 0.7 percent of the population did not hold insurance. By 1996, this figure had increased slightly to approximately 0.9 percent.[135]

There were 46 competing private insurers operating in the Netherlands just prior to the 1987 reform proposals.[136] Historically, private insurance premiums were community-rated; however, throughout the 1970s, competition in the private insurance market resulted in market segmentation as insurers started to charge higher premiums to the elderly. Unlike the US, where most private insurance is purchased on a group-basis through employers, historically individuals have purchased two-thirds of all private health insurance policies in the Netherlands.[137] Increasingly, however, the trend has been towards group insurance plans.[138]

In 1975, concerns over access to health insurance by high-risk groups resulted in a government proposal for a public insurance system to cover the entire population. Concerns over the level of public expenditures required to finance such a scheme resulted in this proposal's demise.[139] Instead the government decided to simplify the existing public insurance system and to tightly regulate the private insurance market to reduce disparities in premiums and to constrain market segmentation. In 1986, the Health Insurance Access Act was passed. This Act required private insurers to offer high-risk, lower-income persons who were self-employed a standard package of benefits and a price cap was set on the premium for this coverage.[140] In 1989, the government began to require private insurers to provide this package of benefits to all people over 65, who had previously been covered by private insurance.[141] In 1991, other high-risk groups were brought under the government's risk pool arrangements. A system was designed to spread the cost of subsidizing premiums for the elderly and high-risk groups amongst all the privately insured. Private insurers charge a levy to all their policy-holders to pay for the cost of these subsidies. The deficits and levies are then pooled with other private insurers. Schut notes that while this initiative achieved the government's goal of improving access, it also resulted in private insurers losing what small incentive they did have to control utilization rates by policy-holders as the additional costs of insuring high-risk patients was pooled with other private insurers.[142]

Patient charges

Historically, the Netherlands government has resisted pressure from private insurers to introduce user charges as a means of cost-control on the basis that such charges would interfere with the rights of patients to free care at point of service.[143] The compulsory Exceptional Medical Expenses Act imposes some user charges, e.g. residents of a nursing home must contribute the sum they would have had to pay for ordinary living expenses in their own home.[144] Since 1991 patients incur user charges if the pharmaceuticals they purchase are above the indicative price set by government regulation (which will cover the cost of the cheapest drug that is clinically effective). Also, benefits for the privately insured may now not always cover treatment by dentists or pharmaceuticals for home use and cheaper private insurance plans may not cover general practitioner services. In 1997, the Sickness Fund Act was amended to require a system of limited user charges for sickness fund enrollees. However, the annual amount of user charges payable was capped at the very low figure of 200 guilders per annum (100 guilders for the elderly) and there were exceptions for the chronically ill. In 1999, for a variety of political and administrative reasons, this mandatory user charge scheme was abandoned.[145]

The supply of health care services

Hospitals

The vast majority of hospitals in the Netherlands are privately owned. Often private hospitals are affiliated with Protestant, Catholic or non-denominational religious orders. All hospitals operate on a non-profit basis.

Prior to reform, there was a concern that expenditures on hospital care have grown faster than expenditures on primary and preventive care and efforts were made to reduce the proportion of all health expenditures on hospital care.

Throughout the 1970s there were unsuccessful attempts to reduce the bed capacity of hospitals as an indirect means of controlling health expenditures.[146] The Hospitals Tariffs Act 1965 provided for price regulation of hospital costs.

Hospital boards had to demonstrate that their charges reflected their actual costs before the Hospital Tariffs Agency would approve the prices they charged. This reform did not, however, go to the root of the problem, which was that hospitals were paid on a fixed price per bed per day. This payment mechanism provided strong incentives for hospitals to keep patients in hospitals for longer periods than might be strictly necessary and deterred the development of out-patient clinics and day-care units.[147] The Health Care Prices Act, enacted on 1 January 1982, prescribes a process of regulated negotiations through which prices to be charged by hospitals and other institutions and health care professionals are set for the forthcoming year.[148] Since 1983, Dutch hospitals have had to operate under prospective annual global budgets negotiated with representatives of private insurers and the Sickness Funds. These budgets cover both public and private patients and cover nearly all costs incurred by a hospital apart from specialists' fees.[149] This change resulted in its own set of perverse incentives. Hospitals had no incentive to operate more efficiently as there was no financial reward for improved performance, since savings made resulted in a hospital's budget being reduced in subsequent years. Consequently, since 1988, a new formula has been used to fix hospital budgets. First, an estimate is made of what should be the operating costs of a hospital if it were efficient. Second, the sum so fixed is adjusted to allow for changes in the population served by the hospitals and in the volume of operations performed.[150] If the hospital's budget is exceeded in any particular year then the budget is reduced by that amount in the following year.[151]

Have these efforts to constrain hospital expenditures been successful? Relative to the average for OECD countries the Netherlands still spends a high proportion of total expenditures on hospital care but, as Table 3.3 illustrates, this ratio fell significantly over the period 1980–90 and has remained fairly stable since then at just over 52 percent.

Table 3.3 Expenditures on hospital services as a percentage of total health expenditures

	UK	*NZ*	*US*	*Netherllands*	*OECD average*
1960	–	–	37.7%	–	–
1970	–	–	44.0%	55.1%	43.4%
1980	53.5%	72.2%	48.7%	57.3%	49.7%
1990	43.9%	60.4%	43.9%	52.3%	46.1%
1991	44.6%	59.1%	44.3%	52.6%	
1992	43.3%	56.5%	43.9%	52.2%	
1993	42.8%	59.1%	43.5%	52.5%	
1994	42.2%	–	43.0%	52.3%	
1995	42.2%	–	42.6%	54.0%	
1996	–	–	42.2%	52.4%	
1997	–	–	42.0%	52.6%	

Source: OECD Health Data 98: A Comparative Analysis of 29 Countries, (created from variables: Total Expenditures on In-Patient Care and Percentage Total Expenditure on Health). *Ibid.* at 28, Table 4

As Table 3.1 demonstrated, the Netherlands has, relatively, a very high number of hospital beds. The Dutch health care system also records, relative to other OECD countries, a significantly higher average length of stay per patient in hospitals. The average length of stay in Dutch hospitals of 33.8 days is over twice as much as the OECD average. The magnitude of this difference leads one to speculate that it is as a result of the Dutch commitment to financing long-term care and its Exceptional Medical Expenses program rather than an excessive propensity to keep general patients in hospital. Schut, a Dutch health economist, confirms in fact, that the average length of stay in general and academic hospitals was only 9.5 days in 1995 (a steady decline from 13 days in 1980).

Even though hospitals, as private institutions, borrow in the private market, most of their loans are government guaranteed.[152] Other forms of government intervention in the secondary health market included the prohibition on building new facilities without government authorization and the existence of plans for different regions within the Netherlands providing for the distribution of medical specialties amongst various hospitals.[153] The government has promoted the mergers of hospitals in the belief that this will lead to benefits from economies of scale. From 1967 to 1984, 93 hospitals were involved in 43 mergers.[154] The Hospital Facilities Act 1982 required a new general hospital to have a minimum size of 175 beds, in order to qualify for two full-time medical specialists in each of the six "core specialties."[155] Between 1984 and 1988, the average market share of the two largest hospitals in each legally defined health region increased by more than 10 percent to 60 percent of the market.[156]

Physicians

The number of physicians in the Netherlands is around the OECD average per thousand people. With 5.4 visits per capita to a physician recorded in 1991, the Netherlands is below the OECD average of 6.2 and the respective averages of 5.7 in the UK and 5.6 in the US but above the 3.8 visits per capita to a physician recorded in New Zealand.[157]

Remuneration of practitioners varies depending on whether they are paid by the Sickness Funds or by private insurers. Sickness Funds pay general practitioners on a capitation basis, the fee being uniformly set for the whole of the Netherlands by regulated negotiations between representatives of practitioners and the Funds. Each Sickness Fund patient must choose a general practitioner to register with from the list of those that the Fund has contracted with. Prior to recent reforms, the Sickness Funds Decree of 1941 required each Sickness Fund to contract with all the physicians in their region on nationally determined conditions.[158] Thus, physicians did not need to compete for contracts with their local Sickness Fund. In the private sector, physicians are paid on a fee-for-service basis. Prior to managed competition reform, there were statutory guidelines in place prescribing the negotiation of uniform tariffs for physicians, which were binding on all physicians once approved.[159] The

Central Agency on Health Care Tariffs oversees and regulates negotiations between representatives of the physicians, private insurers, and Sickness Funds.[160] More than 90 percent of general practitioners in the Netherlands belong to the National General Practitioners' Association (a division of the Dutch Medical Association) which negotiates on behalf of general practitioners with Sickness Funds and private insurers. Over 95 percent of specialists belong to the National Specialists Association, another division of the Dutch Medical Association.

Approximately, 33 percent of physicians are generalists in the Netherlands[161] compared to 37.5 percent in England,[162] 38.3 percent in New Zealand,[163] and less than 30 percent in the US.[164] As in many other developed countries, general practitioners act as gate-keepers to the supply of more expensive specialist, diagnostic, and hospital services and to drugs. In general, health insurers will only reimburse the cost of specialist care, paramedical services, and outpatient psychiatric care if patients are referred by their general practitioner.[165] Once a patient has obtained a referral from their general practitioner, they are free to choose their specialist or hospital although Sickness Fund patients must select a specialist who has a contract with their Sickness Fund.[166] This gate-keeping role is credited with helping to restrain growth in total health expenditures; however, the large degree of flexibility physicians have had with respect to prescribing has become of significant concern due to the increasing cost of pharmaceuticals. Increasingly this flexibility is being limited so that, for example, only certain specialties are able to prescribe certain drugs and for some drugs, permission to prescribe must be obtained from the Sickness Fund in advance.[167] In 1991, the concept of "reference prices" was introduced. Each class of medicine with the same therapeutic effectiveness was allocated a "reference price." If the real price of the drug is above the reference price the patient must pay the difference from his or her own pocket.[168] This was intended to make physicians and patients more aware of the cost-effectiveness of different medicines.

Historically, the government has regulated the number of specialists in the system. Almost all specialists, apart from ophthalmologists, dermatologists, and psychiatrists, conduct their practices from hospitals.[169] Sickness Funds reimburse specialists for out-patient consultations by way of a fee that entitles the patient in question to one full month of treatment for the particular complaint or condition and if continuation of treatment is required beyond a month, then the specialist receives an additional fee.[170] The Sickness Funds operate a claw-back system. If a specialist bills above an annual sum agreed by the Funds and the National Specialists Association then the specialist must repay one-third of the first 30,000 guilders above the agreed sum and two-thirds of all income earned beyond that.[171]

Private insurers reimburse specialists on a pure fee-for-service basis and only specialists who are employed by university hospitals and by psychiatric institutions are compensated on a salary basis.[172] The Dutch Minister of Health,

Welfare and Sport announced in January of 1995 that the government wished to change the basis of reimbursement for specialists in hospitals from a fee-for-service to a fixed income arrangement (either salary, capitation or some combination thereof) within two years.[173] In 1997, the government introduced a proposal to fully integrate specialists into hospitals by abolishing their ability to directly charge Sickness Funds and patients for their services.[174]

As can be seen from the preceding discussion a very important part of the Dutch health care system has been the process of negotiation at a national level between payers (the Sickness Funds Council and private insurers) and health care providers. None of these groups have historically had any real incentive to be sensitive to the relative costs and benefits of services supplied.[175] The Health Care Prices Act and the Health Care Facilities Act, both passed in 1982 with a view to deregulating the health care sector, actually provided significantly greater powers for government in setting prices as the government was now empowered to impose fee reductions to meet specified expenditure targets.[176] Kirkman-Liff describes the negotiation process as follows.[177] First, the Ministry of Social Affairs and the National General Practitioners' Association and the National Specialists' Association negotiate an acceptable income for physicians. They do this by considering public sector employees' salaries in comparable professions. They also negotiate an acceptable figure for the number of patients a physician would be expected to care for. Next, the Ministry of Welfare, Health Care, and Culture, after considering macro-level forecasts of health care costs, develops directions for the Central Body for Health Care Tariffs. The Central Body issues guidelines for the conduct of negotiations after considering representations by various interested groups. Negotiations between insurers and providers may then proceed in accordance with the guidelines. The Central Body reviews all final agreements. One final step is that the service component of agreements negotiated between the Dutch Sickness Funds and the General Practitioners Association are subject to the approval of the Sickness Fund Council.

The Dekker and Simons reform proposals

Prior to the 1987 reform proposals, the Dutch health care system was characterized as a system where "tight and detailed central regulation of prices, volume, and capacity has been superimposed on an essentially private system of provision and a mixed system of finance."[178] The Committee on the Structure and Financing of Health Care[179] (the Dekker Committee, so named after its chair Dr W. Dekker) produced a report in March 1987 proposing managed competition reform of the Dutch health care system. The Committee identified five problems in the system:[180]

- fragmentation of financing between different insurers resulting in inefficient cost-shifting;

- lack of choice for citizens between the various insurers;
- growing disparities in private insurance premiums as between high- and low-risk patients and a tendency for private insurers to avoid enrolment of high-risk individuals;
- few financial incentives for the Sickness Funds to operate efficiently or to seek out the most efficient health care providers;
- government regulation perceived as being costly, complex and inflexible and central planning incompatible with the fragmentation of financing between the different insurers.

The Dekker Committee recommended shifting towards a system of regulated competition between private insurance plans and eliminating the distinction between private insurers and Sickness Funds. The Committee also recommen-ded a mandatory scheme of national health insurance covering general services for all citizens and for the integration of health care and other related social services. Compulsory basic insurance would cover approximately 85 percent of the cost of expenditures on general health care services for all citizens and could be obtained either from Sickness Funds or private insurers, which would compete with each other for enrollees. The Dekker Committee advocated optional private gap insurance to cover the remaining 15 percent of costs for such goods and services as drugs, dental care for adults, cosmetic surgery, and abortion.

The Dekker reform proposals were inspired by Enthoven's managed competition proposals. Enthoven's proposals required that the government's contribution be set at the lowest-priced insurance package with individuals having to pay all additional costs if they selected a more expensive plan. The Dekker proposals, however, required individuals to pay a two-part premium. About 75 percent of the premium would be set by government at a fixed percentage rate of the individual's income and would be paid to the Central Fund. Thus the vast majority of expenditures would be financed on a progressive basis. The Central Fund would pool all premiums collected and then pay a capitated risk-related premium to the particular insurer chosen by the individual in question. The amount paid on behalf of each citizen would thus have no correlation to the amount paid in by that person to the Central Fund and would reflect their risk of needing health care services as opposed to their ability to pay. The balance of the premium would, however, be paid directly by citizens to their chosen insurer. Requiring all enrollees to pay a small share of the total premium directly to their chosen insurer would result in a small measure of price competition. Each insurer (whether Sickness Fund or private insurer) would have to charge *all* individuals the same flat-rate premium and thus could not charge high-risk individuals higher premiums; however, *between* insurers the rate could be different thus providing an incentive for insurers to compete for enrollees on the basis of price. To ameliorate any incentive for insurers to engage in cream skimming of low-risk individuals, the

Dekker report proposed that insurers must accept all individuals that wished to enrol with them.

Under the reform proposals, Sickness Funds and other insurers would not have to contract with every provider who wished to supply services, i.e. they would be able to engage in selective contracting. It was, however, proposed to leave in place the process of regulated negotiations between insurers and providers that fixed physicians' fees and hospital budgets, but with a proviso that these negotiations would set the upper limit for prices. Legislation would require that a minimum range and quality of health care services be supplied to all enrollees. The Dekker reform proposals also provided for most central planning and investment controls to be abolished and for the abolition of government guarantees of hospital borrowing. It was proposed that government eventually move away from regulating prices in health care services markets but that government would still, when necessary, intervene to prevent monopolistic and collusive behavior. It was also proposed that there would be considerable deregulation of the hospital industry, that the Hospital Facilities Act would be confined to the planning of large hospital facilities and that negotiations between hospitals and insurers would no longer be subject to detailed government guidelines.[181]

Unlike New Zealand and the UK, the Netherlands has not been able to implement its reform proposals within the time frame initially set down. As Schut describes it, the system of coalition government means that the implementation of any government policy is open at various stages to attack or delay tactics initiated by interest groups.[182] This is particularly so in the health sector where historically representatives of insurers and providers, as bilateral monopolies, have negotiated issues such as price and capacity. However, the initial prospects for the Dekker proposal seemed good for, as Schut puts it, the proposal "offered not only a theoretically elegant blueprint of an equitable and efficient health care system but also an ingenious political compromise."[183] The political compromise rested in the fact that the Dekker proposals had aspects that appealed to all major interest groups and while each of these groups opposed some part of the proposal, opposition was not united against any particular part.[184]

The Dekker proposals were first put forward in 1987. In November 1989 there was a change of government. The new center-left government decided to continue with the implementation of the Dekker reforms, but some elements of the proposal were altered particularly with respect to putting greater emphasis on access or what the Dutch refer to as "social solidarity." The plan subsequently became known as the Simons Plan after the former Secretary of State for Health. It was decided that coverage under the compulsory basic insurance should be extended from 85 percent of general health care costs to 96 percent of general health care costs. It was also decided that the proportion of the amount paid by each and every individual to the Central Fund that was fixed as a percentage of the particular individual's income would be increased from

75 percent to 85 percent.[185] This would have the effect of increasing the extent to which the system is progressively financed and reducing the amount payable by those on lower incomes. The new government also stipulated that only non-profit insurers would be able to provide coverage under the compulsory basic benefit package and gave permission for small discounts in the case of group insurance.[186] It was also decided that the reform proposals would be phased in gradually and would not be fully implemented until 1995.

In 1992, the Dunning Committee (Government Committee on Choices in Health Care 1992) argued for a more careful evaluation of what would and would not be included in the basic package of services covered by the proposed compulsory basic insurance plan for all citizens.[187] The Dunning Committee proposed that four criteria be used to effectively sift out those services that should not be included in the basic package of care. These criteria were as follows: first, that the community in general considers the care to be necessary; second, that the services are effective; third, that the services are efficient using cost-effectiveness analyses or cost-utility analyses; and, finally, that it is not appropriate for patients themselves to pay for the health service in question. The Committee concluded that individuals should be free to purchase health care services that were not included in the core package and to buy private insurance to cover the cost thereof. Unlike New Zealand, where the Core Health Services Committee has an on-going role in defining what services should be publicly provided, the Dunning Committee was disbanded after the preparation of its report.

By 1994, some important features of the Dekker and Simons plans had been implemented but many important aspects had not.[188] From 1992, Sickness Funds were free to negotiate their own rates of reimbursement with providers. Prior to this time, it had been illegal to pay higher or lower fees than those set through the Central Tariff Agency. Sickness Funds were also able to offer coverage to individuals in other regions and several private insurance companies obtained permission to establish themselves as Sickness Funds. Individuals were now free to change Funds once every two years during an open enrolment period. In 1992, deregulation allowed general practitioners to locate their practices where they wished. From 1993, the Central Fund stopped reimbursing Sickness Funds for all their costs and shifted toward paying the Funds a partially risk-adjusted per capita payment. However, due to technical difficulties Sickness Funds initially were only held responsible for 3 percent of additional expenditures beyond the lump sum received. In an effort to encourage price competition, Sickness Fund enrollees are now required to pay a flat-rate premium to their chosen Sickness Fund. From 1994, Sickness Funds were no longer obliged to contract with every willing provider in an area. This resulted in some twenty-five cases over the course of the next four years where providers challenged the right of Sickness Funds not to renew or grant contracts to them.[189]

The 1995 health care reform plan

A new government assumed office in 1994 and in March 1995 the new Minister of Health, Els Borst Eilers, published yet another health reform plan. This plan provides for three separate systems within the larger Dutch system dealing with, respectively, exceptional medical expenses, curative basic care services, and amenity or inexpensive services.

The Dekker and Simons proposals had provided for the integration of acute and long-term care and proposed extending the Exceptional Medical Expenses Act so that it covered all general medical expenses. Although there are benefits from the integration of acute and long-term care, there was a concern about how to assess accurately the risk of the need for long-term care services as it requires a projection many years into the future.[190] It seems to be accepted that it may be better for these sorts of services to be provided independently of a competition-oriented scheme.[191] As a consequence, the 1995 reforms provide for the retention of a separate Exceptional Medical Expenses scheme, albeit restricted to long-term care and mental health care. All other goods and services previously covered under the Exceptional Medical Expenses scheme, such as drugs, medical devices, rehabilitation, and hospital-related home care services are now the responsibility of private insurers. In 1998 it was intended to shift the administration of the Exceptional Medical Expenses scheme away from the Sickness Funds and private insurers to a single insurer in each region.[192]

With respect to services considered "curative basic care" the government is proceeding with the Dekker/Simons proposals for managed competition. The government plans to increase the level of risk taken on by Sickness Funds from 3 percent to 65 percent within 3 years. In 1997 the Sickness Funds bore 27 percent and in 1999 35 percent of the risk of utilization.[193] In 1996 and 1997, the Central Fund adjusted the capitation payments made to Sickness Funds to allow for not only differences in the age and sex of the enrollees in a particular Fund but also region of residence and disability status. In 1999, employment and social security status were also factored into the calculations.

The capitation payment does not cover all the expenses of the Sickness Funds and the Central Fund pays a fixed amount that is set below the average expected cost of enrollees in each risk group. On average, this amounted to about 250 guilders per enrollee in 1997.[194] This seems to be stimulating a measure of price competition with

> the cheapest sickness fund charging a 40 percent lower flat-rate premium than the most expensive one, whereas in 1996 this margin was only ten percent. In addition, an increasing number of sickness funds are considering, or have already started, managed care activities...[195]

Schut and Hermans also report that in 1997 the Sickness Fund Act was modified to introduce a system of user charges but note that concern over access resulted in a complicated array of targeted user charges such that any potential cost savings may well be outweighed by administrative costs.[196] In 1999, the mandatory user charge regime was abandoned. It is proposed that the government will eventually stop price and capital regulation and allow managed competition to run its course. Although the government is planning to reform the private insurance sector as well through managed competition, so far it has failed to accomplish this so there is as yet no open enrolment period and no risk equalization payment to cross-subsidize those insurers that serve relatively high risk populations.[197]

Pursuant to the 1995 reform proposals there is now a third sector of health care services which are described as amenity and/or inexpensive care. Using the criteria of the Dunning Commission, any health service that does not pass through the four sieve tests of necessity, effectiveness, efficiency and personal responsibility falls within this sector, the financing and provision of which is left to the unregulated private sector.[198] For example, the government shifted dental care for adults into this sector on the rationale that the costs thereof were low enough that such services should be left to personal responsibility. However, subsequently there was concern about access for people in need of dental prostheses and thus coverage for dental prostheses was transferred back to the social insurance basket of services.[199]

The New Zealand health care system and the 1991 reform proposals

Problems in the system prior to reform proposals

As with many health care systems, problems in the New Zealand system have manifested themselves generally as cost and access issues.

Costs

Concern over rising costs has been the primary justification for health reform in New Zealand. In 1980, New Zealand spent 7.2 percent of its GDP on health care and in 1992, 7.7 percent.[200] While clearly this represents an increase in expenditures, these figures compare favorably with an OECD average of 7.0 percent of GDP in 1980 and 8.1 percent in 1992.

Looking more closely at the period 1980–92, New Zealand's health care expenditures as a percentage of GDP fell between 1980 and 1985, but increased steadily between 1985 and 1991 at a compound annual growth rate in the latter period of 2.6 percent. This is to be compared with an average growth rate of 1.6 percent in the OECD.[201] However, this growth rate may reflect falling real GDP rather than growing health care costs due to the New Zealand share market crash in October of 1987, which saw the market fall to one-third of its pre-crash level.[202] By mid-1992, the market was still not back to half its pre-crash level. During this period of recession relatively fixed expenditures on health care services comprised a larger percentage of real GDP. The compound annual rate of growth in terms of per capita health spending was 5.8 percent for the period 1985–91. This compares favorably with a 6.5-percent growth rate in the Netherlands, 7.3 percent in the UK, 9.0 percent in the US, and an OECD average of 7.6 percent. Muthumula and McKendry note that a major cause of significant increases in nominal expenditures on health care in the period 1985–8 was the removal of the wage-price freeze in 1985.[203]

Although New Zealand's relative expenditures would suggest that cost-containment would not be a significant factor motivating reform, nonetheless the government of the day portrayed health care costs as exploding. The National government stated in its 1991 reform proposal that in real terms, between 1980 and 1991, the Department of Health's budget increased from NZ\$1.1 billion to NZ\$3.8 billion, an increase of some 27 percent more than the increase in consumer prices over the same period.[204] These figures have been contested and appear to have been significantly inflated.[205]

Access and quality

As Table 3.2 on page 61, illustrates with regard to health outcomes, New Zealand generally performs at or around the average for OECD countries. As can be seen, however, New Zealand together with the US performs relatively poorly on infant mortality rates. However, neonatal and perinatal (age up to 28 days) mortality rates are low. The perinatal mortality death rate dramatically improved between 1990 and 1992 falling from 8.4 to 6.9 per thousand.[206] This suggests that post-neonatal infant mortality and Sudden Infant Death Syndrome are the most common causes of infant mortality, the latter being related to primary and preventive care rather than hospital care.[207] As Table 3.2 also illustrates New Zealand has the worst recorded figure of the four countries under study in terms of years of potential life lost.

In a recent study, Grant *et al.* found that user charges act as a barrier to access for primary health care services for some sectors of New Zealand's population.[208] In New Zealand, most people have to pay the full cost of a visit to their family doctor (although 45 percent have private insurance to help cover these costs). There are some government subsidies in place for the poor but they still only pay about half of the fee charged. Grant *et al.*'s cross-national study suggests that New Zealanders are less able to access basic primary care than people in the UK, Canada and Australia. Moreover, these latter countries perform better on health indicators of mean life expectancy, years of potential life lost, and infant mortality rate than New Zealand does.

It is also of note that New Zealand records relatively high mortality rates for ischaemic heart disease, respiratory diseases, breast and bowel cancer, motor vehicle crashes and suicide.[209] Despite overall improvements in New Zealand's mortality rates over the course of the last century there have been different rates of change between social groups. As in many other countries, there is a correlation between low income and poor health.[210] The mortality rate of those in the lowest socio-economic group is about twice that of the highest socio-economic group.[211] Durie and others pointed out startling discrepancies between Maori and European health outcomes in the late 1980s:

> Maori women appear particularly disadvantaged with a rate of lung cancer three times higher than the non-Maori rate, ten times greater for cancer of the cervix, four times higher for coronary artery disease, and three times higher for diabetes. Maori children are eight times more likely to develop rheumatic fever, eight times more likely to die from accidents, and nine times more likely to suffer from ear infection and death. Maori deaths from asthma, obesity, cancer (except bowel), renal disease, and diabetes are all well in excess of the non-Maori population. Mental hospital admission rates are three times as high and broad mental health problems are indicated in other statistics." [212]

There is evidence that, even allowing for socio-economic factors, the health care system does not serve the Maori well.[213] A 1993 study, comparing the period from 1975–7 to 1985–7, found that some progress had been achieved in reducing ethnic differences in mortality in New Zealand men but substantial differences remained for diseases that were amenable to medical intervention. The authors of this study conclude that these differences reflect poor access to appropriate health care services for Maori people.[214] Part of the problem may lie with user charges for general practitioner care. There is also the difficulty that some Maori people are reluctant to use European treatments. Some Maori people believe that they require autonomy in the delivery of health care services in order to provide the services Maori need in an acceptable manner.[215]

Of significant concern in New Zealand has been the growth of waiting lists and, in particular, the length of time spent on waiting lists for non-emergency surgical services. According to the government that initiated internal market reform, waiting lists reportedly increased from 38,501 people in 1981 to 62,000 people in 1991.[216] No nationwide information on the actual length of waiting lists was collected until 1967. The nation's 1967 figure of 31,928 people awaiting surgery gives some indication that waiting lists were already a problem by this date.[217] The length of waiting lists is only a problem if it contributes to an unacceptable time spent waiting for care. On average in 1988, 45 percent of those on waiting lists had to wait less than six months for treatment, while 15 percent reportedly had to wait longer than two years.[218] The government of the day used these figures on waiting times as evidence of how inefficient and inequitable the system was and as justification for the 1991 reform proposals.

There were also significant concerns over physicians' control of waiting lists and, particularly, of inequities in the management of waiting lists. It was noted in the Hospitals Taskforce Report in 1988:

> Waiting lists are not queues in the conventional sense of queuing for a bus, where the order of priority remains the same…Hospitals have great diffic-

ulty in determining patients' priorities. They tend to respond to plaintive pressure from patients, general practitioners, politicians or the media. [219]

Financing of health care services

The role of government

On 2 April 1938, then Prime Minister Michael Savage announced the Labour government's proposals for a national health insurance scheme. Although the public supported this scheme, the medical profession of the day, represented by the British Medical Association (BMA), opposed it.[220] Nonetheless, on 1 April 1939 the Social Security Act 1938 came into effect. However, general practitioners refused to cooperate with the government with respect to the implementation of maternity benefits and primary care that were to be free at point of service for patients.[221] Eventually, the government reached an agreement on the provision of maternity benefits but the BMA held out with respect to the provision of general practitioner services as it opposed the government's plan to pay general practitioners on a capitation basis. In 1941, the government capitulated and general practitioners retained the right to charge patients what they wished for their services over and above whatever the government paid them. The government instead made available a subsidy that could be claimed either by the patient or the doctor, and that almost covered practitioners' consultation fee at that time.[222] The Social Security Amendment Act 1941 effected these changes.

It was in 1941 that a fundamental dichotomy emerged between the provision of hospital and general practitioner care. Since 1938, hospital care has largely been funded by, and provided by, government. Since 1941, government subsidies have failed to keep pace with the charges fixed by general practitioners and an increasing proportion of this care has been privately financed.

Through the 1980s and prior to the 1991 proposals for reform, the government's contribution of funds to total health care expenditures was progressively reduced. In 1980, public expenditures on health care was 88 percent of total health care expenditures but by 1991 it had fallen to 82.2 percent.[223] This trend continued throughout the 1990s so that by 1996 76.7 percent of total health expenditures where publicly funded. In 1980, health care comprised 15.8 percent of total government spending and 12.8 percent in 1990.[224] Prior to the reforms, the New Zealand government still contributed the largest share to the health system, funding almost 100 percent of public hospital expenditures, 72.3 percent of drug expenditures, 52.1 percent of private hospital treatment, as well as 76 percent of public health expenditure.[225] It is important to note, however, that government only paid for 51.5 percent of primary services which included targeted subsidies for regular visits to general practitioners and full subsidies for maternity care, mental health care, and laboratory tests.[226] There were (and remain) inconsistencies in the subsidies provided for primary care. For example, some primary services such as laboratory tests were virtually 100-percent subsidized so that an individual patient paid nothing. Other services, like visits to a general practitioner and x-rays, attracted a far lower level of subsidization.[227]

Although the proportion of expenditures paid by government would seem to provide scope for the effective exercise of strong market power in negotiating with health care providers and for co-ordination there has, historically, been internal fragmentation within government sources that has led to confusion and inconsistency. For example, funding and co-ordination of continuing care for the intellectually, physically and psychologically disabled, and the frail elderly, had historically been distributed among epartment of Social Welfare, Area Health Boards, the Department of Health and other agencies.

The Accident and Compensation Corporation

The Accident and Compensation Corporation ("the ACC") was formed on 1 April 1974 to administer a major public accident insurance fund designed to remove the risk of personal liability due to accident.[228] It is a no-fault scheme that compensates for the full medical costs of accident victims and 80 percent of lost earnings and, until 1992, lump-sum compensation for permanent disability.[229] The 1974 scheme abolished the right to sue for personal injury caused by accidents. Physicians in New Zealand are thus protected from civil claims for damages that arise directly or indirectly from medical misadventure.[230]

Prior to internal market reform, the ACC funded 12 percent of primary services and 9.9 percent of private hospital treatments.[231] Over the period 1980 to 1990 the ACC's share of total health care expenditure increased from 0.7 to 4.2 percent.[232] The growing waiting times for public surgery, and the high cost of reimbursing lost earnings while accident victims were waiting for treatment, resulted in the ACC increasingly buying services from private hospitals in order to treat accident victims more quickly so as to get them back to work. A patient received prompter treatment if he or she had suffered the misfortune of an accident rather than an illness. Also, until 1992, the ACC covered the full cost of consultation by an accident patient's general practitioner, which would otherwise be a cost borne to a large degree by the patient. The proportion of practitioner visits classified as "accident related" rose from 15 percent in 1981/ 2 to 22 percent in 1989/90.[233] This indicates that either the number of accidents in New Zealand had increased, or (more likely) that doctors and patients were seeking to have injuries classified as "accidents" rather than as illness or sickness in order to jump queues in public hospitals and to avoid user charges. In 1990, patients were required to sign a declaration affirming they had in fact suffered an accident.[234] The *Consumer* reports that by 1993 accident claims had dropped by 570,000 compared with the 1990 figure.[235]

The National government reformed the accident compensation system in 1992 by limiting the coverage and benefits available.[236] The most significant change made in 1992 was to introduce the finding of fault back into the no-fault scheme. Apart from a small number of cases classifiable as "medical mishap," New Zealand's "no-fault" scheme now requires a process of fault finding on the part of health providers before patients are entitled to compensation. The 1992 reforms meant also that accident victims no longer received free general practitioner care and must now pay between NZ$10.00 and NZ$15.00 per visit. This still does not provide parity with visits to a general practitioner for illness, which for an adult not entitled to a government subsidy is approximately NZ$35.00–$40.00 per visit. Thus both patients and doctors still have an incentive to expand the ordinary meaning of accident in order to obtain a higher government subsidy.

Further and much more fundamental reform of the Accident Compensation Scheme was proposed in 1998 and was implemented on 1 July 1999. The Accident Insurance Act 1998 provides that the ACC will no longer cover employers for employee's workplace injuries. Instead, employers must choose a new personal injury insurer for their employees' work injuries. These reforms are discussed further below.

Private health insurance

The proportion of the population with private insurance increased from 18 percent in 1975 to 41 percent in 1994 but has fallen somewhat to 37 percent in 1996/7.[237] By virtue of a 1967 amendment to the Land and Income Tax Act, medical insurance premiums began to be treated as a tax-deductible item of personal expenditure; however, these tax benefits were eliminated on 17 December 1987.[238] New Zealanders purchase private insurance in order to avoid long queues for non-emergency surgery in public hospitals and to cover the cost of growing user charges for visits to general practitioners and other primary care services. Although half of households with incomes in the top quarter purchase private insurance, fewer than 20 percent of those in the bottom quarter do so.[239] Those with lower incomes, having less effective political voice, have been left on the waiting lists in the public sector while those with higher incomes have had non-emergency surgical services performed promptly in the private sector.

The proportion of total expenditures paid for by private insurers increased from 1.1 percent in 1980 to 3.5 percent in 1991 and to 6.8 percent in 1996/7.[240] Although overall still a small proportion, private insurance is much more important in the funding of *particular* health care services such as non-emergency surgical services, specialist services, and general practitioner charges.[241] The reason why private insurance comprises only a small percentage of total expenditures, despite the fact that 40 percent of the population have private insurance, is that private insurance does not generally cover expensive acute and emergency care which is provided predominantly by the public hospitals.

Patient charges

Prior to the 1991 reforms, patients paid for a significant proportion of certain health care goods and services. The sums paid by patients amounted to 26.5 percent of expenditures on general practitioner care, 24.7 percent of pharmaceutical expenditures, 21.1 percent of private hospital treatments, 76.5 percent of miscellaneous specialist service charges, 49.5 percent of diagnostics, and 82.2 percent of dental costs.[242] In the period 1980 to 1991, the percentage of total health expenditures financed directly by patients increased from 10.4 percent to 14.5 percent and by 1997/7 had increased to 15.6 percent.[243] A study that compared household expenditures on health care between 1987 and 1991 found spending on health care to be unequally distributed across income groups. In 1991, high-income households spent 3.6 times as much on health care services as low-income households, compared with 3 times as much in 1987.[244]

The supply of health care services

Hospitals

As can be seen from Table 3.3 on page 66, New Zealand has devoted a relatively high proportion of total health expenditures to hospital services. In particular, government spends a very high proportion of total expenditures on hospital services. In 1991, funding for hospitals and other institutions comprised nearly 73 percent of central government health expenditures compared to only 7.9 percent for general practitioner services and 24.3 percent on community care in general.[245]

PRIVATE HOSPITALS

After the enactment of the Social Security Act 1938, the importance of private hospitals sharply declined. However, their importance was re-established pursuant to the Hospitals Act 1957 which required the Minister of Health to encourage the development of private hospitals on the assumption that the growth of private hospitals would ease increasing strains on the public sector. The actual number of private hospitals in existence rose from 152 in 1958 to 200 in 1992, but the number of private beds available more than doubled, rising from 2,565 in 1958 to 7,149 in 1992 (compared with 18,823 beds in the public sector).[246] Private hospitals do not generally provide acute and emergency care, leaving this responsibility to the public hospitals.

Hay notes that the scale and nature of private hospital facilities and the size of financial rewards for various types of surgery meant that doctors in private hospitals tended to concentrate most heavily on "-ectomies" (hysterectomies, tonsillectomies, appendectomies, adenoidectomies, colectomies) rather than on the broad spectrum of surgical procedures.[247] As in the UK, most specialists work in both the public and private sectors, and since working in the private sector is more profitable, specialists have little incentive to reduce public sector waiting lists.[248] Consequently, doctors spend less time engaged in major surgery in public hospitals, which may contribute to lengthening waiting lists in the public sector.

PUBLIC HOSPITALS

Throughout the 1980s twenty-seven locally elected hospital boards were reorganized into fourteen Area Health Boards. Prior to the 1991 reform proposals, Area Health Boards performed the dual functions of managing public hospitals and managing government funds with which to purchase most hospital and other secondary services in their respective areas. Thus, the provider and purchaser functions were combined in one entity for each of the fourteen regions. The Area Health Boards were not, however, generally responsible either for the purchase or provision of primary care.

In 1989 the restructuring of twenty-seven hospital boards into fourteen Area Health Boards was completed. Towards the end of 1989 the New Zealand Health Charter was introduced. This required each Board to sign a performance-oriented accountability agreement with the Minister of Health. The purchasing and provider roles of the Area Health Boards were more clearly defined and the agreements provided the Boards with a clearer understanding of their obligations and the funds within which they had to achieve those obligations on a yearly basis.[249]

Physicians

Since 1941, government subsidies have failed to keep pace with the increased fees charged by general practitioners. In 1992, the real value of the government's subsidy had fallen to less than 20 percent of the total average fee.[250] User charges for general practitioner care in New Zealand are higher than in many other countries.[251] The inconsistency inherent in only partial state funding of general practitioner care and full funding of hospital care had resulted in some people turning to hospitals for "free" (but, in terms of real costs, much more expensive) care, rather than visiting their general practitioner.[252]

Changes in the provision of primary care were made throughout the 1980s. The government's subsidy of general practitioner care was increased in October 1988 and again in September 1990 for children, the elderly, and the chronically ill. From 1 September 1990, practitioners were given the option of joining a contract scheme which offered an inflation-adjusted subsidy for all consultations in return for limits on user charges and the provision of patient information for a national database. This scheme was abandoned by the National government upon its election in 1990.

Internal market reform and the Health and Disability Services Act 1993

The proposals for reform of New Zealand's health system have to be understood in the context of the radical restructuring of New Zealand's economic and political landscape throughout the period 1984–90. By the time the National government was elected in 1990, most state services that conceivably had commercial potential had been restructured in an attempt to mimic private firm behavior. This process was known as "corporatization." It was argued that accountability as well as efficiency would be improved if management functions could be placed at arm's length from the political responsibility of ministers. Many of these corporatized entities, such as Air New Zealand and Telecom, were subsequently sold to the private sector.

Upon its election at the end of 1990 the National government announced the establishment of (yet another) task force to report on the health care system. The terms of reference of the task force reflected a preference for the sort of reform that had already been undertaken in other sectors. For example, the taskforce was asked to explore the need for targeting of government subsidies and the need for greater competition in the purchase and provision of health care services.

In 1991 the Minister of Health produced a policy paper which identified the following problems in the health system:[253]

- public hospital waiting times were too long;
- there was conflict in the dual roles of the Area Health Boards as purchasers and providers of secondary (hospital) health care;
- legislative and operational constraints on the Area Health Boards made it difficult for them to operate efficiently;
- funding of the system was fragmented leading to difficulties in co-ordinating care and perverse incentives being created for providers and patients;
- people on higher incomes and in particular geographic locations had better access to health care services;
- there were few incentives in the existing system to induce both general practitioners and patients to make efficient choices between difference health care services;
- there was a lack of consumer control in terms of too little consultation and too little opportunity for local involvement in the delivery of health care services.

The government said that underlying all these problems was the issue of fairness, and that there were inconsistencies in the existing system. However, in practice the government has seemed more concerned about increases in government costs. They also appeared strongly committed to a system that would provide greater consumer choice and flexibility. The Minister of Health in introducing the Health and Disability Services Bill into parliament noted:

There is also a widespread conviction that something as vital and as personal as our health cannot be serviced by a monolithic system. People want choice and flexibility. A standard, pre-packaged approach is not acceptable, either.[254]

The 1991 internal market reform proposals are listed below:

- A regime of targeted user fees for primary and secondary care that included introducing, for the first time since 1938, partial user fees for public hospital care. Those who qualify for government subsidies for treatment must now carry a "community services card" before they are entitled to obtain health care at a reduced price that reflects a government subsidy. To be entitled to a card, a person must be on a "low income."[255]
- Disbandment of the fourteen Area Health Boards. The Boards had previously been responsible for the purchase of most hospital care and had also managed the major public hospitals. The proposals provided for the separation of the Boards' purchaser and provider roles.
- The establishment of four Regional Health Authorities (RHAs) to act as purchasing agents with available government funds. The Northern RHA is responsible for a population of 1,078,878, the Midland RHA, 683,499, the Central RHA, 855,879, and the Southern RHA, 746,046. The Minister of Health is required each year to enter into a funding agreement with the RHAs and to monitor the performance of those agreements. It was envisaged that RHAs would be responsible for purchasing all services from general practitioners as well as other primary care services and all hospital and other secondary care for illness, accident, and disability on behalf of individuals residing within their respective geographically defined regions. Consolidating funding for illness, accident and disability in the RHAs was done with the goal of ensuring better co-ordination in the purchasing of health care services and reducing the potential for cost-shifting.
- Provision for the eventual establishment of private insurance plan to compete with the RHAs. Eventually, individuals would be able shift between RHAs and private plans with an allotted portion of government funding. In essence, this is the managed competition model.
- Public consultation by a government-appointed committee to define a list of "core health care services" that must be available to all New Zealanders without charge or at "affordable" prices. RHAs and private plans must purchase core health care services as a matter of priority for those individuals residing within their respective geographic regions.
- The separation of responsibility for the purchasing of public health care services from other types of health care services, and the establishment of a government-appointed Public Health Commission to purchase public health care services from public and private providers.
- The amalgamation and restructuring of one hundred public hospitals into twenty-three government-owned corporations to be known as Crown

Health Enterprises (CHEs). It was envisaged that CHEs would compete with each other and private providers for supply contracts with the four RHAs. Unlike the old Area Health Boards, the new CHEs do not operate under global budgets and are not necessarily responsible for ensuring the health of their local populations; this latter responsibility falls on the four RHAs. The CHEs are required, in effect, to mimic the behavior of private firms and compete with each other and private providers. While CHEs are required to exhibit a sense of social responsibility, this is not to limit their requirement to act as a successful and efficient business that supplies health care services.[256]

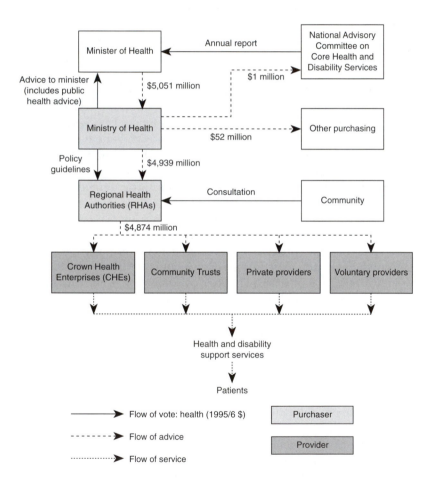

Figure 3.1 The structure of New Zealand's internal market in 1996.

Source: Perfomance Monitoring and Review Section, Ministry of Health in *Health Services 1996: Facts on the Purchasing and Provision of Health and Disability Support Services for New Zealanders* (Ministry of Health: Wellington, 1996) at p. 6

- Subject to economic viability and government approval, small hospitals would be run as community trusts to compete with CHEs and other private providers.

Figure 3.1 depicts New Zealand's internal market in 1996.

As with the Dutch reform experience, some of the 1991 proposals were never implemented and some were implemented but subsequently dropped or significantly modified.

User charges for hospital care, introduced in 1991, were abandoned in 1993 although higher user charges for the majority of the population for primary care services remain in place as does the requirement for those receiving subsidies to carry an entitlement card named the "Community Services Card." The government did subsequently expand upon its original definition of lower income groups entitled to government subsidies for primary services and this resulted in coverage for an additional 100,000 people.[257] In 1996, the Ministry of Health reported that approximately 60 percent of the population are in fact entitled to a Community Services Card but that only 40 percent of the population have one.[258] A Community Services Card does not entitle the holder thereof to free service but a partial government subsidy, which generally for adults only covers half the cost of a general practitioner's fees.

Since 1993, the Core Health Services Committee has abandoned its task of attempting to define a list of prioritized core health care services although, as will be discussed further in the next chapter, it has continued to attempt to prioritize different classes of health need. It is now called the National Health Committee. The Public Health Commission had a brief but active life. Perhaps too active as it was disbanded in July 1995; responsibility for purchasing public services was assumed by the RHAs and a special monitoring unit was created within the Ministry of Health.[259]

In 1996, responsibility for purchasing non-emergency surgical services for accident victims was transferred back from the RHAs to the Accident Compensation Corporation. A report by a government-appointed committee on the 1993/4 performance of the ACC found that the ACC could not influence public hospital surgery schedules or transfer procedures and consequently rehabilitation of accident victims was impeded.[260] The ACC found itself having to absorb rocketing income maintenance costs as accident victims waited with the ill in queues for treatment in the public sector. It estimated that there were between 13,000 and 20,000 accident claimants on waiting lists at this time with an average waiting time of six months, at a cost of between $70 and $100 million in earning-related compensation.[261] As a consequence, purchasing responsibility was transferred from the RHAs and back to the ACC. In 1999, a further change in purchasing responsibility will occur as employers will no longer be covered by the ACC for employees' workplace injuries and will be required to choose a new personal injury insurer for their employees' work injuries. Employers can select any registered private insurer (meeting certain prudential requirements) or a new state-owned enterprise insurer set up by the government. As a result of these changes there will be a significant increase in the number of purchasers (insurance companies) buying health care services for accident victims.[262]

New Zealand's original 1991 proposals for reform envisaged the development of competition between Regional Health Authorities and private plans. This original proposal thus envisaged a transition towards a version of Enthoven's managed competition model. This policy was abandoned because of strong public opposition to what was described as the "Americanization" of the public health service. There were also concerns over the prospect of "cream skimming" i.e. private insurers selecting or attracting low-risk people to their plans and excluding or skimping on care for high-risk people. The dropping of the proposal for private plans has a profound impact on the viability of the managed competition theory underlying and supporting the reform process. Instead of competition between insurance plans indirectly stimulating efficient competition between health care providers, the emasculated reform depended upon RHAs stimulating and micro-managing competition between health care providers through a competitive contracting-out process. Consequently, the incentives RHAs have to negotiate efficient contracts with providers becomes key and this issue and general issues of accountability and governance are dealt with in the following chapter.

Other key issues raised by New Zealand's internal market reform include flexibility and transactions costs (management, administration and contracting costs). With respect to flexibility, the mandatory purchaser-provider split means that the Regional Health Authorities do not have the option of vertically integrating with providers or providing health care services directly and can only ever contract out. The costs and benefits of an inflexible purchaser/provider split are discussed in Chapter 5. With regard to transactions costs, undoubtedly there are additional transaction costs in internal markets which were not incurred in the previous system. In terms of structure, fourteen Area Health Boards have been replaced by four Regional Health Authorities and twenty-three Crown Health Enterprises all contracting with each other, with private for-profit and charitable providers, and with the government. As an example of some of the costs of contracting, one Crown Health Enterprise spent some $93,000 in an unsuccessful bid to run a cardio-thoracic unit that subsequently the local RHA decided not to proceed with.[263] Charitable providers that provide national services, such as Plunket (maternal and baby care) and the IHC (Intellectually Handicapped) Society, have complained about the costs incurred in having to negotiate four separate contracts with the four RHAs. The President of the IHC, Dr Roderick Deane, described the ensuing paper war as "bureaucracy gone mad."[264] Issues of transactions costs, particularly from the perspective of comparing transactions costs in internal markets with those incurred in a managed competition system, are dealt with in both Chapters 4 and 5.

Subsequent to implementation of the internal market reform a significant proportion of general practitioners formed into alliances and groups in order to better negotiate with the RHAs. These entities have were called Independent Practice Associations (IPAs). By 1996, 50 percent of general practitioners had joined IPAs.[265] Subsequently, IPAs have become known as "Budget-holders." Budget-holders are groups of general practitioners who are responsible for purchasing pharmaceuticals, lab tests, and some non-emergency surgery. At the end of June 1997, 71 percent of general practitioners were involved in Budget-holding.[266] If Budget-holders achieve savings on historical consumption patterns, then this is shared between the Budget-holder and the RHA. However, Budget-holders do not (yet) carry any significant financial burden, for when budgets are exceeded these extra costs are paid by the relevant RHA.[267] This type of arrangement is similar to the concept of GP Fundholders in the UK (discussed in the next section) with the difference being that Fundholding was a government-orchestrated initiative whereas IPAs initially sprang up in New Zealand as a response to the consolidation of power on the purchasing side.

In October 1996, a new government was elected in New Zealand. This was New Zealand's first coalition government after a change from "first past-the-post" to a "mixed member proportional representation" electoral system. The new coalition government represented two political parties, National and the Alliance. Pursuant to the coalition agreement between these two parties a number of health policy reforms were required. These included that the four RHAs be replaced by one single funding body, removal of the profit motive of the CHEs, an increased community and regional focus for the CHEs, and free primary care for all children under the age of 6.

On 1 July 1997, the four RHAs were amalgamated (at least technically) into one Health Authority and from 1 January 1998 the Health Funding Authority was established. The amalgamation of the four RHAs into one central purchasing authority was largely in response to what were perceived as rising and excessive transactions costs. However, whether costs will be saved is debatable given that four regional offices are maintained as "branches" of the new Health Funding Authority. Every year the Ministry of Health enters into an "Annual Funding Agreement" with the Health Funding Authority that requires the Authority to seek to achieve the Crown's Statement of Objectives in the health sector. For each of the Objectives there are performance measures designed to demonstrate performance consistent with the Objectives. The Crown's Statement of Objectives for 1998/9, issued pursuant to s.8(1) of the Health and Disability Services Act 1993, still put emphasis on the Authority developing and refining contract methodologies. Thus, the spirit of internal market reform has largely been left intact and there is still an emphasis on contracting out by the Health Funding Authority.

With regard to the impact of internal market reform on costs, the percentage of GDP spent on health care has remained constant in 1992 and 1993 at 7.7 percent and from 1994 to 1996 at 7.6 percent.[268] However, looking at per capita spending (using Purchasing Power Parity in US$), New Zealand experienced an average growth rate of 5.6 percent from 1988 to 1996. This is significantly higher than the OECD average growth rate of 4.1 percent.[269] The rate of growth in private sector spending (user charges and private insurance) has continued to increase significantly.[270]

What has been the impact of internal market reform on issues of access and quality? The reforms did not address one of the key problems in the system, namely the high level of user charges for particular forms of primary care and in particular general practitioner services. The reforms were intended to promote the integration of primary and secondary care but this is quite a challenge when Regional Health Authorities have only a moderate amount of influence in terms of funding primary care. There were, however, signs that some RHAs recognized the benefits of primary and preventive care and they were fully subsidizing this type of care for some groups.[271] The most visible problem of New Zealand's former command-and-control system was implicit rationing through long and growing waiting lists. Despite several cash injections by the government specifically designated to help reduce waiting lists,[272] waiting lists have increased by over 50 percent from 62,000 in 1991 to a reported 93,930 people waiting as of March 1996.[273] Over 18,000 people had been waiting for over two years as at 30 June 1996 compared with 14,901 as at 30 June 1995.[274] The government has decided to change the parameters of the waiting list/ time problem by abandoning waiting lists and implementing a "booking system" in its place. In the new booking system patients are not "booked" in for surgery unless the system can provide the service within two years. Patients whose needs cannot be meet within two years are referred back to the general practitioner to "manage" their condition. Physicians must now determine priorities in booking on the basis of urgency of need and capacity to benefit. On the one hand the benefit of this new system is that people will know for sure whether they will be treated in the public sector instead of languishing in false hope on waiting lists. On the other hand, the criteria employed in determining booking priorities raises issues of discrimination against the disabled, chronically ill, and the elderly.[275]

The UK health care system and the 1989 reform proposals

Prior to internal market reform the UK exemplified the "command-and-control" approach to health care allocation. A command-and-control system is one in which government not only finances the vast majority of services but is also heavily involved in managing the delivery of services. The command-and-control system in the UK has historically relied upon supply-side controls to constrain costs. So, for example, the number of hospital beds, technology, nursing staff, etc. that physicians have to work with are limited either by direct government edict or by tightly controlling the funds flowing into the health care sector. The chief problems with this system, as discussed below, have manifested themselves in terms of rationing through growing waiting lists and times and concerns over whether health resources have been allocated or rationed by physicians in a fair and equitable manner. There have also been concerns that although the UK system controls costs it is not necessarily efficient, as evident by the wide variations in clinical practice that occur across the country.

In the UK there are in fact four slightly different health systems – in England, Scotland, Wales and Northern Ireland. Unless otherwise stated, the discussion will refer to the historical development of and reforms within the National Health Service (the NHS) in England.

Problems in the system prior to reform

Costs

The command-and-control approach is generally associated with the ability to contain total health care expenditures; nonetheless, costs were still a motivating factor for reform in the UK with the government being concerned over rising costs and physicians and other providers arguing that the system was under-funded.

Throughout the 1980s the government expressed concern at the increases in public real expenditures on health care services. In the period 1978–9 to 1991–2 there was a 22-percent increase in expenditures in real terms, without any perceptible impact on the length of waiting lists for surgery and time spent thereon by patients.[276] There was a concern that without change the aging population and increasing technology would exert continued upward pressure on growth in health care expenditures.[277] In contrast to the government's concern over rising costs, there was a strong outcry, on the part of providers and others, that the NHS was under-funded. Discontent grew amongst providers as growth in public expenditures, historically set at 2 percent per annum in real terms, was curbed over the 1980s. Whereas the US has consistently spent more on health care than would be predicted from its real level of GDP, the UK has consistently spent less.[278] For example, in 1990, the UK spent 6.2 percent of GDP on health care services compared with an OECD average of 7.6 percent. This fact coupled with the government's continued desire to cut costs suggests that the UK government has successfully used its monopsony (single buyer) power to control costs. However, stringent cost control is not necessarily a good thing! Stringent cost control may detrimentally affected the quality of the system, or result in cost-shifting, or result in inefficiencies such as losses in improved health care outcomes from slow rates of technology introduction, reduced innovation, or deterring the best and brightest from training to be health care professionals.

Access and quality

Although the UK spends less on health care as a percentage of GDP than would be predicted, it nonetheless performs around the OECD average with regard to health outcomes. Despite an average performance with regard to health outcomes, Spiby notes that the UK does not perform well on specific health indicators compared to its European neighbors. For example, it has significantly higher death rates for ischemic health disease than the former West Germany or France.[279] Together with the Netherlands, it has a high death rate for males from malignant tracheal, bronchial, and lung cancer. It also has a high death rate for women from the same causes, even though the percentage of the population that smokes and the amount of tobacco consumed, while high, is not the highest of OECD countries.[280]

With respect to the quality of care delivered, an issue of significant concern has been the growth and management of waiting lists, particularly for elective (non-emergency) surgery. Waiting lists grew through the 1980s from a reported 700,000 to 900,000 in 1990.[281] The median waiting time was five weeks but 23 percent of patients had to wait 12 months or more for services.[282] As in New Zealand, waiting lists in the UK have been for elective surgery and not for emergency services. Waiting lists, like user charges, are a means of rationing access to health care services, but unlike user charges one would assume that priority on waiting lists would be assigned to those who, objectively, are in the greatest need. However, it appears that this is not always the case and that specialists are influenced by factors other than the objective clinical need of the patient in front of them relative to all other patients. According to Aaron and Schwartz these factors include age, how society perceives the illness, the visibility of the illness, and the cost of treatment.[283] They note that those patients unwilling to accept the consequences of resource limits in the UK have found ways to "work the system" – for example, by jumping ahead of needier people in queues in order to obtain care faster.

Some argue that the issue of waiting lists and times is not a real indication of the system's performance. It is possible that physicians have an incentive to exaggerate the real extent of waiting lists as leverage to argue for more government funding. It is also possible that specialists that are employed in the UK public sector on a salary basis but work part-time in the private sector on an unregulated fee-for-service basis have an incentive to maintain long waiting lists in the public sector. This is because the existence (or even appearance) of long waiting lists in the public sector may enhance demand for their services in the more lucrative private sector. People recorded on waiting lists may be recorded on several lists, may have already died of a pre-existing condition, and may be put on waiting lists before they really need a particular treatment in order to make sure they are further up the "queue" in case they do in fact need the treatment![284] While it is certainly true that the length of a waiting list is not necessarily of concern the time that it takes to clear is of great concern. This is not only because someone's health or chance of recovery may be affected by a delay in treatment but also that patients may suffer a great deal of fear, anxiety, and (depending on their condition) discomfort/pain. Moreover, delay in treating their condition may inhibit their working and social life. These latter costs are hidden costs that are not born by the publicly-funded health care system and thus may be readily overlooked.

Financing health care services

The role of government

After a battle with the medical profession the National Health Service Act 1946 was eventually passed. It provided for universal free access to primary and hospital services, subject only to the express provisions of the Act.[285] Section 1 of the National Health Service Act 1977 requires the Secretary of State for Health to promote the establishment in England and Wales of a "comprehensive health service" in order to "secure improvement in the physical and mental health of the people of those areas and in the prevention, diagnosis, and treatment of illness."[286] The emphasis in the NHS legislation is on service provision as opposed to insurance and government's role extends beyond financing and regulation to delivery. Pursuant to section 3 of the 1977 Act, the Secretary of State, to such extent as she considers necessary to meet all reasonable requirements, has a duty to provide hospital and other like accommodation, medical, dental, nursing and ambulance services, maternity and young child care, preventive, acute and convalescent care, and services required for the diagnosis and treatment of illness.

With respect to the financing of services, since 1946 the government has remained by far the largest financier of health care services. As Table 3.4 demonstrates, although the percentage of health care paid for by the public sector has declined, of the four countries under consideration in this book, the UK had by far the highest percentage of health care services paid for by the public sector.

The budget for the NHS is determined by the British Treasury generally on the basis of previous years' outlays and anticipated inflation and this budget is then approved by the House of Commons. Prior to the 1989

Table 3.4 Percentage of total health expenditures paid for by the public sector

	UK	NZ	Netherlands*	US
1960	85.2%	80.6%	33.3%	24.8%
1970	87.0%	80.3%	84.3%	37.8%
1980	89.4%	88.0%	74.7%	42.4%
1990	84.1%	82.4%	72.7%	40.7%
1991	83.7%	82.2%	74.1%	41.9%
1992	84.5%	79.0%	77.4%	42.9%
1993	84.8%	76.6%	78.3%	43.5%
1994	84.1%	77.6%	77.5%	44.8%
1995	84.4%	77.2%	76.7%	45.9%
1996	84.5%	76.7%	72.1%	46.7%

Source: OECD Health Data 1998: A Comparative Analysis of 29 Countries, Electronic Database

*These figures include the contributions made by employers and employees to government-mandated social insurance schemes. Figures for the amount spent by government from taxation funds is not available for these years but is around 14 percent for the Netherlands.

proposals, the Department of Health allocated the government budget to the fourteen Regional Health Authorities who in turn funded the various District Health Authorities (that purchased hospital services and managed all the public hospitals) and Family Practitioner Committees (that reimbursed the work of general practitioners).

Private health insurance

The proportion of the population with private health insurance has, since 1945, been small but has steadily grown in recent years. In 1980, 6.4 percent of the UK population were covered by private insurance; this percentage rose to 10.5 in 1988 and to 11.5 percent in 1990 and the percentages of professionals, employers and managers with private insurance was significantly higher.[287]

Expenditures by private for-profit insurers as a proportion of total health care expenditures was 3.2 percent in 1990 and 3.5 percent in 1995. By comparison, in New Zealand, the Netherlands, and the US, in 1995, private health insurance as a percentage of total health care expenditures comprised respectively 6.4 percent, 14.3 percent, and 33 percent.[288] The private insurance sector in the UK plays a far larger role than its contributions to total health care expenditures would indicate as it allows those on higher incomes to buy private insurance to avoid rationing by waiting in the public sector. As discussed in Chapter 4, this has significantly reduced political pressures to reduce waiting times and lists. The private sector also provides an additional source of revenue for specialists employed in the public sector, and the fee-for-service basis on which reimbursement occurs in the private sector provides a financial incentive for specialists to provide more services in the private sector than in the public sector.[289]

Patient charges

Despite the parsimony of the UK system, unlike New Zealand, there are no user charges for general practitioner care. This is a key feature of the UK system. It avoids the false economy of people delaying or forgoing the primary care they need because of user charges only to cost the system more if their condition deteriorates. Since 1952, there have been user charges for pharmaceuticals. In 1989, user charges were introduced for eye and dental care.[290] By 1993, user charges had risen to an undifferentiated rate of £4.25 per prescription item; however, 60 percent of the population are exempt from these charges, and over 80 percent of prescriptions are in fact dispensed to those who are exempt.[291] User charges by patients accounted for a mere 3.4 percentage of total health care expenditures in 1990 and actually declined to 2.7 percent in 1995. By comparison, in 1995, user charges accounted for 16.5 percent of total health care expenditures in the US and 22.8 percent in New Zealand.[292]

The supply of health care services

The Secretary of State for Health has historically been accountable to Parliament for the supply of health care services in England.[293] Prior to internal market reform, the Secretary of State appointed Regional Health Authorities, which in turn were responsible for financing government authorities further down the hierarchy, controlling capital investment, and employing senior specialists working in public hospitals.[294] Regional Health Authorities could delegate duties imposed on them by the Secretary of State to District Health Authorities and Family Practitioner Committees, both organizations being established by the Secretary of State. District Health Authorities historically were responsible, within their respective districts, for the supply of public hospital services, and Family Practitioner Committees were responsible for the purchase of general medical, dental, ophthalmic, and pharmaceutical services.[295]

Hospitals

Section 6 of the National Health Services Act 1946 provided for the nationalization of hospitals by providing for the vesting of all private not-for-profit hospitals and all municipal hospitals in the Minister of Health.[296] Prior to the 1989 reform proposals, responsibility for the management and operation of public hospitals had been largely delegated to the District Health Authorities of which there are were about 145, each serving an area with approximately 250,000 people. The direct line of hierarchy between the government and Regional and District Authorities has resulted in government being held accountable at the highest level for small difficulties within the system and has politicized decisions such as the rationalization of the hospital sector.[297] The UK system also has generated little useable information about the cost and benefits of different types of hospital services.[298]

The District Health Authorities had no incentive to contract with the most efficient providers (whether public or private) and thus divert funds from the public hospitals they were responsible for managing.. However, since the mid-1980s, District Health Authorities were required to solicit tenders for the supply of catering and ancillary services. District Health Authorities could not ensure the supply of integrated care, since they could not readily shift funding from hospital to primary care or vice versa as the Family Practitioner Committees controlled the budget for general practitioner care. Public hospitals were funded by way of block budgets based on historical expenditures. Consequently, improving efficiency may have actually proved disadvantageous as it might result in a reduction in the level of government funding in the next financial year and/or might result in more referrals but with no more resources to deal with these new patients.[299] Capped hospital budgets also provided incentives for cost-shifting. For example, specialists based in public hospitals referred patients back to their general practitioners, who were not subject to the same budget limitations, for either the cost of their own services or for the pharmaceuticals they prescribed.[300] Long and growing waiting lists for elective surgery can also be viewed as a form of cost-shifting on to patients.

Prior to the 1990 reforms there were 200 private acute hospital providing about 10,500 beds in the UK.[301] As in New Zealand, private hospitals only provide elective surgery leaving responsibility for acute and emergency care to the public hospitals. In 1986, it was estimated that 16.7 percent of residents in England and Wales undergoing elective surgery (excluding abortion) were treated in the private sector.[302] The Health Services Act 1976 provided for the creation of a Health Services Board to control the establishment of private hospitals in order to safeguard the NHS from what was feared to be too much competition from the private sector. This Board was subsequently dissolved pursuant to s. 9 of the Health Services Act 1980.[303]

Physicians

Prior to the 1989 reform proposals, the supply of general practitioner services was managed through local Family Practitioner Committees (the members of which were government appointed) who were responsible for the funding and delivery of primary health care services. These Committees contracted with general practitioners and prepared a list of NHS practitioners.[304] The Committees were also responsible for making arrangements for the supply of dental services, ophthalmic services for certain groups, and pharmaceutical services.[305]

General practitioners are treated as independent private contractors even although they are publicly financed. Every individual in the UK is enrolled with a general practitioner. Patients are free to select a general practitioner from the NHS list subject to the consent of the practitioner concerned. Where the patient has no particular preference then her Family Practitioner Committee will assign her to a practitioner. The average list size in England in 1991 was 1,900 patients.[306] In 1990, 39 percent of physicians were generalists and by 1995, 35.9 percent were generalists; however, over 90 percent of all episodes of ill health in the UK are treated in general practice. A significant contribution to the NHS's relative cost-effectiveness is that general practitioners act as filters or gatekeepers to the consumption of more expensive hospital, specialist, and other services. The opportunities open to patients to access the system at more expensive entry-points are very limited.

At the time of the creation of the NHS there was a long battle as organized medicine resisted government attempts to reimburse general practitioners on a salary basis.[307] However, by 1966 this resistance had faded and practitioners agreed to adopt a basic salary proposal (described as a "practice allowance") and in subsequent years, practitioners have been among the strongest defenders of salaried reimbursement under the NHS.[308] Prior to the 1989 proposals for reform, Family Practitioner Committees paid general practitioners using a mixture of three methods. First, practitioners received a basic practice allowance or salary (which was larger for practitioners locating in those areas viewed as being under-serviced). Second, they received a capitation payment per registered patient (with three levels of payment depending on the age of the patient). And, finally, they received specific fee-for-service payments for particular preventive services.[309] Fee-for-service payments and payments of costs were pegged to the total average costs for all practitioners, with practitioners being able to keep any moneys they saved below the average.[310] By the mid-1980s about 46 percent of general practitioners' incomes were derived from capitation.[311] Maynard and Walker note that, historically, the prices fixed by the government for the price of labor have reflected to only a very limited degree the relative scarcities of labor.[312]

Specialists in the public sector are paid on a salary basis and also may receive "distinction awards" that can result in an increase of their salary by 40 to 95 percent.[313] Until recent reforms, specialists were paid by and were accountable to the relevant Regional Health Authority rather than to the District Health Authority that managed the hospital. Specialists may work part time in private hospitals although their primary employer remains the NHS. In 1993, Maynard and Walker noted that specialists earned an average of £39,000 from private practice.[314]

Internal market reform and the NHS and Community Care Act of 1990

The presidents of three leading Royal Colleges representing specialists issued a public statement on 7 December 1987 warning that the NHS was in crisis and called for an immediate independent review. This statement was in response to the reduced growth in government expenditures on health care services over the preceding decade and the pressure being exerted upon providers to produce the same standard of care for the population with fewer funds. According to Day and Klein, this statement on the part of the Royal Colleges so angered the then prime minister, Margaret Thatcher, that she announced a review of the NHS in January 1988 without consulting her ministerial colleagues.[315]

Proposals for internal market reform of the NHS were first announced at the beginning of 1989 and encapsulated in a White Paper entitled 'Working for Patients'.[316] Subsequently, the reforms were implemented in the National Health Service and Community Care Act 1990.[317] The stated goal of the reforms was to improve efficiency by creating competition on the supply side of the market between public and private institutions. It is important to note that the White Paper primarily sought to reform the management and delivery of services and not the funding thereof. Thus the government was to remain the primary financier of health care. There were eight important reform proposals:

- The splitting of responsibilities for the purchasing and the provision of hospital services, both functions having formerly been performed by the District Health Authorities. The District Health Authorities were to become purchasers of health care services and to contract with competing public and private providers.

- The establishment of public hospitals as self-governing "NHS Trusts" (which are not trusts in the legal sense but crown corporations) with the power to vary salary packages for employees and to borrow capital within annual financing limits.
- The establishment of groups of general practitioners as "Fundholders" with their own budgets to purchase some diagnostic and elective procedures from public hospitals and other providers.
- The creation of indicative prescribing budgets for those general practitioners not electing to become Fundholders.
- The creation of a hundred new specialist positions within public hospitals to help reduce waiting times.
- The creation of a tax exemption for the purchase of private insurance for those over 60.
- The membership, remuneration, and staffing of District and Regional Health Authorities and Family Health Services Authorities would be reorganized on "business lines."
- Rigorous audits would be introduced throughout the NHS.

Originally it was intended that the existing Regional Health Authorities would perform their role of overseeing and financing the District Health Authorities. However, further reforms on 1 April 1996 resulted in the abolition of the Regional Health Authorities and the merging of District Health Authorities and Family Practitioner Committees into a hundred Health Authorities. These Health Authorities were responsible for purchasing hospital, primary and community health services for varying populations ranging from roughly 125,000 up to just over a million. Overseeing the Health Authorities were eight branches or outposts of the NHS Executive (an agency within the Department of Health).[318]

Prior to the 1989 proposals for reform the Regional Health Authorities were financed pursuant to a formula known as RAWP (Resource Allocation Working Party). This formula was intended to reallocate funding more fairly between various regions to reflect underlying need as opposed to historical expenditures. In order to do this, allocations were based on regional differences in standardized mortality ratios.[319] Subsequently, the RAWP forum was reviewed and refined and was meant to determine the funding received by Health Authorities, although in 1996 the Department of Health was still only allocating 76 percent of the total budget according to this formula.[320] Bloor and Maynard note that the RAWP formula does not apply to primary care which is still largely "demand determined and not case limited: it is a function of the number of general practitioners and their prescribing behavior."[321] Unlike New Zealand, the UK Health Authorities were not responsible for funding disability services. A new regime was introduced in the UK for the purchase of community care for the elderly, the mentally ill, and the mentally and physically handicapped. Budgets were capped and management responsibility was devolved to local authority social services managers.[322]

The key part of internal market reform in the UK, as in New Zealand, is the splitting of the purchaser and provider roles of the District Health Authorities which had formerly been responsible for purchasing all hospital care *and* managing all the public hospitals in their district. In the reformed system Health Authorities were expected to be transformed into active purchasers and engage in hard bargaining for the supply of cost-effective hospital and other secondary services from a range of health care providers. Consequently, it was vitally important to ensure that the Health Authorities had the incentives and necessary expertise to make good decisions and to engage in hard-bargaining. The accountability of Health Authorities and other purchasers are analyzed in Chapter 4.

Section 3 of the National Health Service and Community Care Act ("the Act") allows Health Authorities to enter into "NHS contracts" for the provision of health goods and services.[323] The providers from whom they may choose to contract with include independent public hospitals ("NHS Trusts"), private hospitals and community organizations. Thus the term "internal market" is somewhat misleading as it is intended that both public and private providers will compete in the new market. Section 4 of the Act provides that an "NHS contract" is not in fact a contract in the traditional legal sense. The nature of contracting in the UK internal market is discussed in Chapter 5.

The public hospitals are now managed by "NHS Trusts." These institutions are not trusts in the usual legal sense but crown corporations. NHS Trusts must comply with directions received from, and are directly accountable to, the Secretary of State.[324] An NHS Trust has the freedom to negotiate its own terms of service for its employees instead of being bound by national agreements. Specialists employed by an NHS Trust are employed by and accountable to the Trust itself rather than to the relevant Health Authority as has historically been the case.[325] An NHS Trust is required to carry out its functions "effectively, efficiently and economically."[326] However, there are limitations on NHS Trusts that do not hinder private firms. For example, section 10 of the Act requires that all NHS Trusts ensure that their revenues will meet their outgoings in any financial year and thus Trusts, unlike private firms, cannot carry losses or surpluses forward from year to year. This makes them vulnerable to short-term fluctuations and more likely to stick with the status quo and resist innovation.[327] NHS Trusts must set prices to equal (normally) short-run average costs plus a 6 percent rate of return on capital assets.[328] Trusts can only set prices equal to marginal cost when they have unplanned excess capacity.[329] Anand and McGuire note that efficient prices would be set at marginal cost and that short-run average cost would in fact equal marginal cost if there were constant returns to scale but that the relationship between average cost and marginal cost is unknown in the health care sector.[330] On the other hand, Trusts have an advantage over GP Fundholders (discussed below) and other private providers in that they are exempt from income tax and corporation tax.

Section 14 of the Act provided for the recognition of "GP Fundholders."[331] General practices with more than 5,000 patients (originally, the requirement was 11,000 patients) could apply to a Health Authority to become Fundholders. A Fundholder received a capitated budget (known as an allotted sum) with which to buy drugs and approximately 20 percent of hospital and community services for the patients that are enrolled with them.[332] Consequently, the existence of GP Fundholders provided some competition for Health Authorities in their role as purchasers of health care. The 1989 White Paper claimed that Fundholders would have an incentive to minimize costs in order to retain a surplus from their allocated budgets but would not have an incentive to reduce the quality of care. The White Paper claimed that Fundholders would wish to maintain or improve the range, number, or quality of services provided to attract patients to stay enrolled with them. The financial incentive to contain costs was somewhat muted as GP Fundholders are not allowed to keep surpluses as pure profit. Regulation required them to invest savings back into their respective practices thus, it was hoped, ultimately benefiting patients.[333] The Fundholding initiative was originally seen as a "bolt-on" to the main reforms (being the purchaser/provider split) but quickly assumed increasing importance.[334] In 1997, there were 3,500 Fundholders, involving around 15,000 general practitioners, acting as purchasers for approximately 50 percent of the population for a limited range of health care services.[335]

In 1997 there were three types of Fundholders:

- Practices with 5,000 or more patients enrolled on their lists could apply to central government to be a "Standard Fundholding Practice" (by far the most common form of Fundholding) and, if successful, received an annual budget from which they should pay their own staff and purchase diagnostic, community, outpatient, and elective (e.g. non-emergency) surgical services and drugs, medicines, and listed appliances for all the patients enrolled with them.[336]
- Practices with 3,000 or more patients enrolled on their lists could now apply to be a "Community Fundholding Practice" and, if successful, received an annual budget to pay their own staff, and purchase diagnostic tests, some community health services, and drugs, medicines, and listed appliances for all the patients enrolled with them.
- Seventy practices, each with over 30,000 patients, which were "Total Fundholders," were required to purchase the full range of publicly-funded health care services.[337]

Problems arose as to how to determine the GP Fundholders' budgets. The first issue was whether their budgets should reflect historical use patterns (which would ease transition and cause less disruption but do little to improve efficiency) or whether a formula could be worked out to fund the purchasers on a per capita risk-adjusted basis (which would likely improve efficiency). Initially, the government decided to fix budgets according to historic expenditures, but moving over time to adjust budgets along a formula basis.[338] Thus, section 15 of the Act provided for payment by the relevant Health Authority to the Fund-holder to be determined by such factors as the Secretary of State may direct. In order to enable a Fundholder to manage the actuarial risk of the patients enrolled with the practice, Fundholders' financial liability was capped at £6,000 per annum for any patient and the relevant Health Authority paid for any costs incurred beyond this sum.[339]

The Fundholding approach was conceptually quite different from the balance of the internal market reforms and in particular the mandatory purchaser/provider split. This is because Health Authorities are government agencies and are required to contract out for the supply of all health care services whereas GP Fundholders are private entities and are allowed to provide health care services directly. In Chapter 5, the differences between Fundholding and the mandatory purchaser/provider split enforced in the balance of the internal market are analyzed further.

A new standard contract for general practitioners was introduced on 1 April 1990 which placed greater emphasis on costs and performance than had been historically the case.[340] Financial incentives were provided to encourage practit-ioners to perform minor surgery; to practice in deprived or isolated areas; to undertake child health screening and to encourage health promotion centers; and once a year to make home visits to patients over 75 to assess their health.[341] The importance of capitation was emphasized and the proportion of fees paid through this means increased from 46 percent to 60 percent of general pract-itioners' incomes. Some of the requirements regarding the supply of health promotion services were dropped on 1 April 1993.[342] The reform proposals did not propose to change the way specialists are paid. Maynard and Walker note that specialists continue to receive a salary, may earn a Distinction Award[343] and may earn a significant portion of their income from private practice.[344] The fragmentation of income sources in this manner diminishes the ability of NHS Trusts to hold specialists accountable for their performance in the public sector.

Figure 3.2 depicts the UK internal market as at 1997.

With respect to the issues of cost and access outlined at the outset of this section, internal market reform in the UK has come at a price. Compared to previous years, the 12.2 percent and 13 percent annual percentage increase in total health expenditures recorded in the years 1990–1 and 1991–2 is high.[345] Total health expenditures as a percentage of GDP also significantly increased in these years; a 7.6 percent increase in the 1991–2 year compared with an average rate of growth of 1.7 percent over the whole period 1980–92.[346] Moreover, the growth rate in per capita health spending in US dollars of 11.4 percent in 1991–2 was significantly higher than any other OECD country.[347] The 1992–3 figure of 9.6 percent for the annual percentage increase in total health expenditures, while high, is more comparable to pre-reform growth

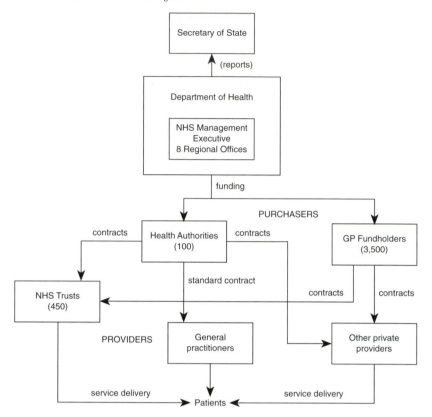

Figure 3.2 The structure of the NHS internal market in 1997.

Table 3.5 Health care expenditures as a percentage of GDP[349]

	1980	1990	1991	1992	1993	1994	1995	1996	1997
Netherlands	7.9	8.3	8.6	8.8	9	8.8	8.8	8.6	8.5
New Zealand	6	7	7.5	7.6	7.3	7.4	7.4	7.4	7.7
UK	5.6	6	6.5	6.9	6.9	6.9	6.9	6.9	6.7
United States	9.1	12.6	13.4	13.9	14.1	13.6	13.6	13.6	13.6

Source: The New NHS: Modern, Dependable, A White Paper, CM 3807, 8 December 1997

figures. More recent statistics show that spending on government-funded health care has continued to increase in real terms by 3 percent per annum over the reform period and that efficiency has fallen.[348] As Table 3.5 indicates, health care spending as a percentage of GDP jumped from 6.0 to 6.9 percent between 1990 and 1992 and stayed at this percentage mark till 1997 when it fell slightly to 6.7 percent.

With respect to access and long waiting lists, unlike New Zealand, the UK internal market had some early success in addressing this problem. The number of individuals waiting for elective procedures fell by 2.9 percent in the period December 1994 to March 1995, at which point there were 1,040,161 people on waiting lists and approximately the same number of people were on waiting lists at 30 September 1995.[350] The number of people waiting for more than twelve months for elective procedures on 30 September 1995 was 27,900 – a reduction of 55 percent since September 1994, when there were 62,300.[351] How much of this improvement is due to the improved efficiency of the system as opposed to additional government expenditures is unclear. Through 1997 waiting lists started to increase once again with 1,207,500 waiting at the end of September 1997 (an increase of 1.5 percent over the previous quarter) and with the number of people waiting for more than 12 months increasing by 24 percent.[352] The numbers waiting had slightly declined by 31 January 1999 with 1,159,400 people waiting and with the number of people waiting more than twelve months dropping to 54,600.[353] However, now there has been growth in the waiting list to get on the waiting list! How this works is that patients are not put on waiting lists for particular treatments until they are seen by a specialist to confirm that they do in fact need the treatment and should be on the waiting list. There were 468,000 people on waiting lists to see specialists at the end of 1998.[354]

New Labour reforms

On 8 December 1997, the newly elected Labour government, under the leadership of Tony Blair, released a White Paper detailing yet further reforms of the NHS. The Health Act (UK) (1999), c.8, passed on 30 June 1999, implements those parts of the New Labour reforms that require primary legislation although many of the reforms had begun to be implemented prior to this date. The new reforms promised to dismantle the internal market and to shift from an emphasis upon competition and choice to an emphasis upon cooperation. The reforms promise to be a "third way" of running the NHS; not the old command-and-control model and not the competitive contracting model but a more collaborative approach "based on partnership and driven by performance."[355]

The New Labour reforms comprise a number of different initiatives but the most significant is the abolishment of GP Fundholders from 1 April 1999 and the creation of "Primary Care Groups" (PCGs). The latter are to be large groups of general practitioners and community nurses, which in addition to managing the budgets for primary and community care will also, eventually, be responsible for purchasing services from the NHS Trusts. On 6 August 1998, it was announced that the Minister of Health had accepted proposals from 480 prospective PCGs.[356] On average, a PCG includes between 50 and 60 general practitioners from 20 or so different practices. PCGs being formed cover populations ranging from 50,000 to 200,000 people but the average, as anticipated, is around 100,000 people each.

At first, PCGs will be under the managerial umbrella of the Health Authorities; however, over time it is envisaged they will evolve to be "freestanding

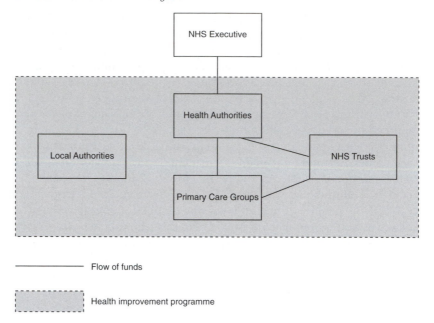

Flow of funds

Health improvement programme

Figure 3.3 The New Labour Reforms of December 1997.

Source: The New NHS: Modern, Dependable, A White Paper, CM 3807, 8 December 1997

bodies" known as Primary Care Trusts. They will still be accountable to the Health Authorities but will have financial responsibility for supplying care (except for specialized mental health or learning disability services) to their particular populations. The PCGs are expected to assumed increasing responsibility as follows:

• at a minimum, advise the Health Authority in purchasing health care services;
• have devolved responsibility, from the Health Authority, for managing the budget for health care in their area;
• become a Primary Care Trust, a freestanding body, responsible for purchasing health care;
• become a Primary Care Trust but with the added responsibility for the provision of community health services.

Each PCG will have available their population's share of the available resource for hospital and community health care services, the budget for prescribing by general practitioners and nurses, and the budget which reimburses general practitioners for the cost of their practice staff, premises and computers. Thus, the PCGs will not control payments to general practitioners for the services they provide and the White Paper emphasizes that general practitioners will retain their "independent contractor status" under the new reforms. Even the proposal that the PCG be responsible for the infrastructure budget for general practitioners has caused consternation amongst the medical profession. The Labour government has thus already agreed that if the PCGs overspend their budgets for hospital referrals or for prescriptions, they will not be allowed to cut back on infrastructure payments to general practitioners.[357]

Although the reforms propose the elimination of GP Fundholders, the new proposals could be viewed as a validation of the Fundholding scheme as it seeks to give financial responsibility for *all* health care services to groups of physicians and community nurses and to align clinical and financial responsibility. The White Paper containing the new Labour proposals notes "[p]rimary care professionals …understand patients' needs and they deliver most local services. That is why they will be in the driving seat in shaping local health services in the future."[358] The difference with the previous system is that people had a choice, even if it were rarely exercised, to leave a Fundholder for another or for a non-Fundholding general practitioner. Now, for better or for worse, people have no choice but to rely on their PCGs to make good decisions. Also of concern is that whereas previously general practitioners determined themselves whether or not they wanted to be Fundholders, now general practitioners and community nurses are being forced to assume clinical and financial responsibility for purchasing a range of health care services. The other key difference between PCGs and Fundholders is that general practitioners who were Fundholders had a much stronger financial incentive to purchase cost-effective care. With PCGs any savings made by one general practitioner would have to be shared amongst 50 to 60 general practitioners and, worse still, may be offset by overspending by other members of the PCG over whom the practitioner has little or no control.[359]

Interestingly, although the rhetoric of the latest raft of reforms is the elimination of the internal market, the New Labour reforms still require a split between the PCGs and the entities that manage the public hospitals, NHS Trusts. Although the language of purchasing and contracting seems to have now been totally ditched, the new reform proposal still requires PCGs to "commission" services from the NHS Trusts. The emphasis is upon longer-term contracts, a minimum three-year term, rather than annual contracts in order to enhance stability. The shift to longer-term, relational contracts was, however, something that was already occurring. Thus, the extent to which the logic of the internal market has truly been eliminated by the New Labour reforms is questionable.

Synthesis and conclusion

This section synthesizes the previous discussion of the structure and dynamics of the four countries under study. The goal is to ascertain the factors that are likely to result in a system that efficiently ensures access for all citizens to some agreed-upon comprehensive range of health care services on the basis of need as opposed to ability to pay. In 1995, White identified what he viewed as international standards for health systems: universal coverage; comprehensiveness of principal benefits; progressive financing (contributions linked to ability to pay rather than utilization); cost control through administrative mechanisms including global budgets and limitations on system capacity; and binding fee schedules.[360] As discussed below, these factors, though important, are insufficient alone. Other mechanisms are needed to address the need to allocate resources between different health needs (balancing societal and patient interests), of ensuring that the most cost-effective service is supplied in response to a particular health need, and of ensuring the technically efficient production of services.

Financing

Looking first at financing, I discuss the issues that arise under the headings of private insurers and progressive/regressive financing, single-payer systems, cost-containment initiatives and comprehensiveness and integration.

Private insurers and progressive/regressive financing

The fact that many countries have proposed more market-oriented reforms of their respective health allocation systems seems at first blush surprising given the high cost and inequities of the US system. The poor performance of the US system highlights the inefficiencies and inequities of a system largely financed by private insurance that is subject only to piecemeal regulation and the problem of a system that is not comprehensive and, as a consequence, allows a great deal of cost-shifting.

Difficulties within the US are often used as evidence against any form of market or competition-oriented reforms and particularly any role for private insurers. This argument is unsound. It is one thing to attempt to use market-style reform as a *means* to improve the efficiency of a system striving towards a social goal (access to health care on the basis of need). It is quite another to accept, as in the US, that health care should be allocated like cable TV service, i.e., if you can pay for it then you will receive it. This is readily apparent when one considers the Netherlands, which accords a relatively large role to private insurers. There is a strong commitment in the Netherlands to what is described as the principle of "solidarity" which in essence is the goal of ensuring universal access on the basis of need as opposed to ability to pay. The Dutch achieve this goal despite the fact that the wealthier 40 percent of the population voluntarily purchase private insurance for general medical services and the poorer 60 percent must purchase insurance from non-profit insurers (Sickness Funds). The whole population is compulsorily insured for exceptional medical expenses. Although, of course, it is difficult to draw linkages between a health care system and health care outcomes, as far as one is able to measure health outcomes such as mortality rates and incidences of disease, the Netherlands has outperformed all the other countries under study. The Netherlands does spend a slightly higher amount on health as a percentage of GDP than would be expected from its level of GDP relative to other OECD countries but significantly less than the US and less than the single-payer system of Canada. A 1990 publication reported that the Dutch were generally satisfied with their health care system and certainly are more satisfied than the citizens in the US, the UK, and (one would strongly suspect although there is only anecdotal evidence) New Zealand.[361] A 1996 study of the European Union found that 14.2 percent of the Dutch population were very satisfied and 58.6 percent were fairly satisfied with "the way health care runs in the Netherlands." By comparison, 7.6 percent of UK citizens were very satisfied and 40.5 percent were fairly satisfied with the UK health care system.[362] It is also notable that the Dutch government ensures access on the basis of need to a comprehensive range of health care services including prescription medication, home care, and long-term care which may not be covered in those countries with a greater degree of public funding.[363] Of course, the Dutch system has its share of problems. One of these problems has been reductions in access as a result of risk-rating on the part of private insurers which has resulted in the need for government regulation and which in part inspired the Dekker-managed competition proposals. The point still stands, however, that discounting totally any role for private insurers on the basis of the US experience is to ignore the relative successes of the Dutch system.

There are some who bring to bear fire and brimstone rhetoric against market or competition oriented reforms.[364] One must, however, be careful to identify demons correctly. From the perspective of distributive justice what is important is that the system is financed largely progressively with contributions being based on ability to pay rather than need for the health care services. It is true that progressive financing is usually assured through public rather than private financing. However, the problem is not directly private insurance or the existence of private insurers but more particularly the fact that private insurers compete for profits by seeking to identify high-risk people and either excluding them completely or charging them higher premiums than they can afford. The managed competition model seeks to change the paradigm for competition between private insurers. It does this by ensuring that the system is largely progressively funded, by fostering competition between private insurers on price and quality dimensions, and by regulating and monitoring to prevent competition on risk exclusion. Thus the goal is that insurers will not be rewarded for avoiding high-risk people but by efficiently managing hospital, physicians and other health care providers whilst being accountable and responsive to the people enrolled with them. The prima facie advantage of a managed competition system over a single-payer system (described further below) is that there are incentives on the demand side to contain costs, improve quality, and be responsive to patients/consumers.

Single-payer systems

The UK and New Zealand systems are often described as "single-payer" systems as government pays for the majority of health care expenditures from general taxation revenues. The term "single-payer" is misleading for even in systems like the UK and New Zealand there is a *mixture* of public and private financing with different proportions being apparent in different health service markets. New Zealand does not perform particularly well with respect to access and health outcomes because of its high reliance on user charges for primary care services. Those on lower incomes entitled to government subsidies have only approximately half of the cost for a visit to a family doctor paid for. By contrast, those who are able to afford top-up private insurance generally have between 80–100 percent of these costs paid. The fact that the actual amount paid for by the private sector as a percentage of total expenditures is small (as the "big ticket" items are all publicly-funded) means that commentators often overlook the significance of private spending in New Zealand. Thus New Zealand is typically portrayed as a system ensuring universal access but the question glossed over is universal access to what? In reality, even though the Dutch system relies to a greater degree on private insurance than New Zealand it ensures better access to basic health care services for low-income people. It achieves this by ensuring there are no user charges for general practitioner services for the poorer 60 percent of the population. Thus, from the perspective of achieving justice, the Netherlands system is a better system than the New Zealand system despite its overall greater reliance on private insurance and private financing.

It seems to be generally true that in systems where governments pays for the vast majority of health care expenditures costs are able to be contained. This is achieved as governments in these systems use their power as the primary purchaser of health care services to negotiate down the prices of hospitals, physicians, and other health care services and to restrict the flow of resources into the system, i.e. new capital, technology, etc. Cost-containment should not, however, be confused with efficiency.[365] Growing waiting times and waiting lists in the UK and New Zealand suggest that costs are shifted from the health care sector to others – for example, employers and employees if people have to be absent from work while waiting for care. As evidence for this, for a short period after post-internal market reform in New Zealand, responsibility for purchasing health care services on behalf of accident patients was transferred from the no-fault accident compensation authority to Health Authorities. Subsequently, accident patients were forced to queue with sickness and disability patients in the public sector rather than having private services brought for them. As a result, the income maintenance costs incurred by the no-fault compensation system sky-rocketed as accident victims languished on waiting lists for months and even years. Eventually, purchasing responsibility was transferred back to the accident compensation authority so that they could purchase more timely services in the private sector. Thus when a public body has to incur some of the lost earnings resulting from lengthy waiting lists and times then they will not be tolerated. This suggests that the ability of the UK and New Zealand systems to control costs is exaggerated by noting the relatively low level of GDP absorbed by health care expenditures.

The fact that one health care system spends less on health care than another cannot mean that it is necessarily a better system or a more efficient system.[366] Taken to its extreme this would mean that Turkey, which has the lowest level of expenditures amongst OECD countries, is the most efficient system in the OECD. One has to look at what is achieved with the system but, of course, this is difficult because of the difficulties of measuring the quality of care delivered and, in particular, of proving the link between the utilization of health care services and health care outcomes. It seems almost impossible to determine whether a country's particular level of health care expenditures is close to a point of allocative efficiency in terms of the amount spent on health care relative to, say, education or defense or telecommunications. Many value judgements are involved in the absence of effective price signals regarding what public services people value highly. McGuire and Anand note that

> the choice of health care systems should be guided by empirical data but this is rarely the case because of the lack of empirical data and the difficulties of testing one system against the other given that each system is a product of its own historical and cultural setting.[367]

Cost-containment initiatives

Throughout the 1980s many OECD countries, particularly single-payer systems, sought to control total health care expenditures by regulating the number of "inputs" into the system, e.g., the numbers of physicians and other health providers, the number of hospital beds, and the distribution of technology. The policy of reducing the resources invested in a health system is based upon the assumption that the more hospitals, health care providers, and technology in a system of full insurance, the greater the increase in cost, irrespective of needs or outcomes. These measures coupled with prospective budgets for hospitals and/or physicians and capped government expenditures, proved successful at containing the percentage of GDP spent on health care services in a number of jurisdictions throughout the 1980s.[368]

A popular initiative in many countries has been to close and/or consolidate hospitals and to reduce the number of hospital beds. Between 1980–95, in nearly every OECD country, the total number of hospital beds per 1,000 population has fallen.[369] This reform initiative has been implemented often with a view to reaping efficiencies from economies of scale and specialization and with a view to shifting resources from expensive acute care to primary and preventive care and home care. It is of interest to note, however, that countries such as the US and Canada, who expend the highest level of GDP on health care, do not have a high ratio of hospital beds relative to other OECD countries. Moreover, it is unclear whether or not a shift to primary and preventive care and home care will in fact be cost-effective and, as Klein notes, such policy appears to be driven largely by faith rather than evidence.[370] However, as discussed further below, cost-containment is not the same as efficiency and may have a detrimental effect on the quality of services supplied. In the shift from caring in hospitals to caring in homes, it is important to quantify not only the costs and benefits of this transition but also who will bear these costs.

Comprehensiveness and integration

Comprehensiveness and integration have been recognized as the key features of an efficient health care system.[371] The US system clearly demonstrates the problems associated with a lack of comprehensiveness in financing. The US system has, historically, been a merry-go-round of shifting costs. Health providers pass on costs to insurers who pass on costs to employers who pass on costs to the government (through the tax subsidy) and to their employees (through lower wages) who in turn believe that the costs are being fully borne by employers. Health providers who provide charity care or who receive lower prices for caring for Medicaid patients pass on part or all of the cost of these services to other privately insured patients.

Although the US system is the most extreme example of cost-shifting, all the health care systems under study have had different financing regimes for different health care services. Often different entities have been responsible for sickness, accident and disability services and there have often been differences in the flow of financing for general practitioner services, specialist services, and hospital services. This has proved problematic as it enabled cost-shifting from sector to sector and made it difficult to ensure that the most cost-effective service is supplied to fulfill a particular health need. Irrespective of the proportion of public and private financing in a system, the rule of thumb would seem to be that where costs can be shifted, be it from payer to payer or from payer to provider or to patients or to society at large, then they will be.[372] In order to foster cost-effective decision-making, financing of health care should cover a comprehensive range of health care services to allow effective substitution by decision-makers.

As part of internal market reform the new purchasing authorities in the UK and New Zealand are responsible for funding a comprehensive range of health care services including hospital and physician services, and in New Zealand they are also responsible for funding disability services. These initiatives are clearly a positive step. The Dutch Sickness Funds (the non-profit insurers that cover the poorer 60 percent of the population) have always been responsible for funding hospital and physician services. As part of managed competition reform proposals it was proposed to make Sickness Funds and private insurers not only responsible for coverage for all general medical services but also the services covered under the compulsory Exceptional Medical Expenses scheme (long-term care). Eventually, this proposal was dropped because of concern of how to fairly finance insurers for providing this type of coverage.

The issue of comprehensiveness raises the question of the boundaries of a health care system and other social service systems. This problem is particularly apparent in many countries with the shift away from hospital care to care in the home. Should services like housekeeping, food preparation and so on in the home all be part of the health care system? Clearly, where such services are substitutes for care that would otherwise have to be supplied by a hospital or institution then such services should be included in the health care system. Extensions of services beyond this point requires consideration of the values citizens place on fulfilling health needs in the home and whether or not these needs could not be met by targeting service delivery to those who would otherwise be unable to afford the services.

Evidence of cost-effectiveness

There is growing awareness that there is little evidence for cost-effectiveness or even effectiveness of many health care services. For example, Culyer notes that the greatest source of inefficiency in all health systems is the production of health care services that are inappropriate, ineffective or not cost-effective.[373] Why has this been the case? Historically, in the health care systems of most developed countries, public and private insurers have not actively purchased services but have either passively reimbursed providers on an unrestricted fee-for-service basis or indemnified patients for their health care costs.[374] Patients have had no incentive to consider the cost of health care services their physician recommends due to the moral hazard associated with third-party financing (be it from public or private insurance). Even when patients did have an incentive to consider costs through the imposition of user charges or deductibles, they likely did not have the information or expertise to ration effectively their own utilization. This would suggest, perhaps, that health care expenditures in most countries could be significantly cut without compromising health care.[375] However, a lack of sensitivity on the part of physicians to the costs and benefits of health care services supplied or recommended seems to be a general problem in all systems, *even those which have tightly controlled the resources available to the system* such as the UK and New Zealand. Experience from the UK and New Zealand systems suggests that simply restricting the flow of resources into the system is insufficient. Leaving politically poisonous rationing decisions in the hands of physicians operating under hard budgets seems to result in growing waiting lists and times, in growing dissatisfaction with the health system, and in costs being shifted to where budgets are softer. In other words, simply tightening budgets may not result in better allocation decisions but more adroitness in cost-shifting to other payers or on to patients or society at large. Capping health care expenditures can only be a short-term answer. In the longer term, a system must concern itself with three factors. First, the decision-making processes whereby health needs are prioritized so as to balance societal interest with patients' interests. Second, the selection of the most cost-effective service to satisfy a particular health need. Third, the technically efficient production of health care services.

An important caveat that I will note at this point and discuss again in subsequent chapters, is that there is a danger in relying too heavily on the fact that there is not significant evidence of the cost-effectiveness of many health care services. This is because the effectiveness of many important health care services may be very difficult to measure. As a society we value very highly the supply of particular health care services that cannot be readily measured in terms of outcomes – for instance, the supply of palliative care and the care of vulnerable populations such as the mentally and physically handicapped. Thus, only focusing on the easily measurable will not result in a health system that a society wants. Moreover, it may be difficult to establish the cost-effectiveness of some primary and preventive services which common sense dictates will be of benefit to society. The benefits of primary and preventive care may not be realized for many years and it may be difficult because of the time-frame involved to identify a causal link between a resulting health benefit and the primary and preventive care provided. Values are important in determining the configuration of a health care system, particularly as the kinds of health care services we value cannot necessarily be measured in health care outcomes. Due to the information asymmetry that exists between physicians and patients, the views of patients and citizens seem to be often discounted, particularly in predominantly publicly-funded systems. There need to be mechanisms in place within a system to determine and implement citizens' values with regard to prioritization of health care needs, the kinds and quality of service necessary to meet those needs, and the method of delivery of services to satisfy those needs.

The shift to proactive purchasing

The problem of passive third-party payers (public or private insurers) has been a problem in all countries under discussion. There has been insufficient pressure on the demand side to ensure optimal decision-making on the part of health care providers. Recent years have seen the growth of managed care plans in the US stimulated by both government and private initiatives. Managed care plans seek to reverse the historical arrangements of passive payers reimbursing providers on a fee-for-service basis. Rather, insurers become proactive purchasers. As managed care plans have grown as a competitive force, traditional insurers have taken steps to contain their own costs, thus reducing the ability of providers to cost-shift. Whether or not managed care can, in the long-term, control escalating expenditure, is a matter for debate. It is important to note that managed care developments in the US are ad hoc and are not part of a comprehensive, integrated, and progressively financed health care system.

Internal market reform and managed competition reform both seek to provide a comprehensive progressively financed health system that seeks to achieve efficiency gains through proactive purchasing, the theory being that this will provoke an efficient supply-side response. The concept of a proactive

Table 3.6 Changing systems

	Pre-1980	1980s	1990s
Role of the purchaser	• public or private indemnity insurer (most systems historically) • no active purchaser	• public insurers shift to block funding for hospitals • capping the total spent but otherwise a passive payer	• proactive purchasing of all health care services • managed care • managed competition • internal markets
Level of competition	• no competition between purchasers or providers	• no competition between purchasers or providers	• seeks to foster competition between providers (internal markets) or between insurer/purchasers offering managed care plans (managed competition)
Paying providers	• fee-for-service payments (retroactive)	• prospective annual budgets for hospitals but still generally fee-for-service for physicians	• a variety of techniques but may pay on a capitation basis (a fixed sum per annum per person)

purchaser is a significant development from the historical role of government and private purchasers as passive "indemnity insurers," reimbursing either provider or patient for all costs incurred on the assumption that no care is supplied or consumed that is not "needed." The transition from passive indemnity insurer to prospective block budgets for hospitals to proactive purchasing of all health care services is depicted in Table 3.6.

In subsequent chapters, I will analyze and compare the managed competition model and the internal market model. Both of these models meet the general requirements that White described of being progressively financed, ensuring universal coverage, and covering a comprehensive range of benefits. The test is the degree to which these models *over time* ensure optimal decision-making from the perspective of prioritizing needs in health care, choosing the most cost-effective service to address a particular need, and ensuring the technically efficient production of services.

It has proven insufficient in the UK and New Zealand to accrue market power on the demand side and to reduce the inputs into their respective systems. Purchasers need incentives in order to be proactive purchasers of health care services and to make optimal decisions. Thus, general issues of accountability and governance have long been overlooked in health systems as the focus has historically been on third-party payers passively financing the supplier of health care services and there was no purchasing or demand-side tension. Once we determine there is a need for a purchasing role, then governance issues become critical. The next chapter deals with these issues.

Notes

1 G. J. Schieber *et al.*, 'Health System Performance in OECD Countries, 1980–1992', (1994) (Fall) 13(4) *Health Affairs* 100 at pp. 101–102.

2 J.-P. Poullier, *OECD Health Systems: Facts and Trends 1960–1991* (Paris: OECD, 1993) at p. 14 (hereinafter *OECD Health Systems: Facts and Trends*) and OECD, *US Health Care at the Crossroads* (Paris: OECD, 1992) at p. 18 and p. 24 (hereinafter *US Health Care at the Crossroads*).

3 Schieber *et al.*, 'Health System Performance in OECD Countries, 1980–1992', *op. cit.*

4 Figures from K. R. Levit *et al.*, 'National Health Spending Trends, 1960–1993', (1994) 13(5) *Health Affairs* 14 at p. 15, Exhibit 1.

5 S. T. Burner, D. R. Waldo and D. R. McKusick, 'National Health Expenditures Projections Through 2030', (1992) 14(1) *Health Care Financing Review* 1.

6 S. Smith et al., 'The Next Ten Years of Health Spending: What Does the Future Hold?', (1998) 17(5) *Health Affairs* 128.

7 T. H. Boyd, 'Cost Containment and the Physician's Fiduciary Duty to the Patient', (1989) 39 *DePaul Law Rev.* 131 at p. 131, notes defensive medicine "refers to a practice in which physicians utilize exhaustive diagnostic and treatment methods of minimum value to ensure the best quality of health care while at the same time erecting an undefeatable defence against liability."

8 See the American Medical Association, *The Cost of Medical Professional Liability in the 1980s* (Chicago, IL: American Medical Association, 1990). The estimates vary as to the impact of the practice of defensive medicine on total health expenditures. D. Dewees and M. Trebilcock, 'The Efficacy of the Tort System and its Alternatives: A Review of Empirical Evidence', (1992) 30(1) *Osgoode Hall Law J.* 57 at p. 83, estimated the total cost of liability-related defensive medical practices in the US to be approximately $11 billion annually but note that this estimate did not include the transaction costs of the tort system, the foregone income and the emotional trauma sustained by physicians involved in malpractice claims, and the public cost of providing the court system. R. N. Rubin and D. N. Mendelson, *Estimating the Costs of Defensive Medicine* (Fairfax, VA: Lewin–VHI, 1993) as cited by J. S. Todd, 'Reform of the Health Care System and Professional Liability', (1993) 329(23) *New Eng. J. of Med.* 1733 suggest that the cost of defensive practices is much less, estimating a figure of $36 billion over 5 years.

9 R. R. Bovbjerg *et al.*, 'US Health Care Coverage and Costs: Historical Development and Choices for the 1990s', (1993) 21(2) *J. of Law, Medicine and Ethics* 141 at p. 155.

10 A. M. Epstein *et al.*, 'A Comparison of Ambulatory Test Ordering for Hypertensive Patients in the United States and England', (1984) 252 *JAMA* 1723.

11 W. P. Welch, D. Verrilli, S. J. Katz and E. Latimer, 'A Detailed Comparison of Physician Services for the Elderly in the United States and Canada', (1996) 275(18) *JAMA* 1410.

12 OECD, *US Health Care at the Crossroads*, *op. cit.*, p. 24 – using OECD purchasing-power-parity

13 White House Domestic Policy Council, *The Clinton Blueprint: The President's Health Security Plan* (New York: Times Books, 1993) at p. 3 (hereinafter *Clinton Blueprint*).

14 Physicians for a National Health Program, press release, 'Number of Americans Without Health Insurance Jumps to 43.2 Million'. Online. Available HTTP: http://www.pnhp.org/press998.html (accessed 17 March 1999).

15 OECD, *US Health Care at the Crossroads*, *op. cit.*, p. 63.

16 See R. J. Baxter and R. E. Mechanic, 'The Status of Local Health Care Safety Nets', (1997) 16(4) *Health Affairs* 7 at p. 12.

17 C. G. McLaughlin and W. K. Zellers, *Small Business and Health Care Reform: Understanding the Barriers to Employee Coverage and Implications for Workable Solutions* (Ann Arbor, MI: Regents of the University of Michigan, School of Public Health, 1994) at pp. 2 and 4.

18 It is estimated that one-quarter of the approximately four million welfare recipients would enter the labor force if health insurance were available continuously – *ibid.*, p. 31 and p. 45.

19 A. M. Rivlin, *et al.*, 'Financing, Estimation, and Economic Effects', (1994) 13(1) *Health Affairs* 30 at p. 31 and p. 44. The authors also refer to one study which estimates that the mobility rate for married men would increase by one-third in the absence of pre-existing condition exclusions.

20 K. M. Langwell and T. Menke, 'Controlling Costs of the US Health Care System: Trends and Prospects' in R. J. Arnould, R. F. Rich and W. D. White (eds), *Competitive Approaches to Health Care Reform* (Washington, DC: Urban Institute Press, 1993) at p. 20.

21 D. Vagero, 'Equity and Efficiency in Health Reform: A European View', (1994) 39(9) *Soc. Sci. Med.* 1203 at p. 1207.

22 Schieber *et al.*, 'Health System Performance in OECD Countries, 1980–1992', *op. cit.*, p. 105.

23 See S. Bishop, 'When Doctors Go Too Far', *The New York Times*, 27 February 1999, A15.

24 OECD, *US Health Care at the Crossroads, op. cit.*

25 National Center for Health Statistics (U.S.), *Health, United States, 1990*, DHHS Pub. No. (PHS) Public Health Service (Washington: US Government Printing Office, 1991) as cited by N. de Lew, G. Greenberg and K. Kinchen, 'Special Report: A Layman's Guide to the US Health Care System', (1992) 14(1) *Health Care Financing Review* 151 at p. 157.

26 R. L. Braithwaite and S. E. Taylor (eds), *Health Issues In the Black Community* (San Francisco, CA: Jossey-Bass, 1992).

27 See A. C. Enthoven, 'The History and Principles of Managed Competition', (1993) 12 (Supplement 1993) *Health Affairs* 24 at p. 25 and Bovbjerg *et al.*, *op. cit.*, at p. 143.

28 J. R. Hollingsworth and E. J. Hollingsworth, *Controversy About American Hospitals: Funding Ownership and Performance* (Washington DC: American Enterprise Institute for Public Policy Research, 1987) p. 32.

29 Bovbjerg *et al.*, *op. cit.*, pp. 143–4.

30 K. R. Levit, G. L. Olin and S. W. Letsch, 'Americans' Health Insurance Coverage, 1980–1991', (1992) 14(1) *Health Care Financing Review* 31 at p. 33, Table 1.

31 Levit, *et al.*, 'National Health Spending Trends, 1960–1993', *op. cit.*

32 For a full appraisal of the economic impact of the tax subsidy on health insurance and health service markets in the US see M. V. Pauly, 'Taxation, Health Insurance, and Market Failure in the Medical Economy', (1986) 24 *J. of Econ. Lit.* 629. He notes at pp. 636–638 that health insurance premiums receive special tax treatment in two ways. First, employer-paid health insurance provided as a fringe benefit is a tax-deductible business expense for the firm and second, consumer payments for health insurance are tax deductible for those taxpayers who itemize where their total medical expenses exceed a certain proportion of income. A. C. Enthoven and S. J. Singer, 'Market-based Reform: What To Regulate and By Whom', (1995) 14(1) *Health Affairs* 105, note that in 1995, the Congressional Budget Office estimated that excluding employer-paid health insurance premiums from federal income and payroll taxes cost the government US $90 billion.

33 U. E. Reinhardt, 'Reorganizing the Financial Flows in American Health Care', (1993) 12 *Health Affairs* 172 at pp. 179–180.

34 J. Gruber and A. Krueger, 'The Incidence of Mandated Employer-Provided Insurance: Lessons from Workers' Compensation Insurance' in D. Bradford (ed.), *Tax Policy and the Economy*, vol. 5 (Cambridge, MA: MIT Press, 1991) as cited by A. M. Rivlin, *et al.*, *op. cit.*, p. 44, fn. 20.

35 Reinhardt, 'Reorganizing the Financial Flows in American Health Care', *op. cit.*, p. 181.

36 The Employee Retirement Income Security Act of 1974, Pub. L. No. 93-406, 88 Stat. 829 (1974) (codified at 29 USC. 1001-1381 (1982)). For a discussion see J. A. Brown, 'ERISA and State Health Care Reform: Roadblock or Scapegoat?', (1995) 13(2) *Yale Law and Policy Review* 339.

37 For a comprehensive discussion of this topic, see W. Shonick, *Government and Health Services: Government's Role in the Development of US Health Services 1930–1980* (New York: Oxford University Press, 1995).

38 Levit *et al.*, 'National Health Spending Trends, 1960–1993', *op. cit.*, p. 21' OECD Health Data 98: A Comparative Analysis of 29 countries (electronic database).

39 D. J. Rothman, 'A Century of Failure: Health Care Reform in America', (1993) 18 *J. Health Polit.Policy Law* 271 at p. 275.

40 R. Munts, *Bargaining for Health: Labour Unions, Health Insurance and Medical Care* (Madison, WI: University of Wisconsin Press, 1967) as cited by W. Glaser, 'Universal Health Insurance That Really Works: Foreign Lessons for the United States', (1993) 18(3) *J. Health Polit.Policy Law* 695 at p. 696.

41 P. A. Corning, *The Evolution of Medicare...From Idea to Law*, (Washington, DC: Department of Health, Education, and Welfare, 1969) as cited by D. Blumenthal, 'Health Care Reform – Past and Future', (1995) 332(7) *New Eng. J. of Medicine* 465.

42 For a comprehensive account of the enactment of Medicare and Medicaid and description of both programs, see Shonick, *op. cit.*, Chapter 10.

43 De Lew, Greenberg and Kinchen, *op. cit.*, at p. 152.

44 For a discussion, see H. S. Luft, 'Medicare and Managed Care', (1998) 19 *Ann. Rev. Public Health* 459 at 462.

45 OECD, *US Health Care at the Crossroads, op. cit.*, p. 63.

46 Bovbjerg *et al.*, *op. cit.*, p. 148.

47 J. K. Iglehart, "The American Health Care System', (1992) 326 *New Eng. J. of Med.* 962.

48 G. King, 'Health Care Reform and the Medicare Program', (1994) 13(5) *Health Affairs* 39.

49 See F. Mullan, M. L. Rivo and R. M. Politzer, 'Doctors, Dollars, and Determination: Making Physician Work-Force Policy', (1993) 12 *Health Affairs* 138 at p. 140. S. A. Schroder, 'Training an Appropriate Mix of Physicians to Meet the Nation's Needs', (1993) 68 *Acad. Med.* 118, notes that fewer than 15 percent of medical students graduating in 1991 and 1992 intended to become generalists.

50 Langwell and Menke, *op. cit.*, p. 25. See also Welch *et al.*, *op. cit.* discussing the price of services for elderly patients.

51 A 1992 OECD report suggests that the resilience of physicians' incomes in this regard must be due to an even stronger increase in the demand for services – OECD, *US Health Care at the Crossroads, op. cit.*, p. 14.

52 Langwell and Menke, *op. cit.*, pp. 22–24. During the late 1980s, price increases accounted for more than half the increases in real expenditures on physician services – OECD, *US Health Care at the Crossroads, op. cit.*, p. 14.

53 See J. E. Fielding and R. Rice, 'Can Managed Competition Solve Problems of Market Failure?', (1993) 12 *Health Affairs* 216 at p. 220.

54 See the discussion in B. R. Furrow *et al.*, *Health Law: Cases, Materials and Problems* (St. Paul, MN: West Publishing Co., 1997) pp. 609–620, particularly 42 USC.A. § 1395nn (Supp. 1995).

55 W. C. Hsiao, D. L. Dunn and D. K. Verrilli, 'Assessing the Implementation of Physician-Payment Reform', (1993) 328(13) *New Eng. J. of Medicine* 928.

56 De Lew, Greenberg and Kinchen, *op. cit.*, p. 155 note that there are approximately 6,700 hospitals in the US including 5,480 community acute care hospitals, 880 specialty hospitals (i.e. psychiatric, long-term care etc.), and 340 federal hospitals open only to military personnel, veterans, or native Americans). Fifty-nine percent of community acute care hospitals are private not-for-profit hospitals, 27 percent are public hospitals, and 14 percent are private for-profit hospitals.

57 Hollingsworth and Hollingsworth, *op. cit.*, p. 86.

58 Langwell and Menke, *op. cit.*, pp. 20–1.

59 D. A. Rublee, 'Medical Technology in Canada, Germany, and the United States: An Update', (1994) 13(4) *Health Affairs* 113.

60 OECD, *US Health Care at the Crossroads, op. cit.*, p. 32

61 In 1974 the federal government introduced the Health Planning and Resource Development Act that required all states receiving federal aid to enact Certificate of Need ("CON") laws regulating capital investment in health care institutions. This legislation was criticized by Pauly and others on the basis that the CON program was captured and dominated by those hospitals that were the subject of regulation and used by them to exclude efficient competition – M. V. Pauly, 'A Primer on Competition in Medical Markets' in H. E. Frech III (ed.), *Health Care in America: The Political Economy of Hospitals and Health Insurance* (San Francisco, CA: Pacific Research Institute For Public Policy, 1988) at p. 39. Subsequently the CON laws were repealed.

62 Langwell and Menke, *op. cit.*, p. 38. M. L. Lassey, W. R. Lassey and M. J. Jinks, *Health Care Systems Around the World* (Upper Saddle River, NJ: Prentice Hall, 1997) p. 59, notes the federal Prospective Payment Commission estimates that Medicare pays only 91 percent of costs and Medicaid pays only 74 percent.

63 De Lew, Greenberg and Kinchen, *op. cit.*, p. 162.

64 G. F. Anderson, 'All-Payer Ratesetting: Down But Not Out', (1991 Annual Supplement) *Health Care Financing Review* 42–4.

65 See H.R. 1200, 103d Cong., 1st Sess. (3 March 1993) (introduced by Rep. McDermott); H.R. 3222, 103d Cong., 1st Sess. (6 October 1993) (introduced by Rep. Cooper); H.R. 3080, 103rd Cong., 1st Sess. (15 September 1993) (introduced by Rep. Michel); S. 1770, 103d Cong., 1st Sess. (22 November 1993) (introduced by Sen. Chafee).

66 For a full description see *Clinton Blueprint, op. cit.*, p. 21.

67 See A. C. Enthoven, 'Why Not the Clinton Health Plan?', (1994) 31(2) *Inquiry* 129.

68 President Clinton as cited by J. K. Iglehart, 'Health Care Reform: The Role of Physicians', (1994) 330(10) *New Eng. J. of Medicine* 728.

69 The reason given in the Clinton proposals for the exclusion of Medicare beneficiaries was that the logistical difficulties were too great in the short term; however, states would eventually be permitted to integrate Medicare beneficiaries into Regional Alliances provided that beneficiaries received the same or better coverage as standard Medicare benefits and that federal financial liability was not increased – *Clinton Blueprint, op. cit.*, p. 216.

70 W. A. Zelman, 'The Rationale Behind the Clinton Health Care Reform Plan', (1994) 13(1) *Health Affairs* 9 at p. 20.

71 *Ibid.*, p. 18.

72 S. H. Altman and A. B. Cohen, 'Commentary: The Need For A National Global Budget', (1993) 12 (Supplement 1993) *Health Affairs* 194 at p. 198.

73 Rivlin, *et al.*, *op. cit.*, pp. 31–32.

74 F. B. McArdle and D. H. Yamamoto, 'Pricing of the Standard Benefit in the Health Security Act', testimony before the House Energy and Commerce Subcommittee on Health and the Environment, 22 November 1993 as cited by J. F. Sheils and L. S. Lewin, 'Alternative Estimate: No Pain, No Gain', (1994) 13(1) *Health Affairs* 50.

75 However, the $44 billion reserve cushion provided for by the Clinton administration for unanticipated increases in spending would be wiped out – *ibid.*, p. 51.

76 Blumenthal, *op. cit.*, at p. 466.

77 A Democratic poll showed that of the 54 percent of voters canvassed who said they were disappointed by Clinton, half cited the fact that he offered a health care reform plan that favored big government – J. K. Iglehart, 'Editorial', (1994) 13(5) *Health Affairs* 5 at p. 6.

78 S. Steinmo and J. Watts, 'It's the Institutions, Stupid! Why Comprehensive National Health Insurance Always Fails in America', (1995) 20(2) *J. Health Polit. Policy Law* 329 at p. 352 and see also K. R. Wing, 'American Health Policy in the 1980s', (1985–6) 36(4) *Case Western Reserve Law Review* 608.

79 Glaser, *op. cit.*, p. 697.

80 See T. R. Marmor, *Understanding Health Care Reform* (New Haven: Yale University Press, 1994) p. 29, noting that a majority of Americans are in favor of a national health insurance scheme.

81 H. J. Aaron, 'Thinking Straight About Medical Costs', (1994) 13(5) *Health Affairs* 8.

82 Bovbjerg, *op. cit.*, p. 150.

83 *Ibid.*, p. 143.

84 42 U.S.C. s 300(e) (1994) (amended 1976, 1978, 1981, 1986, 1988).

85 De Lew, Greenberg and Kinchen, *op. cit.*, p. 156.

86 *Ibid.*

87 D. Mechanic, 'Managed Care: Rhetoric and Realities', (1994) 31(2) *Inquiry* 124 at p. 125.

88 Iglehart, 'The American Health Care System', *op. cit.*, at 965.

89 De Lew, Greenberg and Kinchen, *op. cit.*, p. 157.

90 See generally H. T. Greely, 'Direct Financial Incentives in Managed Care: Unanswered Questions', (1996) 6(1) *Health Matrix: Jnl of Law-Medicine* 53.

91 Figures from J. K. Iglehart, 'Health Policy Report: Physicians and the Growth of Managed Care', (1994) 331: 17 *New Eng. Jnl of Med.* 1167, p. 1168 and Mercer/Foster Higgins, *National Survey of Employer-Sponsored Health Plans* (New York: William M. Mercer, Inc., 1997) at p. 9 as quoted by Smith *et al.*, *op. cit.*

92 J. White, 'Which "Managed Care" For Medicare?', (1997) 16(5) *Health Affairs* 73; H. S. Luft, 'Medicare and Managed Care' (1998) 19 *Ann. Rev. Public Health* 459 at 462, and J. E. Sisk *et al.*, 'Evaluation of Medicaid Managed Care: Satisfactory Access and Use' (1996) 276(1) *JAMA* 50.

93 See Health Care Financing Administration, 'National Survey of Medicaid Managed Care Programs and Enrollment, 30 June 1996'. Online. Available HTTP: http://www.hcfa.gov/medicaid/trends1.htm (accessed 28 March 1999).

94 Managed Care On-Line, Inc., 'Managed Care Facts and Figures – Medicare HMO Enrollment by State'. Online. Available HTTP: http://www.mcol.com/mcfact3.htm (accessed 28 March 1999).

95 Bovbjerg *et al.*, *op. cit.*, p. 153.

96 See R. Miller and H. Luft, 'Managed Care Plan Performance since 1980: A Literature Analysis', (1994) 271(19) *JAMA* 1512 and J. Zwanziger and G. A. Melnick, 'Can Managed Care Plans Control Health Care Costs?' (1996) 15(2) *Health Affairs* 185.

97 Mechanic, *op. cit.*

98 P. D. Ginsburg and J. D. Pickering, 'Tracking Health Care Costs', (1996) 15(3) *Health Affairs* 140. See also Levit *et al.*, 'National Health Spending Trends, 1960–93', *op. cit.*

99 Levit *et al.*, 'National Health Spending Trends, 1960–93', *op. cit.*, p.18.

100 See D. Wholey, R. Feldman and J. B. Christianson, 'The Effect of Market Structure on HMO Premiums', (1995) 14(1) *J. of Health Econ.* 81, and T. M. Wickizer and P. J. Feldstein, 'The Impact of HMO Competition on Private Health Insurance Premiums, 1985–92', (1995) 32(3) *Inquiry* 241, who find that Health Maintenance Organization penetration has a statistically significant negative effect on the rate of growth of premiums charged by traditional indemnity insurers.

101 See Ginsburg and Pickering, *op. cit.*, p. 155.

102 Smith et al., *op. cit.*, p. 133.

103 *Ibid.*

104 U. E. Reinhardt, 'Health System Change: Skirmish or Revolution?', (1996) 15(4) *Health Affairs* 114 at p. 115.

105 US General Accounting Office, 'General Insurance Standards: New Federal Law Creates Challenges for Consumers, Insurers, Regulators', report to the Chairman, Committee on Labor and Human Resources, US Senate, February, 1998. Online. Available HTTP: http://hippo.findlaw.com/healthins.html (accessed 28 March 1999).

106 Health Insurance Portability and Accountability Act 1996, PL, 104–191, 21 August 21 1996, 110 Stat 1936 (HR 3103) § 301.

107 Employee Retirement Income Security Act of 1974 (ERISA) USC.A. § 701 as inserted by *ibid.* § 101. A pre-existing condition restriction can in any event only relate to a medical condition diagnosed or treated some time during the six months preceding the 12-month waiting period and cannot be imposed on new-borns, newly adopted children less than 18 years old, or pregnant women.

108 For a discussion, see B. K. Atchinson and D. M. Fox, 'The Politics of the Health Insurance Portability and Accountability Act', (1997) 16(3) *Health Affairs* 146 at p. 147.

109 US General Accounting Office, 'General Insurance Standards: New Federal Law Creates Challenges for Consumers, Insurers, Regulators', *op. cit.*

110 See 'Statement by the President, The Children's Health Insurance Program One year Anniversary', 1 October 1998. Online. Available HTTP: http://www.hcfa.gov/init/wh-chip9.htm (accessed 28 March 1999) and see generally N. Halfon *et al.*, 'Challenges in Securing Access to Care for Children', (1999) 18(2) *Health Affairs* 48.

111 See Bipartisan Consensus Managed Care Improvement Act of 1999, H.R. 2723, (106th Cong.) (1999) (Sen. Norwood) and Health Quality and Choice Act of 1999, H.R. 2824, (106th Cong.) (1999) (Sen. Coburn). For a brief discussion of the Coburn-Shadegg Bill (Republican) and the

Norwood-Dingell Bill (Bipartisan) see G. Aston, 'Health Plan Liability Erupts at Center of House Battle', Online. Available HTTP: http://www.ama-assn.org/public/journals/amnews/amnews.htm (accessed 20 September 1999).

112 F. Rutten and A. van der Werff, 'Health Policy in the Netherlands: At the Crossroads' in G. McLachlan and A. Maynard, *The Public/Private Mix for Health: The Relevance and Effects of Change* (London: Nuffield Provincial Hospitals Trust, 1982) p. 187.

113 See J. W. Hurst, 'Reforming Health Care in Seven European Nations', (1991) *Health Affairs* 7 at p. 13, Exhibit 1.

114 *OECD Health Systems: Facts and Trends, op. cit.*, p. 19, Chart 3.

115 Schieber *et al.*, 'Health System Performance in OECD Countries, 1980–1992', *op. cit.*, p. 108, Exhibit 5.

116 The figures in this paragraph are from H. P. Uniken Venema, H. F. L. Garretsen and P. J. van der Maas, 'Health of Migrants and Migrant Health Policy: The Netherlands as an Example', (1995) 41(6) *Soc. Sci. Med.* 809 at p. 811.

117 *Ibid.*, p. 815.

118 A. J. P. Schrijvers, 'Letter from Utrecht: The Netherlands Introduces Some Competition into the Health Services', (1991) 266(16) *JAMA* 2215 at p. 2217.

119 OECD, *Health Policy Studies No. 2, The Reform of Health Care: A Comparative Analysis of Seven OECD Countries* (Paris: OECD, 1992) at p. 89 (hereinafter *Health Policy Studies No. 2*).

120 *Ibid.*, p. 92.

121 F. T. Schut, 'Health Care Reform in the Netherlands: Balancing Corporatism, Etatism, and Market Mechanisms', (1995) 20(3) *J. Health Polit. Policy Law* 615 at p. 617.

122 *Ibid.*

123 Ziekenfondswet (Sickness Funds Insurance Act) of 15 October 1964 *Staatsblad* (Official Journal of the State) 392.

124 Algemene Wet Bijzondere Ziektekosten (AWBZ) (Exceptional Medical Expenses Act) of 14 December 1967, *Staatsblad* (Official Journal of the State) 617.

125 F. Rutten and J. van der Linden, 'Integration of Economic Appraisal and Health Care Policy in a Health Insurance System: The Dutch Case', (1994) 38(12) *Soc. Sci. Med.* 1609 at p. 1610.

126 M. L. Lassey, W. R. Lassey and M. J. Jinks, *Health Care Systems Around the World: Characteristics, Issues, Reforms* (Upper Saddle River, NJ: Prentice Hall, 1997).

127 F. T. Schut, 'Workable Competition in Health Care: Prospects for the Dutch Design', (1992) 35(12) *Soc. Sci. Med.* 1445 at p. 1446.

128 Schut, 'Health Care Reform In the Netherlands: Balancing Corporatism, Etatism, and Market Mechanisms', *op. cit.*, p. 618.

129 B. L. Kirkman-Liff, 'Health Insurance Values and Implementation in the Netherlands and the Federal Republic of Germany: An Alternative Path to Universal Coverage', (1991) 265(19) *JAMA* 2496 at p. 2497.

130 Algemene Wet Bijzondere Ziektekosten (AWBZ) (Exceptional Medical Expenses Act) of 14 December 1967, *Staatsblad* (Official Journal of the State) 617.

131 *Health Policy Studies No. 2, op. cit.*, p. 89.

132 Schut, 'Health Care Reform in the Netherlands: Balancing Corporatism, Etatism, and Market Mechanisms', *op. cit.*, p. 619.

133 B. L. Kirkman-Liff, 'Health Care Reform in the Netherlands, Germany, and the United Kingdom' in A. Blomqvist and D. M. Brown, *Limits to Care: Reforming Canada's Health System in an Age of Restraint* (Toronto: C. D. Howe Institute, 1994) at p. 191.

134 C. Ham and M. Brommels, 'Health Care Reform In The Netherlands, Sweden, And The United Kingdom', (1994) 13(5) *Health Affairs* 106 at p. 115.

135 Netherlands Central Bureau of Statistics, 'The Uninsured for Health Care Costs 1985–1992: An Updating', (1993) 12(10) *Monthly Bulletin of Health Statistics*, pp. 9–10 as cited by Schut, 'Health Care Reform in the Netherlands: Balancing Corporatism, Etatism, and Market Mechanisms', *op. cit.*, p. 618. Netherlands Central Bureau of Statistics (CBB), 'The Uninsured for Health Care Costs 1995–1997; an Updating', *Maandbericht*

Gezondheidsstatistiek, October 1998, p.41 reports that the number of uninsured in 1996 was 144,000 and that the total Dutch population was 15.611 million people.

136 W. P. M. M. van de Ven and F. T. Schut, 'Should Catastrophic Risks be Included in a Regulated Competitive Health Insurance Market?', (1994) 39(10) *Soc. Sci. Med.* 1459.

137 Schut, 'Health Care Reform in the Netherlands: Balancing Corporatism, Etatism, and Market Mechanisms', *op. cit.*, p. 619.

138 Kirkman-Liff, 'Health Care Reform in the Netherlands, Germany, and the United Kingdom', *op. cit.*, p. 190.

139 There was also evidence that private insurers were more efficient than public insurers. A study in 1977 showed that privately insured patients required 56 percent fewer hospital-days than the publicly insured, a figure that Rutten and van der Werff claim cannot be fully explained by the higher morbidity rates of the publicly insured – Rutten and van der Werff, *op. cit.*, pp. 191–192.

140 Schut, 'Health Care Reform in the Netherlands: Balancing Corporatism, Etatism, and Market Mechanisms', *op. cit.*, p. 633.

141 *Health Policy Studies No. 2, op. cit.*, p. 91.

142 Schut, 'Health Care Reform In the Netherlands: Balancing Corporatism, Etatism, and Market Mechanisms', *op. cit.*, p. 633.

143 Rutten and van der Werff, *op. cit.*, p. 189.

144 Schrijvers, *op. cit.*, p. 2216.

145 F. T. Schut and H. E. G. M. Hermans, 'Managed Competition Reform in the Netherlands and its Lessons for Canada', (1997) 20(2) *Dalhousie Law Journal* 437 at p. 451. F. T. Schut and W. H. J. Hassink, 'Price Competition in Social Health Insurance: Evidence from the Netherlands'. (Paper prepared for the second IHEA Conference in Rotterdam, 6–9 June 1999) p. 7.

146 Rutten and van der Werff, *op. cit.*, p. 183.

147 *Ibid.*, p. 186.

148 H. Akveld and H. Hermans, 'The Netherlands' in *Medical Law* – Suppl. 6 (March 1995) (Deventer and Boston, MA: Kluwer Law and Taxation Publishers, 1995) p. 25 (§§37).

149 *Health Policy Studies No. 2, op. cit.*, p. 92.

150 *Ibid.* and Akveld and Hermans, *op. cit.*, p. 26 (§§38). J. A. M. Maarse, 'Hospital Budgeting in Holland: Aspects, Trends and Effects', (1989) 11 *Health Policy* 257, notes that about 35 percent of the budget is determined by the number of beds and the specialists in the hospital, 25 percent relates to the size of the population in the hospital's catchment area, and the balance is calculated by costing the number of admissions, patient days, out-patient surgeries, and specialist visits that the institute in question has agreed to provide.

151 Kirkman-Liff, 'Health Care Reform in the Netherlands, Germany, and the United Kingdom', *op. cit.*, p. 189.

152 *Health Policy Studies No. 2, op. cit.*, p. 92.

153 F. Schut, W. Greenberg and W. P. M. M. van de Ven, 'Antitrust Policy in the Dutch Health Care System and the Relevance of EEC Competition Policy and US Antitrust Practice', (1991) 17 *Health Policy* 257 at p. 262, Table 1.

154 Schut, 'Workable Competition in Health Care: Prospects for the Dutch Design', *op. cit.*, p. 1452.

155 *Ibid.*, p. 1451.

156 F. T. Schut, 'Prospects for Workable Competition in Health Care : Dutch Design and American Experience', paper for the Second World Congress on Health Economics, Zürich (10 September 1990), Erasmus University, Rotterdam as cited by Schut, Greenberg, and van de Ven, *op. cit.*, p. 266.

157 Schieber *et al.*, 'Health System Performance in OECD Countries, 1980–1992', *op. cit.*, p. 107, Exhibit 4. The UK figure is from 1989.

158 Schut, 'Workable Competition in Health Care: Prospects for the Dutch Design', *op. cit.*, p. 1450.

159 Schut, Greenberg and van de Ven, *op. cit.*, p. 262, Table 1.

160 *Health Policy Studies No. 2, op. cit.*, p. 91.

161 H. ten Have and H. Keasberry, 'Equity and Solidarity: The Context of Health Care in the Netherlands', (1992) 17 *The Journal of Medicine and Philosophy*, 463 at p. 466.

162 There are 27,000 general practitioners in England compared to 45,000 hospital doctors – P. Day and R. Klein, 'Britain's Health Care Experiment', (1991) 10(3) *Health Affairs* 39 at p. 47.

163 In 1990, there were 6,339 medical practitioners of which 2,428 were general practitioners – Department of Health, *The New Zealand Health Workforce 1990* as cited in E. Consalvi, 'Consalvi Directory of Decision Makers: New Zealand, Public Sector Health' (Auckland: Strategic Information Ltd, 1993) available online by subscription at: http://www.strategicinfo.co.nz.

164 S. A. Schroder, 'Training an Appropriate Mix of Physicians to Meet the Nation's Needs', (1993) 68 *Acad. Med.* 118, notes that less than 15 percent of US medical students graduating in 1991 and 1992 intended to become generalists.

165 Schut, 'Health Care Reform in the Netherlands: Balancing Corporatism, Etatism, and Market Mechanisms', *op. cit.*, p. 619.

166 B. L. Kirkman-Liff, 'Cost Containment and Physician Payment Methods in the Netherlands', (1989) 26 *Inquiry* 468 at p. 471.

167 Rutten and van der Linden, *op. cit.*, p. 1612.

168 *Ibid.*

169 Kirkman-Liff, 'Cost Containment and Physician Payment Methods in the Netherlands', *op. cit.*, p. 471.

170 Rutten and van der Werff, *op. cit.*, p. 175.

171 Kirkman-Liff, 'Cost Containment and Physician Payment Methods in the Netherlands', *op. cit.*, p. 473.

172 Schrijvers, *op. cit.*

173 M. Spanjer, 'Changes in Dutch Health-Care', (7 January 1995) 345 *The Lancet* 50.

174 Schut and Hermans, *op cit.*, p. 454.

175 Schut, 'Health Care Reform in the Netherlands: Balancing Corporatism, Etatism, and Market Mechanisms', *op. cit.*, pp. 626–627.

176 Schut and Hermans, *op cit.*, p. 454.

177 Kirkman-Liff, 'Cost Containment and Physician Payment Methods in the Netherlands', *op. cit.*, pp. 472–473.

178 *Health Policy Studies No. 2*, *op. cit.*, p. 87.

179 Advies van de Commissie Structuur en Financiering Gezondheidszorg (Commission on the Structure and Financing of Health Care), *Bereidheid tot Verandering* (Willingness To Change), ('s Gravenhage: Distributiecentrum Overheidspublikaties, 1987) (hereinafter *Dekker Report*).

180 *Health Policy Studies No. 2*, *op. cit.*, p. 94.

181 Schut, 'Workable Competition in Health Care: Prospects for the Dutch Design', *op. cit.*, pp. 1450 and 1448.

182 Schut, 'Health Care Reform in the Netherlands: Balancing Corporatism, Etatism, and Market Mechanisms', *op. cit.*, p. 638.

183 *Ibid.*

184 *Ibid.*

185 Schut, Greenberg and van de Ven, *op. cit.*, p. 259, fn 2.

186 *Health Policy Studies No. 2*, *op. cit.*, p. 97.

187 See A. J. Dunning *et al.*, *A Report By The Government Committee On Choices In Health Care* (Rijswijk: Ministry of Welfare, Health and Cultural Affairs, 1992).

188 Van de Ven and Schut, *op. cit.*

189 Schut and Hermans, *op. cit.*, p. 457.

190 *Health Policy Studies No. 2*, *op. cit.*, p. 99.

191 Van de Ven and Schut, *op. cit.*, p. 1468.

192 Schut and Hermans, *op. cit.*, p. 458.

193 For 1997 figures, *ibid.*, p. 450. For 1999 figure see Schut and Hassink, *op. cit.*, p.4.

194 F. T. Schut, 'Institutions and Markets in Health Care', paper prepared for the International Conference 'Institutions, Markets and (Economic) Performance: Deregulation and its Consequences', Utrecht University, 11–12 December 1997 at p. 8.

195 Schut and Hermans, *op. cit.*, p. 451.

196 *Ibid.*, p. 457.

197 *Ibid.*, p. 452.

198 *Ibid.*

199 *Ibid.*, pp. 452–453.

200 Figures in this paragraph are taken from Schieber *et al.*, 'Health System Performance in OECD Countries, 1980–1992', *op. cit.*, pp. 101–102, Exhibits 1 and 2, from OECD data and their own estimates.

201 G. J. Schieber *et al.*, 'Health Spending, Delivery, and Outcomes in OECD Countries', (1993) 12:2 *Health Affairs* 120 at p. 121, Exhibit 1.

202 C. James, *New Territory: The Transformation of New Zealand, 1984–92* (Wellington: Bridget Williams Books Limited, 1992) at p. 177.

203 D. Muthumala and C. G. McKendy, *Health Expenditure Trends In New Zealand 1980–1991* (Wellington: Department of Health, 1991) at p. 10.

204 S. Upton, *Your Health and the Public Health: A Statement of Government Health Policy* (Wellington: Minister of Health, July 1991) at pp. 7–8.

205 R. D. Bowie, 'Health Expenditures and the Health Reforms: A Comment', (1992) 105(945) *New Zealand Med. J.* 458, argues that the government's figures are in fact incorrect, and calculates that the increase of health costs above the consumer price index was not 27 percent, as alleged, but rather 7.7 percent. Using what Bowie describes as the conventional measure (339.6/315.1 − 1) × 100 = 7.7 percent. In fact the percentage increase (rounded up) is 7.8 percent calculated as follows:

$$\frac{\{3.807 \times 357/1125 - 1\}}{\{1.121\}} \times 100 = 7.8 \text{ percent}$$

Moreover, he notes that the population increased by 8.4 percent from 3.138 million to 3.401 million over the same period. Therefore, in fact, the per capita consumer price index-adjusted expenditure fell by 0.7 percent.

206 Ministry of Health, *Health Expenditure Trends in NZ 1980–1997* (Wellington: Ministry of Health, 1998) (hereinafter *Health Expenditure Trends in NZ 1980–1997)* at p. 39, Table 8.5. Online. Available http://www.moh.govt.nz (accessed 1 July 1999).

207 Ministry of Health, *Healthy New Zealanders: Briefing Papers for the Minister of Health 1996, Vol. 2, The Health and Disability Sector* (Wellington: Ministry of Health, 1996) (hereinafter *Healthy New Zealanders*) at p. 13.

208 C. C. Grant, C. B. Forrest, and B. Starfield, 'Primary Care and Health Reform in New Zealand', (1997) 110 *New Zealand Med. J.* 35.

209 *Healthy New Zealanders, op. cit.*, pp. 10–11.

210 *Healthy New Zealanders, op. cit.*, p. 13 notes, "In the 1992/93 Household Health Survey, people with a family income of $20,000 or less were more than three times as likely as people with an income of over $30,000 to report their health as 'not so good' or 'poor.'"

211 I. Kawachi, S. Marshall and N. Pearce, 'Social Class Inequalities in the Decline of Coronary Heart Disease Among New Zealand Men, 1975–77 to 1985–87', (1991) 20 *Int. J. Epidemiol.* 393, showed that mortality rates associated with coronary disease have fallen more steeply for men in professional and administrative positions than for unskilled workers. These figures may reflect differences in smoking rates rather than access to care.

212 M. H. Durie, 'Implications of Policy and Management Decisions on Maori Health: Contemporary Issues and Responses' in M. W. Raffel and N. K. Raffel (eds.), *Perspectives on Health Policy: Australia, New Zealand and the United States* (Chichester/New York: John Wiley and Sons, 1997) p. 201.

213 See E. Pomare and G. de Boer, *Hauora: Maori Standards of Health* (Wellington: Department of Health, 1988).

214 N. Pearce, E. Pomare, S. Marshall and B. Borman, 'Mortality and Social Class in Maori and Non-Maori New Zealand Men: Changes Between 1975–7 and 1985–7', (1993) 106(956) *New Zealand Med. J.* 193.

215 E. Murchie, *Rapuora: Health and Maori Women* (Wellington: The Maori Women's Welfare League Inc., 1984) and S. Milroy and A. Mikaere, 'Maori and the Health Reforms: Promises, Promises', (1994) 16(2) *New Zealand Universities Law Review* 175.

216 Upton, *op. cit.*, p. 28.

217 I. Hay, *The Caring Commodity: The Provision of Health Care in New Zealand* (Auckland: Oxford University Press, 1989) at p. 151.

218 Upton, *op. cit.*, p. 28.

219 A. Gibbs, J. Scott and D. Fraser, *Unshackling the Hospitals – Report of the Hospital and Related Services Taskforce* (Wellington: Government Printer, 1988) at p. 8.

220 R. M. Burdon, *The New Dominion: A Social and Political History of New Zealand 1918-1939* (Wellington: A. H. and A. W. Reed, 1965) at p. 249 as cited by I. Hay, *The Caring Commodity: The Provision of Health Care in New Zealand* (Auckland: Oxford University Press, 1989) at p. 110.

221 *Ibid.*, p. 245.

222 Hay, *op. cit.*, p. 121.

223 Muthumala and McKendy, *op. cit.*, p. 44, Appendix 2.

224 *New Zealand Official 1993 Yearbook* (Wellington: Department of Statistics, 1993) at p. 508.

225 Upton, *op. cit.*, p. 44.

226 *Ibid.*, p. 44.

227 *Ibid.*, p. 14.

228 For a description of the history of the scheme and a critique of the 1992 amendments see Rt. Hon. Sir G. Palmer, 'New Zealand's Accident Compensation Scheme: Twenty Years On', (1994) 44(3) *University of Toronto Law Journal* 223.

229 Since 1 July 1992 a "disability allowance" is paid in lieu of lump sum payments. Payments for pain and suffering and loss of enjoyment of life are no longer made.

230 The Accident Compensation Amendment Act 1974 amended the term "personal injury by accident" to include "medical, surgical, dental or first aid misadventure". Patients suffering medical misadventure are still able to initiate common law claims for exemplary damages – Donselaar v. Donselaar, (1982) N.Z.L.R. 97. The 1992 changes to the scheme have revived some private tort actions, such as the tort of emotional shock.

231 Upton, *op. cit.*, p. 44.

232 Muthumala and McKendy, *op. cit.*, p. 25.

233 Upton, *op. cit.*, p. 15.

234 *Consumer*, 'ACC: Adding Insult to Injury', May 1994, No. 326 at p. 6.

235 *Ibid.*

236 S. Todd and J. Black, 'Accident Compensation and the Barring of Actions for Damages', (1993) 1(3) *The Tort Law Review*, 197.

237 *Health Expenditure Trends in NZ 1980–1997*, *op. cit*, p. 23, Table 4.12.

238 Section 59(6) of the Income Tax Act 1986 provides that premiums paid in respect of any policy of personal accident or sickness insurance are not deductible after 17 December 1987. Section 59(6) was added by s. 4(3) of the Income Tax Amendment Act (No. 2) 1988.

239 N. K. Raffel, 'New Zealand's Health System: A Brief Description' in M. W. Raffel and N. K. Raffel (eds), *op. cit.*, p. 135.

240 *Health Expenditure Trends in NZ 1980–1997*, *op. cit*, p. 25.

241 Prior to the 1991 reform proposals, private insurers funded 10 percent of general practitioner services, 6.1 percent of diagnostics, 15.4 percent of miscellaneous specialist services, 2.8 percent of pharmaceuticals, 16.2 percent of private hospital treatments, and 24.5 percent of private hospital treatments excluding psychiatric and geriatric hospitals – Muthumala and McKendy, *op. cit.*, p. 11, p. 32, and p. 55, Appendix 4J.

242 *Ibid.*, p. 32 and Appendix 5J.

243 *Health Expenditure Trends in NZ 1980–1997*, *op. cit*, p. 25.

244 N. J. Devlin, 'The Distribution of Household Expenditure on Health Care', (1993) 106(953) *New Zealand Med. J.* 126–127.

245 Muthumala and McKendy, *op. cit.*, p. 55, Appendix 4J.

246 Figures from New Zealand Board of Health, Clinical and Public Health Laboratory Services, (1974) 22 *Report Series*, p. 14 as cited by Hay, *op. cit.*, p. 163 and *New Zealand Official 1993 Yearbook*, *op. cit.*, p. 162.

247 Hay, *op. cit.*, p. 152.

248 T. Ashton, A. Beasley, P. Alley and G. Taylor, *Reforming the New Zealand Health System: Lessons From Other Countries, Report of a Study Tour Sponsored by Health Boards New Zealand* (April 1991) p. 19.

249 Ashton reports that the 1989 initiatives resulted in *prima facie* productivity improvements. For example, the average length of stay in hospital fell from 15.55 days in 1987 to 13.31 days in 1989, and the throughput of surgical patients increased by 10 percent between 1987 and 1990 – T. Ashton, 'Reform of the Health Service: Weighing Up the Costs and Benefits' in J. Boston and P. Dalziel, *The Decent Society* (Auckland: Oxford University Press, 1992) at p. 150.

250 *Ibid.*, p. 149.

251 Ashton *et al.*, *op. cit.*, p. 18.

252 Ashton, *op. cit.*, p. 149.

253 Upton, *op. cit.*, pp. 11–19.

254 Hon. S. Upton as reported in *Hansard*, 'Health and Disability Services Bill: Introduction', 20 August 1992, 10773 p. 10776.

255 *Healthy New Zealanders*, *op. cit.*, p. 21, notes "low income is defined by a number of thresholds, ranging from $17,134 and below for a single person to $45,692 and below for a family of six."

256 Health and Disability Services Act 1993 (N.Z.) (1993) No. 22, s. 11.

257 Anon, 'Some Lose, More Gain Health Discount Cards', *The New Zealand Herald*, 19 January 1994, s. 1:3.

258 *Healthy New Zealanders*, *op. cit.*

259 See generally the Health and Disability Services Amendment Act 1995 (NZ) No. 84.

260 Noted in P. Pepperell and J. Hodders (eds) (1996) *The Capital Letter* 18(17) at p. 2.

261 *Ibid.*

262 Section 362 of the Accident Compensation Act (N.Z.) (1998) No. 114 provides for coordination in purchasing "public health acute services." However, insurers are free to conclude their own arrangements for all other kinds of care, e.g. elective surgery, general practitioners services, etc.

263 Anon, 'Tendering "A Fiasco"', *The New Zealand Herald*, 23 June 1994.

264 As quoted by Anon, 'Health Bodies Told to Restrain Costs', *The New Zealand Herald*, 14 December 1995.

265 *Healthy New Zealanders*, *op. cit.*, p. 20.

266 *Purchasing For Your Health 1996/97: A Performance Report of the Fourth Year of the Regional Health Authorities* (Wellington: Ministry of Health, 1998). Online. Available HTTP: http://www.moh. govt.nz (under publications) (accessed 20 April 1999) at p. 26.

267 See L. Malcolm and M. Powell, 'The Development of Independent Practice Associations and Related Groups in New Zealand', (1996) 109(1022) *N.Z. Med. J.* 184.

268 *OECD Health Data 98: A Comparative Analysis of 29 Countries* (OECD electronic database).

269 *Health Expenditure Trends in NZ 1980–1997*, *op. cit*, p. 29.

270 Privately funded real expenditures increased by 6.6 percent per annum over the period 1980– 95 whereas publicly funded expenditures increased by 1.2 percent *Healthy New Zealanders*, *op. cit.*, p. 66.

271 *Ibid.*, p. 21 notes "Some RHAs have been able to contract with IPAs for free [General Medical Subsidy] GMS consultations for children under five years. One RHA has also contracted, on a pilot basis, for free mental health consultations with GPs."

272 F. Barber, 'Cash Help to Slash Waiting Lists for Surgery', *The New Zealand Herald*, 14 September 1994.

273 72,647 people were on waiting lists in 1993 and 77,558 people in 1994 – S. Upton, *op. cit.*, p. 28 (1991 figure); *Purchasing for Your Health: A Performance Report on the First Year of the Regional Health Authorities and Public Health Commission* (Ministry of Health: Wellington, 1995), Table 17 at p. 85 (1993 and 1994 figures); L. Dalziel, Opposition Health Spokeswoman as cited by *The New Zealand Herald*, 17 April 1996, s. 1:1 (1996 figures).

274 *Healthy New Zealanders*, *op. cit.*, p. 25.

275 See 'Surgery Booking System "Has Flaws"', *The Press*, 8 March 1999. Online. Available HTTP: http://www.press.co.nz/10/99030803.htm (accessed 5 April 1999).

276 A. Maynard, 'Can Competition Enhance Efficiency in Health Care? Lessons from the Reform of the UK National Health Service', (1994) 39(10) *Soc. Sci. Med.* 1433 at p. 1434.

277 D. Mayston, 'NHS Resourcing: A Financial and Economic Analysis' in A. J. Culyer, A. K. Maynard, and J. W. Posnett, *Competition in Health Care: Reforming the NHS* (Basingstoke: Macmillan Press, 1990) at p. 80.

278 *Health Expenditure Trends in NZ 1980-97, op. cit.*, Figure 6.1, s. 6.5.

279 "Ischemic" is a condition where there is an inadequate amount of blood reaching the heart resulting in inadequate oxygen supply. J. Spiby, 'Health Care Technology in the United Kingdom', (1994) 30(1) *Health Policy* 295 at p. 296.

280 See Schieber *et al.*, 'Health System Performance in OECD Countries, 1980–1992', *op. cit.*, p. 109, Exhibits 6, from OECD data and the authors' own estimates and *OECD Health Systems: Facts and Trends, op. cit.*, Table 3.3.14 and 3.3.15, pp. 94–95.

281 Day and Klein, *op. cit.*

282 *Health Policy Studies No. 2, op. cit.*, p. 120.

283 H. J. Aaron and W. B. Schwartz, *The Painful Prescription: Rationing Hospital Care* (Washington, DC: Brookings Institute, 1984) pp. 97–99.

284 Some of the factors mentioned by B. O'Brien, 'Parallel Public/Private Finance and Waiting Lists' (presentation at the Centre for Health Economics and Policy Analysis, Shifting Involvements: Private and Public Roles in Canada Health Care: Eleventh Annual Health Policy Conference, 28–29 May 1998, Hamilton, Ontario. Unpublished).

285 The National Health Service Act (UK) 1946 9 and 10 Geo. 6, CH 81 enacted 6 November 1946 subsequently repealed and replaced by the *National Health Service Act* (UK) 1977 c. 49.

286 The National Health Service Act (UK) 1977 c. 49, s. 1.

287 Figure for 1988 from W. A. Fitzhugh, *The Fitzhugh Directory of Independent Hospitals and Provident Associations, Financial Information* (London: Health Care Information Services, 1989) at p. 17. Other figures from R. Klein, *The New Politics of the NHS*, (London: Longman, 1995) at p. 155.

288 *OECD Health Data 98: A Comparative Analysis of 29 Countries* (OECD electronic database).

289 A. J. Culyer and A. Meads, 'The United Kingdom: Effective, Efficient, Equitable?', (1992) 17 *J. Health Polit. Policy Law* 667 at p. 675.

290 The National Health Service Act (UK) 1977 c. 49, ss. 78, 79, 79A and regulations enacted pursuant thereto.

291 M. Ryan and B. Yule, 'The Way to Economic Prescribing', (1993) 25 *Health Policy* 25 at p. 31. The National Health Service Act (UK) 1977 c. 49, s. 83A(2) allows regulations to be made exempting individuals from user charges for a number of reasons.

292 Figures are from the *OECD Health Data 98: A Comparative Analysis of 29* Countries (OECD electronic database).

293 R. Loveridge and R. Starkey (eds), *Continuity and Crisis in the NHS: The Politics of Design and Innovation in Health Care* (Buckingham: Open University Press, 1992) at p. 3.

294 *Health Policy Studies No. 2, op. cit.*, p. 113.

295 See the National Health Service Act (UK) 1977 c. 49. ss. 13, 14 and 15.

296 The National Health Service Act 1946 9 and 10 Geo. 6, CH 81 enacted 6 November 1946.

297 A. C. Enthoven, 'NHS Market Reform', (1991) 10(3) *Health Affairs* 60 at p. 62.

298 *Ibid.*, p. 63.

299 *Ibid.*

300 J. Cairns and C. Donaldson, 'Introduction to Economics in the New NHS', (1993) 25 *Health Policy* 1.

301 A. J. Culyer and A. Meads, 'The United Kingdom: Effective, Efficient, Equitable?' (1997) 17 *Journal of Health Politics, Policy and Law* 667 at p. 675.

302 J. P. Nicholl, N. Beeby and B. Williams, 'Role of the Private Sector in Elective Surgery in England and Wales', (1986) 298 *BMJ* p. 243.

303 Health Services Act (UK), 1980, c. 53.

304 The National Health Service Act (UK) 1977 c. 49, ss 29–34.

305 *Ibid.* ss. 35–41.

306 Day and Klein, *op. cit.*, p. 47.

307 See generally F. Honigsbaum, *Health, Happiness, and Security: The Creation of the National Health Service* (London: Routledge, 1989).

308 *Ibid.*, p. 153.
309 Culyer and Meads, *op. cit.*, p. 674.
310 *Health Policy Studies No. 2, op. cit.*, p. 113.
311 Day and Klein, *op. cit.*, p. 49.
312 A. Maynard and A. Walker, 'Managing the Medical Workforce: Time for Improvements?', (1995) 31(1) *Health Policy* 1 at p. 3.
313 See Department of Health Newsletter 98/079, 'Fifth Annual Distinction Awards Report Published', 3 March 1998. Online. Available http://www.coi.gov.uk/coi/depts/GCH/coi8431d.ok (accessed 30 March 1999).
314 Maynard and Walker, *op cit.*, p. 13.
315 Day and Klein, *op. cit.*, p. 45.
316 White Paper, 'Working for Patients', (Cm 555; January 1989).
317 The National Health Service and Community Care Act (UK) 1990 c.19, hereinafter referred to as the NHS 1990 Act.
318 News Release by the Department of Health, 96/106, 1 April 1996, 'Changes to Health Service Structure Release £139 Million for Patient Care'.
319 R. Carr-Hill, 'RAWP is Dead: Long Live RAWP' in Culyer *et al.*, *Competition in Health Care: Reforming the NHS, op. cit.*, p. 192.
320 See the discussion by K. Bloor and A. Maynard, 'Health Care Reform in the UK National Health Service', Paper prepared for the First Meeting of the International Health Economics Association, May 1996, British Columbia, p. 4.
321 *Ibid.*, p. 5.
322 For a critique see D. W. Light, 'From Managed Competition to Managed Cooperation: Theory and Lessons from the British Experience', (1997) 75(3) *The Milbank Quarterly* 297 at pp. 323–325.
323 NHS 1990 Act, *op. cit.*, s. 3.
324 *Ibid.*, Schedule 2, s. 6–8.
325 Kirkman-Liff, 'Health Care Reform in the Netherlands, Germany, and the United Kingdom', *op. cit.*, p. 206.
326 NHS 1990 Act, *op. cit.*, Schedule 2, s. 6.
327 Maynard, 'Can Competition Enhance Efficiency in Health Care? Lessons from the Reform of the UK National Health Service', *op. cit.*, p. 1440.
328 See NHSME, *Costing for Contracting – Acute Services*, FDL (93)51 Annex A, 1993a, and NHSME, *Costing for Contracting – The 1994/95 Contracting Round*, FDL (93)59, 1993b. See also A. McGuire and P. Anand, 'Introduction: Evaluating Health Care Reform' in A. McGuire and P. Anand (eds), *Changes in Health Care: Reflections on the NHS Internal Market* (Basingstoke: Macmillan Business, 1997) at p. 5.
329 Maynard, 'Can Competition Enhance Efficiency in Health Care? Lessons from the Reform of the UK National Health Service', *op. cit.*, p. 1434.
330 McGuire and Anand, *op. cit.*, p. 5.
331 The idea of GP Fundholders was actually conceived by A. Maynard, who has since been less than enthusiastic about its wholesale embrace by the government (See A. Maynard and K. Bloor, 'Introducing a Market to the United Kingdom's National Health Service', (1996) 334(9) *New Eng. J. Of Med.* p. 604).
332 See the report of the Audit Commission, *What the Doctor Ordered: A Study of GP Fundholders in England and Wales* (London: HMSO, 1996) (hereinafter *What The Doctor Ordered*) at p. 6. Standard Fundholders do not purchase the following sorts of hospital care: emergency admissions, inpatient mental health, costs above £6,000 per annum for any patient, accident and emergency, maternity, and medical inpatients.
333 National Health Service (Fundholding Practices) Regulations (UK) 1996, S.I. 1996/76 (hereinafter Funding Regulations 1996)
334 R. Robinson and J. Le Grand, 'Contracting and the Purchaser-Provider Split' in R. B. Saltman and C. von Otter (eds.), *Implementing Planned Markets in Health Care: Balancing Social and Economic Responsibility* (Buckingham and Philadelphia, PA: Open University Press, 1995) 25 at p. 27.
335 A. Harrison (ed), *Health Care UK 1994/95: An Annual Review Of Health Care Policy* (Bristol: J. W.

Arrowsmith Limited, 1995) (hereinafter *Health Care UK 1994/95*) p. 1 noted at this time there were 2,500 Fundholders. *The New NHS: Modern, Dependable*, a White Paper, CM 3807, 8 December 1997, records the number of Fundholders at 3,500. Online. Available HTTP: http://www.official-documents.co.uk/document/doh/newnhs/contents.htm (accessed 30 March 1999).

336 See generally the Fundholding Regulations 1996, *op. cit.*

337 News Release by the Department of Health, 95/485, 18 October 1995, 'GP Fundholding Benefits to be Spread Further'.

338 H. Glennerster and M. Matsaganis, 'The UK Health Reforms: The Fundholding Experiment', (1993) 23 *Health Policy* 179 at p. 182.

339 Fundholding Regulations 1996, *op. cit.*, s. 21.

340 P. Bryden, 'The Future of Primary Care' in Loveridge and Starkey (eds.), *op. cit.*, p. 69, notes that for the first time, performance-related payments were offered for cervical cytology and childhood immunizations. See also Cairns and Donaldson, *op. cit.*, p. 4.

341 A. Haines and S. Iliffe, 'Primary Health Care' in E. Beck, S. Lonsdale, S. Newman, and D. Patterson (eds.) *In the Best of Health?* (London: Chapman and Hall, 1992) at pp. 32–3.

342 T. Scott and A. Maynard, *Will the New GP Contract Lead to Cost Effective Medical Practice? (Discussion Paper 82)* (York: Centre for Health Economics, University of York, 1991).

343 For a criticism of these awards, see Bloor and Maynard, *op. cit.*

344 Maynard and Walker, *op. cit.*, p. 13.

345 Public Expenditure Analyses to 1995-96, Treasury 1993 as cited by Maynard, 'Can Competition Enhance Efficiency in Health Care? Lessons from the Reform of the UK National Health Service', *op. cit.*, p. 1434, Table 1.

346 Schieber *et al.*, 'Health System Performance in OECD Countries, 1980–1992', *op. cit.*, p. 101, Exhibit 1 from OECD data and the authors' own estimates.

347 *Ibid.*, p. 102, Exhibit 1 from OECD data and the authors' own estimates.

348 Public Expenditure Analyses to 1995–6, Treasury 1993 cited by Maynard, 'Can Competition Enhance Efficiency in Health Care? Lessons from the Reform of the UK National Health Service', *op. cit.*, p. 1434, Table 1. For the recent figures see W. Bartlett, 'Regulation, Trust and Incentives: Contractual Relations and Performance in the NHS Quasi-Market', (paper prepared for the conference "Institutions, Markets and (Economic) Performance: Deregulation and its Consequences," Utrecht University, 11–12 December 1997) p. 44. Bartlett cites T. Palleson, *Health Care Reforms in Britain and Denmark: The Politics of Economic Success and Failure* (Aarhus: Forlaget Politica, 1997) for the contention that the efficiency of the UK system actually fell by 5 percent over the reform period.

349 *The New NHS: Modern, Dependable*, a White Paper, *op.cit.*, s. 2.2.

350 Health Care UK 1994/95, *op. cit.*, p. 38, Table 13. There were 1,040,152 people on waiting lists at 30 September 1995 – 9 less than at March 1995 – News Release by the Department of Health, 96/1, 1 January 1996, 'Hospital Waiting List Statistics Published'.

351 News Release by the Department of Health, *ibid.* T. Besley, J. Hall and I. Preston, *Private Health Insurance and the State of the NHS, (Commentary No. 52)* (London: The Institute for Fiscal Studies, 1996) at Figure 3, similarly show a significant decline in the percentage of the population on long-term waiting lists after 1990.

352 J. Snell, 'Action Team Appointed to Tackle Rising Waiting Lists', (20.11.97) *Health Services Journal* 4, as quoted by W. Bartlett *op. cit.*

353 Department of Health, Press Notice 1999/0119, 'Statistical Press Notice – NHS Waiting List Activity Figures 31 January 1999', 2 March 1999. Online. Available HTTP: http://www.coi.gov.uk/coi/depts/GDH/coi2565f.ok (accessed 1 April 1999).

354 See S. Lyall, 'Britain's Prescription for Health Care: Take a Seat', *The New York Times*, 19 April 1999, p. 3.

355 *The New NHS: Modern, Dependable*, a White Paper, *op. cit.*, at section 5. For an explanation of the new legislation see Explanatory Notes to the Health Act (Norwich: Stationary Office Ltd, 1999). Online. Available HTTP: http://legislation.hmso.gov.uk (accessed 24 September 1999).

356 Department of Health, Press Notice 1998/327, 'Minister Welcomes Formation of 480 Primary Care Groups', 6 August 1998. Online. Available HTTP: http://www.coi.gov.uk/

coi/depts/GDH/coi48084.ok (accessed 1 April 1999).

357 See J. Sussex, *Controlling NHS Expenditure: The Impact of Labour's NHS White Papers* (London: Office of Health Economics, 1998) at p. 34.

358 *The New NHS: Modern, Dependable*, a White Paper, *op cit.*, section 5.1.

359 For a discussion see J. Sussex, *op cit.*, p. 29.

360 J. White, *Competing Solutions: American Health Care Prospects and International Experience* (Washington, DC: Brookings Institution, 1995) at p. 271.

361 R. J. Blendon *et al.*, 'Satisfaction with Health Systems in Ten Nations', (1990) *Health Affairs* 185, looked at the level of public satisfaction within ten different countries' health care systems and found that between 41 percent and 47 percent of the Dutch population were satisfied with their health care system. This result was below the 56 percent of the Canadian population who, of all nations, were the most satisfied with their health system, but significantly above the 27 percent of the UK population, and the 10 percent of the US population, reporting themselves to be satisfied. This 1990 publication did not report on the New Zealand health system but the barrage of negative media reports coming from that country would suggest that New Zealanders are not happy with their health care system.

362 E. Mossialos, 'Citizens' Views on Health Care Systems in the 15 Member States of the European Union', (1997) 6(2) *Health Economics* 109 at p. 111, Table 1.

363 See *Health Care in the Netherlands 1996*, pp. 5–6. Online. Available HTTP: http://www.netherlands-embassy.org/hlt-car.htm (accessed 31 December 1998).

364 See, for example, R. G. Evans, 'Going for the Gold: The Redistributive Agenda Behind Market-Based Health Care Reform', (1997) 22(2) *J. Health Polit.Policy Law* 427.

365 See generally, P. M. Danzon, 'Hidden Overhead Costs: Is Canada's System Really Less Expensive?' (1992) (Spring) *Health Affairs* 21.

366 It has been argued in the UK that the health sector has been underfunded for many years – see generally A. Towse, (ed.), *Financing Health Care in the UK: A Discussion of NERA's Prototype Model to Replace the NHS* (London: Office of Health Economics, 1995), and J. Dixon, A. Harrison, and B. New, 'Is the NHS Underfunded?', (1997) 314(7073) *BMJ* 58.

367 McGuire and Anand, *op. cit.*, p. 2.

368 See *OECD 1994 Review of Seventeen Countries, op. cit.*, pp. 37–9. Of 24 OECD countries, only Canada, Finland, Greece, Iceland, Italy and Norway had more rapid rates of growth in health expenditures in the 1980s than in the 1970s.

369 R. B. Saltman and J. Figueras, 'Analysing the Evidence on European Health Care Reforms', (1998) 17(2) *Health Affairs* 85.

370 See R. Klein, 'The NHS and the New Scientism: Solution or Delusion?', (1996) 89(1) *Q. J. Med.* 85 at p. 87.

371 The Health Care Study Group notes that a genuine universal system is an invitation to strategic thinking about the needs and institutions of an entire society and such a system is better able to control costs as it limits cost shifting – see The Health Care Study Group Report, 'Understanding the Choices in Health Care Reform', (1994) 19(3) *J. Health Polit.Policy Law* 499 at p. 501.

372 T. R. Marmor, *Understanding Health Care Reform* (New Haven: Yale University Press, 1994) at p. 26, and M. L. Barer *et al.*, 'It Ain't Necessarily So: The Cost Implications of Health Care Reform', (1994) 13(4) *Health Affairs* 88.

373 A. J. Culyer, 'Chisels or Screwdrivers? A Critique of the NERA Proposals for the Reform of the NHS' in Towse (ed.), *op. cit.*, p. 28.

374 J. C. Dechene, 'Preferred Provider Organization Structures and Agreements', (1995) 4 *Annals Of Health Law* 35, notes that the fundamental flaw in traditional indemnity insurance is the absence of an agreement between the entities responsible for payment and the providers of services, with the goal of limiting costs.

375 Evans, *op. cit.*, at p. 460, notes that students of health care systems believe that there is "a great deal of inappropriate, unnecessary, and sometimes downright harmful care being paid for in all modern health care systems." He goes on to note that the key question becomes one of moving closer to production frontiers.

4 Accountability of health care service purchasers

Comparing internal markets and managed competition

In this chapter I analyze and compare internal market and managed competition reform from the perspective of the accountability of purchasers (be they government-appointed authorities or competing private insurers) to the citizens they ultimately represent.

Enhancing accountability was cited as a goal of internal market reform of the former command-and-control systems of the UK and New Zealand.[1] Although improving accountability is often cited as a key goal of health care reform, it is often unclear what exactly is meant by accountability. This chapter explores to whom and for what a decision-maker is accountable.

Improving accountability should improve the quality of decision-making by reducing agency costs between decision-makers and the public she/he represents. What is the scope of "accountability?" In the health sector it is possible to identify at least three spheres of accountability: political, market, and professional.[2] This book focuses primarily on how to ensure accountability through political and market mechanisms. However, reference is made to professional accountability and this is further developed in Chapter 7, which discusses mechanisms to ensure the quality of health care services supplied. In this chapter I will:

- argue that a series of difficult agency questions and public choice problems arise with respect to the accountability of government-appointed purchasers in the UK and New Zealand, and that there are not the incentives in place necessary to ensure that government-appointed purchasers are responsive to the citizens they represent;
- evaluate the prospects for the use of political "voice" by citizens as a means of reducing agency costs between citizens and the government-appointed purchasers that represent them;
- canvass the advantages and disadvantages of some of the possible means of enhancing voice and the limits of voice as an accountability and efficiency enhancing mechanism.

In addition to political voice, I examine "exit," a market mechanism, as a means of improving accountability. In managed competition proposals in the

Netherlands and the US, consumer choice of insurers in a regulated market is viewed as the means through which to ensure accountability and efficiency. Citizens must choose an insurer/purchaser offering a managed care plan that best suits their needs and, should they become dissatisfied, may "exit" to another insurer/purchaser with a risk-adjusted share of public funding. I will discuss the relative costs and benefits of exit as a means of reducing agency costs and ensuring accountability.

Although managed competition and internal market models are prima facie different, there is a convergence as internal market systems move towards managed care arrangements. Government-appointed purchasers and private insurers in *all* systems may wish to shift financial risk to groups of health providers offering managed care plans. They shift risk by paying groups of providers on a capitated basis (a lump sum per person to cover all health care service needed by that person regardless of how many services that person actually needs or uses). In such a case, the group of providers can take on three functions. First, the *insurance* function, as it bears the costs and risk of utilization of services by patients. Second, the *purchaser* function, as it largely determines what range and mix of health care services to supply to any individual it covers. And, third, (at its discretion) some of the *provider* functions if it actually owns the hospitals or employs the providers who provide services to patients. Consequently, the roles of the public and private sectors and of insurers, purchasers, and providers in all systems are shifting, changing, and becoming less compartmentalized.[3]

Agency and public choice

In the political sphere, Donahue defines accountability as being where:

> government action accords with the will of the people the government represents – not the will of individuals who happen to work in the government and not what those individuals think the citizens should want but what the people, by their own criteria, count desirable.[4]

Thus, accountability may also be described as the level of responsiveness by public institutions to their citizenry. The question that arises is the level of agency costs existing between citizens and their elected representatives. Donahue argues that the question of agency engages the root social challenge of accountability, and devices such as the law, ethics, and the market may all be utilized with a view to ameliorating the problem.[5]

Agency costs arise when one person or organization (the principal) contracts with another person or organization (the agent) for performance of a service. The performance of this service requires the delegation of some decision-making authority from the principal to the agent, but the agent's interests do not match those of the principal.[6] Agency costs are thus the loss to the principal from the agent not acting as instructed or in the principal's best interests.

Factors reducing agency costs between shareholders and managers in publicly-traded companies are not generally present in the public sector.[7] Consequently, agency problems are a great deal more complicated in the public sector than within private firms, particularly because the burden of any inefficiency is diffused over many individuals. Citizens have little incentive to band together into more powerful lobby groups because their own personal share of the public sector's inefficiency is very small and individuals may decline to take any initiatives to lobby for improvement in the expectation that they can free-ride upon the efforts of others.[8] In contrast, members of interest groups who personally have much to gain from a particular government decision will have a greater incentive to lobby the government, but any resultant policy change may not reflect the more diffused interest of the public at large.

The problem of agency cost is closely related to public choice analysis.[9] Public choice is "a perspective that emerges from an extensive application of the tools and methods of the economist to collective or non-market decision making."[10] Neo-classical economists assume that people in the market-place are principally motivated by self-interest. Public choice theory extends this assumption to the actions of politicians, public servants, and interest groups in the public sphere. Although many examples of behavior supporting public choice theory can be found in the literature,[11] examples of governments and public servants not acting out of self-interest (or at least appearing not to) may also be found.[12] This suggests that public decision-makers cannot always be simply assumed to be acting out of self-interest or that what decision-makers perceive as being in their own self-interest may be a much more complicated matrix of factors than simply financial considerations or building or maintaining political power. A sense of public spirit, the law, ethics, culture, moral and social conventions, a desire to embrace good ideas and policy, and ideology are likely to impact on public servants' psyches to a greater or lesser degree, just as they do for everyone else.

Pragmatically, widespread disenchantment with government's performance on the part of those on the left and the right of the political spectrum suggests that public choice problems cannot be ignored when considering the design of a health care allocation system. Balancing the views of both the proponents and critics of public choice, it seems important that there should be, wherever possible, clear financial and political incentives for politicians and public servants to act in the larger public interest.[13] This does not mean that public provision or regulation of markets will be an inferior alternative to an unregulated market (it will depend on the market) or that a sense of public spirit on the part of public servants should not be fostered. Whether or not they will do so naturally, politicians and public servants must pursue the greater public good. Incentives and checks need to be built into the system to ensure that this occurs and to integrate the interests of the general public (the principal) with that of politicians and public servants (the agents). Where discretion is granted, as inevitably it must be, decision-making should be as transparent and open as possible.

How do we operationalize these general observations in a health allocation system? On the purchasing side, what combination of incentives will solve the difficult agency problem of ensuring that purchasers balance society's interests with that of individual patients? Let us begin by looking at the question of to whom and for what the government-appointed purchasers in the UK's and New Zealand's reformed health systems are accountable. Several agency questions arise in these jurisdictions: the question of agency costs between citizens and the government-appointed purchasers, between citizens and the government, and between the government and its own appointed purchasers. A dual agency problem arises in this latter case as, ultimately, the principal in this agency relationship is still the general public, with central government acting on behalf of the public in regulating and monitoring the relevant purchaser's performance.

The lines of accountability

The important areas of responsibility in health care service allocation would seem to be as follows:

- determining the most allocatively efficient level of resources to be devoted to health care services, which requires balancing expenditures on health care services against other needs and recognizing that improved housing, education, nutrition, and increased employment opportunities may have as important an effect on health outcomes as the consumption of health care services;[14]
- satisfying justice in terms of fair access to health care services for everyone but otherwise determining priorities for treatment of health needs on the basis of cost-effectiveness;
- choosing the most cost-effective services or treatments to serve patients' needs;
- ensuring the technically efficient production of services
- ensuring that the quality of services provided is adequate and meets society's expectations;
- ensuring that providers are sensitive to patients' concerns and that a patient's circumstances, values, and attitudes to risk are factored into the decision-making processes at the point of supply.

To an extent these accountability requirements will conflict and thus a balance must be struck between what is in society's interests and a patient's interests and more broadly between equity and efficiency. As discussed below, the lines of accountability drawn in the UK's and New Zealand's reformed systems are too often blurred and there is confusion as to who among central government, purchasers, and providers is ultimately responsible for realization of these goals. Where goals are clearly specified there are often not matching incentives to ensure the realization of those goals.

In the UK and New Zealand systems, central government is responsible for determining how much to tax its citizens and how much to spend on health care services relative to other needs – for example, education and defense. Thus, central government must determine what is allocatively efficient in terms of health care spending and whether or not we would achieve greater satisfaction as a society if fewer or greater resources were devoted to health care. There is no obvious reason to suppose that the government will be able to determine what is an efficient level to spend on health care services although, of course, there is the prospect that resources will be distributed more fairly than in an unregulated private market. Managed competition proposals provide more promise for determining an allocatively efficient level of resources by restructuring and regulating the market for private health insurance and allowing competition between private insurers to determine the total level of resources to be spent on health care. However, in those countries that have proposed or implemented managed competition, priority has been given to containing total costs rather than letting the workings of a managed market determine the most efficient amount in total to spend on health care.[15] President Clinton's (now defunct) proposal for reform did not leave cost control to the workings of a regulated market and instead stipulated that managed competition take place under a global budget.[16] In the Netherlands, despite the partial implementation of managed competition, there has been a marked reluctance to dismantle complex price and capital regulation designed to keep a check on total health care expenditures.[17] This reluctance to dismantle price and total budget caps is because the administrations of these respective countries either do not really believe that managed competition will work or because their overriding concern is to control spending (particularly government spending) even where it would be allocatively efficient to spend more.

Once the central government has determined its annual health budget then in the UK and New Zealand these funds are paid to the various government-appointed purchasers. Upon payment from the central government, the onus is then essentially upon the purchaser to purchase primary and secondary health care services to benefit the people they represent within the budget allocated to them.[18] In contracting for health care services, these government-appointed purchasers are expected to fulfil a complex matrix of responsibilities within a fixed budget. How do we ensure that purchasers perform their functions efficiently and exercise their discretion in the interests of the people they represent?

In the UK, the Audit Commission is required to audit the activities of Health Authorities.[19] The Health Care Act 1999 provides for the oversight of activities by Health Authorities, Primary Care Trusts, and NHS Trusts by a Commission for Health Improvement who may work in conjunction with the Audit Commission. Longley notes, however, that there are no constitutional mechanisms for ensuring that the deliberations of the Audit Commission and similar bodies are taken into account and acted upon by government.[20] In New Zealand, the Audit Office audits annually the Health Authority who must comply with the requirements of the Public Finance Act.[21] These sorts of measures ensure a degree of accountability by reducing opportunities for fraudulent use of public moneys, but further incentives are required to ensure that purchasers are accountable in the fullest sense to the people that they represent.

An initial step towards improving accountability is to clearly specify the goals and objectives of purchasers, both in governing legislation and in transparent management contracts. This should facilitate monitoring by the central government of purchasers' performance relative to those objectives. Moreover, if purchasers' objectives are clearly and publicly articulated then it is difficult for the purchasers and for the central government (as their political masters) to recant from the goals underlying these responsibilities in pursuit of their own self-interest due to the potential for adverse publicity. The difficult question is what objectives and responsibilities should be specified and what weight should be accorded to each.

Prior to the New Labour reforms of 1997, the UK Health Authorities were required to implement directions received from the Secretary of State with respect to the exercise of their functions under the National Health Service and Community Care Act and with respect to the application of government moneys.[22] Apart from directions with respect to special hospitals and the establishment of Community Health Councils (which must be incorporated in regulations), there did not appear to be a legislative requirement that these directions be publicized.[23] A "Code of Accountability" was intended to serve as an informal contract between the central government and the Health Authorities, but the Code does not create any statutory duties.[24] With the 1997 New Labour reforms, Primary Care Groups (PCGs), will be directly accountable to the Health Authority for all aspects of their performance, including financial matters. New Zealand's Health Authority's statutory objectives are couched in general terms, but it is specifically required to meet the Crown's objectives as notified to it.[25] Every such notification is published in the Gazette and tabled in the House of Representatives.[26]

Both in New Zealand and the UK the central government publishes annual guidelines setting out the purchasers' objectives in general terms. The UK government issues in June of each year a policy document informing the Health Authorities of their purchasing intentions for the following year. For the 1997/98 year there are three sets of objectives: long-term objectives and policies; medium-term priorities and objectives for the 1997/98 year; and baseline requirements and objectives for 1997/98 year.[27] In the longer term, performance will be assessed under three headings: equity, efficiency, and responsiveness.[28] Under the 1997 New Labour reforms, Health Authorities are to be responsible for drawing up three-year Health Improvement Programmes, which are to be the framework within which all purchasers and providers operate. It is unclear to what extent guidelines will still flow from the central government to the Health Authorities themselves. Section 17 of the Health Act 1999 (UK) (1999) c. 8 accords wide powers to the Secretary of State to give directions to Health Authorities, Primary Care Trusts, and NHS Trusts. In New Zealand, every year the Health Authority enters into an "Annual Funding Agreement" with the Ministry of Health that requires the Authority to seek to achieve the Crown's Statement of Objectives (issued pursuant to s. 8(1) of the Health and Disability Services Act 1993). For example, the Crown's Statement of Objective for 1998/99 specified targets with regard to improvements in Maori health, mental health and children's health and for the implementation of community health initiatives and a booking system for waiting lists. For each of the Crown's objectives, there are performance measures designed to demonstrate performance consistent with the objectives. In the 1996/97 policy document government set out six principles to provide a framework for purchasing decisions: equity, effectiveness, efficiency, safety, acceptability, and risk management.[29] Somewhat more detailed objectives were specified within those general principles.[30] For example, in terms of acceptability, purchasers (at this time four Regional Health Authorities) were required to improve people's choice and satisfaction and preserve personal dignity and privacy, involve, inform, and consult people and communities, and improve the responsiveness of services to people's diverse needs, preferences and cultural values.[31]

It is not, however, sufficient to simply fix goals and objectives – the obtainment thereof must be monitored. It is significantly easier to focus on objectives that are easy to measure, such as increased turnover or reduced waiting lists, rather than more abstract or broader measures of performance such as people's satisfaction with the health care system or maintaining and improving the quality of services delivered. Undoubtedly a balance must be struck between the benefits of monitoring and the transactions costs associated with monitoring.[32] However, it is important that in monitoring performance central government should give weight to a broad range of performance indices and not simply focus its efforts on those that are the easiest to measure. Prior to the 1997 New Labour proposals, monitoring efforts in the UK's internal market concentrated on a small set of dimensions of output: annual growth in activity, waiting times, and targets for improvements in the health of certain groups of the population.[33] Thus, Health Authorities focused their efforts on those aspects of performance being monitored and not others. The 1997 New Labour proposals promise to broaden performance measures to "things which count for patients, including the costs and results of treatment and care."[34] We will have to wait to see how the new reforms unfold to see exactly how comprehensive the new performance indicators will be, but this is certainly a step in the right direction. The New Zealand government attempted to develop performance indicators to gauge how well Regional Health Authorities met their objectives.[35] By 1995, the monitoring unit of central government was still only able to describe current utilization patterns and there had been no comprehensive evaluation or attempted comparison of purchasers' performances.[36] With the centralization of the purchasing authorities into one Health Authority rather than four, the potential for comparison indicators has been lost. The New Zealand system has worked toward having transparency in performance monitoring. Every year, the Health Authority is required to table a report three months before the end of the year detailing its performance in relation to goals and objectives earlier agreed upon with the government. Subsequently, the government issues a report at the end of the year on the Health Authority's performance.[37]

In addition to setting goals and monitoring the attainment thereof, it is also important to ensure that there are incentives built into management contracts. Allen concluded that the structure of the UK internal market provided no penalties for purchasers that arranged "bad" contracts for supply, yet such arrangements denied patients care in the same way as the alleged inefficiencies of the old command-and-control system.[38] Nothing is likely to change under the New Labour reforms, as there are few if any ramifications for Primary Care Groups that do not perform well. The White Paper outlining the New Labour reforms states "[I]n the rare event that a Primary Care Group got into serious difficulty the Health Authority would have the power to withdraw some or all of the devolved responsibility or require a change in its leadership and management."[39] The mere threat of a loss of power is an incredibly crude incentive by which to seek to ensure performance on the part of Primary Care Groups. In New Zealand, although financial incentives are reportedly included in contracts for managers of the Crown Health Enterprises (government-owned corporations that run the public hospitals), there are no incentives built into contracts for managers of the Health Authority, apart from the prospect of dismissal. The lack of attention to the incentives that influence purchasers is contradictory given that the purchaser's role is crucial to internal market theory, which hinges on astute bargaining by purchasers with competing providers for a variety of health care services. There is also a question of the amount of resources devoted to the purchasing authorities. Due to insufficient investment (in terms of human and capital resources), one manager suggested that the best that can be hoped for on the part of New Zealand Regional Health Authorities was that they would act as a form of passive insurer.[40] This statement is particularly illuminating given that it was intended the Authorities would be anything but passive payers. There is also a question of the skill level of the people who comprise purchasing authorities. Decision-makers need the incentives, skills and the resources necessary to make decisions over time that strike the right balance between patients' needs and societal interest, and between equity and efficiency.

Unlike private firm managers, managers within a government-appointed purchaser do not bear the risk of job loss associated with insolvency or takeover of a private firm. The central government could, however, negotiate management contracts that tie salaries of managers to a comprehensive range of performance measures. A further possibility might be for government to request tenders for management contracts. The greatest difficulty with all measures designed to enhance management's performance lies in objectively measuring and comparing performance with respect to purchasing activities. Smith notes, in reality any system of ensuring performance in health care delivery will be incomplete and imprecise and may encourage providers to "concentrate on the quantifiable at the expense of the unquantifiable."[41] As discussed above, the tendency is for the central government (and thus purchasers and providers) to focus on those aspects of performance that are easiest to measure. One conceivable means around this problem is to tag graduated bonus payments for each and every element of performance with management being paid more or less depending on how they are perceived as having performed by a monitoring unit within the central government. This should help encourage purchasers to compete on those aspects of performance that are more abstract as well as those that are easy to measure.

Despite well-crafted incentives, the central government's propensity to monitor an agency's performance will be limited as it is itself an agent at this level for the general public, and public choice problems arise. Thus, it is important to consider what incentive purchasers have to be directly accountable to the people of the region they represent. Two broad types of incentives, "voice" (political accountability) and "exit" (market accountability), are described further below. Another broad type of incentive is professional accountability. Professional accountability is addressed in more depth in Chapter 7. It is sufficient to note here that professional accountability occurs where a self-regulating profession monitors and regulates the behavior and standards of practice of its members to ensure the quality of care delivered. Professional accountability may, arguably, have protected patients from the worst effects of severe and quickly implemented cost-cutting initiatives in many jurisdictions. The invisible web of collegiality may be what in fact holds many health care systems together. Tuohy notes, for example, that collegial and hierarchical networks of providers continue to be the real directors of the UK health care system despite the imposition of an internal market.[42] Professional accountability is undoubtedly an important mechanism and, historically, has been relied on as a key means by which to ensure the quality and effectiveness of care delivered. On the other hand, professional bodies and collegiality within and between health professions may also serve to protect vested interests and maintain the status quo in terms of the range and quality of health care services supplied, even where it is neither efficient nor fair.[43] Clearly, professional accountability is being increasingly questioned in terms of its effectiveness as a regulatory tool, and other measures to ensure accountability demand consideration.

Hirschman's voice and exit

Albert Hirschman in his celebrated book, *Exit, Voice and Loyalty*, describes how market and political forces can act in tandem as efficiency-enhancing mechanisms in both the public and private sectors.[44] The first concept he describes is that of "exit," which is a means of ensuring the accountability of decision-makers through a competitive market. When a dissatisfied customer shifts custom from one firm to another (exits), she improves her own personal welfare. If a sufficient number of other dissatisfied customers exit, then this action in aggregate sends a clear signal to the firm from which customers are exiting that it must remedy inefficiencies or improve quality or, at the limit, become insolvent. Exit requires no direct communication between the dissatisfied customer and the firm and may thus be a relatively cheap means for an individual to improve her/his own welfare and, indirectly, overall welfare. Exit cannot work, however, as a mechanism in monopoly markets (apart from consumers electing to abstain from consuming the product or service altogether) and may work less well in oligopolistic markets where there is the risk of producer collusion.[45] The success of exit as a mechanism also depends upon the assumption that consumers have all the information they need to make efficient choices.

The second concept that Hirschman describes is that of "voice," which is generally associated with ensuring accountability through political processes.[46] Voice is any attempt to change a firm or organization from within rather than trying to avoid the problem by exit. By comparison with exit, voice is "messy," costly, and its effectiveness is dependent upon "the influence and bargaining power that customers and members can bring to bear within the firm from which they buy or the organizations to which they belong."[47] Unfortunately, those individuals who are most concerned about the quality of an organization's performance and would be most likely to have the political influence necessary to achieve improvement are prima facie also those most likely to exit to another organization when quality declines.[48]

It is important to underscore Hirschman's view that there is no prescription for the combination of exit and voice that will be the most efficiency enhancing. Moreover, over time, as markets and institutions evolve and circumstance change, the appropriate levels of exit and voice will also change.[49] Hirschman also notes that if exit is too easy an option then a crucial number of customers may depart before the firm has had an opportunity to correct its performance. This may result in the insolvency of the firm and, in some instances, welfare losses.[50] Thus, in some firms and organizations, it is important to foster "loyalty" so that individuals will use voice and lobby for improvement and give the organization or firm time to make any necessary adjustments before resorting to exit.

As I will discuss, in internal market systems like New Zealand and the UK, citizens have no choice as to who acts as their purchaser of publicly-funded health care services and thus they rely upon voice to ensure the performance of government-appointed purchasers. The mechanism of voice is, however, diluted by the fact that in both New Zealand and the UK there are supplementary private health insurance schemes covering services that are also provided by the public system.[51] There is some opportunity for exit to work as an efficiency-enhancing mechanism in the context of the UK's GP Fundholders and New Zealand's Budget-holders as, in theory at least, citizens should be able to shift from purchaser to purchaser taking with them a risk-adjusted share of public funding. In managed competition proposals and reforms in the US and Netherlands, exit (in theory) is the primary means by which to ensure the performance of insurer/purchasers offering managed care plans.

Voice and political accountability

How may voice work to improve the accountability of government-appointed purchasers in the UK and New Zealand? Here I will examine five mechanisms to improve voice: devolution, election, consultation, charters of rights, health service commissioners, and capture of the politically influential.

Devolution

The first question to consider is what opportunities do citizens have to influence their purchaser's decision-making processes. As at 1 July 1997, there were four Regional Health Authorities in New Zealand, each responsible for populations of between approximately 680,000 and a million people. On 1 July 1997, the four Authorities were merged into one Central Health Authority, albeit with four branches, responsible for the whole population of 3.78 million.[52] As at 1 April 1996, there were 100 Health Authorities in the UK responsible for varying populations ranging from roughly 125,000 up to just over a million, the operations of which are overseen by eight branches or outposts of the NHS Executive (an agency within the Department of Health).[53] In addition, there were 3,500 GP Fundholders (representing about 50 percent of all general practitioners) responsible for purchasing a limited range of health care services including drugs, diagnostic tests, and elective surgery. The New Labour proposals provide for the abolition of GP Fundholders and for their responsibilities to be taken over by approximately 500 Primary Care Groups. It also provides for the gradual transfer of purchasing responsibility away from the Health Authorities to the Primary Care Groups. These Groups will be responsible for an average of 500,000 people.

The large size of New Zealand's Health Authority and the UK's new Health Authorities is conducive to rationalizing and coordinating the purchase of health care services; however, this benefit must be weighed against the difficulty people may experience in having their voice heard by a large and distant administrative body. Conceivably, responsibility for purchasing services could be further devolved in order to improve opportunities for the use of voice. The difficulty is that devolution will result in additional transactions costs. As discussed further below, this was viewed as a particular problem in the UK with the development of 3,500 GP Fundholders, all acting as purchasers. Devolution may also result in a reduction of monopsony purchasing power.[54] The degree to which diminution of market power on the demand side will be a problem will depend on the structure of the supply side of the health care service market in question. This is likely to be a particular problem in areas that are not densely populated. In these areas the prospects for competition for the market itself (where the sole supplier in the market operates efficiently as a new entrant could easily set up in competition if the supplier did not), seems remote. Nothing would seem to be lost from the further centralization of purchasing power if the large size of purchasers renders voice ineffective as an accountability-enhancing mechanism, yet further devolution is unacceptable because of increased transactions costs and diminution of monopsony power.

The agency problem is complicated by the devolution of purchasing responsibility from the central government to various regional agencies and/or to Fundholders. The public's attention is fragmented between the central government, purchasers, and public and private providers. It thus may be difficult to know to whom complaints and concerns should be addressed and voice is rendered less effective as a mechanism for improving the quality of decision-making. This fragmentation problem is potentially very serious as important areas of responsibility could be avoided successfully by all parties. Thus, somewhat counter-intuitively, voice as a mechanism for enhancing accountability may be aided by the centralization of responsibility for purchasing health care services. Possibly it was hoped that delegating responsibility for health allocation decisions to government-appointed purchasers in the UK and New Zealand would dilute the political ramifications for central government of hard decisions.[55] If this was in fact a goal, it has not been realized, for a clear result of the reform process in both countries has been the continued politicization of health allocation issues at the central government level.[56] This politicization of the health care system is reinforced by the central government's inability to refrain from interfering with the operation of both purchasers and providers in both New Zealand and the UK.[57]

As mentioned above, prior to 1 April 1999 there were 3,500 Fundholders in the UK. Fundholding is a form of managed care and Fundholders receive a capitated budget with which to buy drugs and approximately 20 percent of hospital and community services. Similarly, in New Zealand, there has been a recent rapid growth in the number of Budget-holders. General practitioners are given budgets with which to purchase drugs, lab tests, and elective surgery. Seventy-one percent of general practitioners were involved in some form of Budget-holding at the end of June 1997.[58] However, as Budget-holders do not yet bear any financial risk if they exceed their nominal budgets one cannot describe this as a managed care initiative. Paying by means of capitation and transferring financial risk to health care providers is essentially a way of devolving purchasing responsibility to a local level. Fundholding/Budget-holding can be viewed as separate from the purchaser/provider split that characterizes the balance of the internal market reforms. Fundholders/Budget-holders are both purchasers *and* providers and can substitute, subject to licensing and other regulations, their own services for services they may otherwise purchase from other health providers. By comparison Health Authorities must contract out for the supply of *all* services.

Given a fixed capitated budget with which to buy services on behalf of patients, the physicians who comprise a Fundholder have a prima facie incentive to purchase the most cost-effective mix of services on the part of their patients. One of the positive features of GP Fundholding, as with other forms of managed care, is that it may provide an incentive to provide primary and preventive care so as to keep the Fundholders' enrollees healthy and thus in less need of more expensive acute and institutional services.[59] The attraction of the Fundholding concept is, in theory, that a patient has a close relationship with his or her physician and thus a physician, acting as a purchaser, is more likely to be responsive to a patients' expressed preferences (voice) within the limitations of the physician's budget. Of course, the larger the number of physicians making up the Fundholding consortium the greater the likelihood that any individual physician will be distanced from management decisions. In theory, if a Fundholder is unresponsive to voice then a patient may exit to another Fundholder or exit to a non-Fundholding general practitioner (in which case the relevant Health Authority would purchase all services). In both cases there would be a consequent loss of income for the Fundholder.

The critical question is whether the benefits of Fundholding outweigh the costs. In particular, do improvements in the quality of services from a patient's perspective (shortened waiting times, improved facilities, greater choice) and from a societal perspective (better health outcomes, faster recovery and return to work) outweigh the additional administrative and transactional costs of having so many small purchasers? Unfortunately it is very difficult to quantify in monetary terms the value of improvements in service quality in a publicly financed system. Initially it did appear that Fundholders were achieving improvements in both the quality and range of services purchased for patients. This result may have been, however, only a function of the character of those who initially elected to become Fundholders at the commencement of the reforms. Indeed, increasingly, as the number of Fundholders grew, the reports on Fundholders' performances became far more mixed.[60]

There was a concern that the rapid growth of Fundholding would diminish the Health Authorities' power to plan and coordinate the delivery of services to a large population.[61] Concerns were also raised regarding a perceived lack of accountability of GP Fundholders.[62] Unlike Health Authorities or NHS Trusts, Fundholders were not subject to an annual audit by the Audit Commission. The Audit Commission's 1996 report criticized the lack of monitoring of Fundholders by Health Authorities.[63]

Conceivably, concerns about Fundholders' accountability might have been addressed by the prospect of exit by patients (with a share of public funding) to other Fundholders and to Health Authorities. It seems that it was not part of the UK patient culture for patients to shop around between family doctors. There was no evidence that patients were moving between Fundholders or from non-Fundholding physicians to Fundholders for reasons other than changing address.[64] However, it is not necessary that a great deal of movement between purchasers be apparent for exit to be working as a performance-enhancing mechanism. The mere prospect of exit may be sufficient to inspire performance. The advantages and disadvantages of exit as an accountability-enhancing mechanism are more fully explored in the next section of this chapter. It should be noted that in terms of competition between purchasers, Fundholders had a competitive advantage over Health Authorities for the following reasons:

- Fundholders did not have to compete with respect to a full range of services;
- the budget allocation received by Fundholders was higher than that received by Health Authorities for non-Fundholding patients;
- individuals could only "exit" with their share of public funding to the Health Authority if they could find a general practitioner to enrol with that was not a Fundholder; thus, a bias was created in favor of GP Fundholders as it was impossible for Health Authorities to lure patients back from a Fundholder;
- Health Authorities often had no alternative but to contract with NHS Trusts for the provisions of most services, so that NHS Trusts found it to be to their advantage to offer their best deals for GP Fundholders so as to obtain extra marginal revenue; thus, rather than suffering from the disadvantage of being a small purchaser, Fundholders were able to use this to their advantage.

The New Labour reforms, put forward in December 1997, provide for the elimination of the 3,500 Fundholders. They are now replaced by 500 Primary Care Groups who will also, over time, assume the purchasing responsibilities of Health Authorities. From the perspective of enhancing voice, this initiative can be seen as both devolution and recentralization. Purchasing power is to be devolved away from the 100 Health Authorities to the 500 Primary Care Groups on the assumption that the family doctors and community nurses comprising these groups "know what patients need." On the other hand, purchasing power is being centralized with the dissolution of the 3,500 Fundholders (representing 15,000 family doctors and purchasing on behalf of 50 percent of the population).

The White Paper setting out the New Labour reforms blamed "spiralling" transactions, management, and administrative costs upon the existence of 3,500 Fundholders in the internal market and upon the culture of competition.[65] Tony Blair's government wishes to "end bureaucracy" and reduce administrative, transactions, and management costs. It hopes to achieve this by eliminating Fundholders and replacing them with 500 Primary Care Groups. The 100 Health Authorities will, however, stay in place and are responsible for shaping health outcome targets for their respective regions and for monitoring the performance of Primary Care Groups. Thus, the number of purchasers in the system will be reduced from 3,600 to 600, and possibly fewer, if some Health Authorities can be consolidated as is hoped. The New Labour reforms wished to harness the best aspects of Fundholding, as it was acknowledged that Fundholders were able to secure responsiveness on the part of the NHS Trusts. However, they also wished to discard the worst aspects of it, namely differences in access to services depending on whether an individual was enrolled with a Fundholder or not and high transactions costs. The New Labour reforms seem to gloss over the key question of whether the Primary Care Groups, given their size and their lack of financial incentive to make efficiency gains, can or will be as innovative and responsive to local concerns as the GP Fund-holders were.

As discussed in Chapter 2, many health care allocation decisions center around the values a society has with respect to satisfying health care needs and that is why it is critically important to have public input into articulation of these values. The New Labour reforms largely usurp public consultation in favor of letting doctors and nurses determine these values on behalf of patients and society. The government makes the assumption that family doctors and community nurses will instinctively work together in the best interests of patients and society as a whole and will make good purchasing decisions. There is no evidence at all to suggest this is likely to be the case. The GP Fundholders had incentives to make efficiency gains as surpluses could be ploughed back into their practices. There was also the threat of "exit," for if a Fundholder did not perform an individual could shift their capitated share of public funding to another purchaser. The New Labour reforms do not provide any direct financial incentives for family doctors and nurses making up the Primary Care Groups to improve their performance or to be responsive to the people they represent. It has also eliminated the prospect of exit as, short of leaving the region, all individuals will have no choice but to rely upon their local Primary Care Group to purchase health care services on their behalf.

The creation of Primary Care Groups creates significant agency problems and it is impossible to know at this point how the knowledge and views of individual doctors and nurses will be refracted through a large organization like a Primary Care Group. Doctors and nurses, as two separate groups, with two quite separate ideologies about health care, may have very different opinions about health care priorities and what range and quality of health care services should be purchased/supplied to meet health care needs. Moreover, doctors and nurses have a history of having to deal with each other in a hierarchy. Doctors may ride roughshod over nurses' opinions and values or, alternatively, there could be a great deal of acrimony in reconciling competing opinions. Moreover, even within professional groups there will be very different opinions on what is in the best interests of patients and society. This is clear from the wide variations that occur in service delivery across the country that cannot be explained by underlying differences in health care needs.

Election

One means of improving voice as an accountability mechanism would be for the public to elect the members of the purchasing institutions. Voice is enhanced for the members know that if they are not responsive to their constituents they may well be voted out of power at the next election. Locally-elected members may be more responsive to the exercise by voice of people within the communities they represent and the members therefore may be more representative of the communities they serve. In contrast, Longley notes that members of the business community are disproportionately overrepresented on the UK's government-appointed Health Authorities and that in no sense can it be said that the Authorities are representative of the communities they serve.[66] The same criticism can be levied at the new Primary Care Groups, given that the governing bodies will be comprised of family doctors and community nurses.

The reason often offered for eschewing the possibility of citizens electing the boards of their own purchasers is that government-appointed purchasers will be more independent and this will help to reduce public choice costs. In fact, it is far from clear that devolving responsibility to government-appointed purchasers will reduce public choice problems, given that the appointed members rely on the continued support of the government who appointed them to their positions.[67]

The prospect of being voted out of office every few years might provide some incentives for performance, but the problem arises that the elected members may try to vindicate themselves to voters by concentrating on easy-to-measure performance indicators such as turnover and waiting lists. Thus, simply allowing the election of purchasers every few years could arguably prove too crude a means of ensuring the optimal performance of purchasers. The primary problem with reliance on election as a means of ensuring accountability is that many citizens would have to rely on members for whom they may have not voted and with whose policies they do not agree. Moreover, it is unclear whether the decisions made by an elected body would reflect the preferences of any citizen, or would result in a series of compromises that satisfied no-one. There is also the potential problem that elected boards would be dominated by members of the medical profession, who clearly would have a much greater interest in being so elected than ordinary members of the public. Despite these problems with electing decision-makers, in a democracy this is surely a means of enhancing accountability that must be seriously considered.

Consultation

Imposing a duty on purchasers to consult widely with the people they represent may overcome the problem of a lack of responsiveness on the part of large government-appointed purchasers to the citizens they are meant to represent. In the UK, regulations require Health Authorities to consult with "Community Health Councils"[68] on any proposal that the Authority has under consideration for any "substantial development" or "substantial variation" in the provision of health care services in a particular area.[69] At least half of Community Health Council members have had to be appointed by local government and each relevant local government has one representative thereon. Purchaser or provider interests are not permitted to be represented on the Councils;[70] however, each Health Authority has to make arrangements to obtain advice from "medical practitioners, registered nurses and registered midwives" and "other persons with professional expertise in and experience of health care."[71] The New Labour reforms, proposed in December 1997, although indicating that they wish a strong public voice in health care allocation decisions, in fact rely predominantly upon the expertise of health care professionals to make these value-laden decisions. The New Labour reforms require Health Authorities in conjunction with Primary Care Groups to formulate "Health Improvement Programmes," which are to be "jointly agreed by all who are charged with planning or providing health." There is no mention made of consultation with the public with respect to formulation of these strategic Programmes.

In New Zealand, the Health Authority is required to consult "on a regular basis" with "regard to its intentions relating to the purchase of services" with such of the following as the authority considers appropriate: "(a) Individuals and organizations from the communities served by it who receive or provide health care services or disability services; (b) Other persons including voluntary agencies, private agencies, departments of State, and territorial authorities."[72]

Currently, legislation in New Zealand and in the UK places a similar emphasis on consultation with citizens as it does with health care professionals. The New Labour reforms of December 1997 go a step further and makes doctors and community nurses responsible for purchasing decisions. The policy reason for this is likely the assumption that in a publicly-funded system it is important to obtain the cooperation of health care providers, perhaps so that they will be less resistant to foregoing the financial rewards of an unregulated private sector. However, placing the same weight on consulting providers as on consulting the people that the purchasers are meant to represent may undermine the role of purchasers as agents for those people. Health care professionals obviously have a financial interest in purchasing decisions and purchasers may find themselves "captured" by provider groups. What this means is that, consciously or unconsciously, the purchaser begins to put the interests of provider groups above the more diffused interests of the public and patients that the purchaser is meant to represent. Thus, it may be inappropriate for health care professionals to be ultimately responsible for purchasing decisions or to force purchasers to consult providers. This does not mean that purchasers should not consult health care providers, particularly with regard to information such as the effectiveness or otherwise of particular treatments. In general, however, greater weight must be given to consulting citizens than to consulting health care professionals.

Charters of Rights and Health Service Commissioners

Another means of enhancing voice is to stipulate at a central level what people can expect of their purchasers and increase the amount of information that patients and public receive regarding purchasers' and providers' performances. Establishment of an independent commissioner or ombudsperson also provides a forum for people to voice their concerns.

In the UK, the Patients' Charter sets out the national standards regarding what patients can expect in terms of access and treatment from the publicly-financed system. At the regional level, Health Authorities and NHS Trusts (which manage the public hospitals) are encouraged to negotiate even higher standards and every year Health Authorities publish an annual report on each hospital's performance on Charter standards. The Patients' Charter, introduced on 1 April 1995, expressly states (amongst other things) how long patients should expect to have to wait for various services.[73] The Charter also sets out patients' rights and expectations with respect to general practitioner, community, ambulance, dental, optical, and pharmaceutical services. The New Labour reforms of December 1997 proposed to expand and enrich the Patient's Charter to "tell people about the standards of treatment and care they can expect of the NHS. It will also explain patients' responsibilities."[74] At the time of writing, details of the proposed expansion to the UK Patients' Charter were not available.

The UK's Health Services Commissioner may investigate a complaint from a person who "has sustained injustice or hardship" as a consequence of:

> a failure in a service provided by a health care service body, a failure of such a body to provide a service, which it was a function of the body to provide, or maladministration in connection with any other action taken by or on behalf of such a body.[75]

The scope of the Commissioner's authority was extended in 1996 to allow her or him to hear complaints regarding all aspects of publicly funded health care services and to hear complaints regarding the clinical judgements of doctors, nurses, and other clinical professionals.[76] The list of bodies subject to investigation has also been extended to include private providers. However, the Act continues to expressly provide that the Commissioner is unable to question the merits of a decision taken by a body in the course of exercising any discretion vested in that body except in the case of maladministration.[77] This provision is consistent with case law reflecting a general reluctance on the part of the courts to intervene in the rationing and allocation decisions made by government authorities and providers within the UK's National Health Service.[78]

In New Zealand, a code of rights for health and disability service consumers was brought into force on 1 July 1996.[79] The ten rights provided for in the code are couched in very general terms.[80] Unlike the UK Patients' Charter, there are no specific statements of rights and expectations with respect to waiting lists and waiting times. The code frames rights in the context of the consumers' relationships with health care providers and not in the context of consumers' relationships with purchasers. Moreover, the Act states that providers will not be found in breach of the code if they have taken "reasonable actions in the circumstances to give effect to the rights, and comply with the duties" in the code. The onus is on the provider to prove that in fact its actions were reasonable.[81] Consumers have recourse to a Health and Disability Services Commissioner in the event of a failure to implement these rights.[82] The powers of the Commissioner are relatively limited.[83] She may, however, refer a matter to the Director of Proceedings who in turn may institute disciplinary proceedings before the Complaints Review Tribunal who has power to award damages, make declarations and order and grant such other relief to the complainant as the Tribunal thinks fit.[84]

The use of charters and codes of rights is one way of providing information to patients.[85] However, entitlements in both the UK and New Zealand are framed in the context of the patient/provider relationship rather than the citizen/purchaser relationship. Without discounting the need for the former, there is also a need for formal codification of minimum entitlements and rights of a citizen vis-à-vis his or her purchaser. Presently, in both the UK and New Zealand, a Health Services Commissioner does not have jurisdiction to critique the performance of purchasers like the Health Authorities.

Capturing the voice of the politically influential

In both the UK and New Zealand, citizens may purchase private insurance to cover the cost of private services and user charges imposed in the public sector. The existence of private insurance covering services that are meant to be available to all in the publicly funded system may dilute the use of voice on the part of those holding private insurance who, as a consequence, have less of a vested interest in the public system.[86]

As discussed in Chapter 3, one of the strongest criticisms made of the UK and New Zealand's former command-and-control health systems was the growth of waiting lists and times for non-emergency treatments. Concomitant with the increase in waiting lists for elective surgery in New Zealand has been an increase in the estimated proportion of the population with private insurance, which increased from 18 percent in 1975 to 41 percent in 1994 but has fallen somewhat to 37 percent in 1996/97.[87] The percentage of total health expenditures paid for by private insurance has, unsurprisingly, more than doubled from 2.75 percent in 1990 to 6.18 percent in 1994.[88]

Applying Hirschman's model of voice and exit to the New Zealand system we can see that those individuals who are concerned about quality in terms of increased waiting times are *not* using their influence or their "voice" to press for improvements in the public sector. Instead, if they can afford too, they are exiting to the private sector to get more timely treatment. The effects of this are even more pernicious than might at first be envisaged because of what Hirschman describes as the "lazy monopoly" problem.[89] A lazy monopoly (which in general operates in a market where there is no competition for the market itself) may in fact have an incentive to encourage those that would otherwise be likely to use their voice in criticizing the monopoly to move to another market. This phenomenon sounds like "exit" but in truth it is not because the decision-maker suffers no financial consequences as a result of the movement of the quality-conscious and politically influential to another market. Hirschman's description of a lazy monopoly fits both New Zealand's Regional Health Authorities and the UK Health Authorities (and, for that matter, the new Primary Care Groups). This is because none of these bodies loses any public funding as a result of the shift by disgruntled citizens into the private sector for more timely treatment. Thus, there is more scope for productive inefficiency or slack as the purchasers have fewer demands placed upon their resources once quality-conscious individuals have exited to the private sector. There is also the question of distributive justice as those individuals who buy private insurance or private services may not be those who are, clinically, in the greatest need of (or would benefit most from) elective surgery.

As in New Zealand, most private insurance in the UK is used to cover the cost of non-emergency treatment. As discussed in Chapter 2, in contrast with New Zealand's striking failure to reduce waiting lists, the UK seems to have been relatively more successful (at least in the early stages of the reform process) in reducing both waiting lists and waiting times for elective surgery. However, since the change of government in 1997, and with the clear signal that the NHS would be in for yet another round of reforms, waiting times and lists have begun to grow once more.

The impetus to deal with waiting lists and times appears to have originated with the UK government. Through top-down control, the goal of containing waiting lists and times became a primary goal in the priorities set by the central government for purchasers to follow and, consequentially, in agreements between purchasers and providers. Patients are now also clearly informed of what they can expect in terms of waiting times in the Patients' Charter. Clearly, while an undue fixation on waiting lists and times at the expense of other goals may cause its own set of problems, such a focus demonstrates that the system is anchored in reality and not just in rhetoric to satisfying end-users.

Why has the UK system, at least for a time, been more proactive than the New Zealand system in controlling waiting lists? There are two possible reasons. First, there is the possibility that the presence of GP Fundholders in the UK system resulted in more aggressive bargaining for the supply of timely elective surgery. The evidence for this to date is mixed although arguably the mere prospect of competition between GP Fundholders and Health Authorities helped to improve the performance of the system overall. Secondly, unlike New Zealand, the vast majority of people in the UK rely on the public system for the delivery of *all* their services, such that the political ramifications of not dealing with the waiting list problems have become too high. Voice is thus being used by a sufficient number of politically influential people to maintain and improve the quality of the public health system.

There has been empirical work conducted in the UK examining the linkage between length of waiting lists and uptake of private insurance. Besley, Hall and Preston found that there is a positive association between the purchase of private health insurance and length of local NHS waiting lists.[90] They also found that individuals who express dissatisfaction with the NHS are more likely to purchase private insurance and that the privately insured tend to be "better off, better educated, middle-aged and more inclined to support the Conservative party."[91] This provides some evidence for the thesis that those who are most sensitive to quality issues and are most likely to have the political connections with which to exercise voice are more likely to "exit" by buying private insurance. Nonetheless, although the percentage has grown in recent times, in 1993 only 11.3 percent of the UK population had private insurance.[92] This is a relatively small percentage compared to the estimated 40 percent of New Zealand's population with private insurance. In the UK, where nearly 89 percent of the population is totally dependent on the public system to meet all their health care needs, arguably significant political pressure is brought to bear to reduce waiting times. By comparison, in New Zealand only 60 percent of the population is totally dependent upon the public system and thus one would expect less political pressure. It seems highly unlikely, for example, that the UK government would get away with a proposal similar to the present New Zealand government's solution to waiting lists. It plans to abolish the present lists, and introduce a system of booking whereby patients will not be put on a waiting list unless the system can meet their needs within six months.[93] If the patient's needs cannot be met in this timeframe then she/he will simply be referred back to their general practitioner for management of their condition. If successfully implemented, this booking system will artificially deflate waiting lists. I would suggest that if the entire New Zealand population were wholly dependent on the public sector for all their health care needs such an initiative would never be politically feasible.

How could one change the incentives inducing quality-conscious and wealthier individuals to buy private insurance covering services available in the public sector and enhance the use of voice? One method would be to make exit more difficult. The first step is to remove all government subsidies of private insurance and private supply of services that are already provided in the public sector. On this basis, one must question the wisdom of the 1990 UK reform whereby private insurance premiums became a tax-deductible item of expenditure for those aged over 60 (although this was repealed in 1997) and the UK government's announcement in March 1997 that it will subsidize private insurance covering long-term care for the elderly.[94] Taking matters a step further, government could seek to reduce the incentive to obtain private insurance for services that are provided in the public sector by imposing a surcharge on premiums that purport to provide coverage for those classes of services.

A more radical step would be to prohibit private insurance covering those services that are available in the public sector. This is what Canada does, albeit on a province-by-province basis.[95] Exit is made more difficult as only those individuals who can afford to pay directly for the cost of private care are able to exit the public sector. Evidence suggests that as a consequence voice is strongly used as a mechanism to enhance the quality of Canada's health care system and to protect what are perceived as being core values.[96] Certainly, waiting lists are less of a problem in Canada than in the UK and New Zealand. The Fraser Forum estimates the number of Canadians on waiting lists for surgical procedures in 1995 to be 165,472.[97] As I have noted elsewhere, this equates to approximately 0.56 percent of the Canadian population, which is a significantly smaller proportion than the 1.78 percent of the UK population and the 2.62 percent of the New Zealand population on waiting lists.[98] Some might wish to argue for supplementary private insurance on the basis that the US system relies predominantly on private insurance and does not appear to have a problem with waiting lists. This is, however, comparing apples with oranges, as the US does not attempt to achieve a universal insurance system ensuring access on the basis of need as opposed to ability to pay.

Some argue that advocating the reduction of private insurance is untenable, as the existence of a private insurance market covering services provided in the public sector eases pressure on and demand for publicly-funded services and, thus, waiting lists will be reduced. Indeed, on the basis of this assumption governments in predominantly publicly-funded systems often subsidize the purchase of private insurance and private care. However, Davis found that where there is a high percentage of surgical beds in the private sector, the length of waiting lists for public surgical beds proves to be at least twice as long as is likely if no private surgical beds are provided.[99] This is plausible when it is considered that only a portion of the population can or will utilize private care as only a portion of the population have health insurance or can afford to pay for private care themselves. Recent experience in New Zealand indicates that according a significant role to private insurance covering services that should be provided in the public system is *not* associated with a reduction in waiting lists in the public system. Empirical analysis would be required to identify the independent effect of the take-up of private supplementary insurance on the length of waiting lists but it is possible that the former is in fact exacerbating the latter. The fact that in New Zealand and the UK specialists are employed both in the public sector (where they are generally paid on a salary basis) and in the private sector (where they are paid on a fee-for-service basis), may also be a factor contributing to the waiting list problem. This incentive combination may mean that specialists are well served by long waiting lists in the public sector, which will increase demand for their services in the private sector.

Conclusions on voice and political accountability

In this section I have tried to address the various mechanisms through which to enhance voice and thus political accountability to render purchasers in internal markets more accountable to the citizens they ultimately represent. As Hirschman predicted, the use of voice is "messy" and there are no easy or clear-cut solutions. Devolution of purchasing responsibility is one means of improving voice and accountability, but the benefits thereof have to be weighed against the extra transactions costs and, perhaps, diminution in purchasing power associated with increasing the number of purchasers. Consultation is another means of improving accountability but there are difficulties with ensuring that vested interest groups do not "capture" purchasers. There is also a need for incentives to make sure that purchasers give more than lip service to a requirement to consult. Election of members of purchasing boards is, in a democracy, the most obvious way of ensuring accountability. There are problems, however, as more complex measures of performance such as the quality of services supplied may be lost in the political process. Moreover, although the majority of the population may be satisfied with the members of the purchasing board they have elected, there will still be a significant portion of the population who will not be satisfied. Health service commissioners and charters of rights are important mechanisms through which to improve accountability but presently they seem to be geared towards the patient/provider relationship rather than the patient/purchaser relationship. A key means by which to improve voice in a publicly financed system is to capture the quality-conscious and politically influential individuals therein. In New Zealand, the fact that 40 percent of the population hold supplementary private insurance, allowing them to jump long queues for elective surgery in the public sector, diminishes political pressure brought to bear on government-appointed purchasers to remedy the problem.

It is possible that the many different mechanisms for voice could be combined into an internal market system that would ensure the accountability of government-appointed purchasers to the citizens they ultimately represent. What has been seen to date in the UK's and New Zealand's internal markets is a significant level of rhetoric but insufficient attention to the goal of improving the accountability of purchasers except in terms of cost-containment.

Exit and market accountability

In addition to political accountability, purchasers' accountability to the people they ultimately represent may be enhanced through a competitive market for purchasers. If individuals were (to use Hirschman's terminology) entitled to "exit" from purchaser to purchaser taking with them a risk-adjusted share of government funding then, prima facie, there would be unambiguous financial incentives encouraging the performance of purchasers. Distributive justice concerns would be satisfied as the system would be largely progressively financed. This is the premise of managed competition reform proposals.

Offering consumers the choice of competing private purchasers is the mechanism through which both efficiency and accountability are claimed to be enhanced in Enthoven's model of managed competition reform, in the partially-implemented Dutch reforms, and in President Clinton's defunct reform proposals in the US. Limited competition between public and private purchasers is being encouraged in the UK and New Zealand. In the UK, GP Fundholders (in theory) competed with each other and Health Authorities with regard to the purchase of a limited range of services. In New Zealand, there have been some initiatives, similar to the UK Fundholders. Groups of general practitioners formed into groups known as Independent Practice Associations and received budgets for a limited range of health care services. This development has now been formalized by the government which is seeking to encourage the growth of what has become known as Budgetholding. Thus limited competition between purchasers in the UK's and New Zealand's internal markets was incrementally introduced albeit from the "bottom up," as opposed to the "top-down" process envisaged in managed competition models.

The concept of exit as an accountability and efficiency-enhancing mechanism is very appealing because of its apparent simplicity, particularly when compared with the messy and varied mechanisms needed to improve voice. Its elegance is that of the spontaneous order of competitive markets envisaged by neo-classical economists. However, in managed competition proposals distribution inequities have been corrected by every individual receiving a fair share of public funding which they may shift between competing purchasers, sending a clear signal to competing purchasers as to their relative performance. The theoretical appeal is obvious but, as will become clear, the goal of redistribution means that government must regulate and manage competition, and consequently issues of political accountability cannot be avoided.

In all proposals for managed competition, the process of competition between purchasers is managed or regulated by what Enthoven terms "sponsors." Enthoven notes that managed competition reform requires "intelligent, active, collective purchasing agents contracting with health care plans on behalf of a large group of subscribers and continuously structuring and adjusting the market to overcome attempts to avoid price competition."[100] In Enthoven's model, a sponsor may be a governmental agency, an employer, or a purchasing cooperative. Clinton's proposals for reform required government-appointed Regional Health Alliances to collectively oversee health coverage for over 80 percent of the population under the age of 65.[101] In the Netherlands, the Central Fund (a government agency) is required to act as a sponsor. In the UK, the Health Authorities were responsible for monitoring Fundholders' activities and similarly will be responsible for overseeing the new Primary Care Groups. Similarly, in New Zealand, it is the Health Authority's responsibility to administer managed care initiatives.

The apparent simplicity of the exit mechanism belies many of the problems that have to be surmounted before it can be effectively operationalized. These problems include:

- the incentive for competing purchasers to "cream-skim" healthy enrollees and avoid enrollees with high health costs or with a high risk of such costs in the future;
- determining the rules for price competition between purchasers;
- the need to define "core" services, i.e. the range and quality of services purchasers will compete to provide (or, from the other side of the coin, the need to define consumer entitlements);
- the question of whether consumers have or will have sufficient information to choose wisely between competing purchasers;
- the problem of transactions costs;
- the problem of supply side monopoly.

These problems are discussed more fully below.

Cream-skimming

When a citizen exits from one insurer/purchaser to another there is a risk that she/he is moving as a result of cream-skimming. This would be inefficient as it would be rewarding insurer/purchasers who compete on the ability to avoid risk as opposed to the ability to compete on price and quality. The technical difficulties, importance, and need for effective resolution of this problem are generally underestimated in managed competition proposals.

In an unregulated private health insurance market, high-risk individuals may be either priced out of, or simply excluded from, the insurance market. For example, Fuchs notes that in the US the competitive revolution in health care has caused Blue Cross and Blue Shield, who have historically fulfilled a de facto social insurance function, to cease community rating and engage in risk rating.[102] As a consequence, a growing number of people are left without health insurance. Similarly, in the Netherlands, prior to managed competition reform, there was increasing concern that risk-rating by private insurers was making insurance unaffordable for elderly and/or unhealthy people and that some high-risk groups were being denied coverage altogether.[103]

Managed competition reform proposals seek to satisfy justice and equity concerns by providing for mandatory universal coverage for a comprehensive range of health care services. A sponsor, perhaps a government agency, collects premiums on an income-related basis. In other words, the system is financed according to ability to pay as opposed to need. Citizens' contributions do not depend upon their health cost and/or risk profile. The sponsor pays, on behalf of every individual, a fixed annual premium to that individual's chosen purchaser in return for which the purchaser undertakes to cover all of that individual's health care needs for a comprehensive range of services (as defined by regulation) in that year. This is in effect a sophisticated voucher scheme. However, if competing purchasers receive the same premium for each insured individual then they have an incentive to cream-skim. In other words, they have a financial incentive to spend time and resources trying to attract low-risk people to enroll with them and to dissuade people with high health costs and/or a high risk of incurring such costs in the future.[104]

In order to minimize cream-skimming, managed competition models require purchasers to accept all who seek to enroll in their plan; however, cream-skimming behavior may be more subtle. One tactic may be to contract with certain types of providers in certain locations and not with others (e.g. electing not to contract with the local facility specializing in oncology services). Another may be to locate the only insurance office on the top floor of a building with no wheelchair access in an affluent white suburb. Such overt tactics will usually (at least eventually) be detectable. Managed competition models require sponsors to oversee and regulate purchaser behavior and require that consumers exercise their right to change purchasers through the agency of their sponsor (i.e. the sponsor acts as an individual's agent in effecting the switch).[105] This arrangement reduces opportunities for purchasers to use subtle cream-skimming tactics. A sponsor must also monitor movement by individuals between purchasers to ensure that such movement is not the result of cream-skimming behavior.[106] Another measure would be to license health purchasers on the condition that they undertake not to engage in cream-skimming behavior with penalties being enforced for violation of this condition. A related idea would be for the government to define cream-skimming tactics as per se in breach of competition law on the basis that allowing firms to cream-skim may result in the demise of other firms that are better able to compete on price and quality. All of the preceding suggestions for curbing cream-skimming are open to the criticism that purchasers will simply invent more sophisticated and undetectable methods of cream-skimming. Thus, sponsors must be continually monitoring competition and putting in place new measures to reduce cream-skimming incentives.

Aside from regulations and sanctions, a potentially less intrusive means of reducing cream-skimming is to correct the financial incentives which encourages it. This requires the sponsor to risk-adjust the premiums paid so that competing purchasers are compensated for the risk they bear as a result of the risk profiles of the people that have chosen to enroll in their particular plan. An adjustment in this regard must be effected in any event to ensure the continued viability of those purchasers who have attracted a disproportionate share of enrollees with high health care costs. Appropriately risk-adjusting premiums is essential to ensure fair competition. If this is not done then those purchasers that are adept at cream-skimming may receive greater income than competitors who perform better on price and quality dimensions. The premiums must be adjusted so that each purchaser receives a premium per enrollee that reflects their *perceptions* of the particular individual enrollee's risk of utilization of health care services. It is purchasers' perceptions of risk that is important as opposed to what the risk in truth may be for this is, given the current state of knowledge, unascertainable.

In the Netherlands, managed competition reform requires the Central Fund to collect income-related sums and from this pay 85–90 percent of a risk-adjusted premium on behalf of each and every individual to that individual's chosen purchaser/insurer. The difficulty is that, to date, the Central Fund has not appropriately risk adjusted the premiums paid. In 1993 and 1994 premium payments were differentiated on the basis of age and gender alone and did not include risk factors that could be readily ascertained by competing purchasers, such as an individual's chronic health status or medical history.[107] Van de Vliet and van de Ven found that if age and gender are the only factors used for risk adjustment then there is a strong financial incentive to cream-skim.[108] They note that it is easy for purchasers to identify those individuals with the greatest non-catastrophic health care expenditures in any year. Ten percent of these individuals can be predicted to have per capita expenditures four years later that are on average nearly double the per capita expenditures within their age-gender group.[109] The inequity of inadequately risk-adjusted premiums has been acknowledged in the Netherlands. As a consequence, in 1993 and 1994, the government only required the Sickness Funds to be financially responsible for just 3 percent of the difference between their actual expenditures on health care services for their enrollees and the total premiums received from the Central Fund.[110] However, as the factors used to calculate risk were extended to region, disability status, employment and social security status this percentage was subsequently increased to 14 percent in 1996, 27 percent in 1997, 29 percent in 1998 and 35 percent in 1999.[111]

Van de Ven and Schut contend that three misunderstandings lie at the root of why the Netherlands initially failed to implement a system of adequately risk-adjusted payments.[112] The first misunderstanding is the assumption that age, gender, and region will explain a large proportion of the variance in health expenditures whereas, in reality, these factors only explain 10–20 percent of the predictable variance in health expenditures for any individual.[113] Similarly, in the US, it has been estimated that 5 percent of all the aged entitled to the government's Medicare program account for over 50 percent of the total costs of the program and 36 percent of those covered do not make any claims.[114] Thus, clearly, age is but one factor in ascertaining who are high-risk individuals. Adjustments for age, sex, and location may more satisfactorily explain variations between very large groups, but risk-adjustment must occur at the individual level for the purposes of managed competition reform as it is through the individual's decision to exit that competing purchasers are held to account.

The second misunderstanding noted by van de Ven and Schut is the assumption that the incentive to cream-skim would be minimized because of the ability to reinsure risks. This assumption is flawed as reinsurance companies will themselves generally charge risk-adjusted premiums to purchasers, thus leaving in place the original incentive to cream-skim.[115] The third misunderstanding is the assumption that if perfectly risk-adjusted premiums were paid then purchasers would have no incentive to operate as efficiently as possible.[116] Van de Ven and Schut believe that this argument is also flawed for two reasons. First, given the current knowledge base, it is only possible for purchasers to predict *partially* the risk of any individual's future needs. The cream-skimming incentive only arises where there is a *discrepancy* between what risk factors are considered by purchasers and what risk factors are incorporated into premiums paid by sponsors. If all known risk factors were incorporated into premium payments then purchasers would still have to manage the unpredictable risk of utilization, the latter being much more significant than the former in determining future patterns of use. Van de Ven and Schut also argue that adequately risk-adjusted premiums will not act as a disincentive for efficiency as any savings are captured by purchasers (at least in the private sector) as profit. This latter argument is more tenuous as, given risk-adjusted premiums, private purchasers have an incentive to compete to improve the quality of services provided so as to attract enrollees but no incentive to compete on the level of premiums as the price is effectively determined by the sponsor. This issue is discussed further below under the problem of facilitating price competition.

Another type of financial incentive that may deter cream-skimming is the use of "risk corridors" where the risk of high utilization is shared between the sponsor and purchasers. This was the situation for the UK's GP Fundholders. They bore financial liability for up to £6,000 per annum for any patient. The Health Authority paid for any costs incurred beyond this sum.[117] Such a measure capped the Fundholders' financial liability, thus diminishing (but not eliminating) the incentive to cream-skim, but also removed any incentive Fundholders had to be sensitive to the cost of the services they purchased past the figure of £6,000. There was, in fact, no evidence that cream-skimming was a serious problem in Fundholding practices; however, the Audit Commission did find an inverse relationship between the proportion of Fundholding practices in an area and the average degree of social deprivation to be highly significant statistically.[118] In other words, Fundholding was more likely to be established in areas where on average their patients were likely to be healthy. Even if cream-skimming was not a problem in the UK it is difficult to know whether this is due to the use of risk corridors. The lack of cream-skimming behavior could also be attributed to the ethical norms of physicians deterring them from cream-skimming, or to the fact that there was little real financial pressure upon Fundholders.

Undoubtedly, cream-skimming is a potentially serious problem. However, it must be remembered that such behavior on the part of purchasers sends a signal not only to those individuals whose risk has crystallized but also to other individuals that this particular purchaser is untrustworthy at the time that it is needed the most. Thus, the need to maintain a good reputation in the market-place will inhibit cream-skimming behavior. One can envisage that the need to maintain a good reputation will be more salient for those health care services and patients that most people can identify with. Thus, cutting the quality of health care services for the elderly or for patients with heart disease or cancer is likely to provoke concern on the part of most people, who can imagine they or their family needing such services. Services for small vulnerable populations or stigmatized health care services may be more at risk in a managed competition system. This is because people may hide their heads in the sand believing that their own risk, for example, of psychiatric disease or of giving birth to a disabled child, is much lower than it really is. Or it may simply be because the health care need only truly does arise in a small segment of the population. A sponsor will need to emphasize in published data how well purchasers treat the most vulnerable groups. Such reporting may foster a sense of solidarity between the general populace and vulnerable groups within it. In such a case, low-risk individuals may signal their dissatisfaction with how a purchaser treats vulnerable groups by the use of either exit or voice. There still will be, however, a need for a sponsor to be particularly vigilant with regard to the quality of services supplied to small vulnerable groups as one cannot rely upon "exit" to protect their quality.

Reform advocates must recognize that adequately dealing with the issue of cream-skimming is the key to managed competition reform and absolutely necessary in terms of protecting vulnerable populations. The role of sponsors is crucial in this regard. Will government-appointed sponsors be up to the task and how will they be kept accountable? Will they have the information needed to calculate risk-adjusted payments? In the former command-and-control health systems of the UK and New Zealand, relatively little accessible data was on service usage. In these countries, the initial costs of setting up information-gathering systems may be significantly higher and the transition more disruptive than in countries like the Netherlands and the US which have historically relied to a greater degree on private insurers and private providers.

Price competition

If the sponsor determines the payment or premium to be received by competing purchasers, then will there be any scope for price competition? The Netherlands' reform proposal attempts to stimulate price competition by requiring that a fixed percentage of the premium (currently 10 percent) be paid by each enrollee directly to his or her chosen purchaser.[119] The purchaser may set this fixed annual fee at any level but it must be the same fee for all enrollees (i.e. it cannot be risk rated). Enthoven's proposal for managed competition reform requires that the premium paid by the sponsor be pegged to the premium of the lowest priced purchaser, with individuals having to bear the full cost of a decision to select a purchaser with a higher priced plan.[120] By contrast, Clinton's managed competition plan required that the sponsor's contribution be pegged to the average price of all plans for fear that to tie contributions to the lowest-priced plan would result in lower-priced plans being "ghettoized" – in other words, low-quality plans for poor people.

   In order to foster price competition, it appears that one has to sacrifice a total commitment to progressive financing of the system. The greater the percentage of the premium directly paid by any individual to his or her purchaser, the greater the incentive for the purchaser to compete on the basis of price. However, as a result, the financing of the health system becomes more regressive as the poor will have to divert a greater percentage of their income than the rich to paying a fixed fee. The purchaser will, in this case, have a greater incentive to cream-skim as this fixed payment will not be risk-rated – it would be the same fee for all enrollees. Allowing a margin for price competition brings with it the risk of increasing the potential for cream-skimming and adversely affecting distributive justice. Thus, the margin allowed for price competition must be restricted to a relatively small component of total costs. This problem has to be put in context and one will recall from Chapter 3 that presently most systems have some proportion of their system privately financed. A comprehensive managed competition system requiring a small premium payment every year on the part of each citizen is arguably as fair if not fairer than a command-and-control system imposing user charges on basic care such as prescription drugs, general practitioner care, ambulance services etc.

Defining core services/defining entitlements

Defining what range and quality of health care services will be made available by competing purchasers and what citizens should be able to expect to be entitled to is important to managed competition reform. Ideally, citizens should be free to move between purchasers in search of the best premium price and/ or quality of services knowing that an adequate range and minimum quality will always be provided.[121] There have been various attempts in the Netherlands, New Zealand, and in the state of Oregon, US, to define the range of "core" services to be available in the public system. Acknowledging that resources are limited, there have been attempts to prioritize services in terms of importance, in order to assist in allocation decisions. This task has proved to be quite elusive in practice.

The original Dekker proposals for reform in the Netherlands required the legal definition of a standard package of benefits to be available to all as part of the reformers' goals to improve access and solidarity (equity).[122] It was proposed that insurance contracts would be different forms of the legally defined standard package. Contracts would vary only with respect to the list of providers able to be visited and the conditions that must be fulfilled in order for costs to be covered (such as a referral slip from a general practitioner).[123] In 1991, the Dutch cabinet essentially skirted the hard issues of what should and should not be included in the basic package by deciding that 95 percent of health care services previously provided should be included in the standard package.

In 1992, the Dutch government's Committee on Choice in Health Care produced a report (which subsequently became known as the Dunning report), dealing with rationing health care services.[124] The Committee did not produce a prioritized list of services to be included in the standard package but recommended that all services satisfy four criteria before being included in the standard package. These criteria were described using the metaphor of a funnel with four sieves, with only those services that managed to pass through the four sieves (or tests) to be included.[125] The sieve approach provides guidance on what services should be provided in the public system but applying these principles in practice is an enormously difficult task requiring information on cost-effectiveness and consideration of community values. After producing its report the Dunning Committee was dissolved and no other organization appears to have explicit responsibility for determining what services should and should not be included in the basic package using the sieve principles.

The Oregon Basic Health Services Act, passed in 1989, was designed to extend coverage of the Medicaid package in Oregon to include all those at or below the poverty line, primarily by means of explicitly rationing the services provided.[126] In determining what priorities should be given to different health care services in the standard package, the Oregon Health Service Commission solicited public input through consultation.[127] The priorities accorded to services as a result of this process were the subject of much criticism. In particular, health care providers criticized the process that resulted in the ranking of low-cost services, such as correction of crooked teeth, thumb sucking, lower back pain, toothaches, migraine headaches, and salmonella poisoning, over possible life-saving treatments such as liver and bone marrow transplants.[128] Health providers were particularly concerned that the ranking violated the ethical "rule of rescue" requiring physicians to act in the case of a life-threatening situation. As a result of these criticisms the Commission recompiled the list of priorities using a methodology that largely eliminated cost considerations and diluted the influence of public input. The Commission re-ranked services based on the treatment's perceived value to the individual patient, its value to society, and the medical necessity of the treatment. This reordering resulted in life-saving treatments being accorded a much greater priority.

The Oregon experience highlights a number of important issues. If one assumes physicians were not acting solely out of self-interest in advocating high-cost life-saving procedures, but were driven predominantly by a moral imperative, then this suggests there must be rights to health care services that should trump more utilitarian concerns.[129] Arguably individuals should have certain basic rights such as a right to life and a right to freedom from incapacity, pain, and suffering that should trump more utilitarian cost-benefit consider-ations that might give greater societal priority to fixing crooked teeth. The great difficulty is that all such rights must be limited to some degree otherwise millions of dollars could be spent on potentially life-saving treatments that have only a remote chance of success. The conundrum is how to balance individual needs with what is in society's best interests. The Oregon process is interesting for the degree of community participation that it entailed. However, one must question whether the results would have been the same if the com-munity had actually been determining the priorities for health care services for their own consumption as opposed to those below the poverty line. I suspect that such explicit rationing would not have been tolerated. This re-engages the earlier discussion of voice and political influence. In short, if all citizens are wholly dependent on a system for satisfaction of their health care needs, then there will be the political will to ensure access to a comprehensive range of high-quality services for all citizens.

New Zealand's National Advisory Committee on Health And Disability was initially constituted with the intention of defining a list of prioritized core services to enable better comparison of competing purchasers.[130] Notwithstand-ing that the proposal for managed competition between Regional Health Auth-orities and private purchasers has been put to one side, the Committee has continued with its work. It is contributing to the debate as to what are cost-effective services, what sorts of general health care services should be given priority, and what services should be excluded from the publicly funded sector. The Committee has, however, found it impossible to develop a specific list of priorities in treatment.[131] Significant discretion was thus left in the hands of the Regional Health Authorities which found it easier to revert to the default option of largely maintaining the service patterns that have historically existed in their regions.

In the UK, there is no equivalent body to that which existed in the Netherlands and Oregon and currently operates in New Zealand. However, increasingly there are calls in the UK to develop explicit rationing criteria.[132]

The difficulties that have arisen should not deter continued attempts in all jurisdictions at defining and prioritizing a core package of services to be universally available. The complexity of rationing issues must be dealt with by all types of health care systems whether reformed along competition-lines or not, unless it is proposed, as has historically happened, to leave these kinds of determinations to the value judgements of individual health care providers. These issues must begin to be addressed by communities, as the growth of costly technology coupled with aging populations and increasing expectations will stretch the ability of systems to meet demands for health care services. Some may argue that determining core services is a misguided endeavor that will stymie innovation and result in inflexibility in the system.[133] From this perspective, the approach taken in New Zealand where priorities are set in terms of general health needs (i.e. Maori health, primary care etc.) may be a more fruitful one. However, as all systems move towards managed care systems there would seem to be a need to more specifically define entitlements and standards and it is difficult to see how to avoid this. What is clear is that this process must be an ongoing one with continual adjustment being made at the margins to the services that are to be publicly-funded. Due to the value judgements involved in determining the relative priorities for purchasing services, it is crucial that the public at large be consulted and that the decision-maker in question be receptive to their opinions.

Citizen choice

One must consider the key question of whether citizens can make effective choices between competing purchasers in a managed competition system. The argument is sometimes made by opponents of the concept of managed competition that citizens are not capable of distinguishing between the merits of competing purchasers. Certainly it appears that in the present US system, many Americans do not understand the differences between health plans and thus may not be making effective choices although, reportedly, the vast majority (70 percent) are satisfied with the choices they have made in the past.[134] In any event, the US experience is not necessarily translatable to a managed competition system, where a sponsor would facilitate citizens choosing purchasers. There would still be, of course, potential for purchasers to confuse consumers, with fine print in their policies limiting and restricting access to, and the quality of, services. As the action of individual exit is the primary means of ensuring accountability in managed competition systems it is vital that sponsors vigilantly monitor the policies offered by purchasers to consumers.[135] There should be an insistence on plain language and a requirement that any limitations on coverage be clearly spelt out on the front page of the policy. Consumers should be entitled to expect, in the absence of express limitations, that the coverage they have historically enjoyed will be available to the same degree. Purchasers may offer to provide a greater range of services or better quality services in order to distinguish themselves from competitors, but this may make it difficult for consumers to compare purchasers.[136] To ameliorate this problem, sponsors could require that any additional benefits to the basic package be listed on a separate page of the policy.

The issue of choosing an insurer/purchaser in a managed competition system must be put in context. In internal market systems it is assumed that government agents can be sufficiently astute and have the necessary information to act as the purchasers of care. Surely it can also be assumed then that they are capable of disseminating this information to consumers? Individuals make difficult decisions about when to visit their doctor, which doctor to visit, and which treatment option is preferable. In reality these sorts of choices are arguably more vexatious in terms of a lack of information and making decisions at a difficult time, than choosing a purchaser once a year.

There is a great deal of anecdotal evidence that unacceptable restrictions of choice are occurring in the US as a result of managed care.[137] Again this problem has to be put in context. The US system has been described as a "parody of excess and deprivation"[138] with historically well-insured patients being able to access the system at any point, e.g. through specialists, hospitals, etc. The concern expressed in the US regarding the diminution of choice might in fact be reflective of a gearing down of expectations to accord more with other developed countries rather than imposing any serious threat to the quality of health care supplied. In any event, a managed competition system does not in and of itself dictate the degree of restriction placed on patients' choice of providers. Sponsors could regulate purchasers if it was considered that insurer/purchasers were unacceptably restricting patients' choice of providers.

Sponsors will also have to monitor and disseminate information to consumers on the quality of various plans offered. This is a task fraught with pitfalls as the quality of services offered is a difficult matter to measure given that the relationship between the consumption of health care services and ultimate health outcomes is often ambiguous. Problems arise, for example, in comparing the different mortality rates of hospitals, as high mortality rates may not be a function of the quality of the service provided but indicative of the characteristics of the patients admitted. Without seeking to understate the burden that will be placed on sponsors in managed competition reform, it is important to note that monitoring quality will be a problem in *all* systems reformed along competition-oriented lines. Thus, for example, New Zealand's sole Health Authority must monitor the quality of competing health care providers. Consequently, the difficulties associated with monitoring quality cannot be used as a justification for not developing competition between purchasers if the alternative is for a government-appointed purchaser to stimulate competition between health providers, as in internal market reform. Consideration must be given to providing for the needs of individuals who are physically and mentally handicapped or who are chronically or terminally ill. These individuals may be particularly vulnerable to reductions in the quality of health care services,[139] as it is particularly difficult to measure and monitor performance in terms of providing services that are primarily of a caring rather than a curative nature. This is a critical issue in any system that seeks to foster competition, whether between purchasers (as in managed competition models) or directly between providers (as in internal market models). Quality assurance issues are discussed further in Chapter 7.

Transactions costs and the problem of supply side monopoly

One must consider the transactions costs inherent in offering a choice of competing purchasers. The greater the number of purchasers, the greater the choice for consumers and the greater the competitive vigor (provided that sponsors are able to prevent cream-skimming). However, a large number of purchasers results in the prospect of higher transactions costs and a diminution of purchasing power vis-á-vis health care providers.

In order to be able to manage the risks associated with providing a comprehensive range of health care services, competing purchasers will find it necessary to provide coverage for a relatively large population. Very small groups carry a significantly greater percentage of utilization risk as, generally, a relatively small number of individuals in any particular group account for the lion's share of health expenditures.[140] Also, purchasers will wish to be of a relatively large size to enhance their market power vis-á-vis health providers.[141] For example, in response to the prospects of competition between purchasers there has been an integration of sickness funds and private insurers in the Netherlands. Amongst Sickness Funds, from 1987 to 1991, thirteen mergers took place involving thirty-three Sickness Funds, so that the number of independent Sickness Funds was reduced from forty-six to twenty-six.[142] Industry observers predict that eventually there may only be ten to fifteen national chains of health insurers serving the Dutch population of 15 million.[143] Thus, transactions costs in the Dutch reformed health allocation system may eventually be significantly less than they have historically been. The problem may not prove to be one of having too many purchasers but rather too few, with competition law having to be invoked to ensure that there is real competition between large purchasers in all regions and to prevent the maintenance or creation of cartels.[144] As purchasers transform into more aggressive buyers of health care services, creating a tension on the demand side never felt before, then the response on the supply side may be to consolidate to create matching or greater market power. Consequently, effective anti-trust legislation will be required to maintain workable competition on the supply side.

As with the other problems of managed competition, the issue of transaction costs must be put in perspective. These costs seem unlikely to be greater in a managed competition system that requires competition between purchasers for the supply of *all* publicly-financed services than, for example, the UK internal market system that allowed 3,500 GP Fundholders to act as smaller purchasers in addition to the 100 Health Authorities. There were so many Fundholders because they do not have to purchase the full range of publicly-funded health care services but only a very limited range of relatively low-cost services. The New Labour reforms propose the abolition of the 3,500 Fund-holders and replacement with 500 Primary Care Groups. Together with the 100 Health Authorities this will still result in 600 purchasers in the UK. In 1996 in New Zealand, there were four Regional Health Authorities, one Accident Compensation Corporation purchaser and 61 Independent Practice Associations, which all acted as purchasers of health care services.[145] Since that time, although the Regional Health Authorities have been merged into one Health Authority, nearly 71 percent of general practitioners have shifted to a "budget-holding" scheme where they are responsible for purchasing a limited range of health care services. Consequently, the number of purchasers in New Zealand has increased significantly. Thus, as managed care flourishes in these internal markets (or for that matter in any system) the effective number of purchasers increases and consequently transactions costs will increase. Moreover, the present number of government-appointed purchasers in the UK and New Zealand has been centrally determined and there does not appear to be any particular economic or planning reasons for the present number of purchasers in either jurisdiction. It may well be that economies of scale would dictate that there be fewer competing purchasers in a managed competition system.

Undoubtedly, the problem of monopoly supply is a serious one and an inc-rease in the number of purchasers in a market may exacerbate the problem. The problem and mechanisms with which to address this problem, such as regulation, competition law, public ownership of monopolies, and joint bargain-ing on the part of purchasers with monopolies, are the focus of discussion in Chapter 6. It is sufficient to note for present purposes that the problem of monopoly supply will also be a problem in internal market systems or any other form of system seeking to encourage managed care where purchasing responsibility and financial risk is devolved to integrated groups of health care service providers.

The residual role of voice

The preceding analysis shows that the role of the sponsor is crucial in managed competition models. Sponsors may be government appointed. Where the sponsor is not government appointed but is, as proposed in the Clinton plan, a large employer, the government still has to monitor and ensure that the sponsor is performing its difficult, yet vital, regulatory role. Thus, one can see that the role of government in a managed competition system, while different, is no less crucial than in any other health care allocation systems that seek to ensure access to health care services on the basis of need as opposed to ability to pay.

There is also a residual need for voice or political accountability as a means of enhancing accountability of competing purchasers in a managed system. This is because patients may be trapped with a particular insurer/purchaser, and/or provider affiliated with that insurer/purchaser, that they are dissatisfied with until the next point in time when they can exit. This may have serious implications if patients are demanding a service or quality of service that their particular purchaser is resisting providing. Time may clearly be of the essence in these types of disputes. Thus, charters of rights, access to a Health Commissioner or ombudsperson, and associated remedies remain relevant.[146] These administrative processes are all means by which enrollees are able to exercise their voice to protect the quality of services received.

Conclusion

Where government-appointed purchasers do not face competition, the system relies on political accountability or voice to render purchasers accountable. Significant and complex agency questions arise in this respect. The theory of internal market reform requires purchasers to be accountable to the citizens that they ultimately represent in purchasing services, but in practice this is given little weight in either New Zealand or the UK. At the time the reforms were proposed there was a great deal of rhetoric emphasizing improving consumer choice and enhancing public participation; however, neither the regulatory framework nor the allocation of resources reflects these goals. There is potential for management contracts between government and purchasers to be designed to reward efficient performance; the great difficulty is how to measure performance and to resist focusing only on those performance indicators that are the easiest to measure. The present lack of incentives for purchasers seems to indicate a lack of commitment in both the UK and New Zealand to the purchasing role. However, the purchaser's role is crucial to internal market theory, which hinges on astute bargaining between purchasers and competing public and private providers.

This chapter has canvassed a range of possibilities for strengthening the use of voice on the part of the public as a means to ensure the accountability of both purchasers and government in internal market systems. Arguably, although not straightforward, mechanisms for voice could be sufficiently refined to ensure the accountability and efficiency of purchasers. As Longley notes, an institutional framework is required to ensure that efforts in this regard are more than mere tokens and that the public interest is properly taken into account.[147] Possibilities include further devolution of purchasing power, mandatory consultation, local elections of purchasers, and providing consumers with more information regarding the level of service they can expect and demand as a matter of course. Ultimately, I argue that for voice to operate effectively it is crucial to ensure that those with political influence have a vested interest in the performance of government-appointed purchasers. The growth of private insurance covering some of the services that are also supplied in the public sector reduces the incentives of the politically influential to protect the quality of publicly-financed services. The movement of dissatisfied individuals into the private insurance market looks like "exit" but in reality it is not for there are no financial consequences for the government-appointed purchasers. As a result, voice is diminished as an efficiency-enhancing tool and inequities are increased.

Ensuring accountability through voice seems messy by comparison with the prima facie simplicity of the exit or market mechanism. Managed competition reform is essentially a sophisticated form of voucher scheme. It is appealing in theory as it offers the spontaneous order of competitive markets but with distribution inequities corrected. Individuals dissatisfied with their current purchaser may "exit" to another, taking with them a risk-weighted share of public funding. However, "exit" is not as appealing as it first appears because of the continued need for government intervention to facilitate competition on price and quality dimensions.

A managed competition system seems to have some advantages over an internal market system for the following reasons described below:

- There is no conflict of interest in government regulating and monitoring purchasers as they are not government-appointed.
- Incentives do not need to be designed and included in management contracts in an attempt to induce performance on the part of government-appointed purchasers.
- There are arguably clearer lines of accountability with a direct line of accountability between purchasers and their enrollees and with sponsors and purchasers having more clearly defined roles, the former being largely a regulator and the latter being left to manage the supply of health care services.
- Individual preferences are given expression through the individual action of exit whereas ensuring accountability only through voice satisfies the preferences of the majority or those with political clout.
- Managed competition reform provides scope for the use of both exit and voice as efficiency-enhancing mechanisms on the part of citizens whereas a pure internal market system relies solely on voice. Hirschman notes that the use of voice as an efficiency-enhancing mechanism is diminished if citizens are not able to threaten, at the limit, to exit.[149]
- Managed competition provides roles for the private sector and harnesses private sector creativity, but not in the diminished way, as in New Zealand and the UK, in terms of creaming off the wealthy (and relatively healthy) and supplying them with top-up insurance to cover the failings of the public system (such as long waiting lists for elective surgery).
- There is a potential for greater innovation in contracting with purchasers and the option of vertical integration with providers should this prove

more efficient. In other words, the exact forms of managed care arrangements are not dictated centrally but are left to evolve in the face of incentives to compete on price and quality dimensions.

The Achilles' heel of managed competition reform is whether or not sponsors have the ability to adequately deal with the cream-skimming problem so as to encourage price and quality competition. Sponsors are required to risk-adjust the premiums paid so that competing purchasers are compensated for the risk they bear as a result of the characteristics of the people that have chosen to enrol in their particular plan. In the absence of purchasers receiving a premium on behalf of each enrollee that reflects that enrollee's risk of subsequent utilization of health care services (as can be assessed by purchasers), the incentive is for purchasers to engage in cream-skimming tactics. The technical difficulties, importance, and need for effective resolution of this problem are generally underestimated in managed competition proposals. Solving this problem is crucial in order to protect vulnerable populations in managed competition systems. Without seeking to understate the problem, it is important to note that cream-skimming is not solely a problem for managed competition systems. Increasingly, internal market systems and other more traditional health care systems are encouraging managed care where integrated groups of providers carry the financial risk of utilization by patients, thus resulting in an incentive for health care service providers to cream-skim.[149] Similarly, the need to determine how to ration health care services and to assess what services are cost-effective is not solely a problem for managed competition systems.

The most significant advantage offered by an internal market system with government-appointed monopsony purchasers over a managed competition system is potentially that of lower transactions costs and increased market power on the demand side. First it must be noted that extra transactions costs are only a problem if they are not offset by concomitant efficiency gains. It is of course difficult to calculate the efficiency gains of a managed competition system, as one has never been fully implemented. It must also be recognized that the problem of transactions costs has increasingly become a problem in internal markets as they shift to managed care arrangements. For example, prior to the New Labour reforms, there were 3,500 Fundholders acting as purchasers in the UK in addition to the 100 Health Authorities. With the recent changes there will be 500 Primary Care Groups together with 100 Health Authorities. By comparison, in the Netherlands (where managed competition is slowly being implemented), in 1999 there were only 50 private insurers and 27 Sickness Funds. Moreover, according to Schut most private insurers and Sickness funds cooperate in holding companies or chains with the 10 largest chains comprising 80 percent of the insurance market in 1998.[150] In the UK and New Zealand, the tendency has been a desire to align clinical and financial responsibility by devolving financial responsibility to groups of physicians (and now, in the UK, community nurses). One must question this approach given that the ethical norms of health care professionals may be severely tested as they are put under increasing financial pressure in their role as purchasers. In order to protect the role of physician as patient advocate it may be better to encourage competition between large purchasers and regulate the degree to which purchasers can shift financial risk down to small groups of health care providers.

A managed competition system offers the prospect of a mix of regulatory, political (voice) and market (exit) mechanisms that can be tailored to ensure the accountability of purchasers. Dranove argues in favor of competition or exit, for "[a] regulated approach will lock in existing institutional arrangements, with all future changes dictated by the whims of the political process, rather than by the demands of consumers."[151] But a politics-free health allocation system is an impossible goal unless one is willing to sacrifice the goal of redistribution. In managed competition models, government must manage or regulate competition between purchasers to: ensure universal coverage; to eliminate cream-skimming; to stimulate competition on price and quality dimensions; to facilitate choice by consumers among competing purchasers; and to ensure that the quality of services provided is of an adequate quality.[152] It is a serious mistake to assume that the government's role is not as critical where there are competing purchasers as it is where governmental agencies act as the sole purchasers of services. Political accountability and voice continue to have a large and important role to play.

In the next chapter, I will move to more closely scrutinize internal market reform as implemented in the UK and New Zealand and in particular the rationale for the "purchaser/provider split." This requirement for a purchaser/provider split will be compared with the managed competition model that allows competing insurer/purchasers to determine their own arrangements with providers, be it contracting out, vertical integration or some other sort of arrangement on the continuum between those two polar options.[153]

Notes

1 The White Paper outlining internal market reform of the UK's health system said the two objectives of reform were to give patients better health care and to provide greater rewards for those working in the National Health Service (NHS) who "successfully respond to local needs and preferences" (Department of Health, *Working for Patients*, Cm855 (London: HMSO, 1989). Similarly, in introducing his health reform proposals in 1993, New Zealand's then Minister of Health declared that there were three reasons to support the Bill, the first being that it would greatly improve the accountability of the public health system (*Hansard Reports*, 20 August 1993, 10773).

2 See E. J. Emanuel and L. L. Emanuel, 'What is Accountability in Health Care?', (1996) 124 *Ann. Intern. Med.* 229.

3 See generally W. P. M. M. van de Ven, F. T. Schut, and F. F. H. Rutten, 'Forming and Reforming the Market for Third-Party Purchasing of Health Care', (1994) 39(10) *Soc. Sci. Med.* 1405.

4 J. D. Donahue, *The Privatization Decision: Public Ends, Private Means* (New York: Basic Books, 1989) at p. 23.

5 *Ibid.*, p. 10.

6 M. J. Trebilcock, *The Prospects for Reinventing Government* (Toronto: C. D. Howe Institute, 1994) at p. 8.

7   E. Fama, 'Agency Problems and the Theory of the Firm', (1980) 88 *Journal of Political Economy* 288 at pp. 291–293.

8   Donahue, *op cit.*, pp. 49–51.

9   For an introduction and overview of the theory, see I. McLean, *Public Choice: An Introduction* (Oxford: Basil Blackwell, 1987). See also M. Kelman, 'On Democracy-Bashing: A Sceptical Look at the Theoretical and "Empirical" Practice of the Public Choice Movement', (1988) 71 *Va. L. Rev.* 199 at p. 268; D. A. Farber, 'Democracy and Disgust: Reflections on Public Choice', (1991) 65 *Chi. Kent L. Rev.* 161; and D. Farber and P. Frickey, *Law and Public Choice: A Critical Introduction* (Chicago, IL: University of Chicago Press, 1991).

10 J. Buchanan, *Liberty, Markets and State: Political Economy in the 1980s* (New York: New York University Press, 1985) at p. 19.

11 In the health sector, McAuslan gives the example of senior consultants in the UK's National Health Service awarding themselves publicly funded merit awards – P. McAuslan, 'Public Law and Public Choice', (1988) 51(6) *The Modern L. Rev.* 681 at p. 689.

12 For example, the notion that politicians are only interested in expanding their own political empires does not rest well with the phenomenon in all industrialized countries where governments across the political spectrum have actively tried to either down-size or privatize public organizations. Clearly, ideas (or at least ideology) have some currency here.

13 G. Brennan and J. M. Buchanan, 'Is Public Choice Immoral? The Case for the "Noble" Lie', (1988) 74 *Va. L. R.* 179 at pp. 187–188, argue that public choice theory becomes problematic when it is used in the positive sense as a predictive model of behavior in political roles. They argue that the proper role of public choice theory should be in the normative sense of institutional reform, meaning improvements in the rules under which political processes operate.

14 See generally R. G. Evans, M. L. Barer and T. R. Marmor (eds), *Why Are Some People Healthy and Others Not?: The Determinants of Health of Populations* (New York: Aldine De Gruyter, 1994).

15 For a discussion, see W. P. M. M. van de Ven, 'Regulated Competition in Health Care: With or Without a Global Budget', (1995) 39(3) *European Economic Review* 786.

16 White House Domestic Policy Council, *The Clinton Blueprint: The President's Health Security Plan* (New York: Times Books, 1993) (hereinafter *Clinton Blueprint*).

17 See W. van de Ven and F. Rutten, 'Managed Competition in the Netherlands: Lessons from Five Years of Health Care Reform', (1995) 18(1) *Australian Health Review* 9.

18 It should be noted that in New Zealand significant user charges apply for general practitioner, drugs, and outpatient services and in the UK user charges apply to drugs.

19 The National Health Service and Community Care Act (UK) 1990, c. 19, s. 20 (hereinafter NHS 1990 Act).

20 D. Longley, *Health Care Constitutions* (London: Cavendish Publishing, 1996) at p. 112.

21 The Public Finance Act (NZ), 1989, No. 142.

22 NHS 1990 Act, *op. cit.*, s. 17 and s. 97(7) (as amended by the Health Authorities Act (UK) 1995, c. 17, s. 47.)

23 *Ibid.*, s.18.

24 A. Belcher, 'Codes of Conduct and Accountability for NHS Boards', (Summer 1995) *Public Law* 288; Longley, *op. cit.*, p. 121.

25 NZ Health 1993 Act, (NZ), No. 22, s. 10 (hereinafter NZ Health 1993 Act).

26 *Ibid.*, s. 8(5).

27 See *Priorities And Planning Guidance For The NHS: 1997/98* (Leeds: NHS Executive, June 1996) (hereinafter *UK Planning Guidance 1997/98*).

28 Six medium term priorities were set for the 1997/98 year: working towards developing a primary care led system; to review and maintain progress on the effective purchasing and provision of comprehensive mental health care services; improving the clinical and cost-effectiveness of services; giving greater voice and influence to users; ensuring that integrated services are in place to meet the continuing health care needs of the elderly, disabled, vulnerable people, and children; and encouraging public organizations to be good employers. Baseline requirements and objectives set include: the attainment of specific goals relating to the reduction of the incidence of coronary heart disease, stroke, cancers, suicide, gonorrhea, and accidents

and the attainment of specific targets for waiting times for health care services. – *ibid.*, pp. 11–21.

29   Minister of Health, *Policy Guidelines For Regional Health Authorities 1996/97* (publication details not given in the document but presumably published in Wellington by the Ministry of Health in November 1995) (hereinafter *1996/97 NZ Policy Guidelines*) pp. 11–12.

30   As an example, in terms of equity, the Regional Health Authorities are required to "improve access…to health and disability services in terms of waiting times, geographical accessibility, and affordability" and give "relatively greater weighting to health gain for those people with lower health status in all population groups, and…greater weighting to Maori and child health gain". In terms of efficiency, Regional Health Authorities are required (amongst other things), where a choice of effective services for addressing a given health problem exits, to choose the most cost-effective service – *ibid.*, p. 11.

31   *Ibid.*

32   A. Mason and K. Moran, 'Purchaser-Provider: The International Dimension', 310(6974) *BMJ* 231.

33   C. Propper, 'Agency and Incentives in the NHS Internal Market', (1995) 40(12) *Soc. Sci. Med.* 1683 at p. 1685.

34   *The New NHS: Modern, Dependable*, a White Paper, Cm 3807, 8 December 1997. Online. Available HTTP: http://www.official-documents.co.uk/document/doh/newnhs/contents.htm (accessed 15 March 1999).

35   See *Purchasing For Your Health: A Performance Report on the First Year of the Regional Health Authorities and Public Health Commission* (Wellington: Ministry of Health, 1995) (hereinafter *Performance Report*) pp. 10–11.

36   *Ibid.*, p. 142.

37   See, for example, *Purchasing For Your Health 1996/97: A Performance Report of the Fourth Year of the Regional Health Authorities* (Wellington: Ministry of Health, 1998). Online. Available HTTP: http://www.moh.govt.nz (under publications) (accessed 20 April 1999).

38   P. Allen, 'Contracts in the National Health Service Internal Market', (1995) 58(3) *The Modern Law Review* 321 at p. 339.

39   *The Modern NHS: Modern, Dependable, op. cit.*

40   Dr R. Naden, 'Contracting to Purchase Health and Disability Services: An RHA Perspective', in *Contracting in the Health Sector*, papers presented at a seminar held by the Legal Research Foundation at the University of Auckland, 6 July 1994, 64 at p. 66.

41   P. Smith, 'Information Systems and the White Paper Proposals', in A. J. Culyer, A. K. Maynard and J. W. Posnett (eds), *Competition in Health Care: Reforming the NHS* (Basingstoke: Macmillan Press, 1990) at p. 119.

42   C. H. Tuohy, *Accidental Logics: The Dynamics of Change in the Health Care Arena in the United States, Britain and Canada* (Oxford: Oxford University Press, 1999) p. 202. For a discussion of this in the context of management of infectious diseases in the NHS internal market see P. Allen, B. Goxson, J. A. Roberts and S. Crawshaw, 'The Management of Infectious Disease Related Risk in the NHS Internal Market' (Paper presented to the Economic and Social Research Council Risk and Human Behaviour Conference, London, 17 September 1999) p. 14.

43   Evans has made the point for many years that all money that is spent on health care services in one form or another results in income for health care service providers – *Strained Mercy: The Economics of Canadian Health Care* (Toronto: Butterworths (Canada), 1984) at p. 281, and seventeen years later see R. G. Evans, 'Going for the Gold: The Redistributive Agenda Behind Market-Based Health Care Reform', (1997) 22(2) *J. of Health Polit.. Policy Law* 427 at p. 440.

44   See generally A. O. Hirschman, *Exit, Voice, and Loyalty: Responses to Decline in Firms, Organizations, and States* (Cambridge, MA: Harvard University Press, 1970).

45   C. M. Flood, 'Prospects for New Zealand's Reformed Health System', (1996) 4 *Health Law Journal* 87 at p. 100.

46   *Hirschman, op cit.*, pp. 30–43.

47   *Ibid.*, p. 40.

48   *Ibid.*, p. 51.

49 *Ibid.*, p. 124 notes: "(i)t is very unlikely that one could specify a most efficient mix (of exit and voice) that would be stable over time. The reason is simple: *each recovery mechanism is itself subject to the forces of decay, which have been invoked here all along.*"

50 *Ibid.*, p. 24.

51 See C. M. Flood, 'Will Supplementary Private Insurance Reduce Waiting Lists?', (1996) 11 *Canadian Health Facilities Law Guide* 1.

52 The estimated resident population for the year ending 31 December 1997 was 3,781,300. Online. Available HTTP: http://www.stats.govt.nz (accessed 11 March 1999).

53 News release by the Department of Health, 96/106, 1 April 1996, 'Changes to Health Service Structure Release £139 Million for Patient Care'.

54 In the US, several studies have shown that large insurers are able to extract discounts from providers. See, for example, F. A. Sloan and E. R. Becker, 'Cross-subsidies and Payment for Hospital Care', (1984) 8 *J. Health Polit. Policy Law* 660. In those countries where government expenditures accounts for the great majority of total health expenditures, government has been able to use its monopsony purchasing power to control costs – see the Health Care Study Group Report, 'Understanding The Choices in Health Care Reform', (1994) 19(3) *J. Health Polit. Policy Law* 499.

55 K. Hawkins (ed.), *The Uses of Discretion*, (Oxford: Clarendon Press, 1992) at p. 12 notes that "(s)ometimes, of course, law-makers want to remain as silent as possible on controversial or complex matters of public policy; in these circumstances, awards of discretion to legal bureaucracies allow legislatures to duck or fudge hard issues."

56 For example, A. J. Culyer and A. Meads, 'The United Kingdom: Effective, Efficient, Equitable?', (1992) 17 *J. Health Polit. Policy Law* 667 at p. 684, note that the absence of locally elected Health Authorities, rather than eliminating politics from the decision-making process, simply transmits the problem to higher levels of government. Similarly, G. Wilson notes that the reformed New Zealand system has not managed to depoliticize decisions in primary or secondary care – G. Wilson 'Health Purchasing: A Regional Health Authority Perspective', (1995) 18(1) *Public Sector* 11. See also Longley, *op. cit.*, p. 123.

57 For examples in New Zealand, see C. M. Flood, 'Prospects for New Zealand's Reformed Health System', (1996) 4 *Health Law Journal* 87 at p. 105, fn 72.

58 *Purchasing For Your Health 1996/97: A Performance Report of the Fourth Year of the Regional Health Authorities, op. cit.*, p. 26.

59 The validity of this proposition is discussed in more detail in Chapter 7.

60 See in general, the Audit Commission, *What the Doctor Ordered: A Study of GP Fundholders in England and Wales* (London: HMSO, 1996) (hereinafter *What the Doctor Ordered*).

61 J. Shapiro and C. Ham, 'The New Health Authorities', (1996) 2(2) *Health Services Management Center Newsletter* (University of Birmingham) 1.

62 See A. Harrison (eds), *Health Care UK 1994/95: An Annual Review of Health Care Policy*, (Bristol: J. W. Arrowsmith Limited, 1995) (hereinafter *Health Care UK 1994/95*) at p. 4, which notes, "GPs are independent contractors: their contracts are broadly drawn, giving them massive scope for exercising discretion in the way they use the resources at their disposal, a discretion which they are currently able to use without being called to account."

63 *What The Doctor Ordered, op. cit.*, p. 63 and generally pp. 64–79.

64 See K. Thomas, J. Nicholl and P. Coleman, 'Assessing the Outcome of Making it Easier for Patients to Change General Practitioner: Practice Characteristics Associated With Patient Movements', (1995) 45(400) *British Journal of General Practice* 581.

65 See *The New NHS: Modern Dependable*, a White Paper, *op. cit.*, at s. 2.18–2.19.

66 Longley, *op. cit.*, p. 116 and p. 122.

67 See generally J. A. Morone, 'The Ironic Flaw in Health Care Competition: The Politics of Market', in R. J. Arnould, R. F. Rich and W. D. White (eds), *Competitive Approaches to Health Care Reform* (Washington, DC: Urban Institute Press, 1993) p. 207.

68 There appear to be 207 Community Health Councils in the UK. Online. Available HTTP: http://www.ukpc.org/pub/chclist.htm (accessed 9 March 1999).

69 See generally the Community Health Councils Regulations (UK)1996, S. I. 1996/640, s.18. Section 18(3) provides that there is no duty to consult where the Authority is satisfied that "in the interest of the health care service" a decision has to be taken without allowing time for consultation.

70 However, prior to 1 April 1996, UK purchasing agencies were under a wide duty to recognize local advisory committees representing different health professions in the relevant district or region and to consult with these committees – see the Health Authorities Act (UK) 1995, c. 17, ss. 4–5, and Sch. 6.

71 The National Health Service Act (UK), 1977, c. 49, s. 12(1) as amended by *ibid.*

72 NZ Health 1993 Act, *op. cit.*, s. 34.

73 The Charter notes that patients can expect to be seen immediately in Accident and Emergency Departments, to be seen within 18 months for inpatient or day care services, within 12 months for coronary revascularisations and associated procedures, and within 26 weeks for a first consultant outpatient appointment, with 90 percent of patients being seen within 13 weeks – *NHS Waiting Times Good Practice Guide, January 1996*, (Leeds: NHS Executive, May 1996) p. 2.

74 *The New NHS: Modern Dependable*, a White Paper, *op. cit.*, at s. 4.20.

75 The Health Service Commissioners Act (UK), 1993, c. 46, s. 3.

76 See the Health Services Commissioners (Amendment) Act (UK), 1996, c. 5.

77 The Health Service Commissioners Act (UK), 1993, c. 46, s. 3(4) and s. 3(5).

78 For a discussion of these cases see J. H. Tingle, 'The Allocation of Healthcare Resources in the National Health Service in England: Professional and Legal Issues', (1993) 2 *Annals of Health Law* 195. More recently, see *R. v. Cambridge Health Authority, ex p B.*, (1995) 2 All ER 129 (CA) p. 130, where it was noted "(the judiciary)…was not in a position to decide on the correctness of the difficult and agonizing judgements which had to be made by health authorities as to how a limited budget was best allocated to the maximum advantage of the maximum number of patients."

79 See the Health and Disability Commissioner (Code of Health and Disability Services Consumers' Rights) Regulations (NZ), 1996/78.

80 The ten rights are: to be treated with respect; to freedom from discrimination, coercion, harassment, and exploitation; to dignity and independence; to services of an appropriate standard; to effective communication; to be fully informed; to make an informed choice and give informed consent; to support; to make a complaint about the provision of health or disability services; and for the code of rights to apply when a consumer is participating or it is proposed that the consumer participate in teaching or research.

81 The Health and Disability Commissioner (Code of Health and Disability Services Consumers' Rights) Regulations (NZ), 1996/78, s. 3.

82 See the Health and Disability Commissioner Act 1994 (NZ), 1994, No. 88.

83 She has the power to investigate a complaint that there has been a breach of the code. She may refer the matter to an "advocate" to resolve the complaint. If after an investigation the Commissioner resolves that there has been a complaint then she may, amongst other things, report her opinion and recommendations to a health professional body and/or make a complaint to that body. If after a reasonable time no action is taken the Commission may make public comment thereon and/or report the matter to the Minister of Health – *ibid.*, ss. 36, 42, 45, and 46(2).

84 *Ibid.*, s. 49 and s. 52.

85 B. Ferguson, 'Progress of the UK Health Reforms and the Role of Information: What Can the "Dismal Science" Contribute?', Discussion Paper 145, January 1996, Center For Health Economics, The University of York p. 13.

86 This argument has been made before in earlier writing: see C. M. Flood and M. J. Trebilcock, 'Voice and Exit in New Zealand's Health Care Sector', in *Contracting in the Health Sector, op. cit.*, p. 37; Flood, "Will Supplementary Private Insurance Reduce Waiting Lists?", *op. cit.*; Flood, 'Prospects for New Zealand's Reformed Health System", *op. cit.*, p. 101.

87 *Health Expenditure Trends in NZ 1980-1997*, (Ministry of Health: Wellington, 1998) at p. 23, Table 4.12. Online. Available HTTP: http://www.moh.govt.nz (accessed 31 December 1998).

88 D. Muthumala and P. S. Howard, *Health Expenditure Trends in New Zealand 1980–1994* (Wellington: Ministry of Health, 1995) at p. 58, Appendix 4, fn 88.

89 Hirschman, *op. cit.*, p. 59.

90 T. Besley, J. Hall and I. Preston, *Private Health Insurance and the State of the NHS*, (*Commentary No. 52*) (London: The Institute for Fiscal Studies, 1996).

91 *Ibid.*, p. 1.

92 W. Laing, 1993 figures estimated in *Laing's Review of Private Healthcare 1994* (London: Lain and Buisson Publications, 1994), p. 140, Table 3.1

93 *1996/97 NZ Policy Guidelines, op. cit.*, pp. 24–25.

94 The Finance Act (UK) 1989, c. 26, s. 54. See *The Economist* (15 March 1997) p. 18.

95 See, for example, Alberta Health Care Insurance Act R.S.A. 1980 c. A-24, s.17, and Ontario Health Insurance Act R.S.O. 1990, c. H.6, s. 14. However, Newfoundland, Nova Scotia, New Brunswick, and Saskatchewan do not appear to have explicit legislation prohibiting private insurance that overlaps the public scheme.

96 The National Forum, *Canada Health Action: Building on the Legacy* (Ottawa: National Forum on Health, 1997) at p. 5 concluded in 1997 "…the health system has always engendered strong support among Canadians. In recent years, however, its significance has broadened into symbolic terms as a defining national characteristic."

97 C. Ramsay and M. Walker, *Waiting Your Turn: Hospital Waiting Lists in Canada* (Vancouver: The Fraser Institute, 1996) at p. 6.

98 See Flood, 'Prospects for New Zealand's Reformed Health System', *op. cit.*

99 P. Davis, *Health and Health Care in New Zealand*, (Auckland: Longman Paul, 1981) at p. 135.

100 A. C. Enthoven, 'The History and Principles of Managed Competition', (1993) 12 *Health Affairs* 24 at p. 29.

101 See the American Health Security Act of 1993, H.R. 3600, 103d Cong., S. 1757, 1st Sess., (1993).

102 V. R. Fuchs, 'Economics, Values, and Health Care Reform', (1996) 86(1) *American Economic Review* 1 at p. 20.

103 *Factsheet: Health Care Reform in the Netherlands*, (Ministry of Welfare, Health and Cultural Affairs, Fact Sheet, V-5-E 1993) (hereinafter *Factsheet*) p. 2.

104 For a discussion of cream-skimming, see J. P. Newhouse *et al.*, 'Adjusting Capitation Rates Using Objective Health Measures and Prior Utilization', (Spring 1989) *Health Care Financing Review* 41; F. T. Schut, 'Workable Competition in Health Care: Prospects for the Dutch Design', (1992) 35(12) *Soc. Sci. Med.* 1445; R. C. J. A. van Vliet and W. P. M. M. van de Ven, 'Towards a Capitation Formula for Competing Health Insurers: An Empirical Analysis', (1992) 34(9) *Soc. Sci. Med.* 1035; W. P. M. M. van de Ven and R. C. J. A. van Vliet, 'How Can we Prevent Cream-skimming in a Competitive Health Insurance Market? The Great Challenge for the 90's', in P. Zweifel and H. E. Frech III (eds), *Health Economics Worldwide* (Boston, MA: Kluwer Academic Publishers, 1992) at p. 23; R. C. J. A. van Vliet, 'Predictability of Individual Health Care Expenditures'. (1992) LIX(3) *The Journal of Risk and Insurance* 443; R. C. J. A. van Vliet and W. P. M. M. van de Ven, 'Capitation Payments Based on Prior Hospitalizations', (1993) 2 *Health Economics* 177; W. P. M. M. van de Ven, R. C. J. A. van Vliet, E. M. van Barneveld and L. M. Lamers, 'Risk-Adjusted Capitation: Recent Experiences in the Netherlands', (1994) 13(5) *Health Affairs* 120; W. P. M. M. van de Ven, F. T. Schut and F. F. H. Rutten, 'Forming and Reforming the Market for Third-Party Purchasing of Health Care', (1994) 39(10) *Soc. Sci. Med.* 1405; J. P. Newhouse, 'Patients at Risk: Health Reform and Risk Adjustment', (1994) 13(1) *Health Affairs* 132; M. Giacomini, H. S. Luft and J. C. Robinson, 'Risk Adjusting Community Rated Health Plan Premiums: A Survey of Risk Assessment Literature and Policy Applications', (1995) *Annu. Rev. Public Health* 401; E. M. van Barneveld, R. C. J. A. van Vliet and W. P. M. M. van de Ven, 'Mandatory High-Risk Pooling: A Means for Reducing the Incentives for Cream-skimming', (1996) 33(2) *Inquiry* 133; and J. P. Newhouse 'Reimbursing Health Plans and Health Care Providers:: Efficiency in Production Versus Selection' (1996) 34, *Jnl. of Econ. Lit.* 1236.

105 See for example Enthoven, *op.cit.*, p. 33.

106 J. E. Fielding and R. Rice, 'Can Managed Competition Solve Problems of Market Failure?', (1993) 12 *Health Affairs* 216 at p. 222, suggest "...(o)ne thing that might help is for plans to report the use and cost experience of disenrollees; this could be made public, alerting consumers that certain plans have a tendency to 'dump' sick patients."

107 Van Barneveld, van Vliet and van de Ven, *op. cit.*

108 Van Vliet and van de Ven, 'Towards a Capitation Formula for Competing Health Insurers', *op. cit.*

109 Van de Ven *et al.*, 'Risk-Adjusted Capitation: Recent Experiences in the Netherlands', *op. cit.*, p. 123

110 W. P. M. M. van de Ven and F. T. Schut, 'The Dutch Experience with Internal Markets', in M. Jerome-Forget, J. White, and J. M. Wiener (eds), *Health Care Reform through Internal Markets: Experience and Proposals* (Montreal: IRPP, 1995) 95 at p. 104.

111 F. T. Schut and W. H. J. Hassink, 'Price Competition in Social Health Insurance: Evidence from the Netherlands', (paper prepared for the 2nd iHEA Conference in Rotterdam, 6–9 June 1999), p. 4.

112 Van de Ven and Schut, *op. cit.*, pp.110–111.

113 *Ibid.*, p. 110.

114 S. S. Wallack *et al.*, 'A Plan for Rewarding Efficient HMOs', (1988) 7(3) *Health Affairs* 80 at p. 84.

115 Van de Ven and Schut, *op. cit.*, pp. 110–111.

116 *Ibid.*, p. 111.

117 National Health Service (Fund-Holding Practices) Regulation (UK), 1996, S.I. 1996/706, s.21.

118 *What The Doctor Ordered*, *op. cit.*, p. 10.

119 In 1994 this averaged to approximately 200 guilders (US$120) per person per annum – van de Ven and Schut, *op. cit.*, p. 102.

120 Enthoven, *op. cit.*, p. 32.

121 L. A. Berthgold, 'Perspectives: Benefit Package', (1993 Supp.) 12 *Health Affairs* 99 at p. 100.

122 *Factsheet*, *op. cit.*, p. 3.

123 Van de Ven and Schut, *op. cit.*, p. 101.

124 Government Committee on Choices in Health Care, *Choices in Health Care* (Rijswijk: Ministry of Welfare, Health and Cultural Affairs, 1992) (English version).

125 The Committee notes "(t)he first sieve retains care that is unnecessary, based on a community-oriented approach. The second sieve selects on effectiveness, allowing only care confirmed and documented as effective. The third sieve selects on efficiency, which can be measured by such methods as cost-effectiveness analysis. The fourth sieve retains care that can be left to individual responsibility. The Committee feels that any care that is retained in one of the four sieves does not need to be in the basic benefit package' – *ibid.*, p. 19.

126 The Oregon Basic Health Services Act, Or. Rev. Stat. §§414.705–414.750 (1993). Prior to implementation of this Act only those individuals who satisfied family status requirements and had incomes equal to or less than 51 percent of the poverty line were eligible – Oregon Health Services Commission, *Prioritization of Health Services: A Report to the Governor and Legislature* (1991) at p. xvii as cited by C. J. Halligan, '"Just What The Doctor Ordered": Oregon's Medicaid Rationing Process and Public Participation in Risk Regulation', (1995) 83(7) *Georgetown Law Journal* 2697.

127 For a fuller description of the processes, see Halligan, *ibid.*, pp. 2708–2711.

128 See *ibid.*, pp. 2711–2712.

129 Support for this view comes from Sweden where the notion of deploying resources to help many people with mild disorders instead of a few with severe injuries and the notion of giving priority to those patients who are considered to provide important contributions to society, were both firmly rejected by a body constituted to consider priorities in health care – Swedish Parliamentary Priorities Commission, *Priorities in Health Care*, (Stockholm: Ministry of Health and Social Affairs, 1995).

130 NZ Health 1993 Act, *op. cit.*, s.6.

131 *Core Services for 1995/96: Third Report of the National Advisory Committee on Core Health and Disability Support Services* (Wellington: The National Advisory Committee On Core Health

And Disability Support Services, 1994).

132 See the (1996) 312 *BMJ* edition which is devoted to moving the debate forward on the rationing of health care in the UK. See also A. Maynard and K. Bloor, *Our Certain Fate: Rationing In Health Care*, (London: Office of Health Economics, 1998).

133 See M. Rachlis, 'Defining Basic Services and De-Insuring the Rest: The Wrong Diagnosis and the Wrong Prescription', (1995) 152(9) *Can. Med. Assoc. J.* 1401 at p. 1403. See also, R. Deber, 'Beyond the Canada Health Act: The Public-Private Mix', paper presented for the Ninth John Olin Annual Conference in Law and Economics, Canadian Law and Economics Association, 26 September 1997.

134 See S. L. Issacs, 'Consumers' Information Needs: Results of a National Survey', (1996) 15(4) *Health Affairs* 31 at p. 35.

135 E. W. Hoy, E. K. Wicks and R. A. Forland, 'A Guide to Facilitating Consumer Choice', (1996) 15(4) *Health Affairs* 9, conclude that consumer choice of plans can be facilitated if sponsors "(1) create a level field for comparison through standardized benefits and structured enrolment processes; (2) offer a limited number of plans that meet appropriate selection criteria; (3) provide comprehensive, objective and reliable consumer information; (4) support this process with education; and (5) hold plans accountable through uniform reporting of performance data."

136 J. E. Fielding and R. Rice, 'Can Managed Competition Solve Problems of Market Failure?', (1993) 12 *Health Affairs* 216 at p. 222.

137 See generally G. Anders, *Health Against Wealth: HMOs and the Breakdown of Medical Trust* (Boston, MA: Houghton Mifflin, 1997).

138 A. C. Enthoven and R. Kronick, 'A Consumer-Choice Health Plan for the 1990s: Universal Health Insurance in a System Designed to Promote Quality and Economy, I', (1989) 325 *New England J. of Health* 854.

139 See the comments of M. Schlesinger and D. Mechanic, 'Perspective, Challenges for Managed Competition from Chronic Illness', (1993) 12 *Health Affairs* 123 at pp. 130–131.

140 For example, S. S. Wallack *et al.*, *op. cit.*, p. 84, note "Medicare claims data suggest that for a random sample of 20,000 aged beneficiaries, the 95 percent confidence interval is plus or minus about 4 percent ($100 in 1987) of the *per capita* cost for a year. Groups comprising only one hundred enrollees would result in a 95 percent confidence interval of plus or minus 66 percent ($1,300 in 1987)."

141 See *OECD Health Policy Studies No. 2, The Reform of Health Care: A Comparative Analysis of Seven OECD Countries* (Paris: OECD, 1992) p. 99.

142 F. Schut, W. Greenberg and W. P. M. M. van de Ven, 'Anti-trust Policy in the Dutch Health Care System and the Relevance of EEC Competition Policy and US Anti-trust Practice', (1991) 17 *Health Policy* 257 at p. 266.

143 As noted by van de Ven and Schut, *op. cit.*, pp. 97–98 and pp. 105–106.

144 See F. T. Schut, *Competition in the Dutch Health Care Sector*, (PhD Thesis, Health Economics, Erasmus University, Rotterdam, 1995) p. 224.

145 See 'Report on Ministry of Health, Managed Care Conference, 2-4 May 1996, Managed Care Applied'. Online. Available HTTP: http://www.enigma.co.nz/hcro/9607/9607/s07.htm (accessed 1 November 1998).

146 For example, E. D. Kinney, 'Protecting Consumers and Providers Under Health Reform: An Overview of the Major Administrative Law Issues', (1995) 5 *Health Matrix* 83 at p. 126, notes that of all the proposals for health reform that abounded in the US between 1993/94, President Clinton's proposal provided the most detailed framework for adjudicating disputes between purchasers and enrollees.

147 Longley, *op. cit.*, p. 155.

148 Hirschman, *op. cit.*, pp. 82–83.

149 See M. Matsaganis and H. Glennerster, 'The Threat of 'Cream-skimming' in the Post-reform NHS', (1994) 13(1) *J. of Health Economics* 31.

150 Personal correspondence with Erik Schut, Erasmus University, Rotterdam, 21 September 1999.

151 D. Dranove, 'The Case for Competitive Reform in Health Care', in R. J. Arnould, R. F. Rich and W. D. White (eds), *op. cit.*, p. 79.

152 For a comment on the problems inherent in Clinton's managed competition plan, see generally L. D. Brown and T. R. Marmor, 'The Clinton Reform Plan's Administrative Structure: The Reach and the Grasp', (1994) 19(1) *J. Health Polit. Policy Law* 193.
153 A version of this chapter first appeared in *Dalhousie Law Journal* (1997) 20(2) p. 470.

5 The interface between health care service purchasers and providers
Contracting out versus integrated production

Internal market reform and managed competition reform both seek to achieve efficiency gains through proactive purchasing. The concept of a proactive purchaser is a significant development from the historical role of government and private insurers as passive indemnity insurers. In a managed competition system, competition between insurers is managed or regulated to provide incentives for insurers to compete along price and quality dimensions in purchasing and/or providing care. Insurers are expected to act as proactive purchasers and/or managers of the supply of care rather than traditional insurers, although they are still expected to manage financial risk within certain parameters. Managed competition models generally assume that insurer/purchasers will implement managed care arrangements, which are one or more of a variety of methods designed with the goal of influencing the clinical decision-making of health care providers. In a managed competition system, insurer/purchasers are free to choose the most efficient supply arrangement and, subject to anti-trust laws, may or may not be vertically integrated with health care providers. By contrast, the Health Authorities in the internal markets of the UK and New Zealand are precluded from supplying health care services themselves and *must* contract out for the supply thereof. The goal of internal market reform is to stimulate competition directly between health care providers rather than, as in the managed competition model, between insurer/purchasers.

This chapter will consider and contrast the costs and benefits of these two distinct approaches: the mandatory contracting out required by internal market reform and the more flexible approach of managed competition. This chapter will draw upon the theory of the firm to evaluate the configuration of purchasers and providers in internal market and managed competition models. The chapter will then move on to consider contracting in the UK and New Zealand internal markets and whether or not the reforms have resulted in more efficient systems than those previously in place.

The purchaser/provider split

In the UK and New Zealand, a key structural feature of the internal markets is a rigid split in the purchaser and provider functions in all health care service markets. Prior to internal market reform in both the UK and New Zealand, the purchaser and provider roles were integrated rigidly for all publicly funded hospital services. The concern was that the old Health Authorities, which were responsible both for managing the budgets for hospital services in their respective regions *and* for managing public hospitals, were likely to favor the public hospitals they managed. Thus, there was no competitive spur for public hospitals to operate efficiently.

In New Zealand, the internal market reform proposals of 1991 provided for the establishment of four Regional Health Authorities (RHAs). Funding of health services were consolidated so that the RHAs were responsible for purchasing all publicly funded health and disability services. As the reforms progressed, responsibility for purchasing public health services was also transferred to the RHAs but responsibility for purchasing accident services was transferred back to the Accident Compensation Corporation. In 1997, the four RHAs were merged into one central Health Funding Authority, albeit with four branches. The RHAs (and now the new central Health Funding Authority) are required to purchase health care services and are precluded from providing health care services or owning (vertically integrating with) health care service providers. Management of the public hospitals is now the responsibility of twenty-three government-owned corporations, known as Crown Health Enterprises (CHEs), which must compete with each other and private providers for supply contracts with the central Health Authority. Thus, a radical shift occurred, with the purchaser and provider functions for hospital services being completely integrated prior to internal market reform, and post reform being rigidly split.

In the UK, as a result of internal market reform, there are 100 Health Authorities, which are responsible for purchasing health care services. On the other side of the split, the public hospitals are now managed by 450 independent NHS Trusts, which are statutory corporations reporting to the Secretary of State. In addition to the Health Authorities there were, until 1 April 1999, 3,500 GP Fundholders acting as small purchasers for a limited range of health care services. From 1 April 1999, 500 Primary Care Groups (PCGs) replaced the 3500 Fundholders. Ultimately, it is expected that the Health Authorities will transfer to these Groups, representing all family doctors and community nurses in a region, responsibility for purchasing hospital services from the NHS Trusts. Thus, despite the promise of the New Labour reforms to abolish the internal market, the key feature of the internal market – a rigid split between the purchaser and provider functions for hospital services – is maintained. However, both the old Fundholders and the new PCGs are purchasers *and* providers in the sense that they could choose to treat a particular health need themselves rather than to, for example, admit the patient to hospital. The difference is that Fundholders had clear financial incentives to supply the most cost-effective care to meet a particular health need whereas the new PCGs face very weak incentives to purchase cost-effective care. Nonetheless, one can argue that the existence of Fundholders and PCGs runs counter to the thesis of the efficacy of splitting the purchaser and provider functions. Our understanding of the costs and benefits of the enforced split of the internal market will be enhanced by comparing the reasoning behind and development of Fundholding and PCGs with the balance of the internal market reforms.

Both the UK and New Zealand imposed a mandatory and rigid purchaser/provider split between Health Authorities and the providers of care in order to reduce managerial conflicts of interest that were perceived to exist in the old vertically integrated Health Authorities. The old vertically integrated Health Authorities were seen as having incentives to sustain inefficiencies in the public hospitals they were responsible for managing rather than to contract out to other potentially more efficient providers. The new government-appointed purchasers in both jurisdictions are, through proactive purchasing pressure, meant to ensure efficient performance on the part of public and private providers. The purchaser/provider split is, however, at odds with the international trend towards managed care and/or integrated delivery systems wherein the purchaser and provider roles *may* be combined.

It is important to note that there is nothing inherent in a managed care arrangement or, for that matter, in a managed competition system, which dictates whether insurer/purchasers will choose to be vertically integrated with or contract out with health care providers. All other things being equal, insurer/purchasers are free to negotiate the most efficient supply arrangement with health care providers. In some instances, depending on market conditions and the nature of the health care services in question, it may be easier for insurer/purchasers to influence providers' decision-making when they are in a close relationship. Managed care plans link the financing and supply of medical care. This may be through contracts between insurers and hospitals and physicians or by insurers owning hospitals or employing physicians. When an insurer is vertically integrated with (i.e. owns) hospitals and employs physicians on a salary basis, cost controls are achieved within the firm. When an insurer contracts out to health care providers then contracts must incorporate the ability for insurers to monitor providers' treatment recommendations and contain incentives for providers to make cost-efficient treatment decisions. The current emphasis in health care policy is, however, upon "integrated delivery systems." The appeal of an integrated delivery system is the concept that different health care providers work together in order to coordinate the supply of the most cost-effective care in response to any particular health need. The key to successful integration is that financial risk is shared, as it is only in this case that different health care providers have an incentive to coordinate their different skills. Thus, this suggests that vertically integrated institutions may be generally preferable to looser contractual arrangements.

Theories of the firm and reasons for and against vertical integration

Internal market reform assumes that the process of government-appointed purchasers contracting out to competing health providers will be more efficient than the rigid vertical integration of the old system. It is helpful to return to first principles at this point and consider the reasons that private firms contract out or vertically integrate and see if we can extrapolate from this to contracting out in the public sector. As Williamson noted in 1975, attention to the internal organizations of private firms will likely prove fruitful in attempting to study the conduct and performance of quasi-market and non-market organizations.[1]

Most discussions of the theory of the firm begin with Coase's observation in 1937 that some economic activities are organized in markets and others are organized internally within a firm.[2] A firm may buy goods or services as inputs for production in a market (contracting out) or it may extend its own boundaries to include production of the inputs (in-house or in-firm production). For example, a pharmaceutical company many choose to contract out for the supply of chemicals it needs to manufacture drugs from other firms or it may choose to make the chemicals itself. In the latter case it may buy the firm that it would otherwise have to buy the chemicals from or it may buy the assets needed for controlling the factors of production. In either case, it would then be "vertically integrated," with one managerial hierarchy.

Coase addressed the question of why, if the market is the most efficient means to allocate resources, do firms exist at all? If complete contracting were viable or efficient in all circumstances there would be no need for the existence of firms.[3] Coase concluded that profit-maximizing behavior requires that a firm expand its own boundaries rather than contract out in a market when the costs of going to the markets becomes larger than the costs of management within the firm. He identified different costs with respect to the process of in-house production and with respect to the process of contracting out for the supply of products or services to other firms. The three costs he identified as associated with contracting out in a market were:

- the costs of discovering the true market price for the required good or service;
- the costs of negotiating a separate contract for each good or service required;
- the costs associated with writing a long-term contract where one or both parties are unsure and/or unable to specify what will be required of the other in the future.

These types of costs are generally referred to as "transactions costs."

Coase identified the costs of in-house production by firms in rather vague terms. The costs he identified included:

- the rising costs "of organizing additional transactions within the firm;"

- the entrepreneur's failure "to make the best use of the factors of production;"
- the increase in the price of supplies because the "other advantages" of a small firm were greater than those of a large firm.

Coase described the first two types of in-house costs as falling within an economic definition of "diminishing returns to management."[4]

Williamson is the scholar most generally associated with developing Coase's theory that transactions costs determine whether production of goods or services occurs within a firm or is contracted out to other firms. He explored whether one could predict when the costs of contracting in the market would be greater than the costs of in-firm production.[5] Williamson makes two behavioral assumptions. The first is that individuals have "bounded rationality;" the second is that individuals may act opportunistically in transactions.

With respect to the assumption of "bounded rationality," Simon, an organizational psychologist, is credited with first having observed that "(t)he capacity of the human mind for formulating and solving complex problems is very small compared with the size of the problems whose solution is required for objectively rational behavior in the real world."[6] Consequently, whilst individuals generally intend to be rational, their actions may not accord with their intentions. In the relevant literature, this problem is often (unclearly) tied to the problem of identifying future risks and contingencies and the ability to specify in contracts appropriate responses thereto. Depending on the degree of uncertainty involved in any particular transaction it may be very difficult for parties to foresee all risks and contingencies. Even if complete information was available, parties to a contract may still not use rational means to solve the puzzle of what provisions to incorporate in the contract to address future risks and contingencies. Alternatively, it might cost too much to solve the puzzle relative to the discounted risk of waiting to see what events unfold.

The second assumption Williamson makes is that individuals may act opportunistically in transactions, i.e. with a lack of candor or honesty or with guile in pursuing their own self-interest. Generally, Williamson considers this behavioral tendency to be of little consequence as long as there is a competitive market for the particular good or service required. However, when a party to a contract has made specific investments in assets or skills to produce the goods or services required and these specific assets are not readily acquirable elsewhere then this party has significant incumbency advantages at the contract renewal juncture. Williamson refers to this problem as a case of "asset specificity."[7] The market, at the point in time at which the contract is open for renewal, is significantly less competitive than it was at the outset and the incumbent may effectively have been transformed into a monopoly. By the same token, the incumbent may also be vulnerable to exploitation by the purchaser as it may be very difficult or impossible for the incumbent to use the specialized assets or skills for other purposes. A bilateral monopoly situation may thus arise.[8]

The outcome of negotiations between parties to a bilateral monopoly will depend on the relative susceptibility of each party to holdout tactics. In such a case, vertical integration may be a more efficient choice for one or both parties than short-term or long-term contracting. The key to understanding this, as Flannigan notes, is to realize that, by vertically integrating, the firm avoids the opportunism or exploitation problem "by moving the contracting interface to a competitive (large-numbers) market."[9] Thus, rather than contracting with a supplier who controls specialized assets, an integrated firm (which now controls the specialized assets) can contract in competitive markets for the factors required for production using those specialized assets. Vertical integration reduces opportunism problems as then neither firm has a pre-emptive claim on profits and the integrated firm's internal control mechanisms can be more extensive and refined than that which was feasible through contracting.[10] Williamson also notes that the decision to vertically integrate can reduce any information asymmetry problems, e.g. where one party opportunistically relies on information that the other party does not have regarding costs, quality or other underlying conditions germane to the trade.[11]

Williamson argues that unlimited integration will not occur due to the costs associated with increasing firm size. These costs associated with increasing firm size include:

- loss of information regarding the real value and scarcity of production factors that is signaled through market prices;[12]
- the creation of incentives within the firm for non-pecuniary forms of opportunism (such as slacking on the job) on the part of employees;
- loss of management control because of the scale of the enterprise;
- the deadlines and delays of hierarchies;
- other bureaucratic costs associated with internal firm management.[13]

The unresolved issue remains of how to move beyond abstract generalizations of the costs of increasing firm size (or, conversely, the costs of contracting-out) to making predictions in a particular market of what is likely to be the most efficient firm configuration.

Thus far the discussion has been limited to consideration of the private sector. Does the theory of the firm have relevance where one or more of the parties to the contract is the government or are government agents, as in the UK's and New Zealand's internal markets? Some scholars argue that, due to inherent inefficiencies of government operation, government should always contract out to the private sector for the supply of services or goods.[14] The theory of "contestable markets" suggests that even in the case of a monopoly on the supply side it is more efficient to contract out to the private sector. It is argued that the process of competitive bidding for the contract to supply public goods/services for a fixed period will drive prices down from the monopoly to the competitive level.[15] Thus, while competition *within* the market may result in wasteful duplication of resources, competition *for* the market results in the necessary competitive rigor to ensure efficiency without costly regulation. Williamson,[16] Priest,[17] and Goldberg[18] have, respectively, criticized this theory of contestable markets. Williamson notes that, just as in the private sector, in the public sector it is not possible to fully predict future contingencies prior to entering into a long-term contract. As a consequence, ongoing negotiation and agreement between the parties is necessary and there is scope for opportunistic behavior by both parties. Moreover, Williamson argues that long-term contracts often require the deployment of specialized assets, which cannot be readily utilized for other purposes or obtained elsewhere. As a consequence, incumbent suppliers have an advantage at contract renewal junctures as new entrants will not be easily able to acquire the assets they need and contracting with a new entrant may result in a lag time in the production process.

Trebilcock concludes from the literature of the theory of the firm that governments will find it more efficient to contract out for the supply of services or goods rather than produce the good or service itself when:

- the desired product or service is easily described and its volume and quality can be specified in advance;
- the costs of negotiating contracts is relatively inexpensive (and, one might add, the cost of monitoring and enforcement of contractual performance is relatively low);
- production involves few economies of scale or scope but large returns to specialization.[19]

Using Trebilcock's general criteria, one may conclude, given the information asymmetry and contestability problems that appear to be apparent in many health care service markets, that *any* form of competition-oriented reform will be inefficient, be it internal market or managed care reform. This is not, however, necessarily the case. We may use some of the general theories regarding contracting-out to consider the costs and benefits of the rigid purchaser/ provider split in internal markets. These criteria are of less relevance when it comes to just considering the role of government as sponsor in the managed competition model, where the role of the sponsor is to pool funding, calculate risk-adjusted payments, and regulate competition between competing insurer/ purchasers. None of these regulatory tasks will be easy. However, I would argue that government is better suited to the role of regulator than to that of purchaser or provider. As a purchaser of health care services, government is expected to engage in the micro-management of different and dynamic health care service markets and different health care providers. Essentially one must determine what is the most appropriate role for government, and a factor influencing this decision is that if government is left as a purchaser then there are potential efficiency losses from enforcing a rigid purchaser/provider split in order to avoid conflicts of interest.

In order to assess whether the rigid purchaser/provider split of the internal market model is efficient, one has to consider two factors:

a) the degree of the information asymmetry problem; and
b) the degree of asset specificity.

If the information asymmetry problem is acute and the degree of asset specificity is high then, in general, it will be inefficient for government to contract out rather than to produce the services in-house. The next section will examine the degree of asset specificity and information asymmetry in health care service markets with a view to determining what, if any, generalizations can be made when choosing between in-house production and contracting out.

The varying characteristics of health care service markets

Whether or not government or a private firm should contract out for the supply of a good or service or produce, that good or service itself depends on the nature and conditions of the market in question both in the short and (in the foreseeable) long run. Consequently, it is important to consider the characteristics of different health care service markets. In particular, we must consider the scope for opportunism arising in health markets due to investment in specialized assets and to information asymmetry.

Where a provider invests in resources for which there are no ready substitutes in order to secure a contract then, at the point of contract renewal, the incumbent provider will have significant advantages over other potential competitors. Incumbency advantages occur as switching providers might subject the purchaser to an unacceptable lag in supply. Also if the purchaser is the sole purchaser of the service (in economic terms, a monopsony) then a new entrant to the supply market is unlikely to make the necessary capital investments without the guarantee of a long-term contract. From the incumbent supplier's perspective, it is now dependent on the purchaser as it is unable to readily transfer its specialized investments to other uses. The market is no longer competitive and there is potential for opportunistic behavior on the part of both contracting parties.

Crocker and Masten note that investment by providers in assets can take at least four general forms.[20] These are physical-asset specificity, site or location specificity, human-capital specificity, and dedicated assets (which are investments made to support a particular contract which are not specific to the purchaser but which would result in substantial excess capacity if the contract were not renewed). In addition, Crocker and Masten note that the need for timeliness in supply may result in the threat of delay being an effective strategy for achieving bargaining concessions. As I will seek to demonstrate, the threat of hold-out and the relative abilities of contracting parties to withstand hold-out is key to understanding how bargaining between bilateral monopolies in internal markets is likely to occur.

All types of asset specificity noted by Crocker and Masten may be present in certain health care service markets. However, broad generalizations about health care service markets are difficult if not impossible, as there are distinct markets for different services. Let us take three general types of health care services to illustrate this point – emergency services, general practitioner services, and mental health care services.

In the case of emergency services, a hospital and the technology employed therein may not be readily able to be deployed for other purposes, which makes the owner of the hospital dependent on the purchaser. On the other hand, whether the hospital is publicly or privately owned, it will be absolutely critical to the purchaser to have an ongoing relationship with the hospital in order to ensure timely access for patients. The purchaser's vulnerability in this regard will depend on surplus capacity within the hospital and the number of other hospitals located nearby. The purchaser may consider that it is unacceptably compromising the safety of local patients should it contract with a hospital that is more than, for example, thirty minutes drive from the population it serves. In terms of negotiations between a purchaser and the incumbent provider, arguably it will be the purchaser who will be most vulnerable to threats of hold-out by the provider. This problem will be exacerbated by the provider having significantly better information than the purchaser will about the costs of production.[21] A purchaser's vulnerability to opportunistic hold-out tactics will not be as critical for elective (i.e. non-urgent) surgical services as presumably the criteria of proximity to the population will not be marked and thus more hospitals will be potential competitors. In terms of human-capital specificity, a hospital employs skilled staff, which could in certain circumstances make it difficult to switch hospitals. For example, one could imagine a hospital holding a monopoly in a particular new and innovative surgical technique because of the fact that they employ or contract with a particular surgeon who is one of the few to have developed and refined this technique. Should a hospital hold a monopoly in the supply of a particular service, then this may provide it with scope for opportunism in concluding contracts for the supply of other contestable services by cross-subsidizing its operations in contestable markets with profits made in markets where it holds market power.

With respect to general practitioner services, investments in physical capital are presumably relatively small and easily diverted to other production purposes, for example the office lease. Moreover, while in some rural or remote areas a general practitioner may hold a monopoly, one would predict that, subject to the training and retention of sufficient doctors, patients would generally have a choice of practitioner within a reasonable traveling distance and/or that the market is contestable.[22] In many jurisdictions there is a problem with attracting general practitioners into rural areas because of a variety of professional and life-style factors.[23] Where physicians are paid on a fee-for-service basis this allows them to locate in an urban area with a high number of physicians and still earn a sustainable income as they can influence demand for their own services. If physicians are paid on a capitation basis they may find themselves forced to relocate from areas with high numbers of physicians in order to attract a sufficient number of enrollees as they will not be able to top up their incomes by simply seeing the same people more often. General practitioners who develop long-term relationships with patients may, in a sense, develop specialized human assets through acquiring information about the history and preferences of patients. However, one would envisage that practitioners could be prevented from monopolizing this information if adequate medical records were required to be kept and required to follow the patient upon their exit to another general practitioner.

With respect to mental health care services, one sees in practice significant investments in specifically designed institutions which could not be readily deployed to other uses, although rehabilitative and continuing care services may not require such specialized investment.[24] The proximity of the provider of mental health care services to the population it serves may not be as crucial as for emergency services. However, proximity to local communities is still an important element of the quality of the service supplied in terms of integration of the patient into local communities. The supply of some mental health care services may require investment in specialized knowledge in terms of a provider's familiarity with a patient's medical history. It may also require that there be continuity in the supply of services to patients if relationship-building and trust are considered imperative aspects of quality.

In some health care markets, the paucity of information available regarding future contingencies hinders both long-term planning and the ability to conclude long-term contracts. Problems of information paucity are exacerbated in former command-and-control systems, like the UK and New Zealand, as historically there been no systematic emphasis on the collection and dissemination of information on the cost and quality of services. In these countries, the administration and transactions costs incurred have been low but perhaps at the cost of information regarding performance.

In many health care markets, providers will have information regarding production costs and quality that a purchaser (be it a public or private insurer or individual patient) will not have. This is a function of the fact that in many systems allocation decisions have been left in physicians' hands so there has been little need to elicit this information. It is also a function of the lack of good information about the linkages between health care services and outcomes. For example, for some services of a caring nature it will be difficult if not impossible to gauge performance by way of measurable health outcomes.[25] However, the degree of these problems will vary significantly depending on the health care service markets in question. Stipulating, measuring and monitoring quality in contracts, for example, for some mental health care services, palliative care services and disability health care services, may be difficult due to the lack of any readily measurable criteria for performance. By comparison, assessing the quality of an appendectomy seems relatively straightforward in terms of removal of the offending appendix, the lack of complications or readmission required thereafter, and the patient's recovery time.

The clear lesson from these examples is that to assume homogenous health care service markets is erroneous.[26] A survey by Ashton released in 1996 of the New Zealand system (consisting of interviews with management of purchasers and providers) suggests that there are significant variations in transactions costs *depending on the health care service market in question.*[27] In particular, the transactions costs associated with contracting out of acute mental health care services are perceived as being much higher than for other services. By comparison, transactions costs for rest home services were perceived as being low. She contends that consequently it appears that transaction costs rise as asset specificity, frequency of transactions, uncertainty, and problems of measurement increase. This work generally supports the argument that different markets warrant different treatment.

Health care service markets vary in their characteristics such that there are some services where contracting out might be the more appropriate option and others where in-house production would be more appropriate. One cannot even make general predictions about service areas, such as mental health care services or general practitioner services, as much will depend upon the particular conditions of smaller markets within those general categories. For example, the mental health care service market can be broken down into at least three further markets: forensic mental health care services (for criminals and/or those who are a danger to themselves or the community); acute/intensive mental health care services; and rehabilitation and continuing care mental health care services.[28] Each of these markets will exhibit different levels of asset specificity, information problems, and scope for opportunistic behavior. Moreover, the characteristics of these markets are dynamic and are liable to change over time. For example, developments in technology may reduce the fixed costs of surgery and thus the monopoly characteristics of hospitals. Keyhole surgery allows significantly faster patient recovery time and overall reduces the average number of beds and staff required in hospitals by negating the need for many patients to stay overnight, thus reducing the overall fixed costs of operation. This highlights the need for a flexible system that responds to changes in technology and the production process on the supply side.

Williamson noted that opportunism problems arising from asset specificity and information asymmetry are not of significant concern provided there is a competitive market. Miller notes from his study of fifteen US communities that insurers initiated only a limited amount of integration with hospitals. He advances the thesis that in a period of excess hospital bed supply, "it can be cheaper for insurers to 'buy' rather than to 'make' hospital services."[29] Thus, the extent to which rigid contracting out will be efficient will depend on the level of competition on the supply side.

The theory of the firm seeks to explain the size and structure of firms. The size and structure of purchasers and publicly-owned providers in internal markets have been fixed by government fiat and have not evolved as responses to market forces. In many government-controlled systems, such as the UK, New Zealand and Canada, recent emphasis has been placed upon consolidating hospitals generally on the assumption that efficiencies from economies of scale will be reaped. However, Schut concludes that empirical research does not support the belief that the larger the hospital the better and, in fact, that moderate-sized hospitals are characterized by constant returns to scale.[30] New Zealand's internal market provides a good illustration of how government has fixed the size and scope of hospital operations. In New Zealand the Auckland CHE (one of twenty-three Crown Health Enterprises or CHEs) manages six hospitals on six separate sites with a total of 1,420 beds. By comparison, the Health Waikato CHE is responsible for fourteen hospitals on fourteen sites with a total of 1,501 beds and the Lakeland Health Ltd CHE is responsible for one hospital with 260 beds.[31] The Auckland CHE's six hospitals cover a wide range of specialties: Auckland Central (specializing in neurosurgery, opthamology, oncology); Starship (for children's medicine); Greenlane (specializing in cardiothoracic surgery and respiratory medicine); National Women's (specializing in gynecology and obstetrics); and the Mason Clinic (for secure psychiatric patients). It is difficult to ascertain whether the size and structure of the CHEs is optimal in terms of the number and types of hospitals they are respectively responsible for. However, much does seem to turn on hospitals' geographic proximity to each other and does not appear to be related to the manageability of the institutions or coordination between health care service needs. The result is that although neighboring hospitals may in fact be potential competitors in a number of health care service markets, when they are under the administrative and managerial umbrella of one CHE, the potential for competition is negated. As government determines the size of purchasers and providers in both the UK and New Zealand, potential competition is artificially suppressed in both jurisdictions. As a result a bilateral monopoly situation often arises, with a single buyer (monopsony) on the demand side and a single seller (monopoly) on the supply side. The results of negotiations in a bilateral monopoly situation are difficult to determine. The risk is that there will be no efficiency gains from the new arrangements but instead there will be increased transactions or administrative costs arising from mandatory contracting out.

Contracting in internal markets

The contract appears to be, as Allen notes, the fulcrum of the internal market model for it performs the function of formalizing the agreement between purchasers and providers as to the range and quality of health care services to be delivered and at what price.[32] This is in contrast to the managed competition model and, indeed, to the general ethos of managed care where, all other things being equal, there are a variety of relationships, contractual and proprietary, that may exist between insurer/purchasers and health care providers.

The rationale underlying the purchaser/provider split in the UK and New Zealand is that prior to internal market reform it was easier for the management of the old integrated institutions to purchase services from the public hospitals they managed even when there were other more efficient private providers.

The problem in both the UK's and New Zealand's former command-and-control systems was that there were no incentives for management within these integrated institutions to choose the most cost-efficient range of services and to purchase from the most efficient provider supplying services of an adequate quality. Rather than directly tackling the problem of the lack of incentives for purchasers, reformers in both New Zealand the UK have focused their energies on minimizing the discretion accorded to decision-makers by indiscriminately splitting the purchaser and provider roles and requiring purchasers to contract out for the supply of services. The contract is used in internal markets as a managerial device to minimize discretion.[33]

The primacy in internal markets of contracting out as opposed to hierarchical or administrative arrangements would seem to reflect the preference of neo-classical economists for allocation through the market as opposed to by government. This preference is based on the assumption that contracts are voluntarily entered into and the parties thereto are fully informed. Thus the welfare of the parties thereto must be improved or else they would not have entered into the contract. However, as discussed in the following section, these assumptions cannot be made with respect to the contracts concluded in the UK's and New Zealand's internal markets.

Contracts in the UK's internal market

Contracts in the UK's internal market violate the assumptions that economists usually make about contracts in the private sector in a number of important respects, to the extent that it is a misrepresentation to call the process "contracting."

The UK Health Authorities have no choice but to contract out for the supply of health care services and thus, as they do not enter contracts voluntarily, the resultant contracts cannot be assumed to be welfare enhancing. It is not yet apparent what impact the new Primary Care Groups will have on purchasing activity but, at least prior to 1 April 1999, the Health Authorities purchased the vast majority of health care services and thus many providers have had no choice but to contract with Health Authorities. Moreover, in the absence of regulatory restraints, there is the possibility that the Health Authorities could use their monopsony power to engage in opportunistic behavior at the expense of health care providers and, ultimately, patients.

As Health Authorities are government-appointed, there is both direct and indirect pressure not to disrupt established entitlements and to maintain the status quo in contracting arrangements. In private markets, managers have incentives to conduct their business efficiently otherwise there is the risk of insolvency and consequent job loss. Both purchasers and providers know that in the UK's internal market the government will be unwilling to sack the management of inefficient Health Authorities, the new Primary Care Groups, or the NHS Trusts. As one example, the previous Conservative government allocated extra funding to the Thames region to mitigate the effects of a fall in funding as a result of the new contracting process and prevented some purchasers from switching to cheaper providers to protect incumbents.[34] Bloor and Maynard concluded that political considerations influenced the UK government's decision to reallocate 76 percent (rather than 100 percent) of health funds on the basis of needs indices that had been reviewed and refined over some time.[35] This decision resulted in benefits to South and Home Counties and, as Bloor and Maynard record, became known as the "mid-Surrey effect...due to the coincidental benefit to the then Secretary of State's Constituency."[36] If governments continually intervene in internal markets to blunt the effect of competition then, as Ham and Maynard note, the result may be the worst of the command-and-control system and the free market system: bureaucratic controls coupled with high transaction costs.[37]

Prior to 1 April 1999, "NHS contracts" were contracts between a Health Authority and an NHS Trust or a GP Fundholder and an NHS Trust. Rather than being free to make any bargain they choose, a prospective party to an NHS contract who considered that the other party was taking advantage of an unequal bargaining position could refer the matter to the Secretary of State for Health. The Secretary of State could specify the terms to be included in any proposed arrangement and direct the parties to proceed with it.[38] Moreover, unlike ordinary commercial contracts, NHS contracts were not enforceable in law and any dispute arising in relation thereto was not heard before the regular courts but by the Secretary of State (or her or his appointee).[39] The Secretary of State was permitted to vary the terms of the arrangement in dispute or terminate the arrangement, powers beyond the regular UK courts in the resolution of ordinary commercial contracts.[40] The New Labour reforms require purchasing responsibility to be eventually transferred from the Health Authorities to Primary Care Groups. The new Primary Care Groups will, however, still be expected to contract with the NHS Trusts with the stipulation that contracts are of at least three years' duration.[41] Where disputes arise between Primary Care Groups and NHS Trusts or other providers, the White Paper setting out the reforms states that the Health Authority will have the power to resolve these disputes. No details are given of what principles Health Authorities will use in the resolution process. However, what is clear is that in the internal market, both pre and post the New Labour reforms, NHS contracts will not be enforceable in the general courts. Maynard argues that this absence of legal redress in the UK's internal market may have been of little significance as many private sector commercial agreements are settled out of court.[42] However, this argument overlooks the fact that in the private sector it may be the threat of litigation that provides an incentive for the parties to negotiate a compromise. Also the determination of disputes through the courts creates a line of precedent that parties in dispute may turn to for guidance in reaching settlements (although UK regulations, prior to the New Labour reforms, did require that the reasons for a particular decision be given and thus a line of administrative precedent could emerge).[43]

The UK government regulates the prices negotiated between the Health Authorities and the NHS Trusts by requiring that the prices charged by NHS Trusts reflect their respective average costs. Presumably, this practice will continue with the transfer of purchasing power from Health Authorities to Primary Care Groups. Marginal costing may only be used where there is surplus capacity above and beyond that predicted to be needed to fulfill the volumes of services required by purchasers in that year and can only be applied during the actual financial year that the spare capacity arises.[44] NHS Trusts cannot negotiate differential rates, notwithstanding the fact that there may be significant differences in the volumes of services demanded by different purchasers.[45] As McGuire and Anand note, unless there are constant returns to scale, average costs do not equal marginal costs and consequently insisting on prices being fixed at average costs will be inefficient in some markets.[46] This provides further confirmation that there are many different health care service markets and they cannot all be treated in the same way.

NHS Trusts are expressly prohibited from cross subsidizing one contract, procedure, or specialty from another and are only allowed to make a return of 6 percent per annum on their net assets. NHS Trusts are not able to carry forward surpluses into the next financial year, and the government regulates and prescribes the amount of private capital able to be borrowed. Moreover, progress was slow in enabling NHS Trusts to negotiate employee contracts.[47] These sorts of restrictions leave the NHS Trusts at a competitive disadvantage compared to private providers who are under no such restrictions, but are understandable given the monopoly held by NHS Trusts in many health care service markets.

Regulation of competition in the UK internal market before 1 April 1999 was not the responsibility of the usual institutions of competition policy (i.e. the Office of Fair Trading and the Monopolies and Mergers Commission) but was left to the government in the form of the NHS Management Executive. On 12 December 1994 the Department of Health published guidelines intended to inform participants in the UK's internal market of current government policy with respect to mergers and anti-competitive behavior.[48] Given that the New Labour reforms of December 1997 emphasize cooperation and collaboration rather than competition, presumably the guidelines for anti-competitive behavior will now be largely redundant.

Given that "contracts" in the UK's internal market are not legally enforceable and that the government controls both purchasers and most hospital providers, the rhetoric of "contracts" may disguise the real fact that the result is simply new hierarchical arrangements within the old UK bureaucracy. As Checkland puts it "(t)he reality of contracting has been that the word is shorthand for a complex social process which has been evolving steadily since the reforms were introduced."[49] This leads to the insight that there is not necessarily a clear choice between contracting out and vertical integration. In truth there is a continuum of options in the context of public/private relationships. The case of the UK's internal market both pre and post the New Labour reforms falls closer towards the pole of vertical integration than towards the pole of contracting out as normally understood in the private sector. Even within the internal market, government-appointed purchasers and providers may vary in the extent to which they treat relationships between them as hierarchical or administrative or as arms-length market transactions to be formally codified in contracts.[50]

Some commentators argue that, rather than fostering increased devolution of power and "less" government, internal market reform in the UK has in fact resulted in increased centralization. Harrison notes in the King's Fund Policy Institute report *Health Care in the UK 1994/95*:

> If we look at actions rather than words, it would be easier to regard the new NHS not as a competitive structure, but rather one in which providers are increasingly having to respond to central targets set for the reduction of waiting lists and other requirements of the Patient's Charter, for the introduction of higher rates of day case surgery, and for the reduction in costs or cash releasing efficiency savings. Targets are set nationally in the best traditions of Soviet-style planning and are then faithfully passed on by purchasers to their main providers, often unamended in the light of local circumstances or to the scope of savings in particular forms of care.[51]

However, Harden argues that it would be a mistake to think that the contractual approach offers nothing new. He argues that:

> The new element is not "consumer sovereignty," however, nor greater rights for individuals. Rather, it is the fact that the parties to the contract have separate interests. In this sense 'competition' is inherent in the contractual approach; not competition between different purchasers, or different providers of services, but in the contractual relationship itself. The public interest – i.e. the overall functioning of the public service in question – is not the responsibility of a single unitary organization, but instead emerges from the process of agreement between separate organizations, none of which has responsibility for the public interest as a whole…(it) is this which is essential to the creation of a structural bias towards minimizing discretion and a focus on performance/outputs rather than process/inputs.[52]

Despite Harden's arguments, it is, in my opinion, difficult to see how competition *within* the contractual relationship will further the public's interest. Surely there is a significant risk that this sort of "competition" will be nothing but a contest to avoid accountability and responsibility and maintain the status quo in order to ensure political longevity? As Maynard (blisteringly) describes it, "(t)here is a risk that the (internal market) reform process has created a quasi-centralized bureaucratic confusion dressed up in the rhetoric of market competition."[53] Is the minimization of discretion, through contracts or otherwise, necessarily a good thing? The theory of the firm suggests that having the discretion to be vertically integrated would, in some health care service markets, be efficient.

Another way to view "minimization of discretion" is as fragmentation of accountability as central government, government-appointed purchasers, and providers all point to each other as being responsible for any failures in performance. Minimizing discretion also fails to acknowledge that purchasers themselves need incentives to in turn ensure the most efficient performance on the part of providers. If purchasers do have incentives to ensure the efficient supply of health care services then mandating a rigid purchaser/provider split reduces the potential for innovation and change.

Contracts in New Zealand's internal market

In New Zealand, there has been a concerted attempt to reform public hospitals into government-owned corporations (Crown Health Enterprises) that seek to mimic private firm behavior. Unlike the UK, in New Zealand's internal market:

- there is no explicit government regulation of pricing;
- there is no prohibition on cross-subsidization by Crown Health Enterprises (CHEs) or, for that matter, other providers;
- there is no explicit regulation of private borrowing by the CHEs;[54]
- regulation of competition is left to the general competition authorities;[55]
- all contracts are enforceable through the regular courts in the usual manner.

Thus, the purchaser/provider split in New Zealand has been more rigorous and real than in the UK. Nonetheless, contracts between the Health Funding Authority (previously four Regional Health Authorities) and the CHEs still contradict the assumptions that neo-classical economists generally make about contracts in the private sector. In New Zealand's internal market, the Health Funding Authority *must* purchase through contracts a comprehensive range of services for the entire population. Thus, the contracts concluded cannot be *assumed* to enhance welfare as one would normally assume in the private sector. If the Health Funding Authority was able to supply its own health care services rather than being forced to contract out then the range and terms of the contacts it entered into might be different. Moreover, health care providers have little real choice but to contract with the Health Funding Authority. In addition, the Minister of Health may compel CHEs to supply health care services.[56] The Health Funding Authority is also entitled by statute to give notice of the terms and conditions upon which it will make payments to public and private health providers and acceptance of such payment is deemed to constitute acceptance of those terms and conditions.[57] The powerful position of the Health Funding Authority as purchaser is arguably demonstrated by the gap between prices paid and CHEs' actual costs.[58] Management of the four Regional Health Authorities (centralized into one Health Authority in 1997) blamed the central government for not funding them to a sufficient degree so that they were able to pay prices that covered providers' costs.[59]

In the private sector, management that do not perform efficiently face the risk of their firm's insolvency and concomitant job loss and damage to their credibility in the management job market. These sorts of incentives do not act upon management in the CHEs. To date, CHEs that are failing have been propped up through deficit funding. In other words, the government injects funds and that sum is then treated as debt to be repaid over the longer term (perhaps past the horizon point where current managers envisage themselves staying in their positions). Part of the problem has been that the CHEs were saddled with unrealistic debt burdens at their inception. The debt, accrued historically by the old Area Health Boards, was simply transferred to the new CHEs.[60] This reportedly caused serious motivational problems for staff, as any savings made through efficiency gains were diverted to debt repayment as opposed to service enhancement. This deficit funding also means that the Health Authority need not be unduly concerned that opportunistic behavior on their part will result in the insolvency of a CHEs.

Despite the rhetoric of contracts and competition, implying as it does "less" rather than "more" government intervention, there has been significant political interference in New Zealand's internal market. For example, the government intervened on various occasions to prevent the closure of surgical wards and hospitals and set up a $130-million fund to be administered by the government (as opposed to the Regional Health Authorities) to encourage CHEs to introduce a new system of booking patients for surgery.[61] According to management within CHEs, this places them between a rock and a hard place with, on the one hand, the expectation that they will conduct the CHEs along private firm lines and yet, on the other, the difficulty of so operating given central government interference.[62] Managers for CHEs were actively head-hunted from the private sector with a strong emphasis being placed on hiring those with general management skills as opposed to a particular knowledge or experience in the health sector. Since the commencement of the reforms, twelve of the twenty-three CHEs have had their chief executive officers resign.[63]

Benefits of internal markets

What have been the benefits of introducing the purchaser/provider split and mandatory contracting out in the UK and New Zealand systems?

Firstly, it is important to note that, as a result of the reforms in both the UK and New Zealand, there has been no significant change in how health needs are prioritized, the sorts of health care services supplied, or the providers who are supplying these services.[64] This should not be that surprising given that the structure of the internal market is essentially that of bilateral monopoly. Generally, in both the UK and New Zealand, contracting continues to consist of "block contracts" (a fixed sum for an unspecified number of services).[65] Acute and emergency care, mental health care services, and primary care providers, are generally provided pursuant to block contracts.[66] The use of a prospective capped payment is no different from the payment regime under the old command-and-control system. Cost and volume contracts are used for elective surgery so that essentially providers receive a fee for each service provided but the total amount they can receive in a particular period is capped. In New Zealand there was much consternation when this method of payment resulted in some CHEs providing all contracted elective surgery in a relatively short-time period and then closing down surgical theaters for the rest of the year.[67] Due to the adverse media publicity, clauses were subsequently included in contracts requiring CHEs to pace the delivery of their services over the course of the year. Cost-per-case or fee-for-service contracts are used for a small number of services. For example, in one contract between a New Zealand Regional Health Authority and a CHE, fee-for-service payments applied to maternity services, termination of pregnancy, postnatal primary care and school dental services.[68]

Söderlund found in the UK that efficiency gains, including lower hotel costs per episode and significantly lower direct treatment and diagnostics costs, occurred when hospitals became NHS Trusts rather than being directly managed by the Health Authority.[69] This is in contrast to New Zealand where it has been acknowledged that internal market reform has not resulted in public hospitals achieving anywhere near the 30 percent efficiency gains envisaged prior to reform, and that performance may, if anything, have weakened.[70] Söderlund, however, notes that it is impossible to say whether the hospitals that became NHS Trusts would have become more efficient anyway (i.e. the more efficient hospitals sought to become NHS Trusts first). Since initially NHS Trusts were a self-selected group, Söderlund considers this hypothesis plausible. He also notes that it is impossible to know whether the transition is a real "one-off" efficiency gain or a permanent and persistent change in organizational functioning. Moreover, the fact that the NHS Trusts operate more efficiently than hospitals managed directly by Health Authorities does not mean that the system as a whole is more efficient. The total costs for the system may still be greater where hospitals are NHS Trusts as opposed to directly managed by Health Authorities. For example, empirical work conducted in South Africa suggests that private for-profit hospitals are able to produce more outputs at lower cost than directly managed public hospitals.[71] However, when the *total costs* faced by the government in contracting out are included in the analysis (such as the extra administrative costs in negotiating contracts), costs per episode of care are more costly for the private for-profit hospitals than for directly managed hospitals. In any event, the argument developed here is not that contracting out to independent institutions will never be an efficient choice in any particular market. The point is that purchasers should in general have the incentives to choose the most efficient configuration both initially and as market conditions evolve. As Williamson notes:

> Whichever way the assignment of transactions to firm or market is made initially, the choice ought not to be regarded as fixed. Both firms and markets change over time in ways that may render inappropriate an initial assignment of transactions to firm or market.[72]

The primary benefit of internal market reform has been that of generating information about the costs and benefits of services. Ashton notes that improved information systems assist purchasers in monitoring the performance of providers, thus improving provider accountability and assisting management in quality improvement.[73] The cost of generating this information has been high and there is no evidence as yet that the cost of information generation is outweighed by the benefits of use of this information to improve service purchase and production. However, an efficient system will require information about the costs and benefits. Consequently, an internal market system might be viewed as a transitional system where information-gathering systems are put in place and the system as a whole reorients itself to considering costs and benefits. One manager of a New Zealand Regional Health Authority described the benefits of internal market reform as follows:

- it has made CHEs focus on what they are doing in terms of services, volumes and costs; in the past their information on each has been poor and there have been failures to link costs to services and volumes;
- it has created a currency for service debates; we now have some way of doing trade-offs between services;
- the purchaser now has a currency to use in its resource-allocation work across services;
- the contracts have quality requirements, which encourage CHEs to monitor the quality of their services.[74]

A report prepared for the incoming New Zealand government in 1996 noted that internal market reform had "enabled greater focus on evidence-based practice, increased service integration, increased accountability for primary care and the development of better information within the health system."[75] One should note that "increased service integration" and "increased accountability for primary care" can be attributable to integration of financing for secondary and primary services and could have been achieved independently of the "purchaser/provider split."

Costs of internal markets

Many commentators have expressed concern over the increased transactions costs associated with enforced contracting out in New Zealand and in the UK.[76] Although the magnitude of transactions costs are often assumed to be indicative of inefficiency this is not necessarily true. The important question, often overlooked, is whether the efficiency gains hoped to be realized from the reformed system outweighs the extra transactions costs. A system could have high transactions costs but still be more efficient than an alternative configuration with lower transactions costs but higher internal management costs. The crucial questions are: first, whether the internal market system, with its enforced purchaser/provider split, is relatively more efficient than the old vertically-integrated hierarchies and, second, whether there is a better institutional arrangement for the allocation of health care services. The problem is that comparison is difficult, given the lack of information regarding costs and benefits in the old command-and-control systems and apparent government resistance to seriously analyze the effects of internal market reform in New Zealand and, to a lesser extent, in the UK.

In the UK, the New Labour reforms of December 1997 responded to concerns over increased transactions costs in the internal market by mandating a shift to long-term contracts with NHS Trusts of at least three years in duration.[77] Similarly, in New Zealand, greater emphasis is now being given to cooperation and long-term contracts. One of the New Zealand government's performance expectations is that the Health Funding Authority will ensure that contracting agreements are based on effective relationships and negotiations carried out in good faith.[78] Ashton argues that given the concern over the increased transactions costs in New Zealand's internal market, the development of long-term, informal, and cooperative relationships between purchasers and providers in New Zealand's internal market will be the most appropriate development in cases where contestability on the supply side is limited.[79] This is known as "relational contracting."[80] Macneil developed the idea that the relationship between parties to a "relational contract" would result in "a mini-society with a vast array of norms beyond the norms centering on exchange and its immediate processes."[81] Thus, the argument runs, contracts in internal markets should be not be viewed through the lens of spot or discrete private sector contracts. As Allen points out, long-term contracts in the private sector often vitiate economists' usual assumptions about contracts but their continued existence is likely to mean that they are efficient.[82] In such a case, as Llewellyn notes, the contract only provides an adjustable framework

> which almost never accurately indicates real working relations, but which affords a rough indication around which such relations vary, an occasional guide in case of doubt, and a norm of ultimate appeal when the relations cease in fact to work.[83]

However, the idea of developing closer relations between purchasers and providers as a means of reducing the transactions costs of the purchaser/provider split while still seeking to preserve the benefits of contracting out in contestable markets is problematic. One of the primary reasons motivating the purchaser/provider split was so that public authorities would not prefer to procure health care services from the institutions they themselves managed as opposed to other potentially more efficient providers. Developing the close relationships needed to sustain long-term contracts between purchasers and providers increases the likelihood that providers will capture purchasers. In other words, incumbent providers will be preferred over other potentially more efficient providers because of personal relationships that have sprung up between the regulator or purchaser and provider.

The development of close relationships between purchasers and providers undermines the rationale for a rigorous purchaser/provider split and in particular the goal of reducing any managerial conflicts of interest. Moreover, although longer-term cooperative relationships may well be efficient for some services, as mentioned earlier, different health care service markets exhibit different characteristics. Large government-appointed providers in the UK and New Zealand supply many different sorts of services, some of which may be more efficiently supplied pursuant to long-term relational contracts and others of which may be more efficiently supplied by contestable spot-markets.

Williamson notes that business people may adapt to institutional problems and develop norms of behavior which reduce the transactions costs associated with uncertainty, opportunism, and small-numbers contracting without the need for vertical integration.[84] He discusses the need for business-people to maintain their reputation as one incentive that counteracts the incentive to act opportunistically at contract renewal junctures. This explains why long-term contracting may occur in the private sector. However, it is important to note that the need for business-people to maintain their reputation is a key factor absent from internal market contracting. For this reason I am doubtful that there is any real prospect of efficiency gains from relational contracting in internal markets. Government-appointed purchasers and government-owned/controlled health care providers have few incentives to be concerned about the reputational effects of their own opportunistic behavior in the internal market. They know that the other party (whether due to the lack of competition in the market or due to government fiat) has no choice but to contract with them. As both purchasers and providers are government-owned, there is also no threat that either party could take the other over. For example, in New Zealand, despite the fact that contracts sometimes were not signed between the Health Authority and the relevant CHE until part way through the financial year, if at all, hospital services were still delivered. [85]

In New Zealand, the contracts that are signed seem generally to cover no more than one year. [86]The New Labour reform proposal assumes that contracts concluded in the UK internal market have generally not been for more than one year, although there is some evidence that in certain parts of the country contracts were concluded for terms of three years.[87] However, the length of contract term is not necessarily reflective of a truly cooperative relationship. Nor is the length of the relationship necessarily reflective of a truly cooperative relationship. Purchasers and providers in internal markets are *already* in long-term relationships irrespective of the form of contract – they have no choice about this given that they are ultimately under government control and are required by legislation to, respectively, purchase and provide services. Contracts may be of short or of longer duration but that is largely beside the point. The existence of a long-term relationship, compelled as it is by circumstance and government requirement, is quite different from the idea of relational contracting in the private sector, the latter fostering trust as part of mutual economic need.

Clearly, it is a mistake to consider the merits and costs of contracting in the UK's and New Zealand's health sector independently of the political milieu in which contracting is occurring. The motivations of both purchasers and providers cannot be assumed to be survival in a competitive market as they can generally be in the private sector. Rather, the motivations of purchasers and providers are more clearly linked to the political incentives in play given that they are funded by government monies and are government appointed or government owned. For example, CHEs and NHS Trusts have been able to politicize the negotiating process by arguing that a government-appointed Health Authority is underfunding them or making cutbacks or sacrificing quality in order to save money.[88] The political nature of the system may also result in resistance to change as it is much safer, politically, for management within the government-appointed purchasers and government-owned health providers to maintain the status quo than to take risks that may jeopardize one's political life. The political incentives are all geared to strongly punish mistakes whilst only weakly rewarding gains and achievements. This results in stickiness in the system, as historical utilization patterns are simply rolled over.

In both New Zealand and the UK, the year prior to internal market reform was used as a benchmark for price, volume, and quality standards, resulting in entrenchment of historical inefficiencies. In the first year of operation of the UK's internal market (1991/92), pre-existing arrangements for supply were rolled over. From April 1992, the UK Health Authorities were free to selectively contract with providers; however, Hughes concludes that "although the nature of developments varies from Health Authority to Health Authority, there is no evidence of any general movement of resources away from the acute sector."[89] Similarly, in New Zealand, for the first year of operation (1993/94), pre-existing arrangements for supply were rolled over. As a more specific example, in the 1994/95 contract between the Southern Regional Health Authority and the Canterbury Health Limited CHE, the contract specifically states that "(w)e (the RHA) acknowledge that the quality standards outlined in this section are intended to describe and quantify quality levels equivalent to which you provided in 1993/94 and at no additional cost."[90] The inertia problem is compounded by the fact that budgets set for the UK Health Authorities and New Zealand's Regional Health Authorities were based on historical consumption patterns, although there are efforts underway in both countries to distribute funds on a per-capita weighted basis.[91] In sum, although there have been small movements at the margins, the historical configuration of providers and service patterns have largely remained intact in both New Zealand and the United Kingdom.

Managed care in internal markets

The GP Fundholding scheme, a form of managed care, resulted in some of the most significant changes to the UK's system. Similarly, in New Zealand, it has been argued that Independent Practice Associations are the key to effecting real change.[92] Glennerster concludes that GP Fundholders were better contractors than Health Authorities as they had better information about health care needs and more motivation to improve service standards. Because Fundholders were relatively small, they could also switch their contracts without resulting in a financial loss for NHS Trusts and other providers. If, however, a Health Authority shifted their contracts away from a NHS Trust, this would have serious financial consequences for the Trust and there would likely be political influence brought to bear not to upset the status quo.[93]

As a result of the Fundholding scheme, which involved over 3,500 Fundholders and 15,000 general practitioners, there was a shift in the balance of power from hospitals and specialists to general practitioners. Through the contracting process, Fundholders were able to secure better quality care for their particular patients, such as quicker access to surgery, etc. This, however, raised the specter of a two-tiered system. This was one of the primary motivations for the New Labour reforms to abolish Fundholding. The interesting point, from the perspective of contracting out versus in-house production, is that the Health Authorities and GP Fundholders did not compete on a level playing field. Health Authorities incur relatively greater transactions costs as they must contract out for the supply of all health care services. GP Fundholding was a form of managed care as each Fundholder received a fixed annual fee to care for all its enrollees. A practitioner who was a Fundholder member could, subject to other regulations and licensing requirements, decide whether to attend to the patient's needs in-house or to contract out for the supply of services from specialists, hospitals, and other providers.

The evidence suggests that, overall, the Fundholding initiative was not efficient as the transactions costs involved outweighed efficiency gains.[94] For the year ending 1994/95, the Audit Commission calculated that Fundholders received a total of £232 million of public monies to cover the costs of staff, equipment, and computers needed for managing Fundholding. On the other side of the ledger, the Audit Commission reports that Fundholders made efficiency savings of £206 million over the 1994/95 year.[95] Once this is deducted from the total costs, there is a shortfall of £26 million. The actual shortfall may be even greater, however, because the Commission was not able to calculate the management and transaction costs incurred by Health Authorities and health providers in dealing with Fundholders. The Commission did note that the average direct cost incurred by NHS Trusts (which are responsible for managing public hospitals) in dealing with GP Fundholders was £5,900 a year per Fundholder. The Commission also referred to the estimate of one NHS Trust that it cost four times as much to negotiate contracts with thirteen Fundholders, accounting for 4 percent of the Trust's incomes, as it did with the Health Authority, accounting for 91 percent of its income.[96]

This should not necessarily be taken as evidence that all managed care arrangements will be inefficient. Part of the reason for the high transactions costs associated with Fundholding is that there were so many small Fundholders that the various Health Authorities and NHS Trusts had to do business with. One would predict that if larger integrated delivery systems (really) competed with each other, the transactions costs would not be of the same magnitude, as these systems would have an incentive to minimize internal transactions costs. It is also to be noted that the incentives that the Fundholders responded to were more complex than a simple for-profit motive, as the disposal of surplus was regulated and had to be used to further patient amenities.[97] The new Primary Care Groups, proposed by the New Labour reforms of December 1997, are a step in the right direction to the extent that they are increasing the size of purchasers. However, the new Primary Care Groups will not compete with each other and have no explicit financial incentives to engage in good decision-making.

Conclusion: a flexible approach

The purchaser/provider split in the UK and New Zealand was adopted in order to prevent government-appointed purchasers from purchasing services from the public hospitals they managed at the expense of other (perhaps) more efficient public and private providers. It also sought to restructure public hospitals into institutions that were, to varying degrees, more like private firms. The goal of internal market reform was thus to minimize the discretion of decision-makers and to encourage them to enter into contracts for supply with efficient health care providers. However, this focus did not tackle the real problem, namely a lack of incentives for purchasers to enter into the most efficient supply-side arrangements. The problem in the previous rigidly integrated health authorities of the UK and New Zealand was not that they were integrated with hospitals but that they did not have incentives to purchase well. Thus, attacking the potential conflict of interest in being both the purchaser of government-funded health care services and being a significant provider attacked the symptom but not the root of the problem. Moreover, it is likely that in some health care service markets the most efficient arrangement may be or could evolve to be that of vertical integration. Flexibility is key.

One might argue that a purchaser/provider split in internal markets is acceptable, as reducing scope for opportunistic behavior is one of the key reasons why firms tend to vertically integrate in the private sector. The tendency towards opportunism in internal markets on the part of purchasers and providers is tempered by the political milieu in which they must operate.[98] Government-appointed purchasers and providers in the UK and New Zealand know that threats of hold-out and overt opportunistic behavior will not be tolerated. However, in the absence of specifically designed managerial incentives, the political incentives to which government-appointed purchasers and providers respond has led to maintenance of the status quo and perpetuation of inefficient historical patterns of supply. Thus, the risk of opportunism is not one of private firms seeking monopoly rents, but of government-appointed decision-makers not performing their role of purchasers as well as they could or should.

Some commentators advocate long-term relational contracting between purchasers and providers as a means of reducing transactions costs in internal markets. The development of such a relationship raises the specter of purchasers being "captured" by providers, which is in large part what motivated the indiscriminate split between purchasers and providers in the first place. By prohibiting purchasers in internal markets from providing health care services, the discretion and power of government-appointed monopsonies is checked. However, I argue that it was not the level of discretion accorded in the first place that was the key problem, but rather the lack of incentives, institutional support, and information needed for purchasers to be pro-active purchasers.

The rationale behind the purchaser/provider split runs counter to the international trend towards managed care arrangements and of integrated delivery systems. Government-appointed purchasers in internal markets could seek to purchase managed care from competing groups of providers. This is in fact what happened in the UK with GP Fundholders. However, Fundholding was a central government initiative and Fundholders were lured into participation with relatively generous budgets. Independent Practice Associations in New Zealand evolved in response to the potential for aggressive purchasing behavior on the part of Regional Health Authorities. However, neither the UK's Health Authorities nor New Zealand's Health Funding Authority have incentives to encourage managed care arrangements. Moreover, as they cannot provide services or integrate with other providers, they must wait for providers to initiate managed care plans. The large health care providers with the resources to implement large-scale managed care plans are largely government-owned institutions who have strong incentives to maintain the status quo.

Simon's assertion that individuals operate under bounded rationality is particularly appropriate for anyone who struggles with issues of institutional design. As soon as one feels that she or he has discovered an important piece to the puzzle of what constitutes the best institutional design, one finds that it does not quite interconnect with the other pieces located. So, the evaluation of alternative institutional arrangements becomes more of an art than a science and it is difficult to move past abstract generalizations about likely incentive effects in the absence of rigorous empirical data. One point is clear in the health care sector: the configuration of any health system will have to constantly evolve to respond to changing needs.[99] The need for continual change has been historically shown in all systems. Even the command-and-control systems of the UK and New Zealand have undergone successive reform after reform. Maynard refers to the successive "redisorganizations" of the National Health Service[100] and the same can be said of New Zealand. No sooner has one set of reforms been implemented than another is introduced. These periodic government-imposed upheavals dampen the morale of people working within the health sector. Moreover, little effort is expended on evaluating past reforms or fully evaluating the likely effects of new proposals. There is no perfect or easy solution to what constitutes the best institutional design. However, a paradigm shift is needed so that the health system in question is constantly and incrementally evolving without top-down structural reforms. The managed competition model offers more promise in this regard than the internal market model.

Notes

1   O. E. Williamson, *Markets and Hierarchies, Analysis and Anti-trust Implications: A Study in the Economics of Internal Organization* (New York: The Free Press, 1975) at p. 8.

2   R. H. Coase, 'The Nature Of The Firm', (1937) 4 *Economica* 386.

3   For a discussion, see T. E. Olsen, 'Agency Costs and the Limits of Integration', (1996) 27(3) *RAND J. of Econ.* 479.

4   Coase, *op. cit.*, p. 395.

5   See generally Williamson, *Markets and Hierarchies: Analysis and Anti-trust Implications, op. cit.*, and O. E. Williamson, *The Economic Institutions of Capitalism: Firms, Markets, Relational Contracting* (New York: Free Press, 1985).

6   H. A. Simon, *Administrative Behavior: A Study of Decision-Making Processes in Administrative Organization,* (2nd edn), (New York: Free Press, 1965).

7   See O. E. Williamson, 'Comparative Economic Organization: The Analysis of Discrete Structural Alternatives', (1991) 36 *Admin. Sci. Q.* 269 at pp. 281–282.

8   H. Imai, 'Bilateral Price-Setting in a Bilateral Monopoly Model', (1986) 24 *J. Econ. Theory* 311; S. R. Williams, 'Efficient Performance in Two Agent Bargaining', (1987) 41 *J. Econ. Theory* 154; J. C. Rochet, 'Some Recent Results in Bargaining Theory' (1987) 31 *Europ Econ Rev* 326.

9   R. Flannigan, 'The Economic Structure of the Firm', (1995) 33(1) *Osgoode Hall Law J.* 105 at p. 124 and p. 128.

10   See Williamson, *Markets and Hierarchies: Analysis and Anti-trust Implications, op. cit.*, p. 10.

11   *Ibid.*, p. 14.

12   O. E. Williamson, 'Hierarchical Control and Optimum Firm Size', in O. E. Williamson, *Economic Organization: Firms, Markets and Policy Control* (New York: New York University Press, 1986) pp. 32–53 (first published as an article in 1967 in the *J. of Political Economy*).

13   Williamson, *The Economic Institutions of Capitalism: Firms, Markets, Relational Contracting, op. cit.*, pp. 133–135.

14   See W. Baumol, J. Panzer and R. Willig, *Contestable Markets and the Theory of Industry Structure* (New York: Harcourt Brace Jovanovich, 1982), and W. Baumol, 'Contestable Markets: An Uprising in the Theory of Industry Structure', (1982) 72 *American Econ. Review* 1.

15   *Ibid.*

16   Williamson, *The Economic Institutions of Capitalism: Firms, Markets, Relational Contracting, op. cit.*, Chapter. 13.

17   G. L. Priest, 'The Origins of Utility Regulation and the "Theories of Regulation" Debate', (1993) 36(1) *J. of Law and Econ.* 289.

18   V. Goldberg, 'Regulation and Administered Contracts', (1976) 7 *Bell J. of Economics* 426.

19   M. J. Trebilcock, *The Prospects for Reinventing Government* (Toronto: C. D. Howe Institute, 1994) at p. 13. Another way of stating this would be that government will find it more efficient to contract out than to produce the service itself where, first, information asymmetries between the parties are small and there is adequate information available on costs, prices, and quality, thus reducing the scope for opportunistic behavior and, second, there is competition within or for the market (which depends to a large measure on the degree of investment in specific assets and substitutability thereof).

20   K. J. Crocker and S. E. Masten, 'Regulation and Administered Contracts Revisited: Lessons from Transaction-Cost Economics for Public Utility Regulation', (1996) 9(1) *J. of Regulatory Econ.* 5.

21   Possibly this problem of hold-out could be mitigated by locally based clinics with staff capable of triage and with ambulance and helicopter providing transport to larger centers with a number of hospitals. The viability of this option will depend on the cost and the impact on patients' safety and cost.

22   By this I mean that a new general practitioner (having satisfied all relevant licensing requirements) could readily enter the market as a supplier.

23   For a discussion see M. L. Barer and L. Wood, 'Common Problems, Different "Solutions": Learning from International Approaches to Improving Medical Services Access for Underserved Populations', (1997) 20(2) *Dalhousie Law Journal* 321.

24 Although the sale in the latter part of 1996 by South Auckland Health (one of the 23 Crown Health Enterprises) of the Kingseat psychiatric hospital for $6.8 million suggests that it is indeed possible to actually dispose of specifically designed institutions. The relevant question is the value realized in the sale relative to the original investment, discounted by the number of years in service.

25 S. R. Smith and M. Lipsky, 'Privatization in Health and Human Services: A Critique', (1992) 17(2) *J. Health Polit. Policy Law* 233 at p. 237: "...most services cannot be judged on the basis of decisive client outcomes. They cannot be standardized in their treatment approaches, nor can auditors effectively intrude into the interactions between workers and clients to determine whether decisions were made appropriately and consistently with existing policy."

26 See T. Ashton, 'Contracting for Health Services in New Zealand: Early Experiences', paper presented at the International Health Economics Association Inaugural Conference, Vancouver, 19–23 May 1996, and T. Ashton and D. Press, 'Market Concentration in Secondary Health Services Under a Purchaser-Provider Split: The New Zealand Experience', (1997) 6(1) *Health Economics* 43 at p. 43.

27 Ashton, 'Contracting for Health Services in New Zealand: Early Experiences', *op.cit.*

28 See the New Zealand's Commerce Commission Decision No. 275, ISSN No. 0114-2720, 1 August 1995 (application by the Midland Regional Health Authority and Health Waikato Limited for authorization under the Commerce Act (NZ) 1986, No. 5, s. 58, p. 32).

29 R. H. Miller, 'Health System Integration: A Means to an End', (1996) 15(2) *Health Affairs* 92 at p. 100.

30 F. T. Schut, 'Workable Competition in Health Care: Prospects for the Dutch Design', (1992) 35(12) *Soc. Sci. Med.* 1445 at p. 1452.

31 *Core Services for 1995/96: Third Report of the National Advisory Committee on Core Health and Disability Support Services* (Wellington: National Advisory Committee on Core Health and Disability Support Services, 1994). Appendix 12, pp. 137–139.

32 P. Allen, *A Legal Perspective on Contracts in the NHS Internal Market* (Bristol: S.A.U.S. Publications, University of Bristol, 1995) at p. 2.

33 A. Fox, *Beyond Contract: Work, Power and Trust Relations* (London: Faber, 1974) p. 62.

34 C. Ham and A. Maynard, 'Managing the NHS Market', (26 March 1994) 308 *BMJ* 845.

35 K. Bloor and A. Maynard, 'Health Care Reform in the UK National Health Service', (paper prepared for the First Meeting of the International Health Economics Association, May 1996, Vancouver, British Columbia).

36 *Ibid.*, p. 4.

37 Ham and Maynard, *op.cit.*, p. 846.

38 See the National Health Service and Community Care Act (UK) 1990, c. 19, s. 4.

39 *Ibid.*, s. 4(3).

40 Allen, *op. cit.*, p. 10. See also D. Hughes, J. V. McHale and L. Griffiths, 'Settling Contract Disputes in the National Health Service: Formal and Informal Pathways', in R. Flynn and G. Williams (eds), *Contracting for Health: Quasi-Markets and the National Health Service* (Oxford: Oxford University Press, 1997) and J. McHale, D. Hughes and L. Griffiths, 'Conceptualizing Contractual Disputes in the National Health Service Internal Market', in S. Denkin and J. Michie (eds), *Contracts, Competition and Cooperation* (Oxford: Oxford University Press, 1997).

41 *The New NHS: Modern, Dependable*, a White Paper, Cm 3807, 8 December 1997, section 6.17. Online. Available HTTP: http://www.official-documents.co.uk/document/doh/newnhs/contents.htm (accessed 30 March 1999).

42 A. Maynard, 'Can Competition Enhance Efficiency in Health Care? Lessons from the Reform of the UK National Health Service', (1994) 39(10) *Soc. Sci. Med.* 1433 at p. 1438.

43 See the National Health Service Contracts (Dispute Resolution) Regulations (UK), 1991, S.I. 1991/725.

44 Allen, *op. cit.*, p. 6.

45 *Ibid.*

46 A. McGuire and P. Anand, 'Introduction: Evaluating Health Care Reform' in P. Anand and A. McGuire (eds), *Changes in Health Care: Reflections on the NHS Internal Market* (Basingstoke: Macmillan Business, 1997) at p. 5.

47 A. Harrison (eds), *Health Care UK 1994/95: An Annual Review of Health Care Policy* (Bristol: J. W. Arrowsmith Limited, 1995) (hereinafter *Health Care UK 1994/95*) at p. 6, notes that although the intention was that NHS Trusts should set their own arrangements for pay at a local level, the government accepted in February 1994 the Pay Review Bodies' recommendations for clinical staff of across-the-board rises of 3 percent.

48 For a discussion, see D. Dawson, *Regulating Competition in the NHS: The Department of Health Guide on Mergers and Anti-Competitive Behaviour, Discussion Paper 131* (York: Centre for Health Economics, 1995).

49 P. Checkland, 'Rhetoric and Reality in Contracting: Research in and on the National Health Service', in R. Flynn and G. Williams (eds), *Contracting for Health: Quasi-Markets and the National Health Service* (New York: Oxford University Press, 1997) at p. 115.

50 See D. Hughes, L. Griffiths and J. McHale, 'Purchasing in the NHS: Administered or Market Contracts?', in A. McGuire and P. Anand (eds), *op. cit.*, 55 at p. 56.

51 *Health Care UK 1994/95*, *op. cit.*, p. 7.

52 I. Harden, *The Contracting State* (Buckingham: Open University Press, 1992) at p. 33.

53 Maynard, *op. cit.*, p. 1437.

54 Although they have only recently been able to supply services to private purchasers and there are government guidelines in place which effectively regulate this source of income.

55 There was a transition period of nearly two years where key players were exempt from these requirements. The Minister of Commerce issued a statement under the Commerce Act (NZ) 1986, No.5, s. 26 in June 1993 stating that, when considering competition issues in the health sector, the Commerce Commission should take into consideration the major changes underway and give the industry time to work through the transitional arrangements in place. The notice was withdrawn in May 1995.

56 The Health and Disability Services Act (NZ) 1993, No. 22, s. 40.

57 *Ibid.*, s. 51.

58 The Auckland Healthcare (a CHE) board chairman, Graeme Hawkins, is quoted as saying that the money paid to it often fell well short of its actual costs. Examples include: one young heart disease patient cost just under $80,000 to treat but the CHE received $1,868 in payment; a child with acute bronchitis cost just under $40,000 to treat but the CHE received $1,561, and a child with pneumonia stayed in the CHE for 32 days, costing nearly $30,000, but the hospital was paid only $17,928 – see A. Young, 'Health Chiefs Hit Back', *New Zealand Herald*, 4 December 1996, A19. Of course, what really needs to be shown is that the CHE's costs do not reflect inefficiencies in production and that the CHE's average cost falls below the average price paid by the Regional Health Authority.

59 E-mail letter from J. Webster, Manager, Central Regional Health Authority, 4 April 1997 – on file with author.

60 In 1994 it was reported that the Crown Health Enterprises had debts totally $1,256 million and operating deficits of $180 million – A. Stone, 'Health Budget Boost "Inadequate"', *New Zealand Herald*, 24 February 1994, s. 1:5.

61 See, for further examples, C. M. Flood, 'Prospects for New Zealand's Reformed Health System', (1996) 4 *Health Law Journal* 87 at p. 105, fn 72.

62 Letter from John Luhrs, Manager, Canterbury Health Limited, 15 May 1996, at p. 2 – on file with the author.

63 Interview with L. Mckenzie, Manager Medical and Surgical Services, Central RHA on 22 November 1996, Wellington, New Zealand.

64 In the UK see D. Hughes, S. McClelland and L. Griffiths, '"Cinderella" Services in the NHS Internal Market: Does Contracting Make a Difference?', (1997) 20(2) *Dalhousie Law Journal* 400 at p. 402, who note in particular that the two studies considered by them "provide no evidence of any significant transfer of expenditure from the acute sector towards primary care and community health care services, and highlight certain pressures that continue to pull resources towards acute care."

65 McGuire and Anand, *op. cit.*, p. 4, note that block contracts dominate in the UK.

66 In New Zealand, see Ashton, 'Contracting for Health Services in New Zealand: Early Experiences', *op. cit.*, p. 9. See also the 1994/95 contract between the Southern Regional Health Authority and Canterbury Health Limited signed respectively by the parties on 17 October 1994 and 19 October 1994 – on file with the author (hereinafter Canterbury Health 1994/95 Contract).

67 See B. Orsman, 'Bolger Shares Dim View of Hospitals: Closing Doors for Surgery Undermines Confidence', *New Zealand Herald* 17 April 1996, p. 5.

68 See for example, Canterbury Health 1994/95 Contract, *op. cit.*, cl. D04.

69 N. Söderlund, 'Hospital Casemix, Costs, and Productivity in the NHS Internal Market', paper presented at the International Health Economics Association Inaugural Conference – Vancouver, 19–24 May 1996, p. 15.

70 Crown Company Monitoring Advisory Unit, *Crown Health Enterprises: Briefing to the Incoming Minister*, (Wellington: Crown Company Monitoring Advisory Unit, 1996) at p. 21.

71 J. Broomberg, A. Mills and P. Masobe, 'To Purchase or to Provide? The Relative Efficiency of Contracting Out Versus Direct Public Provision of Hospital Services in South Africa', paper presented at the International Health Economics Association Inaugural Conference – Vancouver, 19–24 May 1996.

72 Williamson, *Markets and Hierarchies: Analysis and Anti-trust Implications*, *op. cit.*, p. 10.

73 P. Howden-Chapman, 'Doing the Splits: Contracting Issues in the New Zealand Health Service', (1993) 24(3) *Health Policy* 273; P. Howden-Chapman and T. Ashton, 'Shopping for Health: Purchasing Health Services Through Contracts', (1994) 29(1) *Health Policy* 61, and T. Ashton, 'Contracting the Kiwi Way: Costly or Constructive?', paper presented at the CHEPA 10th Annual Health Policy conference, Hamilton, Ontario, 21–23 May 1997, p. 7.

74 Letter from L. Mckenzie, Manager Medical and Surgical Services, Central RHA, 18 March 1997 – on file with author.

75 Minister of Health, *Healthy New Zealanders: Briefing Papers for the Minister of Health 1996: Vol. 1, Key Policy Issues*, (Wellington: Ministry of Health, 1996) at p. 5.

76 See Ashton, 'Contracting the Kiwi Way: Costly or Constructive?', *op. cit.*

77 *The New NHS: Dependable, Modern*, a White Paper, *op. cit.*, s. 9.11–9.17.

78 See Ministry of Health, Evaluation of the Performance of the Health Funding Authority for the Period 1 January–31 March 1998'. This information is available in 'Crown's Statement of Objectives 1998/99' (July 1998) from the Ministry of Health's website under Online Publications at http://www.moh.govt.nz (accessed 9 August 1999).

79 T. Ashton, 'Voice and Exit in New Zealand's Health Care Sector – Commentary', in *Contracting In The Health Sector* (Papers presented at a seminar held by the Legal Research Foundation at the University of Auckland, 6 July 1994) at p. 42.

80 The distinction between classical, neo-classical and relational contracts was first advanced by I. R. Macneil, 'Contracts: Adjustment of Long-Term Economic Relations Under Classical, Neo-classical and Relational Contract Law', (1978) 72(6) *Northwestern University Law Review* 854.

81 *Ibid.*, p. 901.

82 Allen, *op. cit.*, pp. 332–335, notes that long-term contracts do not proscribe in detail the parties' rights and obligations and often parties accept the unwritten laws of the particular trade. Even when problems do arise between the parties they rarely resort to the courts.

83 K. N. Llewellyn, 'What Price Contract? – An Essay in Perspective', (1931) 40 *Yale Law J.* 704 at p. 737.

84 Williamson, *Markets and Hierarchies: Analysis and Anti-trust Implications*, *op. cit.*, p. 106.

85 The contract for the year 1 July 1994 to 30 June 1995, for the total sum of NZ$150,357,714, between the Southern Regional Health Authority and Canterbury Health Limited (one of the twenty-three CHEs in New Zealand responsible for eight hospitals totaling 953 beds) was not signed until 27 October 1994. The following year, the parties signed a two-page heads of agreement but still had not signed a formal contract by the end of the 1995/96 year – See Canterbury Health 1994/95 Contract, *op. cit.* and Luhrs, *op. cit.*

86 See Canterbury Health 1994/95 Contract, *op. cit.* See also the Brent and Harrow Health Authority Contract with West Middlesex Hospital NHS Trusts dated 8 April 1997 for the contract

year running from 1 April 1997 – on file with author. This contract is only worth £36,000 but the solicitor to Brent and Harrow Health Authority notes that their contracts with their two main acute providers for about £25,000,000 is on similar terms and has not yet been agreed for the financial year – letter from P. Allen, 1 August 1997, on file with author.

87 Dawson and Goddard conclude from their survey in the north of England of contracting by six Health Authorities and a selection of GP Fundholder contracts that, in fact, contracts are predominantly for a three-year terms – D. Dawson and M. Goddard, 'Long-Term Contracts in the NHS: What Will They Achieve?' (1998) Discussion Paper 157, Centre For Health Economics, University of York.

88 This seems to be the case in New Zealand with daily newspaper reports by providers accusing purchasers and the government of underfunding the health sector. In the UK similar complaints of underfunding are made by providers – see S. Lyall, 'For British Health System Bleak Prognosis', *N.Y. Times News Service* 30 January 1997. I do not mean to suggest that there may not be some truth to the claims of underfunding, but that this issue becomes a political one with providers portraying the problem as a simple one of "government underfunding" and government portraying it as another simple problem – "greedy doctors".

89 Hughes, McClelland and Griffiths, *op. cit.*, p. 7.

90 Canterbury Health 1994/95 Contract, *op. cit.*, s. G, p. 112.

91 In the UK, see H. Glennerster and M. Matsaganis, 'The UK Health Reforms: The Fundholding Experiment', (1993) 23 *Health Policy* 179 at p. 182.

92 See L. Malcolm, 'Learning the Health Lessons, and Working Out What to Do Next?', (17 October 1996) *The Press*, Online. Available HTTP: http://ariadne.plain.co.na/42/96101720.htm (accessed 1 November 1998).

93 H. Glennerster, 'GP Fundholding: Wild Care or Winning Hand?', in R. Robinson and J. Le Grand (eds), *Evaluating the NHS Reforms* (London: King's Fund Institute, 1994).

94 See generally Audit Commission, *What The Doctor Ordered: A Study of GP Fundholders in England and Wales* (London: HMSO, 1996)

95 *Ibid.*, p. 7.

96 *Ibid.*, p. 66, Exhibit 26, and p. 82.

97 The National Health Service (Fund-holding Practices) Regulations (UK) 1996, S.I., 1996/706.

98 Williamson, *Markets and Hierarchies: Analysis and Anti-trust Implications, op. cit.*, considers the twin problems of institutional design as being how to limit opportunism and how to economize on bounded rationality.

99 For example, a survey published in 1997 predicts that depression, heart disease, and road accidents will replace respiratory infections, diarrhea diseases and complications of childbearing as the world's leading causes of death and disability. It also predicts that there will be an extraordinary epidemic of tobacco-related mortality and disability, which will claim more than 8 million lives worldwide in 2020. Some would argue that the growth in technology is endogenous to the system in question, but the inescapable fact is that the system itself provides incentives for the growth of certain technologies which in turn place strain on the system itself in terms of increased costs – see C. J. Murray and A. D. Lopez, 'Alternative Projections of Mortality and Disability by Cause 1990–2000: Global Burden of Disease Society', (1997) 394(9064) *Lancet* 1498.

100 Maynard, *op. cit.*, at p. 1435.

6 The problems of monopoly supply

In light of the shift to active purchasing in internal market and managed competition systems, does there need to be continued regulation of the supply side or can it be largely left to evolve on its own? To use the rowboat analogy of Osborne and Gaebler, does the government have sufficient steering power in a managed competition model that it can leave the private sector to row?[1] Although the rowboat metaphor has the power of simplicity, in the real world, things are often murkier and less clear-cut than policy-makers, economists and other rationalists would like to assume.

First, it is important to note that governments may wish to continue to regulate inputs on the supply side in order to contain total public expenditures, irrespective of efficiency considerations. Although an internal market system or a managed competition system may achieve a level of spending on health that is allocatively efficient, this efficient level may be above that which a government is prepared to fund from public moneys. As Schut and Hermans note in the Netherlands:

> the government faces the dilemma that while managed competition may improve efficiency and reduce unit costs, it may not guarantee the realization of macro-economic cost-containment goals. This is because managed competition may not only lead to lower production costs but also to higher productivity and a higher responsiveness to consumer preferences or patient needs.[2]

The difficulty is that although distributive justice considerations support financing of health expenditures on a progressive basis, which is generally achieved by financing from general taxation revenues, historical overruns in public sector borrowing mean that expenditures have to be curbed now to compensate for past excesses. Squeezing expenditures on health care goods and services, which citizens value higher than other goods and services, will result in all manner of perverse incentives and costs. It results in creeping privatization of the system as citizens look to have their values satisfied in the private sector. Naturally enough, governments tend to argue that retrenchment of public spending is efficient and will not lead to injustice and that enough money is being spent on health care. There may be very little one can do to counter these political realities except to make a plea to maintain the integrity of a progressively financed system and for governments to acknowledge that reducing public spending is a short-term solution brought about by the necessity to reduce public deficits. A social insurance-based system for health care financing, such as that envisaged in a managed competition system, would be better able to protect the system's integrity as then financing of health care would be separated from other government expenditures and from general taxation revenues.

In Chapter 4, I discussed the crucial need for incentives for purchasers in both internal markets and managed competition in order that they make wise purchasing decisions from public and private providers. However, even if the right mix of incentives is in place for purchasers there is still a problem if there is monopoly on the supply side. There may be monopoly on the supply side due to economies of scale in production. Particularly in the former command-and-control UK and New Zealand systems, monopoly may also be due to government policy geared to consolidating hospitals and reducing hospital beds. On the other hand, there is the prospect that the presence of a number of competing purchasers in a managed competition system will aggravate the problem of monopoly on the supply side. This is because a monopoly provider may be in a better negotiating position vis-á-vis a number of competing insurer/purchasers as opposed to a single government purchaser. There is thus the opportunity for the monopoly provider to engage in cost-shifting tactics. More-over, if a monopoly provider will not deal with a particular insurer/purchaser then the latter will not be able to offer its plan to local residents. Managed competition requires that insurer/purchasers offer their services to all individuals within a defined region. Consumer choice of insurer/purchasers may be a mirage if the reality is that a consumer must pick a particular insurer/purchaser because it is the only one that has a contract with the local monopoly hospital. One must also recognize that health care systems are dynamic and there will be a supply side response to proactive purchasing behavior, with health care providers merging and/or collaborating in order to gain market power.

Thus one can see that an important supply side issue that requires resolution in any system that seeks to promote competition between health care providers is the problem of monopoly supply. This chapter will explore the problem of monopoly supply and analyze various possible solutions.

Competing purchasers and the problems of monopoly supply

What's wrong with monopoly?

The problem of monopoly supply is that a monopoly provider (being a single seller or group of sellers behaving like a single seller in any particular market) will prefer to produce fewer services and at a higher price than otherwise would be charged in a competitive market.[3] From a socio-political perspective, monopoly is objectionable as it results in the transfer of resources from the ultimate consumers to the owners of the monopoly. Consumers are generally portrayed as having less power and wealth than owners of monopoly. Of course this stereotype may be true in the case of some products but may not be the case in others where consumers themselves are large corporations. From a purely economic perspective monopoly is objectionable as it results in a "dead-weight loss" to society or, in other words, a misapplication of society's limited resources. This occurs because consumers have an incentive to purchase alternative services at a cheaper price but, in fact, these alternative services cost more to produce than those produced by the monopoly. Thus, for example, rather than buying a surgical service from the only hospital in the region that charges high prices, a purchaser may choose to buy the service on an outpatient basis from a clinic of doctors. However, although the clinic's prices are cheaper, the clinic's real cost of producing the service is significantly higher than the hospital's. Prices set at a monopoly level send a wrong signal to consumers about how many resources have been taken to produce the service or good. Thus, there is a prima facie case for government intervention to correct the inefficiency that results from consumers buying goods and services that actually take up more of society's limited resources to produce than other goods and services which would be equally satisfactory. However, there is, of course, a cost associated with government intervention. Some economists point out that the cost to society of regulation to prevent inefficiencies arising from monopoly may be greater than the cost of the inefficiencies. [4]

How monopoly arises

Monopoly may arise as a result of a concerted effort on the part of a firm to exclude competitors and/or because of the fact that it is the most efficient competitor. In the latter case, where the monopoly situation is persistent over time, there may be what is known as a "natural monopoly." A natural monopoly occurs where, as production volume increases, long-run average costs tend to decrease. [5] In other words, there are relatively high fixed costs associated with production of even a small number of services or goods. Consequently efficiencies arise when a higher volume of services or goods are produced by a single firm as opposed to many firms as the fixed costs are smoothed over a larger number of units of production. It would be inefficient to encourage competition between many smaller firms within the market as this would result in an inefficient duplication of fixed resources.

One must consider the cost-effectiveness of regulation or other incentives that would ensure that the natural monopoly sets a price closer to that which would be the case in a competitive market. It is important to note that unlike, for example, a telecommunications network or the electricity grid, hospitals may be natural monopolies in some markets and not in others. Thus, for example, a hospital may be a natural monopoly in the supply of heart transplant surgery but face competition in the supply of outpatient services.

Monopoly also arises as a result of government policy. Governments of many OECD countries have sought to control the respective costs of their health care systems by controlling the number of inputs into the system, namely the number of hospitals and other health care providers. Monopoly may have also arisen as a result of government policy to purchase or procure health services from only publicly-owned institutions, thus precluding the potential entry of private competitors. Prior to internal market reform, this was the situation in both the UK and New Zealand.

Cross-subsidy from monopoly to competitive markets

In an internal market system, as government-appointed purchasers are monopsonies (the only buyer in a market), then if there is monopoly on the supply side a bilateral monopoly emerges and it is difficult to predict what will be the result of negotiations.[6] In the UK and New Zealand, the size of (respectively) NHS Trusts and Crown Health Enterprises and the number of hospitals they are responsible for has been centrally determined. Consequently, although individual hospitals may not be monopolies, they are controlled by government-mandated organizations that generally hold monopolies in one or more health care markets. Thus, there is the risk that NHS Trusts and Crown Health Enterprises will cross-subsidize their operations in health care markets where they face competition from others where they hold a monopoly. This is also a risk in managed competition systems as organizations that are providers in a number of health care markets may cross-subsidize from the market in which they hold a monopoly to those markets where they face competition, thus potentially eliminating more efficient competitors in those latter markets.

Control of bottleneck or essential facilities

Due to the presence of a number of competing insurers/providers in a managed competition system, the monopoly supply problem may be greater than in an internal market system where purchasers are monopsonies (i.e. the only buyer in a market). In a managed competition system, the only hospital in a region will have a significant advantage in negotiating supply contracts as it will know that competing insurer/purchasers will have to contract with it in order to provide a full service plan to local residents. If one insurer/purchaser owns the only hospital in a region then it may refuse to supply competing insurer/purchasers. The effect of this is to prevent competitors in the insurance/purchasing market from enrolling individuals into their plans who, if they needed, for example, emergency services, would have to use the hospital's facilities. This is known as market leverage – the use of power in one market (the hospital service market) to gain or maintain power in another related one (the health care insurance/purchase market).[7] In a managed competition model, the goal of the insurer/purchaser that is integrated with a monopoly health care provider would be to force people dependent on that provider to exit from their preferred insurer/purchaser and transfer to it.[8] The societal costs of monopoly are arguably greater when the monopolist controls bottleneck or essential facilities as it has spill-over effects into other related markets.

On the other hand, as discussed in the last chapter, there may be significant efficiency gains that accrue from vertical integration between insurer/purchasers and health care providers. Such integration may improve the ability of insurer/purchasers to control the clinical decision-making of health care providers and to render them more cost-sensitive. Proponents of the managed competition model envisage a system whereby several large insurer/purchasers offering managed care plans would compete on price and quality dimensions. This amounts essentially to the idea of competing "integrated delivery systems" – the new catch-phrase in health policy.[9] Enthoven has said that he now refers to his managed competition model as "managed care-managed competition" to emphasize that what are meant to compete are integrated delivery systems supplying comprehensive care.[10] In an integrated delivery system, a number of different health service providers (hospitals, general practitioners, specialists, nurses, etc.) work within an organizational or contractual arrangement to provide coordinated and seamless care to a particular population. As Miller notes, several types of integration activities "offer the prospect of reduced administration costs; lower medical care prices; utilization, and expenditures; and higher quality of care."[11] Integration and coordination of care is important as it is recognized that where there are a variety of ways in which the needs of patients can be met, some may be more cost-effective than others. For example, a cardiologist could take a patient's blood pressure every month or a nurse-aid could do so without any reduction in the quality of the procedure. As Fuchs notes:

> physicians' decisions are the major determinant of the cost of care. Only in an integrated system, however, do physicians have the incentive, the information, and the infrastructure needed to make these decisions in a cost-effective way. Integrated systems also have an advantage in avoiding excess capacity of high-cost equipment and personnel.[12]

Some might consider these claims to be somewhat exaggerated; nonetheless, an integrated system clearly has many potential benefits.

From a policy perspective, the ideal system may be one in which there is regulated competition between managed care plans. These plans can be thought of as smaller, financially integrated sub-systems that combine the insurance, purchasing and most provider functions into one firm. What is offered is not insurance per se but the management of financial risk and the supply and coordination of health services as and when they are needed. However, where there is monopoly on the supply side the benefits of allowing integration have to be balanced against the cost of decreased competition between insurer/purchasers offering managed care plans. As competition between insurer/purchasers is the key to ensuring the accountability and efficiency of a managed competition system this may have to trump the achievement of efficiency gains from vertical integration where the two are not compatible.

Is there sufficient depth in health care markets so that each insurer/purchaser is able to offer its own integrated delivery system, i.e. its own independent panel of health care providers? A new health plan must establish a large complex network of providers, either by acquiring or contracting with incumbent providers, or by introducing new providers into the market. Without the threat of entry, there is no real competition either in or for the market. In some markets, however, it may be inefficient to duplicate hospitals or technological service providers as they are natural monopolies. The extent to which natural monopoly will exist on the supply side will vary from country to country and within any particular country and between health care markets. In terms of population density, the Netherlands is a very densely populated country with 449 people per square kilometer.[13] The UK is less densely populated with 235 people per square kilometer. By comparison, the US and New Zealand have very low population densities with, respectively, 28 people per square kilometer and 13 people per square kilometer. In both the US and New Zealand, however, there are discrete urban areas which are much more densely populated than outlying areas. For example, one-third of New Zealand's population live in the greater Auckland region. In more densely populated regions there would likely be greater scope for competition between insurer/purchasers offering managed care plans. These sorts of generalizations do not, however, take us very far in terms of considering the design of a system.

Kronick, Goodman and Wennberg estimate that 42 percent of the US population live in areas capable of supporting managed competition with three efficient full-service provider networks, and 29 percent of the population live in areas that could not support more than one efficient full-service provider network. The rest of the population lives in areas that can support limited competition with some sharing of hospital services.[14] In the Netherlands the problem of monopoly on the supply side is diminished because of the uniformly high population density. A natural monopoly is a rare phenomenon in the Dutch hospital market.[15] Nine out of ten hospitals in the urbanized Dutch Randstad area, accounting for about 45 percent of the population, have more than ten potential competitors within a 24-kilometer radius.[16] In the present UK and New Zealand internal markets it is clear that the hospital market is highly concentrated.[17] However, if the present NHS Trusts and Crown Health Enterprises were unbundled then the degree of monopoly on the supply side would be significantly reduced. Propper, for example, argues that there is indeed scope for competition between UK health care providers. She estimates that only 8 percent of a large sample of all acute care providers have no competitors within a 30-minute travel distance in the four specialities of general surgery, orthopaedics, ear, nose and throat (ENT), and gynaecology.[18] New Zealand's population is so dispersed that, although competition between managed care plans in the Auckland region may be viable, in most other areas it seems likely that the problem of monopoly supply may be severe.

As I argued in the last chapter, it is not possible to reach a generalized conclusion as to the potential for competition in a health care system and, for the purposes of this book, it is not necessary to do so. It is sufficient to conclude generally that health care markets differ within any particular system and the specific nature of a particular market will vary depending on its location. Also health care markets are dynamic and advances in technology will alter the mix of capital and other resources required for production. Moreover, in response to proactive purchasing, health care providers will seek to acquire market power. Thus, the important conclusion is that one size does not fit all. Consequently, a model that rigidly assumes competitive or contestable markets system-wide and across many different health care markets is likely to lead to inefficiencies because of its inflexibility. Similarly, a model that rigidly assumes the absence of competitive or contestable markets will result in inefficiencies. The fact that there is not sufficient depth across all health care markets to create integrated delivery systems capable of independently satisfying the needs of enrollees of competing insurer/purchasers does not mean the managed competition model is fundamentally flawed. The important question is, what is the nature and cost of regulation or some other combination of incentives that is required to allow competing insurers/providers to purchase services from natural monopoly providers?

The supply side response to proactive purchasing

In a managed competition system there is the prospect of insurer/purchasers trying to thwart competition from other insurer/purchasers by preventing their patients accessing monopoly hospitals and other facilities. In both managed competition and internal market reform there is also the problem that the threat of proactive purchasing may invoke a response on the part of providers to form into monopolies or, worse still, to collude in order to improve their bargaining power. Thus, one must consider not only the monopoly supply problem in current markets but also how supply markets will respond to pro-active purchasing pressure. For example, Morrisey *et al.* note in the US that providers are forming into (so-called) integrated delivery systems in order to have one institutional voice, with the goal being to increase their market power in contract negotiations with insurer/purchasers.[19] Schut notes in the Netherlands that general practitioners, pharmacists, specialists, and hospitals are independently seeking ways to strengthen their market power by forming into strong regional organizations or cooperations.[20] Similarly, in New Zealand, an important motivation for general practitioners in forming Independent Practice Associations was to improve their negotiating power with the Regional Health Authorities.[21]

Groups of health providers that are formed simply to improve their bargaining power vis-à-vis purchasers are clearly not beneficial. However, if groups of health care providers that wish to form into alliances assume the insurance/purchasing role there is no reason why such alliances should not be permitted.

In assuming the insurance/purchasing role, the alliance of health care providers will bear the financial risk of misapplication of resources, be responsible for managing the delivery of care, and decide upon the mix of health services to supply. Rather than an insurer/purchaser integrating downwards to incorporate health care providers (e.g. owning a hospital), an alliance of health care providers may integrate forward into the insurance/purchasing role.

In the US there has been growth in the number of integrated provider organizations, which are essentially groups of health care providers that offer managed care arrangements to private insurers.[22] These arrangements are often referred to as "integrated delivery systems" even though they are distinguishable from a situation where an insurer vertically integrates forward to incorporate hospitals and physicians into the firm's operations. Not all arrangements that call themselves "integrated delivery systems" are necessarily desirable. The appeal of an integrated health care system is the concept that health care providers (i.e. family doctors, specialists, nurses, hospitals, home care workers, pharmacists, dentists, technicians, etc.) all work to coordinate the application of their varying skills and the care supplied to a patient. The goal is that the patient receives the most cost-effective care and costs are not shifted from provider to provider or on to patients or to society at large. This seems to have been the objective of the New Labour proposals of December 1997, which provided for the establishment of Primary Care Groups (PCGs). These PCGs are large groups of general practitioners and community nurses, which are to be responsible for managing budgets for primary and community care and eventually for purchasing services from NHS Trusts. However, the only repercussion if a PCG runs over budget is that, in the worst case scenario, some or all purchasing responsibility may be transferred back to the relevant Health Authority or a change in its leadership and management may be required.[23] Thus, there are very weak incentives for the PCGs to make cost-effective purchasing decisions. The key to efficient integration is that the group of providers must bear a significant component of financial risk as it is only then that different health care providers have an incentive to coordinate their different skills. Arrangements describing themselves as "integrated delivery systems" that do not exhibit these qualities are not truly "integrated" and may in fact be examples of collusion.

To recap, the problems arising from monopoly on the supply side are as follows:

- how to prevent a health care provider cross-subsidizing from health care markets where it is a monopoly to health care markets where it faces competition;
- how to prevent insurer/purchasers which are vertically integrated with monopoly providers from suppressing competition on the part of other insurer/purchasers by refusing to sell the health care services in which they hold a monopoly and/or causing other insurer/purchasers to inefficiently duplicate facilities that are natural monopolies;

- how to prevent monopoly health care providers from charging prices above long-run average cost and producing fewer services than is optimal from society's perspective;
- how to prevent the formation of monopoly (except where it is a natural monopoly) on the supply side as an attempt to build market power where there are no offsetting efficiency gains.

Solutions to the problem of monopoly supply

There are at least six possible solutions to the problem of monopoly on the supply side. These are collective bargaining on the part of insurer/purchasers with monopoly health service providers, an enforced purchaser/provider split in natural monopoly markets, nationalization of monopoly health providers, employment of the essential facility doctrine, employment of general competition law, and industry-specific regulation of monopolies. In this next section I will discuss the costs and benefits of all six solutions with a view to assessing their ability to solve the four component problems of monopoly supply summarized in the preceding paragraph.

Collective bargaining

Insurer/purchasers in a managed competition system could come together as one bargaining unit when negotiating with monopoly health care providers. Collective bargaining is nothing new in many jurisdictions. For example, in the Netherlands, there were statutory guidelines in place prescribing the negotiation of uniform tariffs for physicians, which were binding on all physicians once approved.[24] This negotiation occurred between representatives of the physicians, the private insurers, and Sickness Funds and is monitored and regulated by government through the Central Agency on Health Care Tariffs.[25] Although this regulated negotiation was criticized as ritualistic and bureaucratic, it was also credited with having suppressed the growth of physicians' fees.[26]

Collective bargaining on the part of insurer/purchasers may occur in a managed competition system irrespective of government initiatives to facilitate it. For example, Robinson reports in the US that employers are forming into alliances to bargain with managed care plans.[27] He uses the example of the Pacific Business Group on Health, an alliance of twenty-seven large firms with 2.5 million employees and dependants and $3 billion in annual health expenditures, that is de facto regulating competition between private managed care plans. Robinson reports that the Pacific alliance is standardizing the benefit package offered across firms and health plans, analyzing risk selection factors, requiring health plans to disclose information, putting in place mandates for improvements in quality, and negotiating premiums on behalf of its members.[28] Robinson does not mention this, but such activity would seem to be open to challenge under general competition laws. Collective bargaining on the part of insurer/purchasers would need to be expressly exempted from general competition laws as such activity would prima facie constitute collusion. Such an exemption would have to make a clear distinction between situations where collective bargaining is necessary to deal with the problem of a monopoly provider and where it is simply a device to extract extra concessions from health care providers.

The problem with collective bargaining as a solution to the problem of monopoly supply is that such a mechanism may provide opportunities for collusion in other areas. Although it may be satisfactory to have insurer/purchasers forming an alliance to negotiate with monopoly health care providers, it is far from satisfactory when it comes to a few large insurer/purchasers competing on price and quality determinants. By standardizing benefits and reducing price competition to a single premium bid, managed competition reform looks to simplify consumer choice; however, it also provides many ripe opportunities for collusive behavior on the part of large insurer/purchasers.[29] Thus, to reduce opportunities for collusive behavior generally, collective bargaining should be discouraged as a matter of policy even where insurer/purchasers could point to offsetting efficiency gains in any particular transaction.

Collective bargaining will not correct the problem where an insurer/purchaser is vertically integrated with a natural monopoly provider – the bottleneck situation. There will still need to be some other means by which to compel the vertically integrated monopoly to supply services to competitors in the upstream market. In a system of managed competition with several large insurer/purchasers competing nation-wide one could argue that they would have to cooperate. Although in some areas an insurer/purchaser may have the advantage of being vertically integrated with a monopoly hospital, in other areas a competitor will hold the upper hand in terms of controlling the monopoly hospital. Again, however, there would seem to be a high risk of explicit or implicit collusion where insurer/purchasers agree to divide up the health insurance/purchasing market and so effectively avoid competition. Thus, what is needed, in fact, is not the facilitation of collective bargaining but vigorous anti-trust enforcement to root out any collusive behavior on the part of insurer/purchasers.

Selective application of the purchaser/provider split

In the previous chapter, I was critical of the rigid purchaser/provider split imposed on internal market systems because of its indiscriminate application to all health care markets in a system regardless of the particular structure of the market. In some markets, an enforced purchaser/provider split may result in additional transactions costs without any prospect of offsetting efficiency gains. The appeal of a managed competition system is that having put in place the framework and necessary regulation to ensure competition between insurer/purchasers on price and quality dimensions, insurer/purchasers are left to determine what is the most efficient supply side arrangement. However, where there is a natural monopoly on the supply side (i.e. there is no prospect of efficient entry by other competitors), one may wish to preclude vertical integration between insurer/purchasers and the natural monopoly. This is in order to allow insurer/purchasers to complete on a level playing field when it comes to negotiation with the natural monopoly. One should be clear here that this is not a suggestion of a system-wide purchaser/provider split, as in internal markets, but a purchaser/provider split only in those markets that are natural monopolies. This argument is similar to arguments for unbundling the network components of the telecommunications and electricity sectors (the natural monopoly elements) from the other competitive or contestable elements of the respective sectors.[30] The difficulty is that a hospital may be a natural monopoly in some markets but not in others and pragmatically it would be difficult to effect a split in only those segments of a hospital's operations in which it held a natural monopoly.

It will be necessary to closely monitor an enforced purchaser/provider split in natural monopoly markets as, over time, the natural monopoly characteristics of the market may disappear and others may occur in new markets. Unbundling or a split between insurer/purchasers and natural monopoly providers will reduce the problem of competing insurer/purchasers using market leverage through their control of natural monopoly providers to exclude competitors. It will not, however, eliminate it as there is the prospect of collusive behavior between an insurer/purchaser and a monopoly health care provider. An enforced split will also not eliminate the problem of a monopoly provider cross-subsidizing from monopoly to competitive markets or of a monopoly producing fewer services at a higher price than is efficient.

Public ownership of monopoly

One possible means of solving the problem of natural monopoly is to nationalize (or leave nationalized) providers that are natural monopolies. Presently, most hospitals in the UK and New Zealand are government-owned through (respectively) the larger umbrella organizations of the NHS Trusts and the Crown Health Enterprises. If these countries introduced a managed competition system of competing insurer/purchasers then these administrative organizations would have to be unbundled and hospitals privatized in order to allow insurer/purchasers to form their own relationships with health care providers. Insurer/purchasers may then enter into whatever arrangements with health providers they consider efficient, e.g. vertical integration, joint ventures, spot, short- or long-term contracts, etc. Arguably, those hospitals that are natural monopolies should remain government-owned thus precluding the option of vertical integration. Government could then direct the natural monopoly hospitals to supply competing insurer/purchasers on reasonable terms. Is public ownership the best means to deal with the incidence of natural monopoly or is there some other means by which to remedy the problem at less cost?

With respect to the costs of public ownership, it is often alleged that there are internal slackness problems and that privatization would result in efficiencies. The trend, in many countries, to privatize public enterprises in a wide range of sectors seems to have resulted, in general, in greater efficiencies.[31] However, there is little empirical data to support the contention that private hospitals are more efficient than public hospitals particularly once case-mix is taken into account. In other words, public hospitals look after sicker people so it is flawed to compare their "performance" to private hospitals. This, of course, is related to how health systems are configured and the fact that private hospitals have no incentive to care for the sickest patients; nonetheless, one cannot find evidence that public hospitals are necessarily more inefficient than private hospitals. Moreover, when considering the efficiencies of privatization, analysts are not comparing private firms with government enterprises where performance incentives have been carefully crafted. Rather they are comparing the performance of private firms with government enterprises where it was naively assumed that public ownership would translate to management working to maximize the public interest. Arguably, a government-owned corporation with a sufficiently refined internal incentive structure could be as efficient as a private firm. Also, what is often not noted is that in a natural monopoly situation we do not want a public firm to act like a private firm as this would result in a monopoly price being set and the quantity produced being too low. The goal is to design incentives so that a publicly-owned (nationalized) hospital is technically efficiently but does not seek monopoly rents or reduce production or lower quality. This is a difficult regulatory task.

Smith and Lipsky note that what are perceived as efficiencies arising from privatization are often only cheaper labor costs.[32] Cheaper labor costs may result only in a transfer of wealth from labor to management and not in real efficiency gains. Moreover, even if cheaper labor costs do actually translate into longer-term efficiency gains, it does not appear that labor costs are actually cheaper in private hospitals. In systems like the UK and New Zealand where government has paid for the vast majority of health costs, governments have been able to tightly control wage increases for labor in the publicly-funded sector. Of course, in these latter systems, private hospitals have had no incentive to be efficient due to financing by private insurers on an indemnity basis for the supply of services "supplemental" to those provided publicly. Arguably, in a managed competition system, privately run hospitals would have incentives to operate efficiently. The same is also true, however, for publicly owned hospitals. A managed competition system offers the prospect of a market (albeit a regulated market) where competing private insurer/purchasers can be expected to bring pressure to bear on both privately and publicly owned providers to perform efficiently.

What are the benefits of government-owned natural monopoly? The most viable alternative to nationalization of natural monopolies is regulation and thus the costs of regulation (discussed below) may be avoided by nationalization. However, if managers of public hospitals are given incentives to operate like private firms then some sort of regulation would also be required, as presumably if a nationalized hospital perfectly mimicked a private firm it would charge a monopoly price and produce fewer services than is optional. One benefit of public ownership is that possibly government may be able to prevent the hospital in question from cross-subsidizing from natural monopoly markets to other competitive or contestable markets. In the UK, the NHS Trusts are specifically prohibited from cross-subsidizing.[33] However, there is no evidence as to whether this prohibition is effective and one must wonder about the degree to which it is possible to monitor and detect cross-subsidization.

Another possible benefit of nationalized hospitals is that presumably they will not be as driven by the profit motive as private for-profit hospitals and thus the quality of services is less likely to be compromised in the competitive process. On the other hand, prior to internal market reform, publicly-owned hospitals in the UK and New Zealand appeared to suffer from internal slackness problems as evidenced by long and growing waiting lists, and public hospitals were perceived as being unresponsive to patients' concerns. Thus, the pursuit of profits may not undermine quality goals in publicly-owned institutions but problems with internal slackness may have a detrimental effect on quality. It may also be possible to inculcate a culture of working towards satisfying patients' needs within a non-profit private institution. More important, however, than whether the hospital or provider is for-profit, not-for-profit, or publicly owned, is a set of unambiguous incentives designed to reward those that meet quality expectations.

Gorringe argues, following Coase, that it is important to base efficiency assessments on actual preferences and not on "objective" measures such as health outcomes.[34] It may be that individuals prefer to have their services delivered by a public hospital notwithstanding the fact that they may be more efficiently delivered by a private hospital. Anecdotal evidence suggests there is strong opposition to the idea of privatization of public hospitals in the UK and New Zealand. On the other hand, Blendon *et al.* found that people in countries where health care services are publicly-funded but privately delivered are generally more satisfied than people in countries with systems that are both publicly-funded and publicly-delivered or privately-funded and privately-delivered.[35] It seems likely that people in the UK and New Zealand are erroneously associating privatization of hospitals with a US-style health care system that rations access on the basis of price and not need. If people were assured that this would not be the result of privatization and this was demonstrated (perhaps by way of incremental privatization in certain parts of the country and monitoring the performance of the privatized entity relative to a nationalized hospital) then preferences may change.

Nationalization of hospitals may be seen in terms of using a sledgehammer to crack a nut. A hospital is unlikely to be a natural monopoly in all the health care markets it operates in. For example, a hospital may hold a monopoly in the supply of accident and emergency services but there is viable competition from the nearest hospital for the supply of elective surgery. Nationalizing the hospital to cure the natural monopoly problem may thus lead to other problems. Again we return to the problem of applying an inflexible and indiscriminate solution to markets that are very different. The ideal solution must be something that is more targeted, selective, and flexible.

Essential facilities doctrine

Another potential means by which to alleviate the problem of monopoly on the supply side is by employment of the "essential facilities doctrine." This is a US doctrine applied pursuant to sections 1 and 2 of the Sherman Act[36] (US competition law). It requires a firm to allow another firm reasonable access to an "essential facility" in the case where the latter firm must obtain access in order to compete in a particular market with the owner of the essential facility.[37]

One must be careful in applying this doctrine to jurisdictions other than that of the US. It does not appear to be a doctrine of general application in the Netherlands, the UK or New Zealand. In those jurisdictions the problem that the doctrine attempts to correct is dealt with through general competition laws (refusal to deal and/or abuse of a dominant position provisions). Even within the US doubt has been raised about the application of the doctrine beyond instances of collusive behavior to single firm conduct.[38] Nonetheless, prima facie, the essential facility doctrine seems particularly apt in the context of the bottleneck problem in a managed competition system and thus is worth discussing.

There are four elements that need to be established in order to rely on the essential facility doctrine in the case of single-firm conduct:

- the monopoly must control the essential facility in question;
- it must be impracticable or unreasonable for a competitor to duplicate the essential facility;
- the competitor must have been denied access to the facility;
- allowing access must not detrimentally compromise the monopoly's own use of the facility.[39]

When is a facility "essential" and what constitutes denial of access? A good or service is essential when it constitutes a factor of production that is crucial to the production of some other good or service.[40] In a managed competition system, in order to be able to offer comprehensive coverage to local residents, all insurer/purchasers will need to buy services from the local monopoly hospital. It may be inefficient for all insurer/purchasers to build their own hospitals in the area as this would amount to an inefficient duplication of resources. In other words, the local hopsital is a natural monopoly. The important question is on what terms to allow insurer/purchasers access to natural monopoly hospitals? What constitutes a denial of access is unclear. Case law does not "indicate to what extent the monopolist must exercise an affirmative duty to negotiate or propose reasonable terms, or in what ways and to what extent the terms of access must be unreasonable to constitute a violation."[41]

Debate arises over how to calculate the price to be paid by competitors for the services offered by an essential facility. Should the price reflect the marginal cost of production, the average cost or production, or should the monopolist be able to include in the price charged to competitors in upstream or downstream markets the monopoly rents lost in those latter markets as a result of entry by competitors? In the US, in Laurel Sand and Gravel v. CSX Transportation, Inc.[42] the court found that the access arrangements did not have to ensure that the plaintiff (the firm wishing to gain access to an essential facility) was able to make a profit. Similarly, in New Zealand, the Privy Council recently condoned Telecom's (a telecommunications monopoly) proposal to charge a new entrant a price for interconnection to essential infrastructure that reflected the loss of monopoly rents suffered by the monopolist in *downstream markets* as a result of the new entry.[43] There are various arguments as to why it is efficient to allow such a prima facie perverse outcome to result;[44] however, it is important to note that the proposed pricing rule in the Telecom case was created on the assumption that the monopoly is regulated so monopoly rent is eliminated over time.[45] The difficulty is (and this was expressly recognized by the Privy Council), that the courts are in no position to perform the on-going regulatory role of eliminating monopoly pricing.[46] Werden argues that:

> if the essential facility is a bottleneck that prevents the delivery of the relevant product to certain customers, mandated access would enhance welfare, but only if the facility is subject to pre-existing regulation that can effectively control the price and other terms of access.[47]

Wenden goes on to argue that the essential facility doctrine should be entirely abandoned in favor of industry specific regulation for three reasons:

- it would allow for a more consistent determination of what constitutes a natural monopoly and when it should be subject to mandatory access;
- unlike general competition laws, regulation can respond to the specific conditions of the industry in question;
- a regulator, rather than a court, is likely to be in a better position to determine complex issues regarding the reasonableness of the terms of access.[48]

Over the course of the last decade, physicians and other health care providers have attempted to employ the essential facilities doctrine in the US.[49] Usually the doctrine is relied upon by physicians trying to gain admitting privileges to hospitals that are limiting the number of physicians practicing at the hospital.[50] These sorts of actions are not often successful as physicians have found it difficult to present a credible story that a hospital is an "essential facility" when they still have financially viable practices despite being denied admitting privileges to the hospital in question.[51] This sort of reasoning undermines the potential of the doctrine to remedy the problem of a vertically integrated insurers/purchaser foreclosing access by other competing insurer/purchasers to a natural monopoly. Competitors may remain solvent notwithstanding access to a local hospital being denied as they are able to compete in other markets. However, in that particular market consumers would not have a choice of purchaser and there would be less incentive for the purchaser to be accountable to local consumers on price and quality dimensions.

In Blue Cross and Blue Shield United of Wisconsin, *et al.*, v. Marshfield Clinic[52] a managed care plan sought to establish access to a hospital owned by another. Posner found that the physician-owned health care clinic was not an "essential facility" for purposes of anti-trust doctrine that would require it to cooperate with a would-be competitor. He noted that the clinic did not control even 50 percent of any properly defined market, even if it operated the only Health Maintenance Organization (a form of managed care plan) in the area, and therefore could not be considered "essential."[53] Posner noted that consumers are not better off if the natural monopolist is forced to share some of its profits with potential competitors as the monopolist will still charge fees reflecting its monopoly. This statement is confusing, however, as surely this would depend upon what terms the monopolist is required to give access to competitors. In a managed competition system, the dynamic and ongoing nature of competition between insurer/purchasers is essential. Allowing a purchaser that is vertically integrated with a natural monopoly to foreclose access to other purchasers would not simply be a case of allowing a monopolist to collect its monopoly rents in a particular health care market. It would impede competition in the insurance/purchasing market that covers *many* health care markets and not just the market the natural monopoly operates in. As an example, if competing insurer/purchasers cannot buy emergency services from a hospital that is a natural monopoly, it cannot offer to local residents a comprehensive plan which would include not only emergency services, but elective surgery, primary care, outpatient care, nursing care, mental health services etc.

A monopolist can successfully defend a claim under the essential facility doctrine on the grounds that it has legitimate business reasons for its actions.[54] Areeda notes, "denial of access is never per se unlawful; legitimate business purpose always saves the defendant."[55] A natural monopoly may be able to demonstrate efficiencies accruing from vertical integration with an insurer/purchaser.[56] A vertically integrated monopolist would have a viable argument that in order to run the hospital or other essential facility efficiently it is legitimate to deny competing insurer/purchasers access to it. The argument would be that in order to provide a coherent and comprehensive managed care plan it cannot allow physicians affiliated with other insurer/purchasers with different styles of practice and management of care to disrupt the hospital's activities.[57]

In summary, there are several potential obstacles to the employment of the essential facilities doctrine as a means to solve the bottleneck problem. The doctrine is of little assistance in correcting the other three monopoly supply side problems.

Competition law

It is beyond the scope of this book to describe in detail the general competition laws in each of the four jurisdictions. Instead this section considers, given the general goals of competition law, whether it is an appropriate method by which to deal with the four problems of monopoly supply. As you will recall these problems are the bottleneck problem, the cross-subsidy problem, the problem of monopoly producing at too low an output and too high a price, and the creation of monopoly in the absence of offsetting efficiency gains.

Bottlenecks

General competition laws deal with access to bottlenecks and essential facilities through refusal to deal and abuse of dominance provisions. As I discussed above in the context of the essential facility doctrine, the key problem with respect to employment of competition law is the ability of competition authorities to set and monitor the terms of access. Issues arise such as whether the price charged by the monopolist for access should be based on marginal cost, average cost plus a fair rate of return on the owner's investment,[58] or whether the price should reflect the loss of the monopolist's profits as a result of new entry by competitors in upstream or downstream markets.[59] Arguably, competition authorities and the general courts are ill-equipped relative to an industry-specific regulator with specialized industry knowledge to undertake the necessary analysis. Competition law may be relied on, however, to prevent anti-competitive arrangements between insurer/purchasers and natural monopolies as this may be caught under the collusion provisions. The general conspiracy or collusion provision will not, however, prevent a vertically integrated entity from foreclosing access to other health providers. For example, in the US, section 1 of the Sherman Act[60] requires that, in order to establish a violation, there be two or more parties participating in the conspiracy. A managed care plan and its wholly owned hospital subsidiary would not be capable of conspiring.[61]

Cross-subsidization from monopoly to competitive markets

General competition laws do not specifically deal with the problem of cross-subsidization by a single firm from one market where it is a natural monopoly to another where it faces competition. General competition laws often contain a section prohibiting "predatory pricing"; however, predatory pricing is normally thought of in the context of a dominant firm in a particular market cutting its prices to below cost in order to drive out competitors. The competition authorities are thus required to analyze a single market. This analysis becomes much more complicated when a firm operates in a number of markets and is cross-subsidizing from its activities in one market to its activities in another. The firm may be able to successfully argue that it is not engaged in predatory pricing as its average costs for its total operation is not above the average price charged in all the markets it operates in. Usually predatory pricing can be detected where the costs of operation are above the price but clearly this is going to be more difficult in an instance of cross-subsidization.

Preventing monopoly profits and output

Can competition law prevent natural monopoly health care providers from charging prices above long-run average cost and producing fewer services than is optimal from society's perspective? General competition laws do not prohibit or prevent the extraction of monopoly rents per se. Competition laws are usually unconcerned with monopoly that has arisen as a result of a superior competitive performance. For example, the US Supreme Court has said in the context of section 2 of the Sherman Act[62] that what is required is "wilful acquisition or maintenance of monopoly power as contrasted with monopoly achieved as a result of historical accident, business acumen, or the like."[63]

The general premise of competition law is that the existence of monopoly rents is part of the dynamic process of competition and will attract new entrants into the market, and that over time the monopoly rents will disappear. The difficulty is that in a natural monopoly market there is no possibility of a new entrant or, if there is a new entrant, this would result in an inefficient duplication of resources. Moreover, general competition laws do not usually empower competition authorities and courts to regulate prices on an ongoing basis.[64]

Preventing the formation of monopoly

It may seem a basic proposition to someone unfamiliar with the health care sector that competition or anti-trust law should be left to regulate the competitive or contestable segments of health care service markets. There are two reasons why this assumption cannot be readily made in the health sector. The first is empirical evidence showing that increased competition is associated with increased rather than decreased costs. The second is the policy goal of having competition between managed care plans offering an integrated and comprehensive health care system to each and every enrollee. These two reasons are discussed further below.

INCREASING COMPETITION AND INCREASING WELFARE

Competition law implicitly assumes that fostering competition will result in lower prices and improvements in overall welfare. The thrust of general competition laws seems antithetical to the regulatory environment in many health care systems that seeks to control the number of inputs (hospital beds, physicians, technology etc.) to the system.[65] In fact, the empirical evidence in health care markets suggests that the stimulation of competition is associated with cost and price *increases*.[66] However, these data have been collected mostly in the US, a fragmented system that relies on private financing to a greater degree than most other countries and where, until the recent managed care revolution, insurers passively reimbursed health care providers on a fee-for-service basis. Consequently, historically, competition between providers has not been on the basis of price or real indicators of quality. Rather, providers have tried to attract consumers, who are not cost-sensitive and have very little information about real quality dimensions, by competing on very rough quality indicators, e.g. the level of technology employed, the skill and numbers of hospital staff, and general amenities. By comparison, in a managed competition system, insurer/purchasers have incentives to compete on price and quality dimensions and thus, if the incentives and overlaying regulation work as intended, competition will be associated with cost reductions and/or improvements in quality. In fact, there is empirical evidence from the US that competition between managed care plans has resulted in cost reductions,[67] although one must not rely on these results alone as the US is not an example of a managed competition system. Within the US's present unplanned, uncoordinated and ad hoc health care system there are many opportunities for cost-shifting from plan to plan, from plans to patients and from plans to society at large.

ENCOURAGING COMPETITION BETWEEN INTEGRATED PLANS

With general competition law's bias towards encouraging competition on the assumption that this will improve overall welfare, it may not facilitate the development of integrated delivery systems. From a policy perspective, what is important is competition between managed care plans offering an integrated and comprehensive service and not necessarily between individual physicians, hospitals, etc. Competition law must be flexible enough to accommodate this objective and not undermine its achievement by preventing the formation of such systems. Let us look here at the application of competition law in the four systems and the potential in each to allow competition between integrated delivery systems.

APPLICATION OF COMPETITION LAW

The countries under study have taken a variety of different approaches to the applicability of competition law to health care markets. After the creation of the UK internal market in 1989, it was decided that general competition laws should not apply. Instead, the Department of Health would oversee mergers and would ensure competition. The Department of Health published on 12 December 1994 the government's guidelines with respect to mergers and anti-competitive behavior.[68] The guidelines cover four areas: provider mergers and joint ventures; providers in difficulty; purchaser mergers and boundary adjustments; and collusion. Dawson notes that the policies outlined in these guidelines are drawn from traditional models of competition policy except that the Department of Health is intended to be the regulator of this policy, rather than the Monopolies and Mergers Commission. She suggests this has created a conflict between the Department's roles in rationalizing capacity in the NHS and in enforcement of competition policy.[69] This is particularly so with respect to the Secretary of State's power to intervene where providers are experiencing financial difficulties. For political reasons, hospitals have not been allowed to fail, yet if the rigor of competition is to improve technical efficiency, providers must know that there is the prospect of failure with all its attendant drawbacks for management and staff alike. Thus, Dawson argues, if the government was serious about stimulating competition, investigations of possible breaches of competition law should have been left to the independent Monopolies and Mergers Commission.[70] The New Labour reforms of December 1997 proposed shifting away from an emphasis on competition to an emphasis upon collaboration. The only mention in the White Paper of mergers provides that:

> [g]iven the intended integration of primary and community health services, merging community with acute NHS Trusts will not generally be encouraged. Nor will amalgamation of small community NHS Trusts be encouraged if this inhibits closer working with local primary care teams. Other mergers arising from local decisions will be considered on their merits, on the basis of demonstrable benefits in health and healthcare, and savings in administration.[71]

This kind of general criterion will provide ample opportunity for decisions that reflect short-term political interests.

In contrast to the UK, New Zealand has elected to generally employ competition law to regulate its internal market. To date there have been very few cases. This probably reflects the nature of the relationships concluded between the formally split government purchasers and Crown Health Enterprises which, as discussed in the last chapter, are mainly one-year contracts as opposed to longer-term contracts, joint ventures, or other initiatives. As purchasers and providers are formally prohibited from integrating, there are commentators who call for purchasers and providers to develop longer-term relational contracts in order to reduce transactions costs.[72] The Commerce Act (NZ) 1986, No. 5, however, treats vertical integration with greater leniency than long-term contracts. In the former case, the test is whether the acquisition will result in the acquiring or strengthening of dominance. New Zealand's Court of Appeal has indicated that the dominance acquired has to be significant.[73] By contrast, a long-term contract falls within the ambit of s.27 of the Act and the lesser test is applied of whether or not the contract substantially lessens competition in the market. In 1995, the Commerce Commission refused clearance for a ten-year build-and-operate contract between a Regional Health Authority and a mental health facility on the grounds that after five years the market may become contestable.[74] Prima facie, the decision seems reasonable; however, the Commission failed to recognize some important health policy considerations relating to the overall efficiency of the proposed contract. These considerations include the benefit of continuity of supply of mental health services and the need for a relationship of trust between purchasers and providers in order to ensure the quality of mental health services supplied. Thus, although New Zealand's Commerce Act (NZ), (1986) No. 5 allows the competition authorities to consider efficiencies clearly there is a learning curve in understanding the factors contributing to short- and long-term efficiencies in various health care markets.[75]

Competition law has not historically been applied to the Dutch health sector for two reasons.[76] First, it was thought that the promotion of competition amongst health insurers would be detrimental rather than advantageous to the public interest, and, secondly, there has historically been an exemption for practitioners and other "learned professions" from the scope of anti-trust legislation.[77] This latter exemption was removed in 1987 but, as the government continued to regulate prices charged by the physicians and hospitals under the Health Care Tariffs Act, there has been little scope for the operation of competition law. In 1992, a significant change occurred. Rather than fixing health care prices, the formal rounds of negotiations between insurers and providers were used to establish *maximum* prices. This opened up the prospect of competition below the maximum prices set. However, the Dutch anti-trust legislation had little teeth at this point. In 1991, Schut, Greenberg, and van de Ven noted that the Economic Competition Act provided for some measures to combat abuse of a dominant position; however, actual enforcement was virtually non-existent. Moreover, there was little prospect of improvement in this situation as there was no scope for the imposition of fines or opportunities for plaintiffs to seek damages. There was also no scope to seek injunctions to stop mergers or takeovers that were likely to breach the Act.[78] On 1 January 1998, a new Competition Act was introduced which seeks to reconcile Dutch competition law with European standards.[79] The Act is to be administered by the Netherlands Competition Authority and covers cartels, abuse of a dominant position, and mergers. A range of penalties are provided for breach of the new Act's provisions including fines of up to 10 percent of the annual turnover of a firm. Competitors or other aggrieved parties may launch a civil action against a firm in breach of the new Act. Thus, the prospects for enforcement of competition laws are enhanced. The abuse of a dominant position provisions do apply to health care goods and services; however, upon application, the Netherlands Competition Authority may exempt providers supplying goods or services servicing a public interest.

Of all the countries under study, the US has had the most experience with the application of competition law to the health sector. Since 1975, the health services market has largely been treated just as any other market would be for the purposes of anti-trust law.[80] Anti-trust law has been used to prevent organized medicine's attempts to thwart the development of managed care. In a series of cases in the late 1970s, that focused on the practice of reviewing dentists' practice patterns, the Supreme Court found that the dentists could not prevent cost-containment efforts on the part of insurers. In 1982, the Supreme Court affirmed in Federal Trade Commission v. American Medical Association[81] that the American Medical Association was required to change its code of ethics that precluded groups of physicians from contracting with managed care plans.[82] In a 1984 case, it was also found that it was not anti-competitive for private insurers to preclude physicians from charging patients user charges in addition to the amount paid by the insurer to the physician.[83] From the case law to date it seems that managed care plans are entitled to select surgeons and physicians with whom they believe they will best compete in the marketplace.[84]

The anti-collusion provisions of the US Sherman Act[85] are generally interpreted using a "rule of reason" test which requires the court to consider all relevant market factors and weigh the pro-competitive and anti-competitive effects to determine whether the arrangement or activity in question unreasonably hurts competition. However, price fixing is perceived as so detrimental that the rule of reason test is not applied and it is considered per se illegal even if pro-competitive justifications are offered.[86] One may, however, envisage situations in managed care plans where price fixing should be allowed as part of the design of an integrated, comprehensive and coordinated system of care. Jacobs notes that collective price negotiation that comprises but one part of a "multifaceted integrative scheme designed to achieve some overall competitive benefit" such as a managed care plan, may be acceptable under US anti-trust law.[87]

It seems to be accepted in the US that vertical integration in the health sector can be an efficient alternative to contracting and other arm's-length market transactions in health care markets.[88] US case law also recognizes that vertical arrangements are usually more benign than horizontal ones. In US Healthcare, Inc. v. Healthsource, Inc., the First Circuit notes:

> no one would think twice about a doctor agreeing to work full-time for a staff HMO, an extreme case of vertical exclusivity. Imagine, by contrast, the motives and effects of a horizontal agreement by all of the doctors in a town not to work at a hospital that serves a staff HMO which competes with the doctors.[89]

A distinction is made in US law between insurer-sponsored managed care plans and physician-run plans. An insurer-sponsored plan is a vertical arrangement between a purchaser (in this case a private insurer) and a group of health care suppliers. In contrast, a physician-sponsored plan is a horizontal arrangement among a group of potential competitors and is therefore subject to anti-trust scrutiny.

In the context of horizontal arrangements between health providers, from a policy perspective we would want to prevent arrangements that strengthen the market power so as to defeat legitimate cost-containment actions on the part of government purchasers in an internal market. On the other hand, we would want to allow horizontal arrangements that create efficiencies, perhaps through the creation of integrated groups of health providers. Integration is not necessarily limited to an insurer integrating vertically downwards with health providers. Health providers may form a nexus and by sharing financial risk essentially take on the risk-management/purchasing role. In this case health providers are not simply forming a horizontal arrangement but integrating forward into risk management/purchasing activities.

Until recently, it was thought in the US that physicians had to share financial risk before horizontal arrangements passed the per se illegality test under the Sherman Act.[90] Physicians had argued that the per se illegality rule, applied to horizontal arrangements between physicians for the purpose of sharing information on prices, should be eased.[91] They argued that this was necessary in order for them to be able to compete with the increasingly larger insurer-sponsored managed care plans.[92] The competition authorities do not accept that physicians should be able to negotiate jointly simply in order to amass market power in order to negotiate better terms with insurers/managed care plans. However, the revised guidelines, issued by the Federal Trade Commission and Department of Justice in 1996, emphasized that providers could act jointly, without sharing financial risk, and this would not be considered per se illegal provided that there was extensive integration among the physician participants. In such a case, whether or not the arrangement is anti-competitive will be considered on a rule of reason basis.[93] These revised guidelines seem to recognize that while vertically integrated operations may be ideal, providers cannot vertically integrate upwards without creating a horizontal arrangement between themselves first. In other words, the creation of horizontal arrangements between providers is a transitional stage in creating an acceptable vertically integrated plan.

From this discussion, one can see that the application of general competition law to competitive or contestable health care markets is far from clear-cut. There is an inherent tension between the desire to allow efficient integration and to prevent the accretion of market power without offsetting efficiency gains. In order to be flexible, the general competition laws of the system must allow for trade-offs to be made between the loss of competition and gains in efficiency. Competition laws that declare certain behavior to be per se illegal are not likely to be useful in the health care sector. If the competition authorities and regular courts are not empowered to make trade-offs between efficiencies from competition and efficiencies of integration, then the development of integrated delivery systems may be impeded. Despite the problem of applying general competition law, it has proven in the US to be flexible enough to allow the development of managed care plans. Moreover, as demonstrated in the UK, allowing the government to fulfil the role that competition authorities would ordinarily undertake is unlikely to remedy the problems that arise in maintaining competition in competitive and contestable markets.

Industry-specific regulation

Let us turn now to consider industry-specific regulation. Having concluded that, despite the difficulties, it is probably appropriate to leave competition law to regulate the competitive or contestable segments of the markets, there is still the outstanding problems of access to bottleneck or essential facilities, regulating the price charged by natural monopoly, and cross-subsidization from monopoly competitive markets. Is industry-specific regulation the means by which to solve these problems?

There are at least five advantages with relying upon an industry-specific regulator:

- General competition authorities may lack the specialized institutional knowledge and capacity to deal with complex industries. Commentators have argued this in the context of telecommunications and electricity sectors and other public utilities. Such an argument would seem to be even more applicable to the health sector due to the severe information asymmetry problem and the associated problems of regulating quality (discussed below).
- The terms of access to a natural monopoly by downstream or upstream competitors will probably require ongoing monitoring that the competition authorities and regular courts are ill-equipped to perform.
- A regulator may be able to deal with access issues industry-wide in a more cost-effective manner than piece-meal competition law litigation.
- A regulator may be able to pre-empt access difficulties by competitors in upstream or downstream markets thus precluding monopolists from collecting monopoly rents in those markets throughout protracted litigation proceedings.
- There is no provision in general competition laws or pursuant to the essential facilities doctrine that would compel a monopolist to expand a hospital or other essential facility to cater to the needs of competitors.

There are also at least five disadvantages with relying upon an industry-specific regulator:

- A specific regulator is more likely to be concerned with outcomes rather than the process of competition. Over time, there is a natural tendency for the regulator to protect those who are subject to regulation rather than the process of competition itself – in other words the regulator will be "captured" by the regulated.
- In order to regulate, a specific regulator must obtain extensive information about the firm(s) being regulated, and the cost and time involved with this may seriously impede rigorous competition in a market and may also provide opportunities for collusive behavior.
- An information asymmetry problem exists between the regulator and the monopoly with management of the monopoly having a much better understanding of the firm and its markets than the regulator does.[94]
- Monopolists will not passively give up their rents and will spend considerable resources attempting to manipulate the regulatory process.[95]
- The remedies available to the general competition authorities and courts pursuant to competition law (injunctions, private damages, criminal

sanctions) would be lost and these remedies could prove more powerful than administrative law remedies.[96]

Some of the disadvantages of regulation will be ameliorated or aggravated depending on the type of regulation undertaken. For example, a regulator faces an information asymmetry problem, as a monopolist will have more information about its own costs of production than a regulator will. Where the regulator uses rate-of-return or cost-plus regulations the regulator "must become involved in micro management of the firm, second-guessing the decisions of management."[97] This clearly can be a costly and time-consuming process. By becoming involved in the micro-management of the firm, there is greater opportunity for the regulator to be "captured" by those being regulated, becoming more concerned with the welfare of the firm being regulated rather than societal welfare.[98] Cost-plus regulation also has the potential to entrench inefficiencies, as there is no incentive to reduce costs and, moreover, may lead to over-investment in fixed costs.

In recognition of the problems associated with rate-of-return or cost-plus regulation there has been a general shift in public utility regulation to price-cap regulation.[99] The benefit of price-cap regulation is that the monopolist is able to keep as profit any cost-savings made below the fixed price thus producing internal incentives for efficiency. One difficulty is how to ascertain the level at which to fix the price. A price-cap is a relatively crude form of regulation and may be insensitive to the differing underlying cost structures faced by monopolists in different areas. At some point, it may be necessary to review the underlying cost structure of firms to ensure that price-caps are set at the most efficient level (essentially a mother-of-all rate-of-return hearings!) The greatest concern in using price-caps to regulate health providers is that in the face of price-caps, monopolists will have incentives to cut the quality of services supplied.[100] In fact, the incentive structure of price-cap regulation is very similar to that which underpins capitation payments. The problem of ensuring the quality of health services will, however, equally be a problem in competitive health care markets and thus, regardless, some independent mechanism or entity will be required to safeguard the quality of services supplied. The issue of how to ensure quality is discussed in the next chapter.

Regulation holds the promise of being more targeted and flexible than nationalization. It allows firms to achieve the benefits of vertical integration but intervenes to the degree needed to prevent insurer/purchasers that are vertically integrated with monopoly health providers from foreclosing competition in the insurance/purchasing markets. A regulator is likely to be better able to deal with a natural monopoly than competition law which is premised on the assumption that the more competition within a market the better.

Conclusion

As one can see from the discussion in this chapter, all the problems of utility regulation are present in the regulation of health care delivery and are, in fact, further complicated by information asymmetry and moral hazard problems.[101]

The least intrusive solution to the problem of monopoly supply is to rely on cooperation. In a managed competition system, an insurer/purchaser may hold the advantage in some markets where it is vertically integrated with monopoly providers and not in others. Thus one can envisage a situation where vertically integrated insurer/purchasers would work out access arrangements for competitors as they know this will need to be reciprocated in other markets.[102] In this scenario the only explicit supply-side regulation that would be required is competition law to prevent any collusion between insurer/purchasers where they explicitly or implicitly divide up the insurance/purchasing market between them. This scenario is, however, based on the assumption that insurer/purchasers are beginning from a level playing field and no one insurer/purchaser has a significant advantage in terms of control of monopoly health care providers. Moreover, collusion can be difficult to root out even where competition laws are vigorously enforced.

The use of competition law to maintain and encourage competition in competitive and contestable health care markets is problematic because as a matter of policy we wish to encourage competition between integrated systems and not individual health providers. These problems support the contention that a specific regulator should regulate not only the natural monopoly but also the competitive segments as it would have a greater understanding of the complexities of the system. However, provided that competition law allows trade-offs to be made between the pursuit of competition and efficiency gains, the US case law suggests that competition law will generally facilitate rather than hinder the development of managed care plans. In an internal market system, where the government appoints the purchasers and owns most of the hospitals, leaving government to regulate competition can result in conflicts of interest. Private competitors may choose not to enter the market given the knowledge that publicly-owned hospitals will not be allowed to fail and will be protected from the rigors of competition.

On balance, industry-specific regulation seems the most appropriate means to deal with the problem of bottlenecks, cross-subsidy, and monopoly rents. Competition law should be left to regulate the competitive and contestable markets. A specialized regulator is more likely to have the institutional capacity to effectively monitor a monopoly over time. It promises to be more flexible to different market conditions and to tailor remedies. No system of incentives will be perfect, yet, of the competing alternatives, specific regulation is more likely to deal with the problems effectively. Although in principle this sounds appealing one must be careful of regulatory ossification of the system. By this I mean that purchasers and providers may become so bogged in regulation that innovation, spontaneity, responsiveness – the best qualities of a competitive market – are lost. As I discussed in Chapter 3, there needs to be regulation in a managed competition system to stimulate competition between insurers on price and quality dimensions. To the greatest degree possible, once this regulation is in place, insurer/purchasers should be left to determine their own supply side arrangements. Thus, government intervention to remedy monopoly supply side problems should be as discrete and selective as possible.

Notes

1 D. E. Osborne and T. Gaebler, *Reinventing Government: How the Entrepreneurial Spirit is Transforming the Public Sector* (Reading, MA: Addison-Wesley Publishers Co., 1992), advocate that government intervention be directed towards steering rather than rowing. However, M. J. Trebilcock, *The Prospects for Reinventing Government* (Toronto: C. D. Howe Institute, 1994) at p. 4 notes that Osborne and Gaebler "leave[s] to others the task of developing the rigorous theoretical frameworks and detailed empirical investigations that would enable hard policy choices to be made among alternative governing instruments in particular sectors of governmental activity."

2 F. T. Schut and H. E. G. M. Hermans, 'Managed Competition Reform in the Netherlands and its Lessons for Canada', (1997) 20(2) *Dalhousie Law Journal* 437 at p. 455.

3 R. Posner, *Anti-trust Law: An Economic Perspective* (Chicago, IL: University of Chicago Press, 1976) at pp. 8–22.

4 See, for example, H. Demsetz, 'Why Regulate Monopoly?', (1968) 11 *J. of Law and Economics* 55.

5 For a discussion of natural monopolies generally, see C. D. Foster, *Privatization, Public Ownership and the Regulation of Natural Monopoly*, (Oxford: Blackwell, 1992), and K. E. Train, *Optimal Regulation: The Economic Theory of Natural Monopoly* (Cambridge, MA: The MIT Press, 1991). See also W. J. Baumol, E. E. Bailey and R. D. Willig, 'Weak Invisible Hand Theorems on the Sustainability of Multiproduct Natural Monopoly', (1977) 67(3) *American Economic Review* 350.

6 H. Imai, 'Bilateral Price-Setting in a Bilateral Monopoly Model', (1986) 24 *J. Econ. Theory* 311; S. R. Williams, 'Efficient Performance in Two Agent Bargaining', (1987) 41 *J. Econ. Theory* 154; J. C. Rochet, 'Some Recent Results in Bargaining Theory' (1987) 31 *Europ. Econ. Rev.* 326.

7 The market leverage theory has been discredited by some as a monopoly-expanding threat – see R. Posner, 'The Chicago School of Anti-trust Analysis', (1979) 127(4) *U. Pa. Law Review* 925, and R. H. Bork, *The Anti-trust Paradox: A Policy at War with Itself* (New York: Basic Books, 1978) at pp. 372–381. For a rejoinder, see L. Kaplow, 'Extension of Monopoly Power Through Leverage', (1985) 85(1) *Columbia Law Review* 515.

8 In terms of consumer choice the effects are even more egregious as individuals would not be able to choose either their purchaser or their provider.

9 See for example M. A. Morrisey *et al.*, 'Managed Care and Physician/Hospital Integration', (1996) 15(4) *Health Affairs* 62; R. H. Miller, 'Health Care System Integration: A Means To An End', (1996) 15(2) *Health Affairs* 92.

10 As quoted by P. Newman, 'Interview with Alain Enthoven: Is There Convergence Between Britain and the United States in the Organization of Health Services', (1995) 310(6995) *BMJ* 1652.

11 Miller, *op. cit.*, p. 92.

12 V. R. Fuchs, 'Economics, Values, and Health Care Reform', (1996) 86(1) *The American Economic Review* 1 at p. 17.

13 The 1991 statistics in this paragraph are calculated using figures for area from *Rand McNally New Cosmopolitan World Atlas* (Chicago: Rand McNally and Company, 1966) at pp. 192–194 and figures for population from J. P. Poullier (OECD), *OECD Health Care Systems: The Socio-Economic Environment Statistical References, Vol. II* (Paris: OECD, 1993) at p. 11, Table A1.1.1.

14 R. Kronick *et al.*, 'The Marketplace in Health Care Reform: The Demographic Limitations of Managed Competition', (1993) 328(2) *New Eng. J. Med.* 148.

15 H. S. Luft and S. C. Maerki, 'Competitive Potential of Hospitals and their Neighbours', (1984) 3 *Contemporary Policy Issues* 89 as cited by F. T. Schut, 'Workable Competition in Health Care: Prospects for the Dutch Design', (1992) 35(12) *Soc. Sci. Med.* 1445 at p. 1451.

16 Although, according to the US Department of Justice 1984 merger guidelines, markets with a Herfindahl-Hirschman Index of more than 1,800 (about six equally sized firms) are regarded as highly concentrated and more than 70 percent of the Dutch hospital markets still exceed this figure. The Herfindahl-Hirschman Index is the sum of the squared market shares of all firms in the same relevant product and geographic market and varies from 0 to 10,000 with a score of 10,000 being indicative of a pure monopoly – Schut, *op. cit.*, p. 1451.

17 In New Zealand, see T. Ashton and D. Press, 'Market Concentration in Secondary Health Services Under a Purchaser-Provider Split: The New Zealand Experience', (1997) 6(1) *Health Economics* 43. In the UK, see C. Propper, 'Market Structure and Prices: The Response of NHS Hospitals to Costs and Competition', (Mimeo, Dept. of Economics, University of Bristol, 1994).

18 Propper, *ibid.*

19 Morrisey *et al.*, *op. cit.*, p. 64.

20 See F. T. Schut, *Competition in the Dutch Health Care Sector* (PhD Book, Health Economics, Erasmus University, Rotterdam, 1995) at pp. 227–228.

21 L. Malcolm and M. Powell, 'The Development of Independent Practice Associations and Related Groups in New Zealand', (1996) 109(1022) *NZ Med. J.* 184 at p. 186.

22 For a discussion of the hype surrounding the growth of integrated systems see M. A. Morrisey *et al.*, *op. cit.*, pp. 65–66.

23 *The New NHS: Modern, Dependable*, a White Paper, Cm 3807, 8 December 1997. Online. Available HTTP: http://www.official-documents.co.uk/document/doh/newnhs/contents.htm (accessed 30 March 1999) at s. 5.24–5.26.

24 F. Schut, W. Greenberg and W. P. M. M. van de Ven, 'Anti-trust Policy in the Dutch Health Care System and the Relevance of EEC Competition Policy and US Anti-trust Practice', (1991) 17 *Health Policy* 257 at p. 262, Table 1.

25 *The Reform of Health Care: A Comparative Analysis of Seven OECD Countries*, OECD Health Policy Studies No. 2, (Paris: OECD, 1992) at p. 91. For a description of the complicated negotiation process, see B. L. Kirkman-Liff, 'Cost-containment and Physician Payment Methods in the Netherlands', (1989) 26 *Inquiry* 468 pp. 472–473.

26 Kirkman-Liff, *ibid.*, p. 478.

27 J. C. Robinson, 'Health Care Purchasing and Market Changes in California', (1995) 14(4) *Health Affairs* 117 at p. 118.

28 Thus they are essentially performing the role of sponsors as envisaged by Enthoven in his managed care model.

29 D. A. Yao, M. H. Riordan and T. N. Dahdouh, 'Anti-trust and Managed Competition for Health Care', (1994) 39(2) *The Anti-trust Bulletin* 301 at p. 317.

30 For a discussion in the context of telecommunications, see generally, G. W. Brock, *Telecommunication Policy for the Information Age: From Monopoly to Competition* (Cambridge, MA: Harvard University Press, 1994). For a discussion in the context of electricity, see M. J. Trebilcock and M. Gal, 'Deregulation of Public Utilities: Experience of the Ontario Natural Gas and Electricity Industries', in M. Richardson (ed.), *Deregulation of Public Utilities: Current Issues and Perspectives* (Melbourne: Centre for Corporate Law and Securities Regulation, 1996) at p. 14.

31 See generally W. Megginson, R. Nash and M. van Randenbororgh, 'The Financial and Operating Performance of Newly Privatized Firms: An International Empirical Analysis', (1994) 49 *J. of Finance* 403.

32 S. R. Smith and M. Lipsky, 'Privatization in Health and Human Services: A Critique', (1992) 17(2) *J. of Health, Polit. Policy Law* 233 at pp. 241–242.

33 National Health Service and Community Care Act, (UK), (1990) c. 19, and P. Allen, 'Contracts in the National Health Service Internal Market', (1995) 58(3) *Modern Law Review* 321.

34 P. Gorringe, 'Secondary Health Care: Contracting, People and Politics', draft of 5 November 1996 prepared for the Central Regional Health Authority, New Zealand, Summary, p. 3.

35 R. J. Blendon *et al.*, 'Satisfaction with Health Care Systems in Ten Nations', (1990) 9(2) *Health Affairs* 185.

36 Act of July 2, 1890, Chapter 647, 26 Stat. 209 (1890) (codified as amended at 15 USC.A. (1994)) [hereinafter Sherman Act].

37 The doctrine is usually traced back to the case of United States of America v. Terminal Railroad Association of St. Louis *et al.*, 224 US 383, (1912). For a discussion of its application, see generally F. A. Edgar Jr., 'The Essential Facilities Doctrine and Public Utilities: Another Layer of Regulation?', (1992–1993) 29(2) *Idaho Law Review* 283. Various commentators have advocated either for restriction or expansion of the doctrine's application – see P. Areeda, 'Essential Facilities: An Epithet in Need of Limiting Principles', (1990) 58 *Anti-Trust Law J.* 841 at p. 852 who advocates for a restrictive interpretation. An advocate for a broader application is J. R. Ratner, 'Should There Be an Essential Facility Doctrine?', (1988) 21 *U. C. Davis Law Rev.* 327 at p. 367.

38 See generally G. Werden, 'The Law and Economics of the Essential Facility Doctrine', (1987) 32(2) *St. Louis Univ. Law J.* 433.

39 MCI Communications Corp. v. American Tel. and Tel. Co, 708 F.2d 1081, 1132–1133 (7th Cir.) cert. denied, 464 US 891, (1983).

40 H. Hovenkamp, *Federal Anti-trust Law: The Law of Competition and its Practice* (St. Paul, MN: West Publishing Co., 1994) at p. 274.

41 Werden, *op. cit.*, p. 456.

42 [1991–1 Trade Cases, sec 69, 312] (4th Cir.).

43 Telecom Corp. of NZ Ltd. v. Clear Communications Ltd. [1995] 1 NZL.R. 385.

44 For a discussion, see C. M. Flood, 'Regulation of Telecommunications in New Zealand: Faith in Competition Law and the Kiwi Share' (1995) 3(2) *Competition and Consumer Law Journal* 199 at pp. 212–214.

45 See W. J. Baumol and J. G. Sidak, 'The Pricing of Inputs Sold to Competitors', (1994) 11(1) *The Yale J. of Regulation* 171, and A. E. Kahn and W. E. Taylor, 'The Pricing of Inputs Sold to Competitors: A Comment', (1994) 11(1) *The Yale J. of Regulation* 225.

46 Telecom Corp. of NZ Ltd., *op. cit.*

47 Werden, *op. cit.*, p. 479.

48 *Ibid.*

49 See generally S. H. Walbolt *et al.*, 'Problems of Access to Health Facilities and Equipment: New Competition for Limited Resources', (1986) 55 *Anti-trust Law J.* 599, and S. D. Makar, 'The Essential Facility Doctrine and the Health Care Industry', (1994) 21(3) *Florida State University Law Review* 913.

50 Makar attributes this phenomenon to an increasing number of physicians, fewer hospitals (as a result of consolidation) and hospitals being selective in employment of physicians in order to avoid medical malpractice liability on the grounds of granting admitting privileges to physicians whose qualifications or work was not of a sufficient standard – *ibid.*, p. 928.

51 See *ibid.*, pp. 932–934.

52 65 F.3d 1406 (7th Cir.1995), cert. denied No. 95-1118.

53 *Ibid.*, p. 1413.

54 In Paschall v. Kansas City Star Co 727 F.2d 692 at 697 (8th Cir. 1983) (en ban), cert. denied, 469 US 872 (1984), the Eighth Circuit said that "[l]iability based on specific intent can be negated where valid business justifications exist for the monopolist's actions." See also Aspen Skiing Co. v. Aspen Highlands Skiing Corp., 472 US 585 at 604–5 (1985).

55 Areeda, *op. cit.* at p. 847.

56 In Smith v. Northern Michigan Hospital Inc. 703 F.2d 942 at 953 (6th Cir. 1983), the court rejected a physician group's challenge of a hospital's decision to award its affiliated clinic an exclusive contract for the supply of emergency services. The physicians argued, relying in part on the essential facilities doctrine, that the hospital and clinic were in a horizontal arrangement and it was an unreasonable restraint of trade to deny the physicians admitting privileges for emergency room services. The court concluded that as the hospital was in a vertical relationship with the clinic it had to staff its one emergency room in the most "effective, efficient and medically prudent manner."

57 Presumably, the monopolist's physicians could perform the operations or services for other insurers' patients but this could lead to continuity of care and management problems for competitors.

58 J. F. Quinn and G. F. Leslie, 'Essential Facilities and the Duty to Facilitate Competition', (Symposium on Competition Law and Deregulation in Network Industries, University of Toronto, Faculty of Law, 14 June 1996) pp. 29–30.

59 See Telecom Corp. of NZ, Ltd., *op. cit.* For a discussion see Flood, *op, cit.*, pp. 212–214.

60 Sherman Act, *op. cit.*

61 This is known as the 'Copperweld' doctrine – Copperweld Corp. v. Independence Tube Corp., 467 US 752 (1984).

62 Sherman Act, *op. cit.*

63 US v. Grinnell Corp., 384 US 563, 570–1 (1966).

64 An exception to this is New Zealand's Commerce Act (NZ), (1986) No. 5, Part IV, which enables goods and services to be placed under the direct price control of the Commerce Commission where the Minister determines that there is limited competition in the market and that it is necessary or desirable for prices to be controlled in the interests of users, consumers and suppliers.

65 W. Greenberg, *Competition, Regulation and Rationing in Health Care* (Ann Arbor, MI: Health Administration Press, 1991) at p. 112.

66 See R. B. Thompson, 'Review: Competition Among Hospitals in the United States', (1994) 27(3) *Health Policy* 205.

67 P. B. Ginsburg and J. D. Pickering, 'Tracking Health Care Costs', (1996) 15(3) *Health Affairs* 140. See also generally, R. J. Arnould, R. F. Rich and W. D. White (eds), *Competitive Approaches to Health Care Reform* (Washington, DC: Urban Institute Press, 1993).

68 *The Operation of the Internal Market: Local Freedoms, National Responsibilities*, (London: Department of Health, 1994 (HSG (94) 55)).

69 D. Dawson, *Regulating Competition in the NHS: The Department of Health Guide on Mergers and Anti-Competitive Behavior, Discussion Paper 131* (York: Centre For Health Economics, 1995).

70 *Ibid.*, p. 6.

71 *The New NHS: Modern, Dependable, op. cit.*, s. 6.26.

72 T. Ashton, 'Voice and Exit in New Zealand's Health Care Sector: Commentary', in *Contracting in the Health Sector* (papers presented at a seminar held by the Legal Research Foundation at the University of Auckland, 6 July 1994).

73 See Clear Communications Limited v. Telecom Corporation of New Zealand Limited *et al.*, (1993) 4 NZBLC 103,341.

74 See the New Zealand's Commerce Commission Decision No. 275, ISSN No. 0114-2720, 1 August 1995 (application by the Midland Regional Health Authority and Health Waikato Limited for authorization under the Commerce Act (NZ), (1986) No. 5, s.58, at 32).

75 The Commerce Act (NZ), (1986) No. 5, s. 61 states that the Commission shall not grant an application approving (amongst other things) a contract that has the effect of substantially lessening competition unless the Commission is satisfied that the agreement "…will in all the circumstances result, or be likely to result, in a benefit to the public which would outweigh the lessening in competition that would result, or would be likely to result or is deemed to result therefrom." Section 3A of the Act provides "[w]here the Commission is required under this Act to determine whether or not, or the extent to which, conduct will result, or will be likely to result, in a benefit to the public, the Commission shall have regard to any efficiencies that the Commission considers will result, or will be likely to result from that conduct."

76 F. Schut, W. Greenberg and W. P. M. M. van de Ven, 'Anti-trust Policy in the Dutch Health Care System and the Relevance of EEC Competition Policy and US Anti-trust Practice', (1991) 17 *Health Policy* 257.

77 Schut, Greenberg and van de Ven, *ibid*, p. 271.

78 Schut, Greenberg and van de Ven, *ibid*.

79 For a very brief overview see Ekelmans Den Hollander, 'The Netherlands'. Online. Available HTTP: http://www.globalaw-group.com/nether.html (accessed 8 May 1999).

80 M. S. Jacobs, 'Recent Developments in Anti-trust Law and Their Implications for the Clinton Health Care Plan', (1993) 21(2) *The J. of Law, Medicine and Ethics* 163, and see Goldfarb v. Virginia State Bar, 421 US 773 (1975).

81 Federal Trade Commission v. American Medical Association, 94 FTC 701 (1979), aff'd 638 F.2d 443 (2d Cir. 1980), aff'd 452 US 960 (1982).

82 For reference to this and other cases see Greenberg, *op. cit.*, p. 113.

83 Kartell v. Blue Shield of Massachusetts, Inc., 749 F.2d 922 (1st Cir. 1984).

84 See the discussion by Greenberg, *op. cit.*, pp. 119–121, who notes citing Patrick v. Burget, 486 US 94 (1988) that managed care plans cannot use this as a pretext to punish or eliminate from the market physicians who are also competitors.

85 Sherman Act, *op. cit.*

86 See Arizona v. Maricopa County Medical Society, 457 US 332 (1982). The 1990 case of FTC v. Superior Court Trial Lawyers Association 493 US 411 (1990) makes it clear that price fixing agreements between professionals are unlawful.

87 Jacobs, *op. cit.*, p. 169.

88 See, for example, K. M. Fenton and B. C. Harris, 'Vertical Integration and Anti-trust in Health Care Markets' (1994), XXXIX: 2 The Anti-trust Bulletin 333 at p. 362.

89 US Healthcare, Inc. v. Healthsource, Inc., 19993-1 Trade Cas. (CCH)_70,142 (1st Cir. 1993) at p. 69,589.

90 See Arizona v. Maricopa County Medical Society, *op. cit.* where agreements for maximum price setting between physicians were struck down as a per se violation of s.1 of the Sherman Act 15 USC. §§ 1–7. The case stands for the principle that financial integration and evidence of risk-sharing are important factors in determining whether a physician joint venture raises anticompetitive concerns.

91 See L. BeSaw, 'Hope for Anti-trust Relief: Actions by Congress, FTC May Help Physicians Form Networks', (1996) 92(6) *Medical Economics* 26 at p. 27.

92 *Ibid.*, p. 28, and see N. K. Whittemore, 'Anti-trust Enforcement and Health Care Reform', (1996) 32(5) *Houston Law Review* 1493 at p. 1511, quoting Anti-trust Issues in the Health Care Industry: Hearings Before the Subcomm. on Medicare and Long-Term Care of the Senate Comm. on Finance, 103d Cong., 1st Sess. 66 (1993) (prepared statement of J. C. Egan, Jr., Director for Litigation for the Federal Trade Commission's Bureau of Competition), p. 73.

93 See Federal Trade Commission, 'Department of Justice and Federal Trade Commission Statements of Anti-trust Enforcement Policy in Health Care'. Online. Available HTTP: http://www.ftc.gov/reports/hlth3s.htm (accessed 8 May 1999).

94 T. A. Abbott, III and M. A. Crew, 'Lessons from Public Utility Regulation for the Economic Regulation of Health Care Markets: An Overview', in T. A. Abbott, III (ed.) *Health Care Policy and Regulation* (Boston, MA: Kluwer Academic Publishers, 1995) p. 16.

95 *Ibid.*

96 See P. Areeda and L. Kaplow, *Anti-trust Analysis: Problems, Text, Cases*, 4th edn, (Toronto: Little Brown and Co., 1988) Ch. 1.

97 Abbott and Crew, *op. cit.*, p. 17.

98 One possible solution is to have the members of the regulatory body appointed on a short-term basis only.

99 Abbott and Crew, *op. cit.*, p. 17.

100 *Ibid.*, p. 19.

101 *Ibid.*, p. 13.

102 This is on the assumption that there is regulation requiring insurer/purchasers to provide coverage to all residents in a particular location and setting limits on distances that residents may be expected to travel in order to access care.

7 Achieving quality in a competition-oriented system

Health care services are not like other essential services, for example electricity or telecommunications, where consumers can easily measure the quality of the service supplied. This problem is linked to an absence of information. Patients may often not have the information with which to judge the quality of a diagnosis made or of the care recommended or provided.[1] Health care providers generally have more information than patients, resulting in an information asymmetry problem and concerns that providers may take advantage of vulnerable patients. There is also a concern, however, that providers themselves lack good information about the effectiveness and cost-effectiveness of many health care services. A lack of information also means that it is difficult and costly for government to directly regulate the quality of health care services.

In response to the perceived costs and difficulties of direct quality regulation most systems have devolved regulatory responsibility to health care professionals themselves. Thus, the medical profession and other health care professionals are generally self-regulating professions. Through legislation they are given powers to set conditions on the training required to enter and remain in the profession, to establish ethical codes and professional standards, and to discipline those members of the profession who do not comply with the relevant codes and standards. By contrast, there has been a greater reliance on direct regulatory control of hospitals. Requiring hospitals to operate on a non-profit basis is another tactic adopted to ensure that quality is not sacrificed in the pursuit of profits and that providers do not take advantage of vulnerable patients. Some jurisdictions, like New Zealand and the UK, have nationalized most hospitals. The implicit assumption in these countries is that public sector management will work in the best interests of patients and, ultimately, in the public interest. Most systems also rely upon the deterrent effect of medical malpractice actions to ensure quality in the delivery of care by health care providers, hospitals and other institutions. Moreover, historically it was thought that the quality of care provided by health professionals and hospitals was assured by the fact that public and private insurers indemnified health care providers on a fee-for-service basis. Thus, hospitals and health professionals had no incentive to reduce or restrict the range, effectiveness, or volume of services supplied.

Increasingly there has been growing concern over the conflicts of interest involved in allowing health care professions to regulate themselves[2] and over the real deterrent effect of medical malpractice actions. The shift in most systems to paying hospitals by way of a fixed annual budget has increasingly meant that hospitals have had to choose between different health care needs. In systems with nationalized hospitals, concern has grown that management was finding it easier to allow waiting lists to grow rather than to strive for improvements in efficiency.[3] There has also been a concern that connections and social status were influencing physicians' decisions regarding treatment and that individuals with connections were able to jump queues. Concomitantly with these trends there has been a growing awareness that quality cannot be measured by the supply of all possible health care services irrespective of costs and marginal health benefits. In fact, this problem was recognized as long ago as 1911, when George Bernard Shaw remarked:

> That any sane nation, having observed that you could provide for the supply of bread by giving bakers a pecuniary interest in baking for you, should go on to give a surgeon a pecuniary interest in cutting off your leg, is enough to make one despair of political humanity.[4]

This chapter begins by exploring the question of what is meant by the word "quality." Patients, purchasers (whether government-appointed health authorities, private insurers, or groups of providers), and society at large all have different perspectives on what constitutes quality. Balancing these perspectives requires a system to be concerned with three quality paradigms: technical quality, quality in terms of service or treatment selection for a particular health need, and quality in terms of prioritizing need.

The new wave of competition-oriented reforms seeks to change the balance of power between purchasers and physicians. Purchasers seek to strongly influence or manage physician decision-making. Both internal markets and managed competition require proactive purchasers to use a variety of managed care techniques to influence the behavior of health care providers in supplying and recommending treatment. "Managed care" covers a number of different types of measures whereby purchasers seek to make health care providers more cost sensitive. Possibly, purchasers may seek to devolve financial risk to health care providers. They may do this by paying providers on a capitation basis – a fixed sum per person for a particular period regardless of the actual cost of services needed by that person. There is a fear, however, that capitation will lead to unacceptable cuts in quality.

This chapter explores the incentive effects of different payment mechanisms (fee-for-service, salary, capitation or some combination thereof) and whether there is a "holy grail" in terms of a payment regime with the right incentive mix. Balancing these perspectives requires a system to be concerned with three quality paradigms: technical quality, quality in terms of service, and quality in terms of prioritization. More generally, it examines what is the most efficient set of incentives or types of regulation that will achieve the three quality paradigms described above.

The meaning of quality

An important initial question is, what is meant by "quality"? As McGlynn points out, to a large extent quality is in the eye of the beholder, and purchasers, providers, patients and the general public all have different views on what constitutes quality.[5]

Physicians' perspectives on quality have traditionally dominated health care systems. Physicians have emphasized the professional skill with which medical services are supplied and the importance of supplying an increasing number, range, and complexity of medical services to achieve better health outcomes. Physicians have been entrusted not only with the responsibility of ensuring patients' best interests but also with the responsibility of allocating society's resources. The concern has been that under the guise of ensuring the quality of services, physicians have supplied a range, mix, and intensity of services that best serves their own interests as opposed to the more diffused interests of the general public. Physicians may argue that supplying an increasing range, volume, and intensity of service, even if they are of small marginal benefit, furthers the interests of the patient they are treating. However, the significant risk of iatrogenic (caused by medical examination or treatment) injuries casts doubt even upon this argument. In any event, ultimately, trade-offs must be made between patient welfare and societal welfare, for, in the extreme, all our resources could be devoted to one patient or all our resources could be devoted to health care with nothing left for education, welfare, defense, consumer goods, etc.

Although quality is often thought of in simple terms as skilful diagnosis and treatment, there are at least three separate quality paradigms that a system needs to address. The first is technical or production quality – skill in providing a particular treatment or service. The second is quality in terms of choosing the most appropriate service for a particular need. The third paradigm is quality in terms of prioritization of health needs. Health care systems have historically focused exclusively on technical quality, largely ignoring the second and third paradigms of quality in a system.

Technical quality

Technical quality is directly linked to skill in performing a particular task. Historically, technical quality has been striven for by devolving self-regulatory power to the medical profession. Representatives of the profession have been given the power to license and discipline members of the profession to ensure minimum levels of training and competence. In addition, technical quality has been striven for by relying on the deterrent effect of medical malpractice actions.

As can be seen, historically, mechanisms designed to achieve technical quality have focused on training and finding fault with an individual provider's actions. However, an important aspect of the technical quality of services produced depends on coordination between different health care professionals. Jost notes that:

> Health care production processes are most clearly evident in complex health care institutions such as the hospital, in which patients are admitted, fed, cleaned, toileted, moved from place to place (for X-rays or surgery, for example), connected to and disconnected from various machines, medicated, observed and monitored, discharged and billed.[6]

This need for coordination reinforces the advantages of integrated delivery systems. In an integrated system, providers with different skills work together to ensure the coordinated supply of services to patients. Ideally, there should not only be a seamless transition between services within institutions but between different types of health care services in the system as a whole. There should also be no institutional barriers to patients receiving the optimal mix of hospital, physician, nursing, physiotherapist, occupational therapy, drugs, X-rays, and other care that most cost-effectively addresses their health need.

The formation of integrated systems also opens up the possibility of a move towards internal "total quality management."[7] This management concept, which has had a significant impact on Japanese production techniques and subsequently upon US production, relies upon a commitment to continual improvement of quality. The goal of management in a total quality system is not to punish or select out particular workers who are not performing. Instead it is to create an environment where workers feel able to discuss mistakes and learn from them, thus contributing to the quality of the production process or of the system as a whole. A move to total quality management would constitute a significant paradigm shift in health care systems that have historically relied primarily upon punitive sanctions of *individual* health providers. The insurer/ purchaser managing an integrated system should be equally liable with health care providers for technical efficiency as it is well placed to put in place system-wide checks and balances for quality.

Ideally, technical quality should be assessed by clinical and health outcomes, such as in the case of surgical services the need for readmission, infection rates, mortality rates, mobility gained, pain eased, etc. In 1966, Donabedian conceptualized three aspects of health care quality: structural elements (such as professional credentials and the years of experience of health care providers, and the amount of technology employed); process elements (what tests, procedures and services are performed); and outcomes of care, both short and long term.[8] Unfortunately, despite the significant strides that have been made in outcome assessment since 1966, it is not possible to measure outcomes of care in many cases and structural and process elements must be used as next best indicators of quality.[9] Eddy discusses five factors that make measuring health outcomes so difficult.[10] The first factor, probability, means that one cannot rely on a single observation to demonstrate the relationship between a service and an outcome, and there is a need for a large number of observations. Related to this factor is that of low frequency. The relatively low frequency of specific health outcomes, such as deaths per number of breast cancer cases, means that it is difficult to get a sufficient sample size with which to judge the performance of a provider or, for that matter, of a purchaser. The third factor Eddy identifies is the long delays between the consumption of a health care service and any measurable health outcome. This is a particular problem for measuring outcomes associated with preventive care services. The fourth factor is the weak control that providers and purchasers have over other variables that will affect measurable health outcomes e.g. socio-economic status, smoking, risky behavior, etc. The fifth and final factor Eddy identifies is comprehensibility. Very detailed performance measures are needed to ensure good scientific research and it is not clear that citizens will be able to use these outcome measures to generalize at the level of making choices between providers or purchasers.

With a rise in the importance of an economic analysis of health care systems there has been an increasing emphasis on examining the "goal" or "outputs" or "product" of systems, which are generally assumed to be "health" or "healthiness."[11] The danger with this approach is that, as discussed in Chapter 2, it is too utilitarian and may result in too great an emphasis on population health at the expense of a fair distribution of access to health care services. A balance must be struck between individual needs for health care and what is in the best interest of society as a whole. Also, focusing too strongly on the output or product of a system may mean that purchasers (be they government-appointed or private insurers) will find it easier to focus on easy-to-measure indicators of performance like the number of operations performed, lives saved, etc. rather than upon more subtle indicators of quality. The quality of services of a caring as opposed to a curative nature, such as services for the terminally ill, the chronically ill, the elderly, the disabled, and the mentally ill, become more at risk in a system focusing on outcomes because of measurement difficulties in these kinds of cases. Providing palliative care may not be a priority from the perspective of improving the population's "health" yet most people value this kind of care and consider it as important, if not more important, than curative or preventive services. Similarly, providing health care services to the mentally and physically handicapped may not improve societal "health", but is still valued highly. It is thus dangerous to lay too great a weight on measurable health outcomes and to do so would result in a skewering of the system towards producing curative services that are easy to measure. A system must allow for the fact that the satisfaction of some health care needs will not be readily measurable in terms of outcomes and devote special attention to ensuring that an appropriate level of resources is devoted to those needs.

Two quality issues falling within the paradigm of technical quality are the lengths of time that patients spend waiting for health care services and any unnecessary trauma, anxiety or pain patients undergo whilst receiving medical services or treatment. Depending on the particular health care need, waiting times may cause unnecessary stress, loss of productivity and lost wages, and may aggravate the underlying condition. It can also result in direct patient costs and thus distributional injustices. For example, in New Zealand, if a patient cannot have surgery within six months then he/she is not put on a waiting list but is sent back to his/her general physician to manage his/her condition. This has a disproportionate financial impact on poorer patients, as in New Zealand there are user charges for physician and pharmaceutical services but not for public hospital services. Another technical quality issue relates to the pain or anguish incidentally inflicted upon a patient receiving medical treatment. Even if the "outcome" of treatment may be satisfactory, the quality of the process of supplying care may be unacceptable if unnecessary levels of trauma, anxiety or pain are incidentally inflicted upon the patient.[12] This may be if a nurse is unnecessarily rough when putting in an intravenous drip or if a physician fails to tell a patient what is entailed in medical procedures about to be administered, causing unnecessary fear and anxiety.

Quality in terms of choosing the most appropriate service for a particular need

The second quality paradigm is deciding upon what services or treatment (if any) to supply in response to a particular health need. In this century, physicians have been allowed to monopolize the diagnosis process on the grounds that the quality of care would suffer if unlicensed providers were allowed to diagnose and treat patients.[13] However, information technology has developed and significant advances have been made in our ability to examine and compare physicians' prescribing practices. We are no longer limited to relying upon the medical profession's assessment of the quality of care prescribed or provided. The results gained from empirical analysis of physicians' prescribing practices are disturbing. In some cases it seems that physicians will be more concerned with their own professional self-interest than with quality, whether from a patient or societal perspective.[14] Self-interest aside, it seems that in many cases physicians themselves lack good information about the costs and benefits of particular treatments. Studies show significant levels of variation in the treatment of medical needs that appear to be unjustifiable from a clinical perspective. Thus, there are potential efficiency gains to be had from greater consistency in prescribing patterns without any apparent detriment to the quality of care delivered.[15]

From a patient's perspective, quality of service in the short term will depend upon receiving the best possible service for a particular need in terms of immediate access, short recovery times, minimal side-effects, minimal risks, and greater chance of survival or full recovery, irrespective of cost. Societal welfare may be enhanced, however, if some of these elements of quality were foregone and resources so freed up were devoted to other needs or wants, e.g. other patients' health needs, preventive care, education, infrastructure, tax reductions, etc. There must be mechanisms within a system to determine whether, for example, to provide a particular kind of treatment at a cost of $10,000 with a 100-percent success rate or a substitute treatment at a cost of $1,000 per person with a 80-percent success rate. In the latter case, eight times as many people would be successfully treated for the same cost as the more expensive treatment. However, before we can make this determination we need to know how society values the consequences of the 20-percent failure rate relative to the other uses these resources could be put. If 20 percent of people died or suffered grave physical harm as a result then, within a developed country, justice will require that everyone be provided with the more expensive service with its 100-percent success rate. If the consequences of failure are less severe, a trade-off may be made between a patient's desire to have the best possible service and societal welfare.

Quality in terms of prioritization of needs

Some of the difficulties inherent in prioritizing health care needs have been discussed in Chapter 4. Prioritizing health care needs is complicated, as purchasers, patients and society at large will value the satisfaction of particular health needs differently. A system's primary goal should be to satisfy societal goals and values. However, this general utilitarian approach must be overridden in some instances, such as in the case of services for vulnerable populations. Fairness and justice requires that, for example, HIV/AIDS services, psychiatric services, and services for the mentally or physically disabled, be provided even though many people in society (rightly or wrongly) consider their own probability of needing these services to be almost zero.[16]

Even within the paradigm of society's goals, prioritising health care needs is difficult. For example, societies seem to strongly value satisfying what has become known as the "rule of rescue."[17] Significant resources are expended on rescuing individuals from imminent life-threatening peril. Examples include the enormous sums of money expended to save a child trapped in the bottom of a well, a skier buried alive at the bottom of an avalanche, a yachtsman who has disappeared in the Pacific. In health care, examples include a child who has a 5-percent chance of survival if he/she receives a heart-and-lung transplant that will cost $1 million. Society often demonstrates a strong preference when directly faced with such a poignant case to finance the child's chance of survival. However, a balance has to be struck between society's desire to satisfy the rule of rescue and society's desire to spend a fair amount on health care services relative to other needs. These kind of value-laden issues will never be easy to resolve in any kind of health care system. Notwithstanding the complexity and difficulty inherent in the process it is imperative that a system continually evaluates priorities given to different health care needs through a body such as New Zealand's Core Health Services Commission.[18] To neglect this evaluation is to effectively leave physicians to determine societal values in terms of different health care needs. In my opinion, such decisions should not depend upon the particular values and biases of individual physicians but upon a set of principles that society has determined in a transparent and democratic way.

Modes of payment for health care providers

There are three general means by which to pay physicians and other health care providers: fee-for-service, salary, and capitation. Variants of these payment mechanisms may also be used to pay competing insurer/purchasers in a managed competition system. This section explores the incentives inherent in a particular payment mechanism and, in particular, the likely impact on the quality of care delivered.

Fee-for-service

Historically, fee-for-service payments have characterized all four systems under study but there is now an increasing tendency to use other payment mechanisms.

In the Netherlands, general practitioners are paid on a fee-for-service basis by private insurers and on a capitation basis by Sickness Funds. Maximum fee levels and capitation payments are set by negotiation between associations representing insurers and physicians and must be approved by the Central Board on Health Care Prices pursuant to the Health Care Prices Act.[19] In New Zealand, physicians have historically been paid on a fee-for-service basis from a variety of sources including government, private insurers, and patients themselves with no government regulation limiting either the fee or the volume of services supplied. Increasingly, however, there have been attempts to pay physicians on a capitation basis. In the US there has been a recent and rapid shift as part of the managed care revolution from fee-for-service to other payment mechanisms such as capitation and "withholds" (monies are held back till the end of the financial year and only paid if agreed utilization targets are met.)[20] Prior to internal market reform, payments to UK general practitioners were comprised of three components: a partial salary (which was higher for physicians in under-serviced areas); capitation payments (with three levels of payment depending on the age of the patient); and specific fee-for-service payments for particular preventive services.[21] The system of capitation payments was eroded over the years until by the mid-1980s only 46 percent of general practitioners' incomes were derived from capitation.[22] Specialists in the UK public sector continue to be reimbursed by salaries and "distinction awards."[23]

Prima facie a physician paid on a fee-for-service basis has an incentive to supply as many services as possible to maximize his/her own income. However, this assumes that physicians are concerned only with maximizing their incomes as opposed to other lifestyle factors. Physicians and other health providers will wish to maximize their utility (as opposed to just their incomes), which may be a combination of financial rewards, prestige, professional status, work hours, promotional opportunities, etc. Consequently, if physicians are paid a higher fee for a particular service they may not necessarily produce more of this service but less as they can earn the same income but have more leisure hours. Therefore the link between a fee-for-service payment regime and production beyond an optimal point is not clear-cut.[24]

As discussed in Chapter 2, the key problem with a fee-for-service payment system is not the problem of physicians supplying increasingly more of their own services. Rather, the key problem is that a fee-for-service system does not offer any incentive for physicians to consider the cost-effectiveness of the various services that they recommend, e.g. prescription drugs, diagnostic tests, specialist referrals, etc. Physicians also do not have any incentive to prioritize health needs in accordance with societal values.

Arguably, given that patients may not have the information necessary to assess the quality of services or treatments being recommended or provided, it is preferable to rely on fee-for-service payments to ensure physicians have no incentive to reduce the quality of care provided because of cost considerations. This is because a fee-for-service payment provides an incentive to provide additional services rather than to reduce the quality of services supplied. However, this argument assumes that overprovision results in simply extra costs and no actual harm to a patient. Given the attendant risks of some procedures this cannot be assumed. Moreover, all systems must be concerned with cost and inefficiency, for overprovision in response to one instance of health need necessarily leads to underprovision in response to another health need or alternatively spiralling health care costs. The goal is to design a system that results in production at the optimum point in terms of trade-offs between quality and cost.

The problem of escalating costs in health care systems is often linked to fee-for-service payments. However, it is not fee-for-service payments per se that contribute to escalating costs but fee-for-service in conjunction with what are known as the "guild" principles of health care allocation – indemnity insurance, free choice of providers, solo practice, and no limits on what physicians may prescribe or recommend as treatment.[25] These guild principles have been actively promoted and protected by physicians in many countries as they are clearly to the profession's advantage in terms of maintenance of income and autonomy. If, however, proactive purchasers have incentives to monitor physicians' decisions then the guild principles may be displaced. In such a case it cannot be assumed that the use of fee-for-service payments by proactive purchasers will result in an inefficient system.

Proactive purchasers in either a managed competition system or an internal market system may use a myriad of managed care techniques to provide incentives to physicians to strive to achieve technical quality but also quality in terms of choosing the most cost-effective treatment and prioritizing health needs. If purchasers paid providers on a fee-for-service basis they may still manage the delivery of care by, as examples, reviewing prescribing patterns and disseminating information to physicians regarding the cost-effectiveness of particular services. Some 87 percent of US Health Maintenance Organiz-ations say they use clinical practice guidelines as a technique for monitoring quality.[26] Some physicians chide this as "cookbook" medicine that undermines and discredits their skills as professionals to tailor treatment to each individual's particular needs. Studies show, however, significant variations in the treatment of medical needs that appear to be unjustifiable from a clinical perspective.[27] Thus, there are potentially significant quality and efficiency gains to be had from greater consistency in prescribing patterns.[28] Another popular technique in the US, as mentioned above, is "withholds" where a managed care plan holds back a proportion of payments throughout the year. The amount withheld is paid out at year's end if utilization goals are met. Such modifications to a fee-for-service payment may result in significantly different incentives than those normally associated with fee-for-service payments in an indemnity insurance system.

Where fee-for-service payment is but one of a number of payment mechan-isms used by a purchaser, then it can be used to encourage provision of services that otherwise would be under-supplied. For example, a purchaser that wishes providers to supply more preventive and primary services can pay the provider for those services on a fee-for-service basis and more of those services will be supplied. Similarly, *at the purchaser level itself*, government could reimburse purchasers on a fee-for-service basis for the provision of some services where there is a concern that not enough of these services would otherwise be brought, for example, public health care services or services for vulnerable populations.

Salary

Paying providers on a salary basis does not provide any direct incentive to diminish the quality of services supplied. On the other hand, as salaries are not tied to production (the number of cases treated or patients seen) there is an incentive to slack on the job which may lead to reductions in quality particularly in terms of waiting times for treatment. There is also no *positive* incentive to supply the most cost-effective service or to appropriately prioritise health care needs. Thus, what providers choose to provide may be the result of what is common practice among their local peers or what was commonplace where and when they were trained. Paying hospitals by way of block budgets (a fixed amount per year regardless of the numbers of patients treated or services provided) results in similar incentive effects to salary payments as remuneration is not linked to production or performance. Thus, one should not be surprised that since Health Authorities in the UK and New Zealand internal markets largely negotiated block contracts with, respectively, NHS Trusts and Crown Health Enterprises, there was little change in the range, nature and quality of services delivered.

University professors are paid a salary and few suggest that their performance could be significantly improved by paying them on a fee-per-lecture basis or an amount per student that they attract into their classes per year. The difference is, however, that physicians are the gatekeepers to the rest of the health care system and make recommendations to patients to use other services such as diagnostic tests, X-rays, drugs, specialists, and hospital services. It is to this decision-making process that incentives must be geared in order to compensate for the fact that physicians will be otherwise insensitive to the cost of the services, goods and treatments they recommend.

On the other hand, there are advantages to salary payments. A purchaser in a managed competition could influence provider performance by, for example, choosing to hire those providers who prefer preventive and primary techniques over more intensive and invasive techniques. The purchaser could create an integrated organization with a culture that promotes supplying and recommending preventive and primary care. It may be easier to translate the purchaser's management practices into physicians' behavior when physicians are employees paid on a salary within an organisation rather than independent contractors. A purchaser may initiate peer review and promotions as incentives for performance. It may pay bonuses when utilization targets are met or it may decide that it is easier to foster a team approach in the absence of crude financial incentives directed towards performance. Some of the earliest Health Maintenance Organizations in the US, generally non-profit organizations, operate on a "staff model" basis and still today pay their physicians on a salary basis.

Capitation

A capitation payment is where a provider or group of providers receives a fixed sum per annum (or biannually) per person enrolled with them and for that sum has to provide any of a range of services that people who are enrolled with them may need.

Posner notes that a capitation payment provides a direct incentive to minimize the procedures performed, since the marginal revenue derived from each procedure performed is zero.[29] Posner's analysis, however, is static as, over the longer-term, providers paid on a capitation basis have an incentive to keep their enrollee population healthy through the use of preventive services. This is because if their enrollees fall seriously ill it will cost the health provider more to service them in the longer term. Of course (and as discussed further below), this advantage of capitation depends on providers not being able to shift the long-term costs of their failure to provide preventive care on to others. Posner's statement also does not acknowledge that in a competitive market there will be a financial incentive to provide services or risk losing enrollee loyalty and consequent revenue as enrollees shift to other providers paid on a capitation basis. Other types of incentives working to ameliorate the propensity of physicians paid on a capitation basis to cut the quality of health care services supplied include the risk of medical malpractice actions and professional disciplinary actions. Interestingly, the medical profession argues that it should be trusted to protect patients' interests in a fee-for-service system and that as professionals they would not respond to the financial incentive to supply or recommend any more care than is really needed. However, the profession in many countries has vigorously opposed the use of capitation and other incentives designed to inject cost-consideration on the ground that it will result in diminished quality – presumably because physicians will ignore their ethical codes and standards and respond to the financial incentives to cut the quality of care.

An advantage of a capitation payment is that it allows a physician or other health provider to tailor the supply of health care services towards the health needs of the people that he/she serves. This means that the provider can be more responsive to the particular needs of the individual he/she serves. For example, in New Zealand, there has been some success with devolving payments by way of capitation to Maori communities and/or Maori physicians within those communities.[30] Particular groups in society may have preferences for different sorts of health care services than the majority of the population prefers and payment by capitation offers the promise of realization of those groups' preferences and needs. This is reflective of how paying on a capitation basis is not only a means by which to transfer financial risk to health providers but also a measure of *purchasing power*. Upon receipt of a capitation payment, a level of discretion may be accorded the health care provider to decide upon *what* service or *mix* of services from that range to buy/supply to any particular patient from their fixed budget.

In a fee-for-service system, the potential is for overprovision beyond the optimal point of trade-offs between cost and quality. With capitation, the potential is for underprovision below the optimal point if the purchaser or provider is confident of being able to shift the costs of failing to provide services of an adequate quality on to others. Insurer/purchasers paid on a capitation basis may encourage the delivery of fewer services than are needed, or less effective services, or services of a lower quality in order to maximize profits. Similarly, providers paid by way of capitation may prescribe fewer services than are needed, or less effective services, or services of a lower quality in order to maximize profits. Thus, the problems of quality are similar in both managed competition systems and in internal market systems if, in the latter case, health authorities seek to pay health care providers on a capitation basis. However, in a managed competition system, if an insurer/purchaser does not ensure the supply of services of sufficient quality there is a risk that citizens will register their dissatisfaction by exiting with their risk-adjusted share of funding to another insurer/purchaser. There is a potential for such an accountability mechanism to operate in an internal market system if government-appointed purchasers ensure that the "money follows the patient." In other words it is ensured that a capitated sum is transferred to the citizen's chosen health care provider(s).

Naturally enough, patients are likely to be more concerned over technical quality issues in a capitation system than they will be about the broader quality issue of unnecessary or unnecessarily expensive care being supplied in a fee-for-service system. Because of the personal consequences patients will have a strong incentive to hold providers paid on a capitation basis to account for the quality of services supplied. By contrast, patients have little incentive to hold to account providers paid on an unlimited fee-for-service basis for supplying unnecessary care or recommending treatment that is not cost-effective. Although patients will have a strong incentive to monitor quality in a capitation system, the difficulty is that patients may not always be able to detect instances of quality reductions and this is explored further below. A further problem is that exit may not work well as an accountability enhancing mechanism for, as discussed in Chapter 4, purchasers or providers may find it easier to compete on risk avoidance and cost-shifting rather than on cost and quality dimensions.[31] Thus, to ensure the quality of services in a managed competition system, insurer/purchasers must have incentives to compete on quality dimensions and regulation is required to prescribe their ability to shift costs and risk to others. Similarly, in an internal market system where groups of providers are paid on a capitation basis, they need to have incentives to compete on quality dimensions and be prevented from shifting the cost and risk of their decision-making to others.

In the US, there are concerns over the quality of health care services supplied by providers paid on a capitation basis.[32] The media has focused on a number of tragic stories where managed care plans have denied patients access to potentially life-saving services.[33] A study by Nelson *et al.* found in 1996 that one in four elderly Americans in a Medicare managed care plan would not recommend their plan to someone with a serious or chronic health problem.[34] One study of US managed care plans noted that 22 percent of sick non-elderly patients reported difficulties in obtaining treatment that they or their doctor thought necessary compared with 13 percent in traditional fee-for-service plans.[35] In response to these concerns legislation has been introduced in many states that aspires to protect access to care, choice of care, quality of care, choice of providers, and basic consumer protections.[36] In the Fall of 1999 several bills were before the US House of Representatives seeking to ensure, for example, access to specialists and emergency care without prior approval from managed care plans. The main difference between the various bills put forward is the degree to which insured individuals will be able to sue insurers/managed care plans for denying or limiting benefits.

Notwithstanding all this legislative activity, there is no definite evidence that Health Maintenance Organizations and other managed care plans in fact supply lower-quality care.[37] However, the fact that there is no clear-cut evidence as to diminished quality may be due to the difficulty of objectively measuring quality, particularly in terms of health outcomes.[38] Focusing solely on indicators of performance in terms of outcomes such as life expectancy, infant mortality rates, readmission rates, etc., is impoverished as it fails to pick up more subtle indicators of quality such as the level of unnecessary pain, discomfort, or distress suffered by patients. Even though in terms of health outcomes, the quality of care supplied to patients in managed care plans does not appear to have fallen, quality as more broadly defined in terms of process does appear to have fallen. Notwithstanding, reductions in technical quality in the US may not be viewed negatively if we accept the proposition that the previous indemnity insurance/ fee-for-service system had resulted in supply beyond the optimum point in terms of cost and quality trade-offs. In other words, increasing resources were being spent on individual patients with very small benefit. Thus, present concerns over reductions in the quality of care in the US may be temporary as provider and patient expectations mesh closer to an optimal point in terms of patient/societal welfare trade-offs.

Problems with access and diminishment in quality associated with US managed care plans are used by some to argue that, in general, reliance upon competition and other market-like incentives will result in diminished access and quality. However, this conclusion cannot be drawn. The US fails to ensure comprehensive care to all its citizens on the basis of their need as opposed to ability to pay and managed care has developed on an ad hoc basis. Consequently, there are many leakages in the present US system allowing managed care plans to compete on risk avoidance and cost-shifting. Initially it was thought that managed care plans would cut costs and improve quality but it now appears that apparent efficiency gains may actually be the result of managed care plans successfully "cream-skimming" enrollees with the lowest risk.[39] In other words, managed care plans look to be performing well but this is because they are successfully avoiding servicing those patients with the most expensive health care needs. There is, however, no comprehensive system of incentives and regulations in place compelling managed care plans to compete on quality and price dimensions. Thus, a sharp contrast can be drawn between the present US system and a system that seeks to ensure universal access to a comprehensive range of health care services (justice goals) but yet uses competition and other market-like incentives to improve the efficiency of the system that realizes these goals.

Finally, one should note that academic, media, and public concern over managed care plans is not necessarily evidence of problems with capitation. M. R. Gold *et al.* note from a sample of 108 US managed care plans that 37 percent of managed care plans used capitation as the primary means of paying physicians.[40] Morrisey *et al.* found in a survey of 1,495 US hospitals in late 1993 that 82 percent of hospitals received 5 percent or less of their patient care revenue from capitation payments.[41] The authors of this study note that, in fact, the majority of HMOs and preferred provider organizations (PPOs) appear to enter into discounted fee-for-service arrangements and/or rely upon fee caps and per diems.[42] Thus, a significant proportion of managed care plans still rely upon fee-for-service (albeit modified through use of withholds and utilization review) as a means of reimbursing health care providers.

The key to ensuring that capitation does not result in unacceptable quality reductions is to prevent provider(s) shifting the costs of bad decisions on to others. If providers paid on a capitation basis are only required to provide a limited range of health care services then they may have an incentive to recommend to their patients treatments and services that they are not financially responsible for. On the other hand, if a provider or a small group of providers is financially responsible for a comprehensive range of health care services then there may be difficulties associated with absorbing fluctuations in expenditures caused by patients' varying utilization rates. For example, if a small group of health providers serves a disproportionate number of patients with chronic illnesses requiring expensive treatments they may quickly deplete the capitated sum received. This provides very strong incentives to avoid treating high-risk patients in the first place and/or to cut costs and quality towards the end of the financial year.[43] Consequently, there are reasons why regulation may be necessary to cap the financial risk devolved to small plans or to place restrictions on the minimum size of a risk-bearing entity paid on a capitation basis.[44]

In the US, the federal government has proposed new rules that will regulate compensation arrangements in Medicare and Medicaid managed care plans, and some states have enacted laws limiting the extent to which financial risk can be transferred to health care providers.[45] The UK government capped the liability of GP Fundholders at £5,000 per patient. This means that Fundholders, as purchasers, had no incentive to be sensitive to the costs of treatment for a patient beyond this sum; however, any incentive to avoid or dump high-cost patients was blunted. As discussed in Chapter 4, the problem of allowing many small groups of providers to be paid on a capitated basis is that this increases transactions costs as each group becomes a mini-purchaser and must enter into arrangements and negotiations with other providers. This suggests that the preferred regulatory approach may be to require a minimum organizational size rather than to restrict the range of services for which they are financially responsible.

Hybrid payment systems

All payment mechanisms have their advantages and disadvantages and much will depend on the configuration of payers, purchasers and other health providers. Ideally, a payment system would not be linked to the production of health care services per se (as fee-for-service is) or per person (as capitation is) but one that is tied to outcomes. Thus, purchasers or providers would be paid on the results they obtain. If it were possible to link a plan's financial incentives to patient outcomes then many agency problems could be reduced. However, as discussed above, it is not feasible to focus soley on outcomes because of the difficulty of measuring the links between the consumption of health care services and treatments and ultimate health outcomes given the presence of so many other variables. Also as some outcomes are more readily measured than others there is a risk that health care plans and providers would divert resources to those aspects of performance that are easily measurable and downplay those that are as important for patient care but harder to measure. Imposing strong financial incentives on health care providers to achieve particular patient outcomes could lead risk-adverse health care providers to avoid complex cases.[46]

Some commentators, such as Pauly and Coyte, advocate a mixed system of capitated and fee-for-service payments.[47] Prima facie, a hybrid payment system may capture the best elements of both capitated and fee-for-service payments systems. On the other hand, if designed poorly, a hybrid system could result in the worst features of both capitation and fee-for-services payments. The devil, as usual, is in the detail.

Managed care is often associated solely with capitation payments, but in reality it covers a wide variety of techniques by which purchasers seek to influence providers' behavior. There are also many permutations of fee-for-service, salary and capitation payments. The incentive effects of various combinations of payments will depend upon the particular health care service market in question and the responses of providers within those markets. For example, a number of years ago the US government started to require that the Medicare program pay hospitals on a per-case basis.[48] Hospitals were paid according to a schedule of rates based on the average costs of producing services nationwide for product lines defined by five hundred Diagnosis Related Groups ("DRGs").[49] This system of payment became subject to what was known as "DRG creep" as physicians began to categorize minor problems into more serious DRG groups. This type of evidence supports the view that it is necessary to periodically change the method of paying physicians as they will have figured out some means to chisel the system to their advantage.[50]

Competing purchasers in a managed competition system may be more quickly able to respond to providers' chiseling behavior than a regulator or a government-appointed purchaser in an internal market. Managing physicians has been likened to herding cats. Competing purchasers in a managed competition system are more likely to be able to take a flexible approach both between health care service markets and over time in a particular market, and to be more creative.[51] The need for flexibility and change over time speaks against mandating a particular form of payment system. If insurer/purchasers have incentives to compete on price and quality dimensions then one should begin with the assumption that they should be left to tailor a mix of payment regimes to balance quality and cost. Prima facie, it seems to make sense for government not to be involved in micro-managing physicians, hospitals and other health providers but to devote its energies to getting the incentives right at the purchasing level. There are, however, difficulties with this solution, as discussed below.

Solutions to quality problems

What is needed is a system that has incentives designed to ensure that:

- health providers efficiently provide services of an acceptable technical quality;
- health providers select the most cost-effective mix of services to deal with a particular health care need;
- health providers meet health care needs in a manner that balances what is in the best interests of society with individual patients.

The remainder of this chapter explores other means by which to achieve these three dimensions of quality aside from regulating the type of payment mechanisms employed. One means discussed is providing insurer/purchasers with incentives to compete on quality dimensions and then leaving them to conclude their own arrangements with health providers. Other possibilities include providing citizens with better information with which to judge quality, encouraging the development of ethical training of physicians, professional self-regulation, medical malpractice actions, and the establishment of an ombudsperson or commissioner to deal with patients' concerns.

Incentives for insurer/purchasers to compete on quality

Competition between insurer/purchasers in a managed competition system prima facie provides incentives to compete on quality dimensions. This assumes of course that citizens are supplied with sufficient information to make decisions regarding quality and this is discussed further below.

A problem that arises with reliance on the exit or market mechanism as a quality-enhancement mechanism is that it may not work well in the case of stigmatized health care services, such as services for people with HIV or psychiatric diseases.[52] The rest of the population may believe that these sorts of diseases are never likely to afflict them or their family and thus will not be motivated to "exit" from an insurer/purchaser if incidents of low-quality services being supplied to HIV or psychiatric patients come to light. As discussed in previous chapters, a very small percentage of the population accounts for by far the largest share of health care costs. Therefore looking at averages in terms of the quality of care and health outcomes for the whole population may mask the situation of those who are most in need. Donelan *et al.* note, drawing an analogy with fire insurance, "the true test of consumer satisfaction with insurance coverage comes not in occasional, routine contacts with the insurance company, but when the house is burning."[53] Extrapolating from this, it is possible to conclude that an important indicator of quality is how well a particular insurer/purchaser serves the most vulnerable when in need.

Specific regulation of competing insurer/purchasers is required to ensure that the quality of the services they are supplying to vulnerable populations is of a sufficient standard. The regulator could develop key performance indicators with special emphasis being given to services provided to vulnerable populations and to those elements of performance that are not readily measurable or are at risk of being overlooked. A regulator could, in disseminating information to citizens about the quality of different plans offered by competing insurer/purchasers, emphasize information regarding how plans treat vulnerable populations. This may, to some extent, help shape citizens' preferences so that they select insurer/purchasers who ensure services of an adequate quality for vulnerable populations. The potential to ignore the interests of vulnerable groups may be used as an argument in favor of relying upon government management rather than upon competition between private insurer/purchasers. However, the goal of ensuring quality for vulnerable populations may be better achieved by an independent regulator rather than by a government not only responsible for this but for micro-managing health providers.

From the perspective of competing insurer/purchasers, the obvious way to avoid making trade-offs between cost and quality is to avoid high-risk or high-cost patients in the first instance. In the absence of a comprehensive system, there will be opportunities for cost-shifting through cream-skimming and otherwise shifting costs to other parts of the system.[54] In such a case, insurer/purchasers who are better competitors on cost and quality dimensions might be squeezed out by others more adept at risk-avoidance and cost-shifting. As discussed in Chapter 4, there is a crucial need to adequately risk-adjust payments to reward those plans that care for high-risk patients and to ameliorate the incentive for plans to compete on their ability to avoid risk rather than to compete on price and quality dimensions. Schlesinger speculates about the possibility of requiring insurer/purchasers in a managed competition system to continue to be responsible for the health care costs of a citizen who has shifted to another competitor.[55] Depending on the degree of financial contribution required this may provide a strong incentive to avoid shifting costs, particularly as the management of the costs will be left to a rival. This is an appealing notion although it may be difficult to determine the length of time an insurer/purchaser should be responsible for the costs of a departing enrollee. It is certainly a tool worth exploring if a government regulator found that it was encountering problems with cream-skimming.

A managed competition system has the potential to be a comprehensive system provided that regulation can be sufficiently refined with other incentives to ensure that insurer/purchasers compete on price and quality dimensions and not on the ability to avoid risk and shift costs.[56] Internal markets as implemented in the UK and New Zealand do not offer a comprehensive system. Managed care arrangements such as the UK's GP Fundholders amounted to piece-meal managed care reform, with enormous room for cost-shifting to other purchasers (i.e. the government-appointed Health Authorities). To be a comprehensive system, all citizens in the UK would have to be enrolled with a GP Fundholder and Fundholders would have to be responsible for the purchase of the vast majority of all health care services. In such a case, an internal market system would take on all the characteristics of a managed competition system. The New Labour reforms of December 1997 seem, prima facie, a very important step in the direction of consolidating purchasing power into larger purchasing groups (500 Primary Care Groups instead of 3,500 Fundholders) for a comprehensive range of health care services. The New Labour reforms also wisely recognize the importance of pursuing broad performance measures with a specific emphasis on the quality of care delivered:

> The New NHS will have quality at its heart…This must be quality in its
> broadest sense: doing the right things, at the right time, for the right people,

and doing them right – first time. And it must be the quality of the patient's experience as well as the clinical result – quality measured in terms of prompt access, good relationships, and efficient administration.[57]

However, while the New Labour reforms promise to align clinical *and* financial responsibility in the hands of the new Primary Care Groups, there are only very weak incentives for the new Primary Care Groups to make efficiency gains and, further, it appears they may overspend their budgets without penalty. There will be no competition between Primary Care Groups for public funds. Thus the government will have to rely upon agreements and "voice" incentives, such as were more fully discussed in Chapter 4, to ensure that the new Primary Care Groups make good purchasing decisions, balancing cost and quality and the interests of individual patients with the broader interests of society. There is little discussion in the White Paper nor the Health Care Act 1999 of how the government will structure these incentives, although the primary focus seems to be on the provision of better information regarding the cost-effectiveness of different services and strengthening professional self-regulation.[58]

Even in a comprehensive managed competition system there is still the problem of competing insurer/purchasers shifting costs to society. Society will benefit if adequate resources are devoted to the detection and early prevention of health problems as citizens will be healthier and in less need of health care services in the long term.[59] However, there may not be sufficient incentives for competing insurer/purchasers to invest in preventive and primary care if they know that an individual is unlikely to remain with their plan for their entire lifetime and thus the longer-term costs are likely to be born by another insurer/purchaser.[60] As McGlynn notes, "(i)t takes years for the preventable complications of many chronic diseases to develop…coronary artery disease may develop after many years of poor lifestyle habits or failure to control blood pressure."[61] All purchasers may potentially benefit from greater spending on primary and preventive care in the long run but because of fear of free-riding, no one purchaser is prepared to invest. This problem was recognized by New Zealand policy-makers in the context of the government's original plan for the internal market system to evolve into a managed competition system.[62] In recognition of the fact that there would be underprovision of public health care services by competing insurer/purchasers, the government appointed a "Public Health Commission" that had a separate budget with which to buy public health care services. The Public Health Commission was dissolved once it was determined that it did not implement a managed competition scheme.[63] The same problem exists in internal market and command-and-control systems, however, as incumbent governments will not reap the advantages in their political life of cost-savings arising in the long-term from spending on primary and preventive care.

This concern of people exiting from competing insurer/purchasers, thus diminishing the incentive to invest in the longer term health of their enrollees, harks back to the discussion of exit, voice and loyalty in Chapter 4. Although a system should allow and encourage exit at the margin to ensure the on-going efficient performance of insurer/purchasers, this must be balanced against the need for most enrollees to remain "loyal" to their particular insurer/purchaser. Those who remain loyal will be more likely to use their "voice" over time to lobby for the improved performance of their particular insurer/purchaser with the ultimate threat of exit at the margin if performance does not improve. For insurer/purchasers to know that a large proportion of individuals enrolled with them will not leave their plan provides incentives to invest in the long-term health of the enrollee population.

Another means by which competing insurer/purchasers can shift the costs of their decisions to society is through externalities.[64] Schlesinger refers to the loss of productivity in society associated with failing to detect disease at an early stage, the burden imposed upon unpaid caregivers if chronic illness is not prevented, and the costs of crime as a result of untreated alcohol or drug addictions.[65] As an insurer/purchaser does not have to internalize these societal costs it may spend fewer resources on these sorts of services than is optimal from society's perceptive. One might again consider this evidence against competing insurer/purchasers as proposed by the managed competition model, but there is little evidence to suggest that government-appointed monopsony purchasers in internal markets internalize these sorts of costs. For example, a trend in many countries is the closure of hospitals, reductions in the number of hospital beds and a concomitant greater reliance on "home care" where the latter is often provided by unpaid family members, often women. Thus, while it may be cost-effective from the perspective of government budgets to rely on home care, this decision-making often does not take into account the wider costs for society and the distribution of those costs.[66]

Given that a managed care plan will not reflect society's optimal allocation of health resources, government may seek to intervene to require that the plan produce certain services that will otherwise be underprovided from a societal perspective. Thus, government could choose to pay competing managed care plans on a fee-for-service basis for preventive services in order to ensure provision closer to a point that is optimal from society's perspective. Similarly, government may want to pay on a fee-for-service basis for certain stigmatized services or for services where quality is particularly difficult to measure. This would be on the assumption that the "exit" mechanism may not be sufficient to ensure the provision of a sufficient guarantee of quality of such services.

One possible means to deter competing insurer/purchasers from making cuts in quality is to require that they operate on a non-profit basis. In the UK, GP Fundholders received a capitation payment to buy a range of services while surpluses were required to be reinvested back into their practices so (the reasoning goes) to benefit patients.[67] Ostensibly, such a mechanism has the potential to enhance professional satisfaction and autonomy while allowing surpluses to be ploughed back into patient benefits. However, there were suggestions that some Fundholders simply invested surpluses in the refurbishing of their offices, so enhancing the value of the practice for later resale.[68] In the Netherlands, the Sickness Funds have historically been non-profit organizations. The early US Health Maintenance Organizations were non-profit institutions. Recently in the US there has been a strong trend to transform not-for-profit to for-profit organizations.[69] This has primarily been because of the desire to access capital markets in order to allow expansion and development. Sage notes that US state regulators are attempting to protect public assets by examining the shift of insurers from charitable status to for-profit plans.[70] He goes on to note that laws have been passed in some states that cap profits for managed care plans and that Massachusetts has gone even further and totally prohibited for-profit health care plans.[71]

Requiring private insurer/purchasers to be non-profit operations may make managed competition a far more palatable political option. This is particularly so for the citizens of the UK and New Zealand who are nervous about allowing the profit motive to infiltrate their health care system, viewing such an infiltration as the "Americanization" (and in essence the ruin) of their respective health care systems. A non-profit institution may also engender more "loyalty" amongst subscribers that in turn will encourage greater investment on the part of insurer/purchasers in the long-term health of the enrollee population. A not-for-profit organization may also find it easier to create a culture amongst the health providers that it contracts with or employs that values and promotes primary and preventive health care services over more intensive and interventionist type of approaches. It may be more difficult to develop a public service ethos in a profit-driven enterprise where an emphasis on primary and preventive health care may be viewed as rhetoric cloaking a cost-cutting agenda. Thus, there is certainly merit to the argument that competing insurer/purchasers be required to operate on a non-profit basis with a requirement that surpluses be reinvested back into health care services or amenities for patients. However, relying *solely* upon non-profit organizations or, for that matter, public organizations or upon health care professionals (as in the case of GP Fundholders and now Primary Care Groups) to balance cost and quality and the interests of patients and society at large is misconceived. No matter what the proprietary nature of the purchaser, it must face external incentives to compel it to operate efficiently whilst achieving quality standards.

Empowering citizens with information

If accountability for quality is to be ensured by citizen choice of purchasers, provision of valid and reliable information regarding the quality of services offered by purchasers is vital. Although the discussion of information asymmetry to date has been in the context of health providers and patients, an information asymmetry also exists between citizens and competing insurer/purchasers in a managed competition system. In a system of full insurance, although patients will not be sensitive to the cost of the services they consume, they will be concerned about the quality of the services they receive. Thus, there are strong arguments in favor of government intervening to attempt to improve available information regarding the quality of services offered. In particular, there is a need to provide evidence of the effectiveness of particular health care services. This is so whether one is seeking to encourage competition between insurer/purchasers (in a managed competition system) or between health care providers (in an internal market system).

Despite the very strong arguments for improving health information, realistically there is a limit to how much information citizens and patients can and will absorb. Even if the flow and quality of information is improved the information made available may not be perfect, may be difficult to understand, may relate to very specific health care services, needs, and providers and may not be used to generalize about similar health care services, needs and providers. Information supplied regarding the quality of individual health care providers may be misleading, as high mortality rates, infection rates, etc. may be reflective of the difficult case-mix dealt with by the particular hospital as opposed to the poor quality of services supplied. Also, particular hospitals may specialize in serious high-risk cases. Zalkind and Eastaugh note that using overall death rates as an indicator of the quality of care offered by hospitals may lead to "substantial predictive error rates, even when adjustment for case mix is excellent."[72]

These difficulties mean that citizens may not always be able to make informed determinations regarding the performance of providers and insurer/purchasers. This problem is generally used to justify excessive paternalism within health care systems. In reality, there are information failures in many industries. One only needs to think of car mechanics where the consequences of inadequate service may result in physical harm or even death. No one suggests, however, that governments supplant consumers in choosing the mechanic to service their car and restricting the kinds of services mechanics can supply. The information problem in health care service markets speaks to the need for government to regulate the flow of information to consumers, not necessarily to supplant them in decision-making. Information brings with it a sense of control, well-being, and enriches autonomy, all valued qualities in a time of ill-health where one might otherwise feel a loss of control. Legal doctrine reflects these social values through the doctrine of informed consent which requires the physician or health provider to disclose the risks of treatment that, objectively, a person in the shoes of the patient would want to know.[73]

Of course, the supply of information is not costless, and one has to make trade-offs here as with the supply of other goods and services.[74] Clearly, at the extreme, each patient would have to be trained as a physician to completely remove the information asymmetry problem. Some argue that even if citizens have good information regarding the quality of services they will be reluctant to use that information in considering the merits of different health providers.[75] But while there may be a few individuals for whom this remains true, in modern society there seems to be a growing resistance to the contention that "doctor knows best." Moreover, with new information technologies, information is cheaper and more readily able to be accessed by a greater number of people.[76]

As yet there is little known about the kinds of information that citizens need in order to be able to make the optimal choice of competing insurer/ purchasers. Information that US citizens said they would use, revealed in a study by Edgman, Levitan and Cleary, includes "information on how a plan works, what it costs, the covered benefits, the quality of care and overall satisfaction with care if it were available."[77] The authors found consumers are most interested in "information about costs of coverage, technical competence, the information and communication provided by physicians, coordination of care, and access."[78] The sorts of information identified by US consumers as important may be reflective of the present system of unregulated, unmanaged and ad hoc competition between over 1,500 insurers. By contrast, and as discussed in Chapter 4, a managed competition system would seek to level the playing field through regulation that would set out the terms of coverage every citizen could expect *regardless of their choice of insurer/ purchaser*. Such regulation should ameliorate most of the concerns identified and provide citizens with the assurance that they may exit to another insurer/ purchaser without compromising access to a range of comprehensive services at an adequate level of quality.

In order to keep competing insurer/purchasers responsive to concerns over the quality of services supplied, citizens need information not just about the "outcomes" of care but also the process of care. In dismissing managed competition reform, Woolhandler and Himmelstein note "(e)mpathy, humanity, and imagination are neither profitable nor readily quantifiable..."[79] However, such attributes will be profitable for insurer/purchasers in a managed competition system if citizens seek out purchasers that aspire to incorporate these attributes into the delivery of their services.

It should be noted that it is not necessary for the efficient working of the system that all citizens be informed, critical purveyors of the quality offered by competing insurer/purchasers. So long as there is a critical margin of informed citizens willing to exit from plan to plan this should ensure that insurer/ purchasers offering those plans responsive to quality concerns.

Ethics and professional self-regulation

Empirical evidence suggests that physicians do respond to financial incentives to a greater or lesser degree and that in a fee-for-service system will supply a range, mix and intensity of health care services above that which is optimal. However, in a capitation system physicians may respond to the financial incentive by cutting the quality of services offered *below* an optimal point. Any financial incentive to cut quality standards may be suppressed to a greater or lesser degree by the ethical rule of *premum non nocere* (above all, do no harm). This ethical norm does not inhibit physicians from supplying services that are not cost-effective or even ineffective provided physicians believe there will be at least some small benefit for the patient (or at least no harm) in providing the service or treatment. By contrast, failing to supply necessary health care services or cutting the quality of services may cause physical harm to a patient. Consequently, a physician in good conscience is more likely to do the former and not the latter.[80]

Training financial incentives upon a physician brings into focus the conflict between the physician's personal financial interest and his or her fiduciary duty to his or her patient/s. The intensity of this conflict will depend upon the strength of the financial incentive and the physician's ethical norms.

Arguably, where physicians have a direct financial incentive to suggest anything other than the best possible care for a particular patient, e.g. they are paid on a capitation basis or receive bonuses for meeting utilization targets, then they have a legal duty to disclose this financial interest to patients. In Moore v. Regents of the University of California the Supreme Court of California held that:

> A physician who is seeking a patient's consent for a medical procedure must, in order to satisfy his fiduciary duty and to obtain the patient's informed consent, disclose personal interest unrelated to the patient's health, whether research or economic, that may affect his medical judgement.[81]

Where physicians operate under strong financial incentives to control the costs of the health care services they recommend or provide, there is the potential that this will erode patients' trust and confidence in their physicians.

To ensure quality of care it may be necessary to have further regulation to prevent excessive financial risk being devolved to small groups of health care providers. In a managed competition system where regulation and incentives are in place, requiring insurer/purchasers to compete on price and quality dimensions, there is unlikely to be excessive devolution of financial risk to small groups of health providers. This is because insurer/purchasers will be concerned about the resulting impact on the quality of care delivered. Of course this assumes that the regulation and incentives required will work as intended.

An important source of information regarding the quality of services supplied will be the patient's physician. It is alleged that US managed care plans are imposing gag clauses upon physicians in an effort to prevent physicians making negative comments about plans and the quality of care offered to patients. It is also alleged that plans are trying to stop physicians advising patients of treatment options that their plan has chosen not to cover. Gag clauses may be explicitly provided for in written contracts or implicitly imposed – the latter being evidenced by termination of a physician's employment contract soon after he or she has publicly criticized a plan.[82] Although managed care plans deny that gag causes are prevalent in the industry,[83] nonetheless some US states have moved to legislate against managed care plans imposing or negotiating "gag clauses" in their contracts with physicians.[84] Gag clauses clearly intrude into the physician-patient relationship and erode the agency relationship.

Essentially, gag clauses seek to make a health provider too responsive to a managed care plan's financial interests as opposed to a patient's best interests.

On the other hand, it is possible that physicians are manipulating patients' concerns over the quality of services supplied to improve their own negotiating position with managed care plans. In that case, gag clauses may be best viewed as an understandable overreaction on the part of insurer/purchasers.

Experience from the US does suggest that the medical profession will use a variety of tactics under the cover of protecting their own financial self-interest in order to advance their own professional interests. For example, in Wilk v. American Medical Association,[85] the court found the American Medical Association guilty of a conspiracy to contain and eliminate the profession of chiropractic. The Association argued that, in establishing a code of ethics that made it unethical for medical physicians to associate professionally with chiropractic physicians, it was simply setting standards to promote the quality of health care provided to patients.[86] The medical profession in the US is not happy with the shifting of the balance of power that is occurring from themselves to insurer/purchasers. A Commonwealth Fund study released in early 1997 of 1,700 US physicians concluded that the majority of physicians were dissatisfied with medical practice in managed care plans and 60 percent had serious problems with external reviews and limitations placed on clinical decision-making.[87] The US Federal Trade Commission has taken a strong stand against the American Medical Association's ethical restrictions that inhibit physicians from working for HMOs and against concerted action on the part of some health providers to resist new types of health care delivery organizations.[88] All this tends to support the argument that although physicians clearly have the expertise to comment on the quality of care of services supplied, it may be difficult to determine when their concerns are real as opposed to related to their own professional self-interest.

Notwithstanding the foregoing concerns, there is a need to protect those physicians, nurses, and other health care providers who act as whistle-blowers on poor performance. Due to the difficulty of measuring and monitoring the quality of care delivered, particularly to very vulnerable patients, such as the mentally handicapped, there must be a protective shield for those health care professionals that alert regulators and other decision-makers to unacceptable declines in quality.

All payment mechanisms contain incentives, be it fee-for-service, capitation, or salary, that may encourage a physician or other provider to prefer their own personal interest over their patients or more generally over society. In any system there is a need to inculcate within physicians strong ethical norms to protect their patients' interests. These norms should include the duty of the physician to advise the patient of the range of treatment options and then to advise the patient of the reasons why the physician is recommending or prescribing a particular treatment. Of course, there will always be tension and a physician, in reality, will strike a balance between her or his patients' needs and resources available. However, the development and enrichment of strong ethical norms for physicians will provide a general assurance to patients that within the confines of the resources received, physicians will do their utmost to satisfy all the needs of their patients in the fairest manner. Moreover, physicians should act as advocates on the part of their patients, ensuring that they receive a fair share of available resources in proportion to their relative health needs. The balance between this advocacy and the incentives to contain costs on the part of competing insurer/purchasers in a sense reflects the need of a system to balance individual patient needs against the larger needs of the population being served by the insurer/purchaser.

The need for the enrichment and strengthening of ethical norms is also in recognition of the fact that changing the financial incentives impacting on physicians may not necessarily change physicians' behavior or at least change their behavior in a way one is able to predict. The reasons for behavior are multi-factorial although I do believe that financial incentives are generally a strong motivation. As Morone notes, as the fourth law in his seven laws of social analysis:

> 4. *Beware of incentives.* Economists and other rationalists restlessly tinker with peoples' incentives. This is a dangerous game. Although incentives are important for understanding problems and fashioning solutions, they are also tricky devils, always veering off in unanticipated ways...People are complicated, social systems almost infinitely so. A great many uninvited incentives lurk in each policy change.[89]

Ethical norms and the bonds of collegiality developed between health providers can undoubtedly help to protect the quality of health care services developed, particularly in times of change and transition within a health system. For example, in the context of New Zealand's internal market reforms, Gorringe notes:

> Luckily, however, cooperation evolved before formal contracting. We can call on such things as commitment of people to professional goals, to caring and to cooperation and loyalty within organizations to bridge the motivational gap left by the incompleteness of contracts and their associated incentive structure.[90]

In sum, it would be unwise to underestimate the importance of physicians' and other health providers' altruistic concerns for patients and the importance of their relationships with each other.

Medical malpractice actions

One possible means by which to protect the quality of health care services supplied is through the deterrent effects of medical malpractice actions.

In these times of constrained resources and moves to put in place financial incentives for physicians to be more cost-conscious, there are also counter-intuitive calls to constrain and limit the ability to bring medical malpractice actions and even calls to introduce no-fault schemes (as presently in place in New Zealand.)[91] Primarily these calls originate from physicians. This is under-standable given that physicians may feel that they are expected to juggle conflic-ting duties. Their duties include that owed to society as a whole to fairly allocate resources, the duty owed to patients to distribute resources fairly between them and the duty to provide the best possible treatment to any particular patient. As physicians are pressured to perform in all these dimensions they do not want to be at risk for legal actions in a system where standards and expectations are shifting.

There is also academic support for the abolition or reform of medical malpractice claims.[92] Due to the high costs of litigation, evidentiary difficulties, and information asymmetry between providers and patients (making it difficult for patients to detect instances of malpractice), reportedly only a small propor-tion of instances of malpractice are litigated upon.[93] This fact does not appear to be well-known by physicians who significantly overestimate the likelihood of being sued. As a consequence of a fear of being sued physicians say they engage in defensive medicine: "a practice in which physicians utilize exhaustive diagnostic and treatment methods of minimum value to ensure the best quality of health care while at the same time erecting an undefeatable defense against liability."[94]

On the one hand, physicians argue that the fear of being sued is driving them to engage in costly defensive medicine. On the other hand, there is also the argument that as a significant percentage of malpractice claims goes unlitigated, medical malpractice actions have little real deterrent effect. These arguments seem somewhat contradictory. One could argue that the high level of malprac-tice going undetected and/or unpunished suggests that reforms are needed to improve detection of malpractice and to facilitate the bringing of claims.

Without delving too far into a debate over the utility of medical malpractice actions it is vital to realize that the empirical work done on the effect of medical malpractice claims has been in the context of indemnity-insurance fee-for-service systems. A very different set of incentives present themselves for consideration in a system characterized by managed care arrangements. In a fee-for-service system of full insurance, the sorts of negligence sought to be deterred are more likely to be due to mistakes, accidents, or acts of incompe-tence. In a managed competition system of capitation payments characterized by managed care, it is possible that negligence may arise from decisions to sacrifice quality for personal financial gain. Such occurrences should be treated very strictly, so sending a clear signal to other health care providers that such behavior will not be tolerated. Thus, the value of medical malpractice suits as a deterrent mechanism should not be readily dismissed.

An interesting question is whether physicians can use a lack of resources as a defense to a medical malpractice action. Physicians may claim they lack resources to deliver care of the required legal standard as a result of government-imposed limitations or as a result of restrictions imposed by insurer/purchasers supplying managed care. US courts have treated the determination by managed care plans of coverage and the determination of medical decisions by physicians as two separate transactions. In the case of Wickline v. State of California it was held that a physician's ultimate responsibility is to his or her patient and this trumps any financial or other obligation to a managed care plan. "The physician who complies without protest to the limitation imposed by a third party payer, when his medical judgement dictates otherwise, cannot avoid his ultimate responsibility for his patient's care."[95] Hirshfeld and Thomason argue that the courts' position on this matter fails to recognize that managed care plans will, through a variety of techniques, seek to make physicians more cost conscious.[96] However, as advocates for the patient, physicians should not be silent in the face of constraints placed upon them by insurer/purchasers. The rationale for this advocacy is *not* that each individual patient should be entitled to the very best that medical science has to offer irrespective of cost or likelihood of effectiveness but that every patient is entitled to a fair share of resources that is proportionate to their health needs.

What of the liability of insurer/purchasers? In the US, the dynamic nature of the market where insurers are forming into managed care plans and performing both the role of the insurer and the role of the provider has resulted in confusion over where liability should fall.[97] As mentioned earlier, the US House of Representatives is currently struggling over whether to allow patients to sue managed care plans. In a managed competition model, responsibility for the supply of quality care should fall equally upon the insurer/purchaser and the physician or other health provider so as to provide a clear incentive to supply care of an adequate quality.

Medical malpractice actions will certainly not be sufficient to ensure the quality of health care services but should be considered part of a package to safeguard quality in a competition-oriented system. Malinowski notes, "(a)lthough legal liability may address some of the most egregious instances of inadequate care and instill incentives for providing quality care, it cannot be relied on to police more subtle and systematic lapses in care."[98] He goes on to note "(t)o protect patients' interests and the discretion of physicians to treat them adequately, clearer ethical standards will have to be established and some regulatory safeguards imposed."

Ombudsperson, commissioners, and other voice mechanisms

Another mechanism through which to protect the quality of health care services supplied from the patient's perspective is to create a Health Commissioner or Ombudspersons' office. This mechanism has already been mentioned in Chapter 4 and I will not repeat what was stated there regarding the advantages of such a mechanism. In order to quickly resolve disputes that arise between insurer/purchasers and citizens, a commissioner or ombudsperson should be empowered to mandate dispute resolution and quick determination. If citizens must instigate lengthy and expensive litigation in order to determine matters that need to be resolved quickly, such as the extent of coverage provided, then insurers/providers could use their size and financial power to make complaint resolution particularly difficult thus preventing complaints being made.

Conclusion

Managed competition implicitly assumes that insurer/purchasers will enter into a variety of managed care arrangements with health care providers. In this respect, there is a convergence with internal market models in the UK and New Zealand that are also moving towards explicit forms of managed care. Proponents of internal markets argue that an internal market system avoids the problems of cream-skimming, transactions costs, and quality control associated with a managed competition system. However, in internal markets there has seemed a strong tendency to encourage managed care arrangements (for example, GP Fundholders in the UK and Budgetholders in New Zealand). Competition between providers paid on a capitation basis in an internal market system will result in the same problems said to arise in managed competition systems and the problem of transactions costs may even be aggravated because of the small size of the managed care plans affected.

Any system that seeks to directly or indirectly foster competition on the supply side carries the inherent risk that competition will occur along the lines of avoiding risk and that quality may be cut. When financial incentives are trained upon individual or small groups of physicians, this acutely brings into focus the conflict between the physician's personal financial interest and his or her fiduciary duty to his or her patient. The intensity of this conflict will depend upon the intensity of the incentive to contain costs being trained upon the physician.

A system needs to contain a series of checks and balances with sufficient tension, to ensure cost-containment but also to maintain the quality of care. It will serve neither society nor patients nor providers to allow significant levels of financial risk to be devolved to small groups of health providers or individual physicians. It will not serve society as it will have to pick up the longer-term costs of physicians electing to cut the quality of services supplied. It will not serve patients as they will bear the individual cost of undertreatment. It will not serve providers as they will find it increasingly difficult to resolve financial incentives with their ethical, legal, and professional responsibilities.

The argument made in this book is that the internal market model is flawed as it pays insufficient attention to incentives operating upon government-appointed purchasers or, in other words, governance issues. The goal of internal market reform is to shift some of the power of resource allocation decisions away from physicians and other providers and into the hands of government-appointed authorities. However, the model fails to ensure these authorities have incentives, the skill and the resources to make these allocation decisions, to balance individual patients' needs with society's interests. The New Labour reforms of December 1997 provides for the transfer of purchasing responsibility to large groups of family doctors and community nurses (Primary Care Groups). By contrast, managed competition provides incentives for insurer/purchasers to compete on price and quality dimensions. I argue that if incentives can be sufficiently trained upon competing insurer/purchasers so that they truly compete on price and quality dimensions then insurer/purchasers will not enter into supply side arrangements that may have the effect of resulting in a reduction of quality. In the absence of such incentives, there is a strong case for limitations on the degree to which insurer/purchasers (in managed competition systems) or government-appointed purchasers (in internal markets) can devolve financial risk on to health care providers. Complementary solutions would be the prohibition of gag clauses and protection of physicians from punitive actions should they speak out about the quality of care offered by particular plans. In addition, the traditional methods of professional self-regulation, codes of ethics, and medical malpractice actions could also be employed.

In a managed competition system, an important role for government would be to ensure the filtering of information to citizens regarding the quality of health care services and to ensure the protection of the quality of services for vulnerable populations that the mechanism of "exit" may not otherwise protect. If sufficient individuals "exit" from a particular insurer/purchaser to another this provides a clear incentive to improve performance; however, where the exit is by a very small number of high-cost individuals (for example, HIV patients) this mechanism may simply be too crude to protect the quality of services.

Government, in the role of sponsor, may be able to help to shape citizen preferences for insurer/purchasers that care for the most vulnerable in society by ensuring the publication of data and rankings on how well an insurer/purchaser cares for the most vulnerable. Although the process of exit ensures that an insurer/purchaser remains responsive to concerns about the quality of care from a patient's perspective, exit may undermine quality in terms of what is optimal for society. It is in society's interests to ensure that individuals do not fall sick in the first instance and thus to invest in primary and preventive care; however, given the propensity to exit, insurer/purchasers may feel they are unlikely to reap the full benefit of investments in primary and preventive care. If primary, preventive and public health care services are perceived to be at risk of underprovision in a system of competing insurer/purchasers then government could buy these services on a fee-for-service basis ensuring greater production thereof. The other possibility is to require competing insurer/purchasers to be non-profit organizations that encourage a culture or ethos directed towards primary and preventive care. Such non-profit organizations may inspire amongst individuals enrolled with them a greater degree of loyalty than for-profit organizations, resulting in quality-conscious individuals using voice in order to improve the performance of their insurer/purchaser before exiting to another.

Notes

1 For a fuller discussion of the information asymmetry problem see Chapter 2.
2 For example, T. Stoltzfus Jost, 'Oversight of the Quality of Medical Care: Regulation, Management, or the Market', (1995) 37 *Arizona Law Review* 825 at p. 835, refers to the "dramatic erosion in the public's confidence in self-regulation."
3 R. V. Saltman and C. von Otter, *Planned Markets and Public Competition: Strategic Reform in Northern European Health Systems* (Buckingham: Open University Press, 1992) at p. 13, identify public resistance to continued rationing by queue of certain elective surgical procedures, particularly for the elderly, as a force that has contributed to health reform initiatives.
4 G. B. Shaw, *The Doctor's Dilemma*, 1911, as cited by N. Barr, 'Economic Theory and the Welfare State: A Survey and Reinterpretation', (1992) XXX(2) *J. Econ Lit.* 741.
5 E. A. McGlynn, 'Quality in a Changing System: Challenges in Measuring Quality', (1997) 16(3) *Health Affairs* 7. See also R. W. Hungate, 'Whither Quality?', (1996) 15(4) *Health Affairs* 111.
6 Stoltzfus Jost, *op. cit.*, p. 841.
7 For a discussion, see D. Blumenthal and R. Bohmer, 'Contending Views of Quality Management in Health Care: Implications for Competition and Regulation', in T. A. Abbott, III (ed.), *Health Care Policy and Regulation* (Boston: Kluwer Academic Publishers, 1995) at p. 205, and Stoltzfus Jost, *ibid.*, pp. 838–839.
8 See A. Donabedian, 'Evaluating the Quality of Medical Care', (1966) 2 *Milbank Memorial Fund Quarterly* 166.
9 McGlynn, *op. cit.*, p. 11.
10 D. M. Eddy, 'Performance Measurement: Problems and Solutions', (1998) 17(4) *Health Affairs* 7 at p. 17.
11 For example, R. G. Evans and G. L. Stoddart, 'Producing Health, Consuming Health Care', in R. G. Evans, M. L. Barer, and T. R. Marmor, *Why Are Some People Healthy and Others Not?: The Determinants of Health of Populations* (New York: Aldine de Gruyter, 1994) at p. 38, note "the growing field of health care services research has accumulated extensive evidence inconsistent with the assumption that the provision of health care is connected in any systematic or scientifically grounded way with patient "needs" or demonstrable outcomes…Accordingly, the greatly increased flow of resources into health care is perceived as not having a commensurate, or in some cases any, impact on health status. Nor is there any demonstrable connection between international variations in health status and variations in health spending."
12 One example is where the "outcome" of a procedure is successful in that a woman had a successful caesarean birth and she and her child are healthy. However, the clumsy application of an epidurial resulted in unnecessary pain and anxiety for the mother as it only worked on her left side. The epidurial had to be administered again causing additional stress to the woman who was aware of the attendant risk of paralysis from injection into the spinal cord.
13 Stoltzfus Jost, *op. cit.*, pp. 828–829. One should note, however, that until the recent managed care revolution in the US, patients were able to "self-diagnose" to an extent as they could access specialists without having to visit a general practitioner first.
14 See the discussion in Chapter 2 regarding the ability of physicians to influence demand for their own services.
15 See the discussion by C. E. Phelps and C. Mooney, 'Variations in Medical Practice Use: Causes and Consequences', in R. J. Arnould, R. F. Rich, and W. D. White (eds), *Competitive Approaches to Health Care Reform* (Washington, DC: The Urban Institute Press, 1993) at pp. 171–172, who note that factors influencing behavior will include education and training, the practice of colleagues and peers, and absorption of ethical norms.

16 This may be justified in economic terms under the idea of a "caring externality" or on grounds of equity – see the discussion in Chapter 2.

17 See M. Schlesinger, 'Regulatory Strategies Under Managed Competition Health Care Reforms', in T. A. Abbott, III (ed.), *Health Care Policy and Regulation, op. cit.,* 45 at p. 61.

18 See the discussion in Chapter 4.

19 F. T. Schut and H. E. G. M. Hermans, 'Managed Competition Reform in the Netherlands and its Lessons for Canada', (1997) 20(2) *Dalhousie Law Journal* 437 at p. 444.

20 Physician Payment Review Commission, 'PPRC Report On Changes In Physician Practices', reprinted in Medicare and Medicaid Guide (CCH) 43,720 at 46,846 (1 September 1995).

21 A. J. Culyer and A. Meads, 'The United Kingdom: Effective, Efficient, Equitable?', (1992) 17(4) *J. Health Polit. Policy Law* 667 at p. 674. Fee-for-service payments and payments of costs were pegged to the total average costs for all practitioners, with practitioners being able to keep any moneys they saved below the average – J. Hurst, *OECD Health Policy Studies No. 2, The Reform of Health Care: A Comparative Analysis of Seven OECD Countries* (Paris: OECD, 1992) at p. 113.

22 P. Day and R. Klein, 'Britain's Health Care Experiment', (1991) 10(3) *Health Affairs* 39 at p. 49.

23 For a criticism of these awards, see K. Bloor and A. Maynard, *Rewarding Excellence?: Consultants' Distinction Awards and the Need for Reform, (Discussion Paper 100)* (York: Center for Health Economics, University of York, 1992).

24 J. Hurley and R. Labelle, 'Relative Fees and the Utilization of Physicians' Services in Canada', (1995) 4(6) *Health Economics* 419, and P. C. Coyte, 'Review of Physician Payment and Service Delivery Mechanisms' (April 1995) *Ontario Medical Review* 23.

25 A. C. Enthoven, 'The History and Principles of Managed Competition', (1993) 12 (Supplement) *Health Affairs* 24 at p. 25.

26 A. G. Gosfield, 'Who is Holding Whom Accountable for Quality?', (1997) 16(3) *Health Affairs* 26 at p. 37.

27 See the discussion by Phelps and Mooney, *op. cit.,* pp. 171–2. See also J. E. Wennberg, 'Practice Variations and the Challenge to Leadership', (1996) 21(12) *Spine* 1472; E. S. Fisher, *et al.,* 'Hospital Readmission Rates for Cohorts of Medicare Beneficiaries in Boston and New Haven', (1994) 331(15) *New Engl. J. Med.* 989, and J. E. Wennberg, 'Unwanted Variations in the Rules of Practice', (1991) 265(10) *JAMA* 1306.

28 Phelps and Mooney, *op. cit.*

29 Per J. Posner in Blue Cross and Blue Shield United of Wisconsin, *et al.,* v. Marshfield Clinic, 65 F.3d 1406 (7th Cir.1995), cert. denied No. 95-1118.

30 See, for example, P. Basket, 'Maori Welfare', *New Zealand Herald,* 15 February 1995, and R. Wharawhara, 'Maoris to Play Bigger Role in Health: Power Sharing as Purchasers and Providers in North', *New Zealand Herald,* 8 November 1995, and L. A. Malcolm and M. Powell, 'The Development of Independent Practice Associations and Related Groups in New Zealand,' (1996) 109(1022) *NZ Med. J.* 184.

31 For a vivid example of cost-shifting to patients by way of quality reductions see the letter by S. S. Baker in (1996) 334(16) *New Eng. J. of Med.* 1062 describing how an HMO refused to authorize the provision of liver-transplantation services to a child at a local center and required her to use a center 1,500 miles from the child's home. The father of the child eventually lost his job due to absenteeism (he visited the child regularly) and with it his HMO coverage. The cost of the child's care had to be paid for by Medicaid. Although the father eventually found another job, the HMO excluded any pre-existing condition so the child's care was not covered.

32 See Gosfield, *op. cit.,* p. 27.

33 See generally G. Anders, *Health Against Wealth: HMOs and the Breakdown of Medical Trust* (Boston, MA: Houghton Mifflin, 1996).

34 L. Nelson, R. Brown, M. Gold, A. Ciemnecki and E. Docteur, 'Trends: Access to Care in Medicare HMOs, 1996', (1997) 16(2) *Health Affairs* 148.

35 K. Donelan *et al.,* 'All Payer, Single Payer, Managed Care, No Payer: Patients' Perspectives in Three Nations', (1996) 15(2) *Health Affairs* 254 at pp. 261–3.

36 Gosfield, *op. cit.*

37   See R. J. Arnould *et al.*, 'The Role of Managed Care in Competitive Policy Reforms', in R. J. Arnould, R. F. Rich and W. D. White (eds), *op. cit.*, p. 100; A. L. Hillman, W. R. Greer and N. Goldfarb, 'Perspectives, Safeguarding Quality in Managed Competition', (1993) 12 *Health Affairs* 110 at p. 114, and M. A. Hall, 'Rationing Health Care at the Bedside', (1994) 69(4) *N. Y. U. L. Rev.* 693 at pp. 715–716.

38   S. R. Latham, 'Regulation of Managed Care Incentive Payments to Physicians', (1996) 22(4) *American J. of Law and Medicine* 399 at p. 407

39   J. A. Morone, 'The Ironic Flaw in Health Care Competition: The Politics of Market', in R. J. Arnould, R. F. Rich and W. D. White (eds), *op. cit.*, p. 213, and see D. A. Stone, 'When Patients Go to Market: The Workings of Managed Competition', (1993) (Spring) *The American Prospect* 109 at p. 110.

40   M. R. Gold *et al.*, 'A National Survey of the Arrangements Managed-Care Plans Make With Physicians', (1995) 333(25) *New Eng. J. of Med.* 1678. Of the 108 plans, the authors found that 29 were group-model or staff-model health maintenance organizations (HMOs), 50 were network or independent-practice-association (IPA) HMOs and 29 were preferred-provider organizations (PPOs). The authors found that 56 percent of the network or IPA HMOs used capitation as the predominant method of paying primary care physicians as compared with 34 percent of the group or staff HMOs and 7 percent of the PPOs. From these figures, I calculate that 37 percent of all plans use capitation as the primary means of paying physicians.

41   M. A. Morrisey *et al.*, 'Managed Care And Physician/Hospital Integration', (1996) 15(4) *Health Affairs* 62 at p. 68.

42   *Ibid.*, at p. 69, citing M. A. Morrisey, *Cost-shifting in Health Care: Separating Evidence from Rhetoric* (Washington, DC: AEI Press, 1994) at pp. 23–24.

43   See generally D. Orentlicher, 'Health Care Reform and the Patient-Physician Relationship', (1995) 5(1) *Health Matrix* 141.

44   See generally H. T. Greely, 'Direct Financial Incentives in Managed Care: Unanswered Questions', (1996) 6(1) *Health Matrix* 53.

45   Federal Register 61 (27 March 1996): 13430. See Minn. Stat., sec. 72A, 20 Subdivision 33 (1995) and 1995 Ga. H. B. 1338. Current bills regulating financial incentives include 1995 Cal. S.B. 1478; 1995 Ill. H.B. 2967; and 1996 Md. S.B. 718.

46   M. V. Pauly, 'Effectiveness Research and the Impact of Financial Incentives', in S. Shortell and U. Reinhardt (eds), *Improving Health Policy and Management* (Ann Arbor, MI: Health Administration Press, 1992), p. 151.

47   See M. V. Pauly, 'Paying Physicians as Agents: Fee-for-Service, Capitation, or Hybrids?', in T. A. Abbott, III (ed.), *op.cit.*, p. 163, and Coyte, *op. cit.*, p. 14.

48   R. G. Evans, *Strained Mercy – The Economics of Canadian Health Care* (Toronto: Butterworths and Co. (Canada), 1984), at p. 378 notes that per-case or episode-based reimbursement is calculated by treating each particular illness as requiring a "package" of treatment and a level of reimbursement is determined for that "package." See also Pauly, *op. cit.*, p. 642.

49   R. J. Arnould *et al.*, 'Competitive Reforms: Context and Scope', in R. J. Arnould, R. F. Rich, and W. D. White (eds), *op. cit.*, p. 10.

50   R. Evans as quoted by A. Maynard, 'Health Care Reform: Don't Confuse Me With Facts Stupid!', in *Four Country Conference on Health Care Reform and Health Care Policies in the United States, Canada, Germany and the Netherlands, Conference Report* (Amsterdam and Rotterdam: Ministry of Health, Welfare, and Sport, 1995) 47 at p. 49 – "the only way to pay 'docs' is to change the payment system every two years because by then they have found their way around its constraints and are once again milking the health care system!"

51   R. H. Miller, 'Health System Integration: A Means to an End', (1996) 15(2) *Health Affairs* 92 at pp. 102–103.

52   See generally S. Rathgeb Smith and M. Lipsky, 'Privatization in Health and Human Services: A Critique', (1992) 17(2) *J. Health Polit. Policy Law* 233.

53   Donelan *et al.*, *op. cit.*, p. 265.

54   The Health Care Study Group notes that a genuine universal system is an invitation to strategic thinking about the needs and institutions of an entire society and such a system is better able to

control costs as it limits cost-shifting – see the Health Care Study Group report, 'Understanding the Choices in Health Care Reform', (1994) 19(3) *J. Health Polit. Policy Law* 499 at p. 501.

55   Schlesinger, *op. cit.*, p. 63.
56   Of course, purchasers would still try to maximize the system to their advantage through other tactics. These tactics would, however, certainly have to be significantly subtler than what is presently occurring in the US, and the likelihood of gaining significant benefits from risk-avoidance and quality-reduction tactics would be reduced because of the risk of detection by the regulator.
57   See *The New NHS: Modern, Dependable*, a White Paper, Cm 3807, 8 December 1997. Online. Available HTTP: http://www.official-documents.co.uk/document/doh/newnhs/contents.htm (accessed 15 March, 1999), s. 3.2.
58   *Ibid.*, s. 7.6.
59   This is a commonly held perception but it is not without its problems. In the context of a fixed government budget on health spending, there is a temporal problem that shifting resources from acute and hospital care now to preventive and primary care disadvantages those individuals who have not benefited from the latter services and are in need of hospital care now. Moreover, the fact that, for example, people live longer healthier lives does not necessarily mean that fewer hospital resources will be required as there will presumably be more people living into old age who will need long-term nursing care and other health care services – see C. M. Flood, 'Conflicts Between Professional Interests, the Public Interest, and Patients' Interest in an Era of Reform: Nova Scotia Registered Nurses', (1997) 5 *Health Law Journal* 27.
60   Schlesinger, *op. cit.*, at pp. 61–63. See also K. N. Lohr, 'Perspective: How Do We Measure Quality?', (1997) 16(3) *Health Affairs* 22 at p. 24.
61   McGlynn, *op. cit.*, p. 13.
62   New Zealand's original 1991 proposals for reform envisaged the development of competition between Regional Health Authorities and private plans. This policy was abandoned because of strong public opposition to what was perceived as a step towards the "Americanization" of the public health care service and because of concerns over "cream-skimming"– See Hon. S. Upton in Hansard, Health and Disability Services Bill – Introduction, 20 August 1992, 10773 at p. 10776
63   See T. A. Krieble, 'The Rise and Fall of a Crown Entity: A Case Study of the Public Health Commission', (paper submitted for the Degree of Master of Public Policy at Victoria University of Wellington, November 1996).
64   For a discussion of externalities in general see Chapter 2.
65   Schlesinger, *op. cit.*, pp. 50–51.
66   For a taxonomy of the costs involved in relying on unpaid family members to provide home-care services see J. E. Fast *et al.*, 'Conceptualizing and Operationalizing the Costs of Informal Elder Care', final technical report to the National Health Research Development Program (NHRDP) 17 March 1997 pp. 4–11.
67   See generally the National Health Care Service (Fund-holding Practices) Regulations (UK) 1996, S.I. 1996/76.
68   See A. Maynard, 'Can Competition Enhance Efficiency in Health Care? Lessons from the Reform of the UK National Health Care Service', (1994) 29(10) *Soc. Sci. Med.* 1433 at p. 1438.
69   See generally (1997) 16(2) *Health Affairs* (a special issue on hospital and health plan conversions from non-profit to for-profit.)
70   W. M. Sage, 'Health Law 2000: The Legal System and the Changing Health Care Market', (1996) 15(3) *Health Affairs* 9 at p. 20.
71   *Ibid.*
72   D. L. Zalkind and S. R. Eastaugh, 'Mortality Rates as an Indicator of Hospital Quality', (1997) 42(1) *Hospital and Health Care Services Administration* 3.
73   For a discussion in the US, see J. A. Martin and L. K. Bjerknes, 'The Legal and Ethical Implications of Gag Clauses in Physician Contracts', (1996) 22(4) *American J. of Law and Medicine*

433 at pp. 450–453.

74 See generally B. Ferguson and J. Keen, 'Transaction Costs, Externalities and Information Technology in Health Care', (1996) 5(1) *Health Economics* 25.

75 T. Rice, 'Can Markets Give Us the Health System We Want?', (1997) 22(2) *J. Health Polit. Policy Law* 383 at pp. 406–407.

76 Committee for Information, Computer and Communications Policy, *Global Information Infrastructure – Global Information Society (GII-GIS): Policy Requirements* (OCDE/GD(97)139) (OECD: Paris, 1997), Introduction.

77 *Ibid.*, p. 44.

78 *Ibid.*

79 S. Woolhandler and D. U. Himmelstein, 'Annotation: Patients on the Auction Block', (1996) 86(12) *American J. of Public Health* 1699 at pp. 1699–1700.

80 See the discussion by D. Orentlicher, 'Health Care Reform and the Patient-Physician Relationship', (1995) 5 *Health Matrix* 141 at pp. 160–161.

81 Moore v. Regents of the University of California 793 P.2d 479, 483 (Cal. 199), cert. denied, 499 US 936 (1991).

82 Martin and Bjerknes, *op. cit.*, p. 442.

83 *Ibid.*, pp. 441–442.

84 See generally *ibid.* See for example, in California, 1993 Ca. S.B. 1832, Stats. 1994 c. 614.

85 Wilk v. American Medical Association 895 F.2d 352 (7th Cir. Ill. 1990), cert. denied, 496 US 927, and cert. denied, 498 US 982 (1990).

86 *Ibid.*, p. 356.

87 Anonymous, 'Managed-Care Docs Dissatisfied – Survey', (10 March 1997) *Modern Healthcare* p. 22.

88 D. A. Yao, M. H. Rirordan and T. N. Dahdouh, 'Anti-trust and Managed Competition for Health Care', (1994) 49(2) *The Anti-trust Bulletin* 301 at p. 311.

89 J. Morone, 'Seven Laws of Policy Analysis', (1986) 5(4) *J. of Policy Analysis and Management* 817 at p. 818.

90 P. Gorringe, *Secondary Health Care: Contracting, People and Politics*, draft of 5 November 1996 prepared for the Central Regional Health Authority, New Zealand, at p. 5.

91 See for example, the no-fault system proposed in the United States discussed by A. Wencl and D. Strickland, 'No-Fault Med Mal: No Gain for the Injured', (May 1997) *Trial: J. of the Assoc. of Trial Lawyers of America* 18. See also R. E. Astroff, 'Show Me the Money!: Making the Case for No-Fault Medical Malpractice Insurance', (1997) 5(3) *Health Law Review* 9.

92 See generally, P. C. Weiler, H. H. Hiatt, J. P. Newhouse *et al.*, *A Measure of Malpractice: Medical Injury, Malpractice Litigation, and Patient Compensation* (Cambridge MA: Harvard University Press, 1993), and D. N. Dewees, M. J. Trebilcock and D. Duff, *Exploring the Domain of Accident Law: Taking the Facts Seriously* (New York: Oxford University Press, 1996).

93 For example, in the US it is estimated that less than 20 percent of malpractice victims actually file law suits – *The Report of the Harvard Medical Practice Study*, *op. cit.* See R. R. Bovbjerg, L. C. Dubay, G. M. Kenney, and S. A. Norton, 'Defensive Medicine and Tort Reform: New Evidence in an Old Bottle', (1996) 21(2) *J. Health Polit. Policy Law* 267 at p. 285 and the references cited there.

94 T. H. Boyd, 'Cost-containment and the Physician's Fiduciary Duty to the Patient', (1989) 39 *DePaul L.R.* 131 at p. 131.

95 Wickline vs. State of California 192 Cal. App. 3d 1630, 239 Cal. Rptr. 810 (Ct. App. 1986).

96 E. B. Hirshfeld and G. H. Thomason, 'Medical Necessity Determinations: The Need for a New Legal Structure', (1996) 6(1) *Health Matrix* 3 at pp. 3–5.

97 See J. M. Liggio, 'Preparing the HMO Case', (May 1997) *Trial: J. of the Assoc. of Trial Lawyers of America* 26.

98 M. J. Malinowski, 'Capitation, Advances in Medical Technology, and the Advent of a New Era in Medical Ethics', (1996) 22(2) *American J. of Law and Medicine* 331 at p. 338.

8 Conclusion

Motivation for health reform

Health reform is ongoing in nearly every OECD country in response to concerns over growing health expenditures. As government is the primary payer in many countries, there has been particular concern over the growth in government expenditures. This concern is aggravated by the prospect of an aging population with high expectations as to the satisfaction of their health care needs and wants. Access concerns have arisen in countries that rely to a greater degree on private finance, such as the US and the Netherlands, as private insurers increasingly refuse to provide coverage to high-risk people or charge them such high premiums that they are unable to afford coverage. In countries where governments have tightly controlled health expenditures, such as the UK and New Zealand, there have been access concerns over growing waiting lists and times, and concerns that the allocation of resources, left to physicians' discretion, is not occurring in a fair or efficient way. Policy makers in all jurisdictions have also become increasingly aware of a body of economic literature emphasizing that there is no evidence of the cost-effectiveness or even effectiveness of many health care services supplied. A general concern has arisen that prioritization of health care needs and the supply of health care services has unduly emphasized acute care and expensive technologies over primary and preventive care. This allocation pattern, it is argued, reflects what is optimal from the medical profession's perspective as opposed to what is optimal for society.

The macro cost-containment approach

Throughout the 1980s, many OECD countries sought to control increasing expenditures on health by limiting the total amount of resources available to their respective health care systems. In single-payer systems this was achieved by capping government expenditures, by changing the method of payment to hospitals from reimbursing for all costs incurred to a prospective annual budget (thus devolving to hospitals a measure of budgetary responsibility), and by reducing the number of hospitals and hospital beds and the numbers of health care providers. This macro cost-containment approach is grounded in the economic intuition that expenditures on health care services equate with incomes for health care providers. Health care providers have an incentive to lobby for an ever-increasing amount of resources to be devoted to the health sector, regardless of real need. This self-interested behavior is often disguised in the rhetoric of an increasing societal need for health care services or the threat of declining quality of services. Thus, the theory runs, because of the large inefficiencies within most health care systems, government can cap or cut the amount of resources devoted to the system without detrimentally affecting "health" and physicians and other providers will of necessity increasingly select the most cost-effective services and prioritize health care needs.

Containing costs through the macro cost-containment approach has been effective in a number of countries from the perspective of controlling the percentage of GDP devoted to health care services. However, in the UK and New Zealand systems, the maxim "If costs can be shifted rather than reduced then they will" has proven correct. Costs have been shifted on to the public at large and to patients in particular by long and growing waiting lists for elective surgery in public hospitals, longer travelling times to general practitioners, specialists, and hospitals, loss of income whilst waiting for treatment, and significant costs (as yet unquantified) on informal caregivers who are required to provide home care. Thus, although some so-called single-payer systems may prima facie appear less expensive, their true costs may be hidden.

The macro cost-containment approach to health reform is also based upon some contradictory assumptions. The story its proponents tell of money-hungry and scalpel-happy physicians taking advantage of ignorant patients and members of the public does not rest well with their subsequent assumption that, when faced with restricted resources, physicians will select the most cost-effective service and appropriately prioritize health needs. Simply restricting the resources available to a system will not necessarily result in selection of the most cost-effective services and movement towards the optimal production frontier. As an example, there is no evidence that the supply of services in the UK is any more cost-effective than in Canada, despite the fact that a significantly lower level of resources is devoted to health care in the UK than in Canada. The common criticism of the present mix of health care services supplied is that there is too great an emphasis on acute care and advanced technology at the expense of primary and preventive care. However, it does not appear that there is any less emphasis in a low-spending country like the UK than a high-spending country like Canada. Thus, it has not been demonstrated that the macro-containment approach will reorient the system so that health care needs are appropriately prioritized as well as the most cost-effective services selected to respond to those needs. It also leaves open many opportunities for cost-shifting on the part of health care providers who find it much easier to maintain the status quo rather than to change or improve their old patterns of practice. They may prefer to shift costs on to other payers or patients in terms of longer waiting lists or times or otherwise less responsive services.

A new paradigm: the proactive purchaser

In all four systems there has historically been relatively little pressure on the demand side to ensure the optimal allocation of resources between different health care needs (balancing societal and patient interests) or to ensure the supply of the most cost-effective service in response to a particular need. In response to this problem, both managed competition and internal market reform models seek to introduce proactive purchasers that will actively influence the allocation of resources to different health care needs and the selection of the most cost-effective service in response to a particular health care need. Both types of reform – often described as market- or competition-oriented reform – may be more constructively thought of as reform models that seek to inject tension on the purchasing or demand side of health care service markets. The new wave of competition-oriented reforms seeks to change the balance of power between purchasers and physicians. Purchasers (be they government-appointed purchasers in internal markets or competing private insurers in managed competition markets) seek to influence or manage physician decision-making.

These types of models respond to justice concerns by ensuring access to a comprehensive range of health care services on the basis of need as opposed to ability to pay. Both managed competition and internal market systems must be largely progressively financed in order to satisfy justice concerns. A managed competition system covering a comprehensive range of health care services of an adequate quality will result in a more equitable system than a so-called single-payer system like that of New Zealand's, which has high user charges for general practitioner services. Covering a comprehensive range of services is not only important from a justice perspective but also from an efficiency perspective so as to allow the most cost-effective service, whatever its nature, to be supplied in response to a particular health care need. Comprehensiveness is also important from the perspective of accountability. If payers/purchasers are only responsible for certain health care needs or services then there is more scope to argue that particular problems or patients do not fall within their jurisdiction and budget.

In order to facilitate a measure of price competition, a managed competition model would require citizens to pay either (as in the Netherlands' model) a small fixed percentage of the total premium or (as in Enthoven's model) the difference in premium price between the lowest-price plan and their selected plan or (as in Clinton's proposals) the difference in premium price between the average-priced plan and their selected plan. There may be a concern that managed competition would consequently result in a two-tier system. However, this is not necessarily true or at least no more true than in many systems (even those described as "single-payer") that rely on private financing for important services such as general practitioner services, drugs, home-care services, etc., or systems where physicians consciously or unconsciously prefer patients and health care needs that they can most identify with (for example, treatment of heart disease rather than prevention of diabetes). In other words, in every country there is in reality a two-tier system and in every country rationing occurs, although this is not frankly acknowledged. In seeking to facilitate price competition there is the potential in managed competition regimes for the ghettoization of lower-priced plans. This may lead one to conclude that there needs to be regulatory control of premium prices to reduce the potential for wide differences between the quality and coverage offered by the lowest- and highest-priced plans. However, the specter of an unacceptable two-tier system is significantly lessened provided a comprehensive range of health care services is included in the publicly-funded basket and the sponsor ensures that the quality of services in even the cheapest plan is at a level acceptable to the majority of society.[1]

Setting an acceptable level of quality or, in other words, determining minimum entitlements is a difficult task. However, this is a problem that all systems must wrestle with unless governments intend to leave allocation and rationing issues within the "black box" of clinical decision-making and rely on the macro cost-containment approach to limit the resources available to clinicians. It seems reasonable that a system needs to create the right combination of incentives so that the most cost-effective service is supplied in response to a health care need. However, this belies the difficulties of measuring the relative importance of needs. For example, would a potentially life-saving operation that costs $25,000 to perform and has a 10 percent chance of success be "effective?" Limiting access to someone's chance of life or full recovery does not fit well with the notion of effectiveness because of the judgements that have to be made with regard to the value of the outcome sought to be obtained. There needs to be an ongoing process in place whereby the general public are involved in determining health spending priorities and the range and quality of health care services to be supplied. The difficulty and sensitivity of this task should not deter policymakers. The fact that this is not an easy task speaks even more to the need for this process to occur through a transparent and public process rather than being determined by individual physicians in their office on an ad hoc basis.

Internal markets

Internal market reform has been implemented in systems previously described as "command-and-control," where government not only played a significant role in financing health care services but also in providing health care services through the nationalization of most hospitals. Although I have been critical of internal market reform in the UK and New Zealand, there have been some significant benefits. An important aspect of reform has been the integration of funding of a wide range of health care services into regional government purchasers. Arbitrary partitioning of funding between different services and needs is characteristic of many health care systems and lessens the ability of purchasers and/or providers to make cost-effective substitutions between different health care services in response to health care needs. Integration of funding is also important as a means of reducing cost-shifting, for if different payers are responsible for different needs or services then the temptation is to simply shift costs. The other significant benefit of internal market reform has been the generation of information regarding the costs and benefits of different health care services. In the previous command-and-control systems of both the UK and New Zealand there was little usable information generated regarding the costs and benefits of different health care services. Information has had to be generated in the new internal markets as both purchasers and providers need to be able to measure their own and each other's performance so as to provide a currency for decision-making.

The primary problem with the internal market model is that although it recognizes the central need for proactive purchasing it does not address itself to the issue of how to ensure that government-appointed Health Authorities and Primary Care Groups will in fact be proactive. To ensure optimal decision-making, these Authorities not only need resources and skills but also sufficient incentives. As internal markets eschew competition between purchasers as a means of ensuring performance, one has to rely solely upon political mechanisms or "voice" to ensure the responsiveness of Health Authorities and Primary Care Groups to the citizens and patients they are meant to represent in their purchasing decisions. Significant and complex agency questions arise in this respect. These issues have not been sufficiently addressed and voice mechanisms are underdeveloped in both the UK and New Zealand.

Unsurprisingly, given the lack of attention to the incentives trained upon purchasers, internal market reform in the UK and New Zealand has resulted in little change in the range of health care services supplied and the health care providers who supply them. Internal market reform does not promote dynamic efficiency as Health Authorities are prevented from taking different responses in different health care service markets; they must contract out even when vertical integration may be the more efficient option. Thus, flexibility and dynamic efficiency is forsaken in the quest for a prima facie simple administrative structure where "one size fits all."

The configuration of the supply side, in particular the number and size of New Zealand's Crown Health Enterprises and the UK's NHS Trusts (which are the administrative organizations that manage hospitals), has been government-determined and is rigid. There appears to be a problem of monopoly supply in hospital services within internal markets, but this is a product of years of the macro cost-containment approach to health reform and, in particular, government consolidation and control of hospitals. Although now ostensibly independent of government, public hospitals that could be potentially in competition with each other are often under the same management umbrella. It is unclear to what degree there would be monopoly on the supply side if these administrative structures were unbundled and hospitals were privatized. The result of monopoly on the demand side and monopoly on the supply side, particularly since both are government controlled and threats of hold-out are politically unsustainable, is essentially stalemate with little real willingness to change or innovate on either side.

The contract has been described as the "fulcrum of internal market reform," symbolizing the new relationships between purchasers and providers. There is not, however, a stark choice between contracting out and vertical integration in quasi-government markets. There is in fact a continuum of options in public/private relationships. The UK internal market, although dressed in the garb of contracting out (at least prior to the New Labour reforms of 1997), fell closer on the continuum towards vertical integration. The UK internal market may be better understood as a new form of hierarchical arrangement within government. New Zealand has made a more serious attempt at contracting out and relies on legally enforceable contracts. Notwithstanding, in both the UK and New Zealand, the most prevalent form of contracting has been "block contracts" resulting in little change from the previous system where hospitals were paid by prospective annual budgets. The rigidity and inflexibility of the UK and New Zealand systems both pre and post reform lend themselves to periodic system reform or, as Maynard describes it, "redisorganizaton." This phenomenon has been recently demonstrated once again with the announcement in both New Zealand and the UK of further reforms that purport, in particular, to reduce the transactions costs of the internal market. The rigidity of the structures in place in these countries means that the whole system must periodically be reformed to catch up with changes in health markets caused by exogenous or endogenous factors. Periodically, the entire system must also be shaken up as one or more of the important players in the system (hospitals, physicians and other health providers, private insurers, government authorities, patients) have figured out how to maximize to their own particular benefit all the loopholes of the existing system configuration. By comparison, a managed competition model promises greater dynamic efficiency as competing insurer/purchasers can more readily respond to different health care service markets and changes within those markets over time.

The most dynamic innovation of internal market reform in the UK and New Zealand has been the development of managed care plans controlled by general practitioners. For example, the UK GP Fundholders negotiated quicker responses on the part of hospitals and other providers than Health Authorities and and so reduced waiting lists and times. These managed care developments are, however, in sharp contrast to the balance of the internal market reforms for two reasons. First, they rely upon private purchasers (consortiums of general practitioners) as opposed to government-appointed purchasers. Second, other internal market reforms require a rigid purchaser/provider split but GP Fundholders (as with all managed care plans) may, in some cases, be able to substitute the supply of their own services in place of buying services from other providers.

The belief is that Fundholders and the new Primary Care Groups have an incentive to give greater emphasis to primary and preventive care in order to keep their enrollee population healthy. However, as with all managed care plans this benefit will only accrue if Fundholders/Primary Care Groups know that they must bear the long-term consequences of their decision-making and that there is at least a serious risk that failure to provide care to their enrollee population will have cost consequences for them. This problem is discussed further below in the context of managed competition, as managed care is integral to the managed competition model. As GP Fundholders were only responsible for purchasing a limited as opposed to a comprehensive range of health care services then this increased the potential for shifting costs on to other payers or purchasers and could have meant that over the longer term Fundholders did not engage in optimal decision-making. By comparison, it is intended that the new Primary Care Groups will be responsible for the budgets for a full range of health care services. However, the new Primary Care Groups face very weak incentives not to run over budget and/or to operate efficiently.

The empirical evidence available suggests that the efficiency gains associated with Fundholding were outweighed by additional transactions and administrative costs. This may have been a temporary phenomenon but it also may be reflective of the fact that purchasing responsibility has been devolved to too low a level and that purchasers should generally serve a larger population than the 5,000 minimum allowed in the UK. The New Labour reforms of December 1997 recognized this problem and is replacing the 3,500 Fundholders with 500 Primary Care Groups.

Although internal markets are often lauded as resulting in lower transactions costs than a managed competition system, it is by no means clear that this is the case. In the Netherlands (population 18 million), there are twenty-five Sickness Funds and fifty private insurers. Moreover, most private insurers and Sickness Funds cooperate in holding companies or chains with the ten largest chains ocomprising 80 percent of the insurenca market in 1998. By comparison, in the UK (population 58 million), there were 3,500 GP Fundholders operating as mini-purchasers in the UK in addition to the 100 Health Authorities. Even with the recent changes there will still be at least 500 Primary Care Groups acting as purchasers and, probably, a significant number of Health Authorities. In the absence of empirical evidence it is simply incorrect to assume that an advantage that internal market reform holds over managed competition reform is lower transactions costs. This stance reflects the common misunderstanding that managed competition is "US-style" reform and that as the US system is well known for its high level of transactions costs then the managed competition model is similarly flawed. Moreover, the fixation with the level of transactions costs misses the point that we should be concerned with whether or not any resulting efficiency gains *outweigh* any concomitant increase in transactions or administrative costs.

Questions may also be raised over the devolution of significant amounts of financial risk on to physicians. On the one hand, the New Labour reforms are lacking an engine for positive change as it does not appear the new Primary Care Groups, although responsible for purchasing all publicly-funded health care services, will actually bear the financial risk associated with that decision-making. On the other hand, it is by no means obvious that general practitioners and community nurses have the managerial and administrative skills necessary to act essentially as small insurers. Devolving significant amounts of financial risk on to physicians would also seem to strike at the heart of and potentially undermine the trust often said to be required in the physician/patient relationship. Arguably, the ethical norms of physicians will mean that it is less likely that physician-run managed care plans would make unacceptable cuts to the quality of health care services or avoid high-risk patients. However, I would argue that on balance excessive devolution of risk on to physicians has the potential to undermine the idea of a physician as an agent and advocate on the part of the patient. Optimally, decision-making processes in a health care system should balance societal interests with patients' interests. Physicians are best positioned to be advocates on the part of their patients and to represent their interests to insurers/purchasers. Although it is recognized that this advocacy may be influenced by their own self-interest it is better to err on the side of caution and let physicians' self-interest be one that is advanced by recommending more services of a higher quality rather than one advanced by unacceptable quality cuts. If insurer/purchasers in a managed competition system have sufficient incentives to compete on price and quality dimensions, it seems unlikely that they would devolve excessive amounts of risk down to physicians without safeguards in place to ensure the standards of care provided. In a managed competition model it would be a sponsor's explicit duty to monitor this process.

It is often argued that internal market reform (with its reliance on government-appointed purchasers who are the only purchasers in a particular region) is preferable to a managed competition system as it avoids the problem of cream-skimming. This occurs when insurer/purchasers compete with each other by trying to avoid servicing high-risk or high-cost individuals. However, cream-skimming is equally a problem in internal markets as government purchasers seek to contract on a capitation basis with groups of providers offering managed care plans. Government-appointed purchasers and private insurers in *all* systems may wish to shift financial risk to groups of health care providers. They shift risk by paying groups of providers on a capitated or block contract basis. In such a case, the managed care plan takes on the *insurance* function as it bears the costs and risk of utilization of services by patients, the *purchaser* function as it largely determines what range and mix of health care services to supply to any individual it covers, and (at its discretion) the *provider* function if it actually owns the hospitals or employs the providers who provide services to patients. The problems generally associated with managed competition systems, such as cream-skimming and additional transactions costs, are in truth problems associated with any system that seeks to devolve financial risk to small groups of health care providers. Policy makers should not be lulled into thinking that these same problems will not exist simply because, as in the UK and New Zealand internal markets, managed care is being encouraged from the bottom up in terms of paying groups of physicians or integrated groups of health providers on a capitated basis rather than competing private insurers. In particular, the problem of cream-skimming is just as serious a problem in this context as it is in competition between large insurer/purchasers. There is a danger that internal markets are allowing the development of managed competition through the back door without sufficient consideration of the important issues of the role of the sponsor, accountability mechanisms, and cream-skimming.

Managed competition

The concept of a proactive purchaser is fundamental to a reorientation of a system by injecting tension into the demand side of health care service markets. Whereas the internal market model relies upon voice as the mechanism through which to ensure the accountability of purchasers, the managed competition model also allows the operation of exit or consumer choice between competing insurer/purchasers. This process of competition is regulated by a government sponsor who requires, through regulation and monitoring, that insurer/purchasers compete on price and quality dimensions and not on their ability to avoid high-risk individuals. The managed competition model generally assumes that private insurers will put in place managed care arrangements that are essentially a variety of techniques whereby insurers seek to influence the clinical decision-making of providers.

The concept of exit or consumer choice of insurer/purchasers is often discounted on the grounds that citizens cannot make good decisions between competing insurer/purchasers offering managed care plans. There is a level of arrogance in some of the rhetoric dismissing the ability of ordinary citizens to make judgements about the activities of purchasers and providers. The information asymmetry suggests that at a micro-level patients will not always be able to monitor providers' performances. However, at macro and meso levels citizens' judgements and preferences would seem to be as valid as any other area with respect to the level of resources to devote to health relative to other needs, which health care needs to give priority to, how well providers respond to patients' needs generally, and difficulties with access, waiting lists and times. Moreover, and as discussed further below, it is not necessary that all citizens shop around from plan to plan. The overall quality of services should be set at a level that the vast majority of society is content with. Provided each plan has a significant number of quality-conscious individuals who will signal their dissatisfaction with a plan's performance by exiting to another, exit should work as a mechanism to enhance the quality of services for all. A sponsor will have to provide citizens with information on the performance of insurer/purchasers, ensure that competition occurs on price and quality dimensions, and ensure that a minimum quality of services is maintained.

There has been a strong shift in many health care systems towards an economic analysis of health care service allocation that focuses on the impact (or lack thereof) of health care services on health outcomes. However, too strong a focus on cost-effectiveness where effectiveness is measured by *health* outcomes will not result in a proper balance nor will such an approach receive the necessary public and political support needed to sustain it. An important component of any health care system is caring services such as care of the mentally and physically disabled, palliative care, care for the frail elderly and care pursuant to the process of healing. Social justice requires that these services be treated as importantly as any other health care service that may have greater benefits from a purely utilitarian perspective of maximizing health. Consequently, richer conceptions of performance are needed. This has been apparent in internal markets where performance has been measured by "easy-to-measure" indicators such as turnover, increased day surgery, number of readmissions, etc. Ensuring that insurer/purchasers are at least in some measure directly accountable to the people they represent ought to help ensure that the more difficult-to-measure indicators of quality that people value are nonetheless taken into account. An excellent feature of the New Labour reforms in the UK is the recognition that broad measures of quality must be pursued – "quality of the patient's experience as well as the clinical result." However, unlike a managed care model the New Labour reforms do not provide for an engine that will drive the pursuit of broader quality objectives.

Some argue that there is no room for exit to work as an accountability-enhancing mechanism, as a very small percentage of the population accounts for the largest share of health expenditures. If insurer/purchasers can cream-skim healthy enrollees and avoid treating costly patients then they will not be operating efficiently nor achieving social justice goals. Where an insurer/purchaser cannot avoid treating a high-risk individual there is a concern that they may cut the quality of the health care services they provide in order to save costs and/or to try to force a patient to shift to another insurer/purchaser.

One method of preventing cream-skimming is to risk-rate the per-capita sum paid to competing insurer/purchasers. As the Netherlands experience demonstrates, however, policy makers lack an understanding of the importance of this issue and incorrectly assume that adequately risk-rating payments will mean that there is nothing to compete on, as insurer/purchasers are reimbursed for all costs. This of course is not correct as the percentage of risk that can be predicted is much smaller than what the risk is in reality. In addition there are also technical difficulties to actually risk-rating per-capita sums paid so that they reflect the *risk of each individual as perceived by insurers*. This requires a sponsor to keep abreast of risk determinants used by insurer/purchasers. A sophisticated regulator is required. There is a certain amount of irony in this point, for the promotion of competition as a means of allocating health care is rooted in a sceptical view of government but, in fact, in order to succeed such competition requires sophisticated governance.[2]

Undoubtedly, cream-skimming is a potentially serious problem. However, it must be remembered that such behavior on the part of insurer/purchasers sends a signal not only to those individuals whose risk has crystallized but to other individuals that this particular insurer/purchaser is untrustworthy at the time that it is needed the most. Thus, the need for managed care plans to maintain their reputation in the market place will inhibit cream-skimming behavior. One can envisage that the need to maintain a good reputation will be more salient for those health care services and patients that *most people can identify with*. Thus, cutting the quality of health care services for the elderly or for patients with heart disease or cancer is likely to promote concern amongst most people able to identify with the fact that they too will grow old and there is a reasonable risk that they or their loved ones will be afflicted with heart disease or cancer. Services for small vulnerable populations or stigmatized health care services (where people use the "head-in-the-sand" approach believing that their own risk, for example, of psychiatric disease or of giving birth to a disabled child is much lower than it really is) may be the services that are most at risk. Thus, there will be a need for the sponsor to emphasize in published data how well plans treat the most vulnerable groups in order to foster a sense of solidarity between the general populace and vulnerable groups within it. In such a case, low-risk individuals may signal their dissatisfaction by the use of either exit or voice with how a plan *treats others who are not similarly situated*. Nonetheless a sponsor will need to be particularly vigilant with regard to the quality of services supplied to small vulnerable groups with whom the rest of the populace has no developed affinity.

It is crucial that decision-makers bear the cost of their own decisions in the short and long term. The problem is that the use of exit and competition between insurer/purchasers may reduce the likelihood of having to bear the long-term costs. On the other hand, a monopoly (be it public or private) may well be unresponsive to concerns and resistant to change. Thus, what is required is a mixture of what Hirschman describes as exit, voice, and loyalty. Insurer/purchasers need to be large in order to pool and manage financial risk and in order to keep transactions and administrative costs down. Exit as an option should not be available at any time but perhaps annually or, as in the Netherlands, biannually, so that insurer/purchasers have an opportunity to improve their performance before many people shift their custom. It may be that insurer/purchasers should be required to be non-profit foundations or organizations in order to encourage loyalty on the part of enrollees and thus the use of voice rather than exit when performance deteriorates. Enrollees should have avenues through which to exercise voice in order to lobby for improvements in their chosen plan, such as the use of a patient ombudsperson or a patient charter of rights, with the ultimate threat of exit being available if performance does not improve.

In order for exit to operate there must be a choice of insurer/purchasers offering managed care plans. In some health care service markets there may be natural monopolies or monopolies that have resulted from previous government policy. The fact that there is not sufficient depth across all health care service markets to create integrated delivery systems capable of independently satisfying the needs of enrollees of competing insurer/purchasers does not mean that the managed competition model is fundamentally flawed. The important question is what degree of regulation or combination of other incentives is required to allow competing insurers/providers to purchase services from natural monopoly providers? As discussed in this book, all the problems of utility regulation are present in abundance in the regulation of health care delivery. On balance, industry-specific regulation seems the most appropriate means to deal with the problems of bottlenecks, cross-subsidy, and monopoly rents. Competition law should be left to regulate the competitive and contestable markets.

There is no perfect or easy solution to what constitutes the optimal institutional design; however, a paradigm shift is needed so that the health care system in question is constantly and incrementally evolving. The managed competition model offers more promise in this regard than the internal market model. However, the managed competition model has not been fully implemented in any jurisdiction and there is little empirical evidence as to how the model would actually work in practice. The model is being slowly implemented in the Netherlands. This slowness is in part due to the Dutch system of coalition government and is not necessarily indicative of the difficulty of implementing managed competition per se. Moreover, it is not necessarily clear that hasty implementation of reform is advantageous. The advantage of reform implemented quickly is often touted to be that vested interest groups have little opportunity to mobilize to resist change. However, change must often be of necessity incremental, responding to and/or building upon what often may be accidents of history or earlier policy decisions. More importantly, the health care system is a service industry and service requires continuity and a meeting of expectations notwithstanding that some may consider these expectations ill-conceived. Expectations can be shaped over time, but the temporal element is key and people need time to redefine their expectations. As an example, it is unrealistic and unfair to shift quickly from a system revolving around acute care to one with significantly greater emphasis on primary and preventive care, particularly since there will presumably be individuals who have not benefited from such primary and preventive care measures in the past.

Managed competition reform is often criticized on the basis that it would result in a US-style system. This is an unwarranted criticism. There is a clear distinction to be made between using market reforms as a means to achieving a broader social goal – namely universal access to a comprehensive range of health care services – and adopting a US-style system of piece-meal access that is regressively funded. Managed competition reform would result in a system significantly different from that presently or historically in operation in the US. It would result in a system that more efficiently achieves the distributive justice goal of ensuring access to a basic level of health care services for all on the basis of need as opposed to ability to pay. The US does not directly acknowledge this goal but nonetheless coverage for the uninsured or government insured is indirectly subsidized by a merry-go-round of cost-shifting. The US system also has resulted in the health care needs of the uninsured being addressed only, if at all, when acute, and thus primary and preventive care, which in the long run may result in significant cost-savings for society, are discounted. The present managed care revolution in the US is resulting in cost-savings but these surpluses are being transferred from physicians and other providers to managed care plans. In the absence of government coordination and regulation any cost-savings are thus accrued as corporate profit and are not pooled and redistributed to fund coverage for all. More importantly, scarce resources are still devoted to the mission of trying to avoid covering or treating high-risk individuals rather than trying to deal most efficiently with their needs. Clearly, although the devil is in the detail in terms of the specific design of a managed competition system, such a system would be a significant improvement upon the present US system. The managed competition model is a relatively complicated model. This complexity may make it difficult to "sell" politically and the Clintons foundered badly in this regard in the face of fierce lobbying and criticisms on the part of insurance and physician groups resistant to any prospect of government control of their incomes or their professional autonomy. This is to be expected. Fierce resistance on the part of the medical profession is a phenomenon characteristic of all health care systems that have implemented or have tried to implement universal health insurance.

There are temptations to implement the managed competition model in a piece-meal fashion and this may create more problems than it solves. Internal market reform is itself piece-meal implementation of the managed competition model, pragmatically adapted for the command-and-control systems of the UK and New Zealand. However, without the driving force of competition between purchasers offering managed care plans, managed competition in a sense loses its engine. With internal market reform we are left with the worst of both worlds – the inflexibility and resistance to change of the old command-and-control system together with the additional transactions and administrative costs associated with the managed competition system.

Capitalist economies implicitly accept the presence of exogenous rules to facilitate transactions that drive the spontaneous order of markets. As discussed in Chapter 2, in health insurance and health care service markets the "free market", as conducted pursuant to general contract, property, anti-trust and other laws, will not ensure the efficient realization of social justice goals in the allocation of health care services. The managed competition model's intellectual appeal is its recognition of social justice goals coupled with its implicit assumption that government is better at setting the exogenous rules for the efficient obtainment of these goals rather than being involved in the production process itself. Thus in managed competition, government sponsors lay down the framework for and regulate competition between private insurer/purchasers offering managed care plans. A key question in health reform and in all institutional design is what decisions are best made by whom? In my opinion, government is less suited to the role of being a purchaser of health care services and negotiating with a range of health providers in a range of health markets than it is to the role of sponsor where it is required to lay down the framework for competition and regulates this process. This is a specific role that builds upon the strengths of government as a policy maker and regulator. By contrast, the role of government as purchaser in internal markets involves micro-managing the supply of care on the part of a number of differing health providers in a number of differently structured and changing health care service markets.

Advocating that government set the exogenous rules for competition and production, however, belies the technical difficulties involved in performing this role well. The successful execution of the sponsor role is critical to the managed competition model. Managed competition is an example of the concept of "smaller but smarter government" but, to put it crudely, can government be smart enough? To use the metaphor of Osborne and Gaebler, although ideally the government's role in health care should be "steering" rather than "rowing", in the sea of health care allocation the currents are very strong due to the strong social justice, economic, and political interests at stake.[3] Evans has said that "the notion that some sort of automatic, self-regulating market-like structure can be established that will substitute for public management and yet achieve public objectives is a fantasy: powdered unicorn horn."[4] It is a serious mistake to assume that the government's role is not as critical in a managed competition system where there are competing purchasers as it is in one where governmental agencies act as the sole purchasers of services. Political accountability and voice continue to have a large and important role to play in managed competition systems. However, while I agree that there is an indisputable role for government in restructuring and implementing a new paradigm for health care service allocation, it is far from clear that it is preferable that government be selectively purchasing or managing discrete health care service markets or managing hospitals. Thus while the *nature* and *scope* of government's participation needs to change, its importance is not undermined and its participation remains key.

Reflections on the Canadian system

The goal of this book has been to compare internal market reform and managed competition reform in the Netherlands, the UK, New Zealand, and the United States. It is, however, appropriate to conclude with some general comments on the relevance of this research to the Canadian system.

The Canadian approach to health reform has primarily been of the macro cost-containment school. This approach has been tried in many countries over the course of the 1980s and has ultimately proved unsatisfactory from the perspective of truly controlling costs or reconfiguring the system towards the supply of cost-effective services. The macro cost-containment approach may be thought of as akin to putting a lid on a fiercely boiling pot (the health care system), where pressure periodically forces the lid up allowing boiling water (costs) to overflow. Canada's and all other health care systems need more creative approaches. Although there are undoubtedly problems and pitfalls with the managed competition model it certainly bears closer scrutiny from a Canadian perspective than a simple dismissal of it as being in the land of "powdered unicorn horn" or as "American-style reform." The very strong resistance to any hint of Americanization of the Canadian health care system, however, means that at least for the foreseeable future an explicit policy promoting managed competition reform is unlikely to be implemented. Moreover, it is true that if a government's goal in health reform is simple cost-containment as opposed to higher productivity and lower production costs then a managed competition model may be unacceptable, as it could conceivably result in high overall expenditures due to higher responsiveness to citizen's preferences and needs. Accepting this, the question arises at to what other measures could be taken to reform the present Canadian system that would be more politically acceptable.

In some provinces there has been a shift to devolving budgets and health allocation responsibility to regional government-appointed authorities. Although this initiative is described as devolution there is also a significant amount of centralization as these regional authorities assume management responsibilities for hospitals, a function formerly performed by hospital boards. Thus, these new regional authorities are both purchasers and providers as they are responsible for buying services and for managing hospitals. These new entities resemble the Area Health Boards and District Health Boards that were in existence in New Zealand and the UK *prior* to internal market reform. In the UK and New Zealand this vertical integration was viewed as problematic as there was no incentive for these regional entities to contract out to other potentially more efficient providers or to shift funding from acute and high-technology care to primary and preventive care. Should Canada consider a move to an internal market system similar to that implemented in the UK and New Zealand? From the perspective of policy makers in other countries, such as Canada, there is much to be learned from critically analyzing the experiences of the UK and New Zealand systems.

On the positive side, there have clearly been benefits that have accrued in internal markets from consolidating funding for a comprehensive range of health care services in regional purchasing authorities. Presently, public funding for hospital and other secondary services is separate from physician services. There is also a significant amount of private financing of drugs consumed outside hospitals, medical equipment, and home care services.[5] Integrating funding for secondary, primary, and drug services in regional authorities would be a first step towards facilitating cost-effective substitutions between services.

The New Zealand and UK systems have experienced enormous upheaval in implementing an internal market through a purchaser/provider split only to see the split incrementally unravelled through managed care arrangements and through developing close relationships between government-appointed purchasers and providers. Recent announcements in both New Zealand and the UK propose the abandonment of internal markets, although in both systems the change seems likely to be more cosmetic than real as the purchaser/provider split, apart from some name changes, is to be left in place. The clear lesson from the UK and New Zealand is that enforcing a rigid purchaser/provider split and mandatory contracting out is not the key or at least is insufficient alone. A rigid purchaser/provider split, just as with rigid vertical integration, can be criticized as application of an inflexible and indiscriminate solution to health care service markets that are very different. What is key is that purchasing or budget-holding entities have the resources, the skills and, in particular, the incentives to purchase and/or provide the most cost-effective range of services and to be responsive to the people in the region they represent. Thus the concerns of accountability and governance that this book has raised are fundamental. In all health care systems, much greater attention needs to be given to ensuring tension on the demand or purchasing side or, in other words, ensuring good governance on the part of these regional authorities or purchasers. It is this issue that demands future research and consideration on the part of policy makers, lawyers, and economists.

Notes

1 Competition on quality dimensions would be those over and above sponsor-mandated minimum requirements. For example, a sponsor may require that all elective surgery be completed within six months, but some health plans may offer to ensure provision of surgery within three months.
2 J. A. Morone, 'The Ironic Flaw in Health Care Competition: The Politics of Market', in R. J. Arnould, R. F. Rich, and W. D. White (eds), *Competitive Approaches to Health Care Reform* (Washington, DC: Urban Institute Press, 1993) p. 207.
3 See D. E. Osborne and T. Gaebler, *Reinventing Government: How the Entrepreneurial Spirit is Transforming the Public Sector* (Reading, MA: Addison-Wesley Pub. Co., 1992).
4 R. G. Evans, 'Going for the Gold: The Redistributive Agenda Behind Market-Based Health Care Reform,' (1997) 22(2) *J. Health Polit.. Policy Law* 427 at p. 462.
5 The National Forum's 1997 recommendations to investigate ensuring universal access in the public system to pharmaceuticals consumed outside hospitals and home care services speaks to the need for comprehensiveness in order to avoid cost-shifting – National Forum on Health, *Canada Health Action: Building on the Legacy Vol. II, Synthesis Reports and Issues Papers* (Ottawa: National Forum on Health, 1997).

Bibliography

General

Aaron, H. J., 'Thinking Straight About Medical Costs', (1994) 13(5) *Health Affairs* 8.

Aaron, H. J. and Schwartz, W. B., *The Painful Prescription: Rationing Hospital Care* (Washington, DC: Brookings Institute, 1984).\

Abbott III, T. A. (ed.) *Health Care Policy and Regulation* (Boston, MA: Kluwer Academic Publishers, 1995).

Akerlof, G. A., 'The Market for "Lemons": Quality Uncertainty and the Market Mechanism', (1970) 84(3) *Quart. J. Econ.* 488.

Arnould, R. J., Rich, R. F. and White, W. D. (eds), *Competitive Approaches to Health Care Reform*, (Washington, DC: Urban Institute Press, 1993).

Arrow, K. J., 'Uncertainty and the Welfare Economics of Medical Care', (1963) 53 *Amer. Econ. Rev.* 941.

Barer, M. L. *et al.*, 'It Ain't Necessarily So: The Cost Implications of Health Care Reform', (1994) 13(4) *Health Affairs* 88.

Baumol, W., 'Contestable Markets: An Uprising in the Theory of Industry Structure', (1982) 72 *Amer. Econ. Rev.* 1.

Baumol, W. J., Bailey, E. E. and Willig, R. D., 'Weak Invisible Hand Theorems on the Sustainability of Multiproduct Natural Monopoly', (1977) 67(3) *Amer. Econ. Rev.* 350.

Baumol, W. J., Panzer, J., and Willig, R., *Contestable Markets and the Theory of Industry Structure* (New York: Harcourt, Brace, Jovanovich, 1982).

Bayliss, F. *et al.* (eds), *Health Care Ethics in Canada* (Toronto: Harcourt Brace, 1995).

Beauchamp, T. L. and Childress, J. F., *Principles of Biomedical Ethics*, 4th edn, (New York: Oxford University Press, 1994)

Blendon, R. J. *et al.*, 'Satisfaction with Health Systems in Ten Nations', (1990) 9(2) *Health Affairs* 185.

Blomqvist, A. and Brown, D. M., *Limits to Care: Reforming Canada's Health System in an Age of Restraint* (Toronto: C. D. Howe Institute, 1994).

Brennan, G. and Buchanan, J. M., 'Is Public Choice Immoral? The Case for the "Noble" Lie', (1988) 74 *Virginia Law Rev.* 179.

Broomberg, J., Mills, A. and Masobe, P., 'To Purchase or to Provide? The Relative Efficiency of Contracting Out Versus Direct Public Provision of Hospital Services in South Africa' (paper presented to the International Health Economics Association Inaugural Conference, Vancouver, 19–24 May 1996).

Buchanan, J., *Liberty, Markets and State: Political Economy in the 1980s* (Brighton: Wheatsheaf, 1986).

Burner, S. T., Waldo, D. R. and McKusick, D. R., 'National Health Expenditures Projections Through 2030', (1992) 14(1) *Health Care Financing Review* 1.

Callahan, D., 'What is a Reasonable Demand on Health Care Resources: Designing a Basic Package of Benefit', (1992) 8 *J. of Contemporary Health Law and Policy* 1.

Canadian Bar Association Task Force on Health Care *What's Law Got to Do with it? Health Care Reform in Canada*, (Ottawa: The Canadian Bar Association, 1994).

Carr-Hill, R. A., 'Efficiency and Equity Implications of the Health Care Reforms', (1994) 39(9) *Soc. Sci. Med.* 1189.

Coase, R. H., 'The Nature of the Firm', (1937) 4 *Economica* 386.

— 'The Problem of Social Cost', (1960) 3 *Economica* 1.

Corning, P. A., *The Evolution of Medicare…From Idea to Law* (Washington, DC: Department of Health, Education, and Welfare, 1969).

Coyte, P. C., 'Review of Physician Payment and Service Delivery Mechanisms', (April 1995) *Ontario Medical Rev.* 23.

Crocker, K. J. and Masten, S. E., 'Regulation and Administered Contracts Revisited: Lessons from Transaction-Cost Economics for Public Utility Regulation', (1996) 9(1) *J. of Regulatory Econ.* 5.

Culyer, A. J., 'The Nature of the Commodity Health Care and its Efficient Allocation', (1971) 23 *Oxford Economic Papers* 189.

Daniels, N., *Just Health Care* (Cambridge: Cambridge University Press, 1985).

Danzon, P. M., 'Hidden Overhead Costs: Is Canada's System Really Less Expensive?', (1992) (Spring) *Health Affairs* 1.

Demsetz, H., 'Why Regulate Monopoly?', (1968) *J. of Law and Econ.* 55.

— 'The Theory of the Firm Revisited', in O. E. Williamson and S. G. Winter (eds), *The Nature of the Firm: Origins, Evolution, and Development* (New York: Oxford University Press, 1991).

Dewees, D. and Trebilcock, M., 'The Efficacy of the Tort System and its Alternatives: A Review of Empirical Evidence', (1992) 30(1) *Osgoode Hall Law J.* 57.

Dewees, D., Trebilcock, M. and Coyte, P. C., 'The Medical Malpractice Crisis: A Comparative Empirical Perspective', (1991) 54(1) *Law and Contemp. Probs.* 217.

Donabedian, A., 'Quality Assessment and Assurance: Unity of Purpose, Diversity of Means', (1988) 25(1) *Inquiry* 173.

Donahue, J. D., *The Privatization Decision: Public Ends, Private Means* (New York: Basic Books, 1988).

Donaldson, C. and Gerard, K., *Economics of Health Care Financing: The Visible Hand* (London: Macmillan, 1992).

Donelan, K. *et al.*, 'All Payer, Single Payer, Managed Care, No Payer: Patients' Perspectives in Three Nations', (1996) 15(2) *Health Affairs* 254.

Dougherty, C. J., 'An Axiology for National Health Insurance', (1992) 20:(1–2) *Law Medicine and Health Care* 82.

Dworkin, R., 'Justice in the Distribution of Health Care', (1993) 38(4) *McGill Law Journal* 883.

Eddy, D. M., 'Performance Measurement: Problems and Solutions', (1998) 17(4) *Health Affairs* 7.

Enthoven, A. C., 'Consumer-Choice Health Plan (First of Two Parts): Inflation and Inequity in Health Care Today: Alternatives for Cost Control and an Analysis of Proposals for National Health Insurance', (1978) 298(12) *New Eng. J. of Medicine* 650.

— 'Consumer-Choice Health Plan (Second of Two Parts): A National-Health-Insurance Proposal Based on Regulated Competition in the Private Sector', (1978) 298(13) *New Eng. J. of Medicine* 709.

— 'The History and Principles of Managed Competition', (1993) 12 (Supp.) *Health Affairs* 24.
— 'On the Ideal Market Structure for Third-Party Purchasing of Health Care', (1994) 39(10) *Soc. Sci. Med.* 1413.
Enthoven, A. C. and Singer, S. J., 'Market-Based Reform: What to Regulate and by Whom', (1995) 14(1) *Health Affairs* 105.
Emanuel, E. J. and Emanuel, L. L., 'What is Accountability in Health Care?', (1996) 124 *Ann. Intern. Med.* 229.
Ettner, S. L., 'New Evidence on the Relationship Between Income and Health', (1996) 15 *J. of Health Econs.* 67.
Evans, R. G., *Strained Mercy: The Economics of Canadian Health Care* (Toronto: Butterworths, 1984).
— 'The Canadian Health-Care Financing and Delivery System: Its Experience and Lessons for other Nations', (1992) 10 *Yale Law and Policy Review* 362.
— 'Going for the Gold: The Redistributive Agenda Behind Market-Based Health Care Reform', (1998) 22(2) *J. Health Polit Policy Law* 427.
Evans, R. G., Barer, M. L. and Marmor, T. R. (eds), *Why Are Some People Healthy and Others Not? The Determinants of Health of Populations* (New York: Aldine De Gruyter, 1994).
Fama, E., 'Agency Problems and the Theory of the Firm', (1980) 88 *J. of Polit. Econ.* 288.
Farber, D. A., 'Democracy and Disgust: Reflections on Public Choice', (1991) 65 *Chi. Kent L. Rev.* 161
Farber, D. and Frickey, P., *Law and Public Choice: A Critical Introduction* (Chicago, IL: University of Chicago Press, 1991).
Flannigan, R., 'The Economic Structure of the Firm', (1995) 33(1) *Osgoode Hall Law J.* 105.
Flood, C. M., 'Will Supplementary Private Insurance Reduce Waiting Lists?', (1996) 11 *Canadian Health Facilities Law Guide* 1.
— 'Prospects for New Zealand's Reformed Health System', (1996) 4 *Health Law Journal* 87.
— 'Conflicts Between Professional Interests, the Public Interest, and Patients' Interests in an Era of Reform: Nova Scotia Registered Nurses', (1997) 5 *Health Law Journal* 87.
— 'The Structure and Dynamics of Canada's Health Care System', in J. Downie and T. Caulfield (eds), *Canadian Health Law and Policy* (Butterworths: Toronto, 1999), 5–50.
— 'Contracting Out for Health Services in the Public Sector', (1999) 31 *Canadian Business Law Journal* 175.
— 'Accountability of Health Service Purchasers', (1998) 20(2) *Dalhousie Law Journal* 470.
— 'Preface', (1998) 20(2) *Dalhousie Law Journal* 313.
— 'Competing Crown Health Enterprises: Efficiency or Waste?', (1995) 118 *Planning Law uarterly: Journal of the New Zealand Planning Institute* 12.
— 'Exit and Voice in New Zealand's Health Care Sector' (with Michael Trebilcock) *Contracting in the Health Sector* (Auckland: Legal Research Foundation, 1994).
Foster, C. D., *Privatization, Public Ownership and the Regulation of Natural Monopoly* (Oxford: Blackwell, 1992).
Frank, R. H., *Microeconomics and Behavior* (New York: McGraw-Hill, Inc., 1991).
Fuchs, V. R., 'Economics, Health, and Post-Industrial Society', (1979) 57(2) *Milbank Mem. Fund Quart.* 153.
— 'The Supply of Surgeons and the Demand for Operations', in V. R. Fuchs (ed.), *The Health Economy* (Cambridge, MA: Harvard University Press, 1986).
— 'Economics, Values, and Health Care Reform', (1996) 86(1) *Amer. Econ. Rev.* 1.
Ginsburg, P. B. and Pickering, J. D., 'Tracking Health Care Costs', (1996) 15(3) *Health Affairs* 140.

Goldberg, V., 'Regulation and Administered Contracts', (1976) 7 *Bell J. of Econs.* 426.

Gosfield, A. G., 'Who is Holding Whom Accountable for Quality?', (1997) 16(3) *Health Affairs* 26.

Greenberg, W., *Competition, Regulation and Rationing in Health Care* (Ann Arbor, Michigan: Health Administration Press, 1991).

Harden, I., *The Contracting State* (Buckingham: Open University Press, 1992).

Hawkins, K. (ed.), *The Uses of Discretion* (Oxford: Clarendon Press, 1992).

Health Care Study Group, 'Understanding the Choices in Health Care Reform', (1994) 19(3) *J. Health Polit Policy Law* 499.

Himmelstein, D., Wolfe, S. and Woolhandler, S., 'Mangled Competition', (1993) *American Prospect* 116(13).

Himmelstein, D. and Woolhandler, S., 'The Deteriorating Administrative Efficiency of the U.S. Health Care System', (1991) 324(18) *New Eng. J. of Med.* 1253.

— 'Correction: The Deteriorating Administrative Efficiency of the US Health Care System', (1994) 331(5) *New Eng. J. of Med.* 336.

Hirschman, A. O., *Exit, Voice, and Loyalty – Responses to Decline in Firms, Organizations, and States* (Cambridge, MA: Harvard University Press, 1970).

Hirshfeld, E. B. and Thomason, G. H., 'Medical Necessity Determinations: The Need for a New Legal Structure', (1996) 6(1) *Health Matrix* 3.

Hurley, J. and Johnson, N., 'The Effects of Co-Payments Within Drug Reimbursement Programs', (1991) 18(34) *Canadian Public Policy* 473.

Hurley, J. and Labelle, R., 'Relative Fees and the Utilization of Physicians' Services in Canada', (1995) 4(6) *Health Economics* 419.

Hurowitz, J. C., 'Towards a Social Policy for Health', (1993) 329(2) *New Eng. J. of Med.* 130.

Hurst, J. W., 'Reforming Health Care in Seven European Nations', (1991) *Health Affairs* 7.

— *The Reform of Health Care: A Comparative Analysis of Seven OECD Countries*, OECD Health Policy Studies No. 2 (Paris: OECD, 1992).

Imai, H., 'Bilateral Price-Setting in a Bilateral Monopoly Model', (1986) 24 *J. Econ. Theory* 311.

Kaplow, L., 'Extension of Monopoly Power Through Leverage', (1985) 85(1–4) *Columbia Law Rev.* 515.

Kelman, M., 'On Democracy-Bashing: A Skeptical Look at the Theoretical and "Empirical" Practice of the Public Choice Movement', (1988) 71 *Va. L. R.* 199 .

King, J., 'No Fault Compensation for Medical Injuries', (1992) 8 *J. of Contemporary Health Law and Policy* 227.

Kronick, R., *et al.*, 'The Marketplace in Health Care Reform: The Demographic Limitations of Managed Competition', (1993) 328(2) *New Eng J. Med.* 148.

Labelle, R., Stoddart, G. and Rice, T., 'A Re-Examination of the Meaning and Importance of Supplier-Induced Demand', (1994) 13 *J. of Health Econs.* 347.

Lassey, M. L., Lassey, W. R. and Jinks, M. J., *Health Care Systems Around the World: Characteristics, Issues, Reforms* (Upper Saddle River, NJ: Prentice Hall, 1997).

Le Grand, J., 'Inequality in Health: Some International Comparisons', (1987) 31 *Europ. Econ. Rev.* 182.

Levit, K. R. *et al.*, 'National Health Spending Trends, 1960–1993', (1994) 13(5) *Health Affairs* 14.

Llewellyn, K. N., 'What Price Contract? An Essay in Perspective', (1931) 40 *Yale Law J.* 704.

Lohr, K. N. *et al.*, 'Use of Medical Care in the RAND Health Insurance Experiment: Diagnosis- and Service-Specific Analyses of a Randomized Controlled Trial', (1986) 25 (Supp.) *Medical Care* 531.

Luft, H. S. and Maerki, S. C., 'Competitive Potential of Hospitals and their Neighbours', (1984) 3 *Contemporary Policy Issues* 89.

Malck, M. *et al.* (eds), *Strategic Issues in Health Care Management* (Chichester: John Wiley, 1993).

Malinowski, M. J., 'Capitation, Advances in Medical Technology, and the Advent of a New Era in Medical Ethics', (1996) 22(2) *American J. of Law and Medicine* 331.

Maynard, A., 'Health Care Reform: Don't Confuse Me With Facts Stupid!', in *Four Country Conference on Health Care Reform and Health Care Policies in the United States, Canada, Germany and the Netherlands, Conference Report* (Amsterdam and Rotterdam: Ministry of Health, Welfare, and Sport, 1995) 47.

McAuslan, P., 'Public Law and Public Choice', (1988) 51(6) *Modern Law Review* 681.

MacNeil, I. R., 'Contracts: Adjustment of Long-Term Economic Relations Under Classical, Neo-classical and Relational Contract Law', (1978) 72 *Northwestern University Law Review* 854.

McGlynn, E. A., 'Quality in a Changing System: Challenges in Measuring Quality', (1997) 16(3) *Health Affairs* 7.

McLachlan, G. and Maynard, A., *The Public/Private Mix for Health: The Relevance and Effects of Change* (London: Nuffield Provincial Hospitals Trust, 1982).

McLean, I., *Public Choice: An Introduction* (Oxford: Basil Blackwell, 1987).

Menzel, P. T., 'Equality, Autonomy and Efficiency: What Health Care System Should We Have?', (1992) 33 *J. of Medicine and Philosophy* 33.

Miller, R. H., 'Health System Integration: A Means to an End', (1996) 15(2) *Health Affairs* 92.

Mooney, G., 'What Does Equity in Health Mean?', (1987) 40 *Wld. Hlth. Stat. Q.* 196.

Morone, J., 'Seven Laws of Policy Analysis', (1986) 5(4) *J. of Policy Analysis and Management* 818.

Mossialos, E., 'Citizens' Views on Health Care Systems in the 15 Member States of the European Union', (1997) 6(2) *Health Economics* 109

National Forum, *Canada Health Action: Building on the Legacy* (Ottawa: National Forum on Health, 1997)

National Health Expenditures in Canada 1975–1994, Summary Report (Ottawa: Health Canada, 1996).

Newhouse, J. P. *et al.*, 'Some Interim Results from a Controlled Trial of Cost Sharing in Health Insurance', (1981) 305(25) *New Eng. J. of Med.* 1501.

Newman, P., 'Interview With Alain Enthoven: Is There Convergence Between Britain and the United States in the Organisation of Health Services?', (1995) 310 *BMJ.* 1652.

Olsen, T. E., 'Agency Costs and the Limits of Integration', (1996) 27(3) *RAND J. of Econ.* 479.

Organization for Economic Cooperation and Development, *OECD Health Policy Studies No. 2, The Reform of Health Care: A Comparative Analysis of Seven OECD Countries* (Paris: OECD, 1992).

— *The Reform of Health Care Systems: A Review of Seventeen OECD Countries* (Paris: OECD, 1994).

— *OECD Health Data 98: A Comparative Analysis of 29 Countries* (Electronic Database).

Osborne, D. E. and Gaebler, T., *Reinventing Government: How the Entrepreneurial Spirit is Transforming the Public Sector* (Reading, MA: Addison-Wesley Publishers, 1992).

Pauly, M. V., 'The Economics of Moral Hazard: Comment', (1968) 58(3) *Amer. Econ. Rev.* 531.

Phelps, C., *Health Economics* (New York: Harper Collins, 1992).

Posner, R., *Antitrust Law: An Economic Perspective* (Chicago, IL: University of Chicago Press, 1976).

— 'The Chicago School of Anti-trust Analysis', (1979) 127 *U. Pa. Law Rev.* 925.

Poullier, J.-P., (OECD), *OECD Health Systems: Facts and Trends, 1960–1991, Vol. 1* (Paris: OECD, 1993).

— *OECD Health Systems: The Socio-Economic Environment Statistical References, Vol. II* (Paris: OECD, 1993).

Priest, G. L., 'The Origins of Utility Regulation and the "Theories of Regulation" Debate', (1993) 36 *J. of Law and Econ.* 289.

Raffel, M. W. and Raffel, N. K. (eds), *Perspectives on Health Policy: Australia, New Zealand and the United States* (Great Britain: John Wiley and Sons, 1987).

Ramsay, C. and Walker, M., *Waiting Your Turn: Hospital Waiting Lists in Canada* (Vancouver: The Fraser Institute, 1996).

Rasell, M. E., 'Sounding Board: Cost Sharing in Health Insurance: A Reexamination', (1995) 332(17) *New Eng. J. of Med.* 1164.

Rawls, J., *A Theory of Justice* (Cambridge, MA: The Belknap Press of Harvard University Press, 1971).

Reinhardt, U. E., 'The Theory of Physician-Induced Demand: Reflections after a Decade', (1985) 4 *Health Economics* 111.

— 'Lineage of Managed Competition', (1994) 2 *Health Affairs* 290.

Reisman, D., *Market and Health* (New York: St. Martin's Press, 1993).

Rice, T., 'Can Markets Give Us the Health System We Want?', (1997) 22(2) *J. Health Polit. Policy Law* 383.

Rochet, J. C., 'Some Recent Results In Bargaining Theory', (1987) 31 *Europ. Econ. Rev.* 326.

Rodwin, M. A., 'Conflicts in Managed Care' (1995) 332 (9) *New Eng. J. of Med.* 604.

Rothschild, M. and Stiglitz, J. E., 'Equilibrium in Competitive Insurance markets: An Essay on the Economics of Imperfect Information', (1976) 90(4) *Quart. J. of Econ.* 630.

Rublee, D. A., 'Medical Technology in Canada, Germany, and the United States: An Update', (1994) 13(4) *Health Affairs* 113.

Saltman, R. B., Figueras, J. and Sakellarides, C. (eds), *Critical Challenges for Health Care Reform in Europe* (Buckingham; Philadelphia PA: Open University Press 1998)

Saltman, R. B. and von Otter, C., *Planned Markets and Public Competition: Strategic Reform in Northern European Health Systems* (Buckingham: Open University Press, 1992).

Saltman, R. B. and von Otter, C. (eds), *Implementing Planned Markets in Health Care: Balancing Social and Economic Responsibility* (Buckingham: Open University Press, 1995).

Schieber, G. J. *et al.*, 'Health Spending, Delivery, and Outcomes in OECD Countries', (1993) 12(2) *Health Affairs* 120.

Schieber, G. J., Poullier, J.-P. and Greenwald, L. M., 'Health System Performance in OECD Countries, 1980–1992', (1994) 13(4) *Health Affairs* 100.

Schulman, K. A. *et al.*, 'The Effect of Race and Sex on Physicians' Recommendations for Cardiac Catheterization', (1999) 340(8) *New Eng. J. Of Med.* 618.

Schwart, F. W., Glennerster, H. and Saltman, R. (eds), *Fixing Heatlh Care Budgets: Experience from Europe and North America* (Chichester; New York: John Wiley, 1996)

Schwartz, R. L., 'Life Style, Health Status, and Distributive Justice', (1993) 3 *Health Matrix* 195.

Sen, A. K., *On Ethics and Economics* (Oxford: Basil Blackwell, 1987).

Smith, S. R. and Lipsky, M., 'Privatization in Health and Human Services: A Critique', (1992) 17(2) *J. of Health Polit. Policy Law* 233.

Stoddart, G. L., Barer, M. L., Evans, R. G. and Bhatia, V., *Why Not User Charges? The Real Issues: A Discussion Paper* (Ontario: The Premier's Council on Health, Well-Being and Social Justice, 1993).

Swedish Parliamentary Priorities Commission, *Priorities in Health Care* (Stockholm: Ministry of Health and Social Affairs, 1995).

Thomson, R. B., 'Review: Competition Among Hospitals in the United States', (1994) 27(3) *Health Policy* 205.

Train, K. E., *Optimal Regulation: The Economic Theory of Natural Monopoly* (Cambridge, MA: The MIT Press, 1991).

Trebilcock, M. J., *The Prospects for Reinventing Government* (Toronto: C. D. Howe Institute, 1994).

Tuohy, C. H., *Accidental Logics: The Dynamics of Change in the Health Care Arena in the United States, Britain and Canada* (New York: Oxford University Press, 1999)

Vagero, D., 'Equity and Efficiency in Health Reform: A European View', (1994) 39(9) *Soc. Sci. Med.* 1203.

Vickers, J. and Yarrow, G., *Privatization: An Economic Analysis* (Cambridge, MA: The MIT Press, 1988).

Vladeck, B. C., 'The Market vs. Regulation: The Case for Regulation', (1981) 59(2) *Milbank Mem. Fund Quart.* 209.

Wagstaff, A. and van Doorslaer, E., 'Equity in the Finance of Health Care: Some International Comparisons', (1992) 11 *J. of Health Econ.* 361.

Wallack, S. S. *et al.*, 'A Plan for Rewarding Efficient HMOs', (1988) 7(3) *Health Affairs* 80.

Walzer, M., *Spheres of Justice: A Defense of Pluralism and Equality* (New York: Basic Books, 1983).

Weale, A., 'Equality, Social Solidarity and the Welfare State', (1992) 100 *Ethics* 473.

Welch, W. P., Verrilli, D., Katz, S. J. and Latimer, E., 'A Detailed Comparison of Physician Services for the Elderly in the United States and Canada', (1996) 275(18) *JAMA* 1410.

Williams, S. R., 'Efficient Performance in Two-Agent Bargaining', (1987) 41 *J. Econ. Theory* 154.

Williamson, O. E., *Markets And Hierarchies: Analysis and Antitrust Implications* (New York: The Free Press, 1975).

— *The Economic Institutions of Capitalism: Firms, Markets, Relational Contracting* (New York: The Free Press, 1985).

— 'Hierarchical Control and Optimum Firm Size', in O. E. Williamson (ed.), *Economic Organization: Firms, Markets and Policy Control* (New York: New York University Press, 1986).

— (ed.) *Economic Organization: Firms, Markets and Policy Control* (New York: New York University Press, 1986).

— 'Comparative Economic Organization: The Analysis of Discrete Structural Alternatives', (1991) 36 *Admin. Sci. Q.* 269.

Yao, D. A., Riordan, M. H. and Dahdouh, T. N., 'Antitrust and Managed Competition for Health Care', (1994) 39(2) *The Antitrust Bulletin* 301.

Zalkind, D. L. and Eastaugh, S. R., 'Mortality Rates as an Indicator of Hospital Quality', (1997) 42(1) *Hospital and Health Care Services Administration* 3.

Zweifel, P. and Frech III, H. E. (eds), *Health Economics Worldwide* (Boston: Kluwer Academic Publishers, 1992).

The Netherlands

Akveld, A. and Hermans, H., *The Netherlands* (Boston: Kluwer Academic Publishers, 1995).

Anonymous, 'Changes in Dutch Health Care', (1995) 345 *The Lancet* 50.

Capsarie, A. F., 'View from the Netherlands', (1993) 2 *Quality in Health Care* 138.

Bos, M., 'Health Care Technology in the Netherlands', (1994) 30 *Health Policy* 207.

Delnoj, D. M. J., *Physician Payment Schemes and Cost Control* (Utrecht: Nivel, 1994).

de Leeuw, E. and Polman, L., 'Health Policy Making: The Dutch Experience', (1995) 40(3) *Soc. Sci. Med.* 331.

Ham, C. and Brommels, M., 'Health Care Reform in the Netherlands, Sweden, and the United Kingdom', (1994) *Health Affairs* 106.

Government Committee on Choices in Health Care, *Choices in Health Care* (Rijswijk: Ministry of Welfare, Health and Cultural Affairs, 1992) (English version).

Lamers, L. M. and van Vliet, R. C. J. A., 'Multiyear Diagnostic Information from Prior Hospitalizations as a Risk-Adjuster for Capitation Payments', (1996) 34(6) *Medical Care* 549.

Kirkman-Liff, B. L., 'Cost Containment and Physician Payment Methods in the Netherlands', (1989) 26 *Inquiry* 468.

— 'Health Insurance Values and Implementation in the Netherlands and the Federal Republic of Germany: An Alternative Path to Universal Coverage', (1991) 265(19) *JAMA* 2496.

— 'Health Care Reform in the Netherlands, Germany, and the United Kingdom' in A. Blomqvist and D. M. Brown (eds), *Limits to Care: Reforming Canada's Health System in an Age of Restraint* (Toronto: C. D. Howe Institute, 1994) p. 167.

Maarse, J. A. M., 'Hospital Budgeting in Holland: Aspects, Trends and Effects', (1989) 11 *Health Policy* 257.

Ministry of Health, Welfare and Sport, *Fact Sheet: Health Care Reform in the Netherlands* (Rijswijk: Ministry of Welfare, Health and Cultural Affairs, 1993).

— *Fact Sheet: The Individual Health Care Professions Act (BIG)* (Rijswijk: Ministry of Welfare, Health and Cultural Affairs, 1994).

— *Fact Sheet: Medical Treatment Contracts Act* (Rijswijk: Ministry of Welfare, Health and Cultural Affairs, 1995).

— *Fact Sheet: Health Care Inspectorate* (Rijswijk: Ministry of Welfare, Health and Cultural Affairs, 1995).

Ministry of Welfare, Health and Cultural Affairs, *Care in the Netherlands 1994* (Rijswijk: Ministry of Welfare, Health and Cultural Affairs, 1996.)

Netherlands Central Bureau of Statistics, 'The Uninsured for Health Care Costs 1985–1992: An Updating', (1993) 12(10) *Monthly Bulletin of Health Statistics*.

Nuijens, W. J. F. I., 'The Collectivisation of Health Insurance', (1992) 34(9) *Soc. Sci. Med.* 1049.

Rutten, F. and van der Linden, J., 'Integration of Economic Appraisal and Health Care Policy in a Health Insurance System: The Dutch Case', (1994) 38(12) *Soc. Sci. Med.* 1609.

Rutten, F. and van der Werft, A., 'Health Policy in the Netherlands: At the Crossroads', in G. McLachlin and A. Maynard (eds), *The Public/Private Mix for Health: The Relevance and Effects of Change* (London: Nuffield Provincial Hospitals Trust, 1982).

Ruwaard, D., Kramers, P. G. N., van den Berg Jeths, A. and Achterberg, P. W. (eds), *Public Health Status and Forecasts: The Health Status of the Dutch Population over the Period 1950–2120* (The Hague: SDU Uitgeverij, 1994) 27.

Schrijvers, J. P., 'Letter from Utrecht: The Netherlands Introduces Some Competition into the Health Services', (1991) 266(16) *JAMA* 2215.

Schut, F. T., 'Prospects for Workable Competition in Health Care: Dutch Design and American Experience', (paper for the Second World Congress on Health Economics, Zürich, 10–14 September 1990), Erasmus University, Rotterdam.

— 'Workable Competition in Health Care: Prospects For The Dutch Design', (1992) 35(12) *Soc. Sci. Med.* 1445.

— *Competition in the Dutch Health Care Sector* (PhD Thesis, Health Economics, Erasmus University, Rotterdam, 1995).

— 'Health Care Reform in the Netherlands: Balancing Corporatism, Etatism, and Market Mechanisms', (1995) 20(3) *J. of Health Polit. Policy Law* 615.

Schut, F. T., Greenberg, W. and van de Ven, W. P. M. M., 'Antitrust Policy in the Dutch Health Care System and the Relevance of EEC Competition Policy and US Antitrust Practice', (1991) 17 *Health Policy* 257.

Schut, F. T. and Hassink, W. H. J., 'Price Competition in Social Health Insurance: Evidence from the Netherlands', (paper prepared for the second iHEA Conference in Rotterdam, 6–9 June 1999).

Schut, F. T., and Hermans, H. E. G. M., 'Managed Competition Reforms in the Netherlands and its Lessons for Canada', (1997) 20(2) *Dalhousie Law Journal* 437.

Sonneveldt, T., *On the Role of Government in Health Care: A General Comparison Between the Debates on Health Care Reform in the Netherlands and the US* (Rijswijk: Ministry of Welfare, Health and Cultural Affairs, 1994).

Spanjer, M., 'Changes in Dutch Health-Care', (7 January 1995) 345 *The Lancet* 50.

ten Have, H. and Keasberry, H., 'Equity and Solidarity: The Context of Health Care in the Netherlands', (1992) 17 *J. of Medicine and Philosophy* 463.

Tymstra, T. and Andela, M., 'Opinions of Dutch Physicians, Nurses, and Citizens on Health Care Policy, Rationing, And Technology', (1993) 270(24) *JAMA* 2995.

Uniken Venema, H. P., Garretsen, H. F. L. and van der Maas, P. J., 'Health of Migrants and Migrant Health Policy: The Netherlands as an Example', (1995) 41(6) *Soc. Sci. Med.* 809.

van de Ven, W. P. M. M., 'Perestrojka in the Dutch Health Care System: A Demonstration Project for Other European Countries', (1991) 35 *European Economic Review* 430.

— 'Regulated Competition in Health Care: With or Without a Global Budget', (1995) 39 *European Economic Review* 786.

van de Ven, W. P. M. M. and Rutten, F., 'Managed Competition in the Netherlands: Lessons From Five Years of Health Care Reform', (1995) 18(1) *Australian Health Review* 9.

van de Ven, W. P. M. M. and Schut, F. T., 'Should Catastrophic Risks be Included in a Regulated Competitive Health Insurance Market', (1994) 39(10) *Soc. Sci. Med.* 1462.

— 'The Dutch Experience With Internal Markets', in M. Jérôme-Forget, J. White, and J. M. Wiener (eds), *Health Care Reform Through Internal Markets: Experience and Proposals* (Montreal: IRPP, 1995) 95.

van de Ven, W. P. M. M., Schut, F. T. and Rutten, F. F. H., 'Forming and Reforming the Market for Third-Party Purchasing of Health Care', (1994) 39(10) *Soc. Sci. Med.* 1405.

van de Ven, W. P. M. M. and van Vliet, R. C. J. A., 'How Can We Prevent Cream Skimming in a Competitive Health Insurance Market? The Great Challenge for the 90s', in P. Zweifel and H. E. Frech III (eds), *Health Economics Worldwide* (Boston, MA/Dordrecht: Kluwer Academic Publishers, 1992) 23.

— 'Capitation Payments Based on Prior Hospitalizations', (1993) 2 *Health Econ.* 177.

— 'Consumer Information Surplus and Adverse Selection in Competitive Health Insurance Markets: An Empirical Study', (1995) 14 *J. of Health Econ.* 149.

van de Ven, W. P. M. M., van Vliet, R. C. J. A., van Barneveld, E. M. and Lamers, L. M., 'Risk-Adjusted Capitation: Recent Experiences in the Netherlands', (1994) 13(5) *Health Affairs* 120.

van der Vilt, G.-J., 'Health Care and the Principle of Fair Equality of Opportunity', (1994) 8(4) *Bioethics* 329.

van Vliet, R. C. J. A., 'Predictability of Individual Health Care Expenditures', (1992) 59(3) *J. of Risk and Insurance* 443.

van Vliet, R. C. J. A. and van de Ven, W. P. M. M., 'Towards a Capitation Formula for Competing Health Insurers: An Empirical Analysis', (1992) 34(9) *Soc. Sci. Med.* 1035.

— 'Capitation Payments Based on Prior Hospitalizations', (1993) 2 *Health Economics* 177.

Wijnberg, B., 'Patients' Rights and Legislative Strategies', (1993) 12 *Med Law* 137.

Ziekenfondswet (Sickness Funds Insurance Act) Act of 15 October 1964, *Staatsblad* (Official Journal of the State) 392.

New Zealand

Ashton, T., 'Reform of the Health Service: Weighing up the Costs and Benefits', in J. Boston and P. Dalziel (eds), *The Decent Society* (Auckland: Oxford University Press, 1992).

— 'Competition Among Hospitals: The Theory and the Practice', (paper presented at the 1993 Residential Winter Conference, New Zealand Association of Economists, 23–25 August 1993).

— 'Voice and Exit in New Zealand's Health Care Sector: Commentary', in *Contracting in the Health Sector:*, (papers presented at a seminar held by the Legal Research Foundation at the University of Auckland on 6 July 1994) (Auckland: Legal Research Foundation, 1994).

— 'Contracting for Health Services in New Zealand: Early Experiences' (paper presented at the International Health Economics Association Inaugural Conference, Vancouver, 19–23 May 1996).

— 'Contracting the Kiwi Way: Costly or Constructive?' (paper presented at the CHEPA 10th Annual Health Policy Conference, Hamilton, Ontario, 21–23 May 1997).

Ashton, T., Beasley, A., Alley, P. and Taylor, G., 'Reforming the New Zealand Health System: Lessons From Other Countries', (Report of a Study Tour Sponsored by Health Boards New Zealand, April 1991).

Ashton, T. and Press, D., 'Market Concentration in Secondary Health Services Under a Purchaser-Provider Split: The New Zealand Experience', (1997) 6(1) *Health Economics* 43.

Bowie, R. D., 'Health Expenditure and the Health Reforms: A Comment', (1992) 105(945) *New Zealand Med. J.* 458.

Collins, D. B., 'The Impact of No-Fault Compensation on the Regulation of Medical Practice in New Zealand', (1993) 12(1–2) *Medicine and Law* 61.

Consalvi, E. *Consalvi Directory of Decision Makers: New Zealand Public Sector Heatlh* (Auckland: Strategic Information Ltd, 1993). Available on-line by subscription at HTTP: http:// www.strategicinfo.co.nz

Core Services For 1995/96: Third Report of the National Advisory Committee on Core Health and Disability Support Services (Wellington: The National Advisory Committee on Core Health and Disability Support Services, 1994).

Crown Company Monitoring Advisory Unit, *Crown Health Enterprises: Briefing to the Incoming Minister* (Wellington: Crown Company Monitoring Advisory Unit, 1996).

Cumming, J., and Salmon, G., 'Reforming New Zealand Health Care', in W. Ranade (ed.), *Markets and Health Care: A Comparative Analysis* (London: Longman, 1998).

Davis, P., *Health and Health Care in New Zealand* (Auckland: Longman Paul, 1981).

Devlin, N. J., 'The Distribution of Household Expenditure on Health Care', (1993) 106(953) *New Zealand Med. J.* 126.

Gibbs, A., Scott, J. and Fraser, D., *Unshackling the Hospitals: Report of the Hospital and Related Services Taskforce* (Wellington: Government Printer, 1988).

Gorringe, P., Secondary Health Care: Contracting, People and Politics, draft of 5 November 1996 (prepared for the Central Regional Health Authority, New Zealand).

Grant, C. C., Forrest, C. B. and Starfield, B., 'Primary Care and Health Reform in New Zealand', (1997) 110 *New Zealand Med. J.* 35.

Hay, I., *The Caring Commodity: The Provision of Health Care in New Zealand* (Auckland: Oxford University Press, 1989).

Holland, M. and Boston, J. (eds), *The Fourth Labour Government: Politics and Policy in New Zealand*, 2nd ed., Chapter 7, reprinted in M. Chen and Rt. Hon. G. Palmer, *Public Law in New Zealand* (Auckland: Oxford University Press, 1993) 242.

Howden-Chapman, P., 'Doing the Splits: Contracting Issues in the New Zealand Health Service', (1993) 24(3) *Health Policy* 273.

Howden-Chapman, P. and Ashton, T., 'Shopping for Health: Purchasing Health Services Through Contracts', (1994) 29(1) *Health Policy* 61.

James, C., *New Territory: The Transformation of New Zealand, 1984–92* (Wellington: Bridget Williams Books, 1992).

Kawachi, I., Marshall, S. and Pearce, N., 'Social Class Inequalities in the Decline of Coronary Heart Disease Among New Zealand Men, 1975–77 to 1985–87', (1991) 20 *Int. J. Epidemiol.* 393.

Laing, P. and Pomare, E., 'Maori Health and the Health Care Reforms' (1994) 29(1–2) *Health Policy* 143.

Malcolm, L., 'Decentralisation of Health Management: A Review of the New Zealand Experience', (1986) 5(3) *Public Sector Research Papers* 4.

Malcolm, L. and Barnett, P., 'New Zealand's Health Providers in an Emerging Market', (1994) 29(1–2) *Health Policy* 85.

Malcolm, L. and Powell, M., 'The Development of Independent Practice Associations and Related Groups in New Zealand', (1996) 109(1022) *NZ Med. J.* 184.

Milroy, S. and Mikaere, A., 'Maori and the Health Reforms: Promises, Promises', (1994) 16(2) *New Zealand Universities Law Rev.* 175.

Minister of Health, *Policy Guidelines for Regional Health Authorities 1996/97* (publication details not given in the document but presumably published in Wellington by the Ministry of Health in November 1995).

— *Healthy New Zealanders: Briefing Papers for the Minister of Health 1996, Vol. 2, The Health and Disability Sector* (Wellington: Ministry of Health, 1996).

Ministry of Health, *Health Expenditures Trends in New Zealand 1980–1997* (Wellington: Ministry of Health, 1998). Online. Available HTTP: http://www.moh.govt.nz

Murchie, E., *Rapuora: Health and Maori Women* (Wellington: The Maori Women's Welfare League Inc., 1984).

Muthumala, D. and Howard, P. S., *Health Expenditure Trends in New Zealand 1980–1994* (Wellington: Ministry of Health, 1995).

Muthumala, D. and McKendy, C. G., *Health Expenditure Trends in New Zealand 1980–1991* (Wellington: Department of Health, 1991).

Naden, R., 'Contracting to Purchase Health and Disability Services: An RHA Perspective', in *Contracting in the Health Sector:*, (papers presented at a seminar held by the Legal Research Foundation at the University of Auckland on 6 July 1994) (Auckland: Legal Research Foundation, 1994) 64.

New Zealand Official 1993 Yearbook (Wellington: Department of Statistics, 1993).

Palmer, G., 'New Zealand's Accident Compensation Scheme: Twenty Years On', (1994) 44(3) *Univ. of Toronto Law J.* 223.

Pearce, N., Pomare, E., Marshall, S. and Borman, B., 'Mortality and Social Class in Maori and Non-Maori New Zealand Men: Changes Between 1975–7 and 1985–7', (1993) 106(956) *New Zealand Med. J.* 193.

Pomare, E. and de Boer, G., *Hauora: Maori Standards of Health*, (Wellington: Department of Health, 1988).

Purchasing for your Health: A Performance Report on the First Year of the Regional Health Authorities and Public Health Commission (Wellington: Ministry of Health, 1995).

Southern Cross Medical Care Society, *One Million Members: A Milestone* (Auckland: Southern Cross, 1988).

Todd, S. and Black, J., 'Accident Compensation and the Barring of Actions for Damages', (1993) 1(3) *Tort Law Review* 197.

Upton, S., *Your Health and the Public Health: A Statement of Government Health Policy* (Wellington: Minister of Health, July 1991).

— Health and Disability Services Bill: Introduction, (29 August 1992) *Hansard* 10773.

Wilson, G., 'Health Purchasing: A Regional Health Authority Perspective', (1995) 18(1) *Public Sector* 11.

United Kingdom

Allen, P., 'Contracts in the National Health Service Internal Market', (1995) 58(3) *Modern Law Rev.* 321.

— 'A Legal Perspective on Contracts in the NHS Internal Market' (Bristol: S.A.U.S. Publication, University of Bristol, 1995).

Anand, P. and McGuire, A. (eds), *Changes in Health Care: Reflections on the NHS Internal Market* (Basingstoke: Macmillan Business, 1997).

Audit Commission, *What the Doctor Ordered: A Study of GP Fundholders in England and Wales* (London: HMSO, 1996).

Barlett, W., 'Regulation, Trust and Incentives: Contractual Relations and Performance of NHS Quasi-Market', (paper prepared for the conference on Institutions, Markets and (Economic) Performance: Deregulation and Its Consequences, Utrecht University, 11–12 December 1997).

Beck, E., Lonsdale, S., Newman, S. and Patterson, D. (eds), *In the Best of Health? The Status and Future of Health Care in the UK* (London: Chapman and Hall, 1992).

Belcher, A., 'Codes of Conduct and Accountability for NHS Boards', (1995) *Public Law* 288

Besley, T., Hall, J. and Preston, I., *Private Health Insurance and the State of the NHS (Commentary No. 52)* (London: The Institute for Fiscal Studies, 1996).

Bloor, K. and Maynard, A., *Rewarding Excellence? Consultants' Distinction Awards and the Need for Reform (Discussion Paper 100)* (York: Centre for Health Economics, University of York, 1992.)

— 'Health Care Reform in the UK National Health Service', (paper prepared for the First Meeting of the International Health Economics Association, May 1996, Vancouver, British Columbia).

Bryden, P., 'The Future of Primary Care', in R. Loveridge and R. Starkey (eds), *Continuity and Crisis in the NHS: The Politics of Design and Innovation in Health Care* (Buckingham: Open University Press, 1992) 65.

Cairns, J. and Donaldson, C., 'Introduction to Economics in the New NHS', (1993) 25 *Health Policy* 1.

Carr-Hill, R., 'RAWP is Dead: Long Live RAWP', in A. J. Culyer, A. K. Maynard and J. W. Posnett (eds), *Competition in Health Care: Reforming the NHS* (Basingstoke: Macmillan Press, 1990) 192.

— 'Efficiency and Equity Implications of the Health Care Reforms', (1994) 39(9) *Soc. Sci. Med.* 1189.

Checkland, P., 'Rhetoric and Reality in Contracting: Research in and on the National Health Service', in R. Flynn and G. Williams (eds), *Contracting for Health: Quasi-Markets and the National Health Service* (New York: Oxford University Press, 1997).

Community Health Councils Regulations (UK) 1996, S. I. 1996/640.

Culyer, A. J., 'Chisels or Screwdrivers? A Critique of the NERA Proposals for the Reform of the NHS' in A. Towse, (ed.), *Financing Health Care in the UK: A Discussion of NERA's Prototype Model to Replace the NHS* (London: Office of Health Economics, 1995)

Culyer, A. J., Maynard, A. K. and Posnett, J. W., *Competition in Health Care: Reforming the NHS* (Basingstoke: Macmillan Press, 1990).

Culyer, A. J. and Meads, A., 'The United Kingdom: Effective, Efficient, Equitable?', (1992) 17 *J. of Health Polit. Policy Law* 667.

Dawson, D., *Regulating Competition in the NHS: The Department of Health Guide on Mergers and Anti-Competitive Behaviour, Discussion Paper 131* (York: Centre For Health Economics, 1995).

Day, P. and Klein, R., 'Britain's Health Care Experiment', (1991) 10(3) *Health Affairs* 39.

Department of Health, *Working for Patients*, Cm855 (London: HMSO, 1989).

— *Managing the New NHS: A Background Document* (London: HMSO, 1993).

— 'GP Fundholding Benefits to be Spread Further', news release 95/485, 18 October 1995.

— 'Changes to Health Service Structure Release £139 Million for Patient Care', news release 96/106, 1 April 1996.

Enthoven, A. C., 'NHS Market Reform', (1991) 10(3) *Health Affairs* 60.

Ferguson, B., 'Progress of the UK Health Reforms and the Role of Information: What Can the 'Dismal Science' Contribute?' (Discussion Paper 145, January 1996, Centre For Health Economics, The University of York).

Flynn, R. and Williams, G. (eds), *Contracting for Health: Quasi-Markets and the National Health Service* (New York: Oxford University Press, 1997).

Glennerster, H., 'GP Fundholding: Wild Care or Winning Hand?', in R. Robinson and J. Le Grand (eds), *Evaluating the NHS Reforms* (London: King's Fund Institute, 1994).

Glennerster, H. and Matsaganis, M., 'The UK Health Reforms: The Fundholding Experiment', (1993) 23 *Health Policy* 179.

Goldbeck-Wood, S., 'Survey Finds NHS Budgets Pushed to the Limit', (1996) 312 *BMJ* 1629.

Haines, A. and Liffe, S., 'Primary Health Care', in E. Beck, S. Lonsdale, S. Newman and D. Patterson (eds), *In the Best of Health?* (London: Chapman and Hall, 1992) 32.

Ham, C., 'Private Finance, Public Risk', (1995) 311 *BMJ* 1450.

Ham, C. and Maynard, A., 'Managing the NHS Market', (1994) 308 *BMJ* 845.

Harden, I., *The Contracting State* (Buckingham: Open University Press, 1992).

Harrison, A. (ed.), *Health Care UK 1994/95: An Annual Review of Health Care Policy* (Bristol: J. W. Arrowsmith, 1995).

Hughes, D., Griffith, L. and McCleeland, S., '"Cinderella" Services in the NHS Internal Market: Does Contracting Make a Difference?', (1997) 20(2) *Dalhousie Law Journal* 400.

Hughes, D., Griffith, L. and McHale, J., 'Purchasing in the NHS: Administered or Market Contracts?', in P. Anand and A. McGuire (eds), *Changes in Health Care: Reflections on the NHS Internal Market* (Basingstoke: Macmillan Business, 1997) 55.

— 'Settling Contract Disputes in the National Health Service: Formal and Informal Pathways', in R. Flynn and G. Williams (eds), *Contracting for Health: Quasi-Markets and the National Health Service* (New York: Oxford University Press, 1997) 98.

Klein, R., 'The NHS and the New Scientism: Solution or Delusion?', (1996) 89(1) *Q.J. Med.* 85.

Klein, R., 'Learning from Others: Shall the Last Be the First?', (1997) 22 *Jnl. of Health Politics, Policy and Law* 1267.

Klein, R., 'Why Britain is Reorganizing its National Health Service – Yet Again', (1998) 17(4) *Health Affairs* 111.

Laing, W., *Laing's Review of Private Healthcare 1994* (London: Lain and Buisson Publications, 1994).

Le Grand, J., 'Internal Market Rules OK', (1994) 309 *BMJ* 1596.

Longley, D., *Health Care Constitutions* (London: Cavendish Publishing, 1996).

Loveridge, R. and Starkey, K. (eds), *Continuity and Crisis in the NHS* (Buckingham: Open University Press, 1992).

Marks, J., 'The NHS: Beginning, Middle, and End?', (1990) 58(4) *Medico-Legal Journal* 217.

Mason, A. and Moran, K., 'Purchaser-Provider: The International Dimension', (1995) 310 *BMJ* 231.

Matsaganis, M. and Glennerster, H., 'The Threat of 'Cream Skimming' in the Post-reform NHS', (1994) 12 *J. of Health Econ.* 31.

Maynard, A., 'Can Competition Enhance Efficiency in Health Care? Lessons from the Reform of the UK National Health Service', (1994) 29(10) *Soc. Sci. Med.* 1433.

Maynard, A. and Bloor, K., 'Introducing a Market to the United Kingdom's National Health Service', (1996) 334 *New Eng. J. of Med.* 604.

Maynard, A. and Walker, A., 'Managing the Medical Workforce: Time for Improvements?', (1995) 31(1) *Health Policy* 1.

Mayston, D., 'NHS Resourcing: A Financial and Economic Analysis', in A. J. Culyer, A. K. Maynard and J. W. Posnett (eds), *Competition in Health Care: Reforming the NHS* (Basingstoke: Macmillan Press, 1990) 80.

McGuire, A. and Anand, P., 'Introduction: Evaluating Health Care Reform', in P. Anand and A. McGuire (eds), *Changes in Health Care: Reflections on the NHS Internal Market* (Basingstoke: Macmillan Business, 1997).

McHale, J., Hughes, D. and Griffiths, L., 'Conceptualizing Contractual Disputes in the National Health Service Internal Market', in S. Denkin and J. Michie (eds), *Contracts, Competition and Cooperation* (Oxford: Oxford University Press, 1997) 195.

Meek, C., '£80 Million Manager Explosion', (March 1994) *BMA News Review* 11.

New NHS: Modern, Dependable, a White Paper, Cm 3907 (8 December 1997). Online. Available HTTP: http://www.official-documents.co.uk/document/doh/newnhs/contents.htm (accessed 30 March 1999).

NHS Waiting Times Good Practice Guide, January 1996, (Leeds: NHS Executive, 1996).

Nicholl, J. P., Beeby, N. and Williams, B., 'Role of the Private Sector in Elective Surgery in England and Wales', (1986) 298 *BMJ* 243.

The Operation of the Internal Market: Local Freedoms, National Responsibilities (HSG (94) 55) (London: Department of Health, 1994).

Priorities and Planning Guidance for the NHS: 1997/98 (Leeds: NHS Executive, 1996).

Propper, C., 'Market Structure and Prices: The Response of NHS Hospitals to Costs and Competition' (mimeo, Dept. of Economics, University of Bristol, 1994).

— 'Agency and Incentives in the NHS Internal Market', (1995) 40(12) *Soc. Sci. Med.* 1683.

Propper, C. and Maynard, A., *The Market for Private Health Care and the Demand for Private Insurance in Britain (Discussion Paper No. 53)* (York: University of York, 1989).

— 'Whither the Private Health Care Sector?', in A. J. Culyer, A. K. Maynard and J. W. Posnett (eds), *Competition in Health Care: Reforming the NHS* (Basingstoke: Macmillan Press, 1990) 48.

Robinson, R. and Le Grand, J. (eds), *Evaluating the NHS Reforms* (London: King's Fund Institute, 1994).

— 'Contracting and the Purchaser-Provider Split', in R. B. Saltman and C. von Otter (eds), *Implementing Planned Markets in Health Care: Balancing Social and Economic Responsibility* (Buckingham: Open University Press, 1995) 25

Ryan, M. and Yule, B., 'The Way to Economic Prescribing', (1993) 25 *Health Policy* 25.

Scott, T. and Maynard, A., *Will the New GP Contract Lead to Cost Effective Medical Practice? (Discussion Paper No. 82)* (York: Center for Health Economics, University of York, 1991).

Shapiro, J. and Ham, C., 'The New Health Authorities', (1996) 2(2) *Health Services Management Center Newsletter* (University of Birmingham) 1.

Smith, P., 'Information Systems and the White Paper Proposals', in A. J. Culyer, A. K. Maynard and J. W. Posnett (eds), *Competition in Health Care: Reforming the NHS* (Basingstoke: Macmillan Press, 1990) 119.

Söderlund, N., 'Hospital Casemix, Costs, and Productivity in the NHS Internal Market', (paper presented to the International Health Economics Association Inaugural Conference – Vancouver, 19–24 May 1996).

Spiby, J., 'Health Care Technology in the United Kingdom', (1994) 30(1–3) *Health Policy* 295.

Sussex, J., *Controlling NHS Expenditure: The Impact of Labour's NHS White Papers* (London: Office of Health Economics, 1998).

Thomas, K., Nicholl, J. and Coleman, P., 'Assessing the Outcome of Making it Easier for Patients to Change General Practitioner: Practice Characteristics Associated With Patient Movements', (1995) 45 *British Journal of General Practice* 581.

Tingle, J. H., 'The Allocation of Healthcare Resources in the National Health Service in England: Professional and Legal Issues', (1993) 2 *Annals Of Health Law* 195.

Towse, A. (ed.), *Financing Health Care in the UK: A Discussion of NERA's Prototype Model to Replace the NHS* (London: Office of Health Economics, 1995).

Watt, I. and Freemantle, N. 'NHS Reforms', (1993) 306(6) *BMJ* 657.

United States of America

Aaron, H. J., 'Thinking Straight about Medical Costs', (1994) 13(5) *Health Affairs* 8.

American College of Physicians, 'Physician-Run Health Plans and Antitrust', (1996) 125(1) *Annals of Internal Medicine* 59.

American Medical Association, *The Cost of Medical Professional Liability in the 1980s* (Chicago: American Medical Association, 1990).

Anders, G., *Health Against Wealth: HMOs and the Breakdown of Medical Trust* (Boston: Houghton Mifflin, 1996).

Anderson, G. F., 'All-Payer Ratesetting: Down But Not Out', (1991) *Health Care Financing Review* 42

Anonymous, 'Managed-Care Docs Dissatisfied: Survey', (10 March 1997) *Modern Health-care* 22.

Arnould, R. J., Rich, R. F. and White, W. D. (eds), *Competitive Approaches to Health Care Reform* (Washington, DC: Urban Institute Press, 1993).

Baxter, R. J. and Mechanic, R. E., 'The Status of Local Health Care Safety Nets', (1997) 16(4) *Health Affairs* 7.

Berk, M. L. and Monheit, A. C., 'The Concentration of Health Expenditures: An Update', (1992) *Health Affairs* 145.

Berthgold, L. A., 'Perspectives: Benefit Package', (1993 Supp.) 12 *Health Affairs* 99.

Blendon, R. J. *et al.*, 'Satisfaction With Health Systems in Ten Nations', (1990) *Health Affairs* 185.

Blumenthal, D., 'Health Care Reform: Past and Future', (1995) 332(7) *New Eng. J. of Med.* 465.

Bovbjerg, R., 'Malpractice: Assessing the Health Security Act', (1994) 19(1) *J. of Health Polit. Policy Law* 207.

Bovbjerg, R. *et al.*, 'US Health Care Coverage and Costs: Historical Development and Choices for the 1990s', (1993) 21(2) *J. of Law Medicine and Ethics* 141.

Boyd, T. H., 'Cost Containment and the Physician's Fiduciary Duty to the Patient', (1989) 39 *DePaul L.R.* 131.

Brown, J. A., 'ERISA and State Health Care Reform: Roadblock or Scapegoat?', (1995) 13 *Yale Law and Policy Review* 339.

Brown, L. D. and Marmor, T. R., 'The Clinton Reform Plan's Administrative Structure: The Reach and the Grasp', (1994) 19(1) *J. Health Polit. Policy Law* 193.

Burner, S. T., Waldo, D. R. and McKusick, D. R., 'National Health Expenditures Projections Through 2030', (1992) 14(1) *Health Care Financing Review* 1.

Callahan, D., 'What is a Reasonable Demand on Health Care Resources? Designing a Basic Package of Benefits', (1992) 8 *J. of Contemporary Health Law and Policy* 1.

Danzon, P., 'The Hidden Costs of Budget-Constrained Health Insurance Systems' (paper presented at the American Enterprise Institute Conference, Washington, DC, 3 October 1991).

Dechene, J. C., 'Preferred Provider Organization Structures and Agreements', (1995) 4 *Annals Of Health Law* 35.

De Lew, N., Greenberg, G. and Kinchen, K., 'Special Report: A Layman's Guide to the US Health Care System', (1992) 14(1) *Health Care Financing Review* 151.

Dranove, D., 'The Case for Competitive Reform in Health Care', in R. J. Arnould, R. F. Rich and W. D. White (eds), *Competitive Approaches to Health Care Reform* (Washington, DC: Urban Institute Press, 1993) 79.

Ellwood, P. M. *et al*, 'Health Maintenance Strategy', (May 1971) *Medical Care* 250–256.

Enthoven, A. C., 'The History and Principles of Managed Competition', (1993) (Supp.) 12 *Health Affairs* 24.

Enthoven, A. C. and Kronick, R., 'A Consumer-Choice Health Plan for the 1990s: Universal Health Insurance in a System Designed to Promote Quality and Economy, I', (1989) 325 *New Eng. J. of Med.* 854.

Enthoven, A. C. and Singer, S. J., 'Market-Based Reform: What to Regulate and by Whom', (1995) *Health Affairs* 103.

Epstein, A. M. *et al.*, 'A Comparison of Ambulatory Test Ordering for Hypertensive Patients in the United States and England', (1984) 252 *JAMA* 1723.

Fielding, J. E. and Rice, T., 'Commentary: Can Managed Competition Solve the Problem of Market Failure?' (1993) (Supp.) 12 *Health Affairs* 216.

Frech III, H. E. (ed.), *Health Care in America: The Political Economy of Hospitals and Health Insurance* (San Francisco: Pacific Research Institute for Public Policy, 1988).

Gabel, J., 'Ten Ways HMOs Have Changed During the 1990s', (1997) 16(3) *Health Affairs* 134.

Ginsburg, P. D. and Pickering, J. D., 'Tracking Health Care Costs', (1996) 15(3) *Health Affairs* 140.

Glied, S., *Chronic Condition: Why Health Reform Fails* (Cambridge, MA: Harvard University Press, 1997).

Gold, M. R. *et al.*, 'A National Survey of the Arrangements Managed-Care Plans Make with Physicians', (1995) 333(25) *New Eng. J. of Med.* 1678.

Glaser, W. A., 'Universal Health Insurance That Really Works: Foreign Lessons for the United States', (1993) 18(3) *J. of Health Polit. Policy Law* 695.

Goldman, D. P. *et al.*, 'The Effects of Benefit Design and Managed Care on Health Care Costs', (1995) 14 *J. of Health Econ.* 401.

Greely, H. T., 'Direct Financial Incentives in Managed Care: Unanswered Questions', (1996) 6(1) *Health Matrix* 53.

Gruber, J., 'State-Mandated Benefits and Employer-Provided Health Insurance', (1994) 55 *J. of Public Econ.* 433.

Gruber, J. and Krueger, A., 'The Incidence of Mandated Employer-Provided Insurance: Lessons from Workers' Compensation Insurance', in D. Bradford (ed.), *Tax Policy and the Economy, vol. 5* (Cambridge, MA: MIT Press, 1991).

Halligan, C. J., '"Just What The Doctor Ordered": Oregon's Medicaid Rationing Process and Public Participation in Risk Regulation', (1995) 83 *Georgetown Law J.* 2697.

Hemenway, D. *et al.*, 'Physicians' Responses to Financial Incentives: Evidence from a For-Profit Ambulatory Care Center' (1990) 322 *New Eng. J. Med* 1059.

Hollingsworth, R. and Hollingsworth, E. J., *Controversy About American Hospitals: Funding Ownership and Performance* (Washington, DC: American Enterprise Institute, 1987).

Hovenkamp, H., *Federal Antitrust Law: The Law of Competition and its Practice* (St. Paul, MN: West Publishing Co., 1994).

Hoy, E. W. *et al.*, 'Change and Growth in Managed Care', (1991 Winter) *Health Affairs* 18.

Hoy, E. W., Wicks, E. K. and Forland, R. A., 'A Guide to Facilitating Consumer Choice', (1996) 15(4) *Health Affairs* 9.

Hsiao, W. C., Dunn, D. L. and Verrilli, D. K., 'Assessing the Implementation of Physician-Payment Reform', (1993) 328(13) *New Eng. J of Med.* 928.

Iglehart, J. K., 'The American Health Care System', (1992) 326 *New Eng. J. of Med.* 962.

— 'Health Policy Report, The American Health Care System: Medicaid', (1993) 328(12) *New Eng. J. of Med.* 896.

— 'Editorial', (1994) 13(5) *Health Affairs* 5.

— 'Health Policy Report: Physicians and the Growth of Managed Care', (1994) 331(17) *Health Policy Report* 1167.

— 'Health Policy Report: Republicans of the New Politics of Health Care', (1995) 332(14) *New Eng. J. of Med.* 922.

Issacs, S. L., 'Consumers' Information Needs: Results of a National Survey', (1996) 15(4) *Health Affairs* 31.

Jacobs, M. S., 'Recent Development in Antitrust Law and their Implications for the Clinton Health Care Plan', (1993) 21(2) *The J. of Law, Medicine and Ethics* 163.

Jensen, G. A., Morrisey, M. A., Gaffney, S. and Liston, D. K., 'The New Dominance of Managed Care: Insurance Trends in the 1990s', (1997) 16(1) *Health Affairs* 125.

King, G., 'Health Care Reform and the Medicare Program', (1994) 13(5) *Health Affairs* 39.

Kinney, E. D., 'Protecting Consumers and Providers Under Health Reform: An Overview of the Major Administrative Law Issues', (1995) 5 *Health Matrix* 83.

Kronick, R., 'A Helping Hand for the Invisible Hand', (1994) 13(1) *Health Affairs* 96.

Kronick, R. *et al.*, 'The Marketplace in Health Care Reform: The Demographic Limitations of Managed Competition', (1993) 328 *New Eng J. Med.* 148.

Langwell, K. M., 'Structure and Performance of Health Maintenance Organizations: A Review', (1990) 11(2) *Health Care Financing Review* 71.

Latham, S. R., 'Regulation of Managed Care: Incentive Payments to Physicians', (1996) 22(4) *American J. of Law and Medicine* 399.

Levit, K. R. *et al.*, 'National Health Spending Trends, 1960–1993', (1994) 13(5) *Health Affairs* 14.

Levit, K. R., Olin, G. L. and Letsch, S. W., 'Americans' Health Insurance Coverage, 1980–1991', (1992) 14(1) *Health Care Financing Review* 31.

Lohr, K. N., Brook, R. H., Kambert, C. J. *et al.*, 'Use of Medical Care in the RAND Health Insurance Experiment: Diagnosis and Service-Specific Analyses of a Randomized Controlled Trial', (1986) 25 (Supp.) *Medical Care* 531.

Luft, H. S., *Health Maintenance Organization: Dimensions of Performance* (New York: John Wiley and Sons, 1981).

— 'Medicare and Managed Care', (1998) 19 *Ann. Rev. Public Health* 459.

Makar, S. D., 'The Essential Facility Doctrine and the Health Care Industry', (1994) 21(3) *Florida State University Law Review* 913.

Managed Care On-Line, Inc., 'Managed Care Facts and Figures: Medicare HMO Enrollment by State'. Online. Available HTTP: http://www.mcol.com/mcfact3.htm (accessed 28 March 1999).

Manning, W. G. *et al.*, 'A Controlled Trial of the Effect of a Prepaid Group Practice on Use of Services', (1984) 310(23) *New Eng. J. of Med.* 1505.

Marmor, T. R., *Understanding Health Care Reform* (New Haven: Yale University Press, 1994).

Martin, J. A. and Bjerknes, L. K., 'The Legal and Ethical Implications of Gag Clauses in Physician Contracts', (1996) 22(4) *American J. of Law and Medicine* 433.

Mechanic, D., 'Managed Care: Rhetoric and Realities', (1994) 31(2) *Inquiry* 124.

— *Inescapable Decisions: The Imperatives of Health Reform* (New Brunswick: Transaction Publishers, 1994).

Mercer/Foster Higgins, *National Survey of Employer-Sponsored Health Plans* (New York: William M. Mercer, Inc., 1997).

Miller, R. H., 'Health System Integration: A Means to an End', (1996) 15(2) *Health Affairs* 92.

Miller, R. and Luft, H., 'Managed Care Plan Performance Since 1980: A Literature Analysis', (1994) 271(19) *JAMA* 1512.

Mitchell, J. M. and Scott, E., 'Physician Ownership of Physical Therapy Services: Effects on Charges, Utilization, Profits, and Service Characteristics', (1992) 268 *JAMA* 2055.

Mitchell, J. M. and Sunshine, J. H., 'Consequences of Physicians' Ownership of Health Care Facilities: Joint Ventures in Radiation Therapy', (1992) 327 *New Eng. J. Med.* 1497.

Morrisey, M. A. *et al.*, 'Managed Care and Physician/Hospital Integration', (1996) 15(4) *Health Affairs* 62.

Mullan, F., Rivo, M. L. and Politzer, R. M., 'Doctors, Dollars, and Determination: Making Physician Work-Force Policy', (1993) (Supp.) 12 *Health Affairs* 138.

Nelson, L., Brown, R., Gold, M., Ciemnecki, A. and Docteur, E., 'Trends: Access to Care in Medicare HMOs, 1996', (1997) 16(2) *Health Affairs* 148.

Newhouse, J. P., 'Patients at Risk: Health Reform and Risk Adjustment', (1994) 1(1) *Health Affairs* 132.

Newhouse, J. P. and The Insurance Experiment Group, *Free For All? Lessons From The RAND Health Insurance Experiment*, (Cambridge, MA: Harvard University Press, 1994).

Newhouse, J. P., Manning, W. G. and Morris, C. M., 'Some Interim Results from a Controlled Trial of Cost Sharing in Health Insurance', (1981) 305 *New Eng. J. of Med.* 1501.

Newhouse, J. P. *et al.*, 'Adjusting Capitation Rates Using Objective Health Measures and Prior Utilization', (Spring 1989) *Health Care Financing Review* 41.

Organization of Economic Cooperation and Development, *US Health Care at the Crossroads* (Paris: OECD, 1992).

Orentlicher, D., 'Health Care Reform and the Patient-Physician Relationship', (1995) 5 *Health Matrix* 141.

— 'Paying Physicians More to Do Less: Financial Incentives to Limit Care', (1996) 30 *Univ. of Richmond Law Rev.* 155.

Pauly, M. V., 'A Primer on Competition in Medical Markets', in H. E. Frech III (ed.), *Health Care in America: The Political Economy of Hospitals and Health Insurance* (San Francisco: Pacific Research Institute For Public Policy, 1988).

Physicians for a National Health Program, 'Number of Americans without Health Insurance Jumps to 43.2 Million', press release. Online. Available HTTP: http://www.pnhp.org/press998.html (accessed 17 March 1999).

Raffel, M. W. and Raffel, N. K., *The US Health System: Origins and Functions* (4th ed.) (New York: Delmar Publishers, 1994).

Reinhardt, U. E., 'Reorganizing the Financial Flows in American Health Care', (1993) (Supp.) 12 *Health Affairs* 172.

— 'Publications and Reports: Health Reform, Lineage of Managed Competition', (1994) 13(2) *Health Affairs* 290.

— 'Health System Change: Skirmish or Revolution?', (1996) 15(4) *Health Affairs* 114.

Rivlin, A. M. *et al.*, 'Financing, Estimation, and Economic Effects', (Spring 1994) 1 *Health Affairs* 30.

Robinson, J. C., 'Health Care Purchasing and Market Changes in California', (1995) 14(4) *Health Affairs* 117.

Rodwin, M. A., *Medicine, Money and Morals: Physicians' Conflicts of Interest* (New York: Oxford University Press, 1993).

Rothman, D. J., 'A Century of Failure: Health Care Reform in America', (1993) 18 *J. of Health Polit. Policy Law* 271.

Rubin, R. N. and Mendelson, D. N., *Estimating the Costs of Defensive Medicine* (Fairfax, VA: Lewin–VHI, 1993).

Rublee, D. A., 'Medical Technology in Canada, Germany, and the United States: An Update', (1994) 13(4) *Health Affairs* 113.

Sage, W. M., '"Health Law 2000": The Legal System and the Changing Health Care Market', (1996) 15(3) *Health Affairs* 9.

Schlesinger, M. and Mechanic, D., 'Challenges for Managed Competition from Chronic Illness', (1993) 12 *Health Affairs* 123.

Schroder, S. A., 'Training an Appropriate Mix of Physicians to Meet the Nation's Needs', (1993) 68 *Acad. Med.* 118.

Schroeder, S. A. and Sandy, L. G., 'Specialty Distribution of US Physicians: The Invisible Driver of Health Care Costs', (1993) 328(13) *New Eng. J. of Med.* 961.

Scott, L., 'Communities Ask, "What's in it for us?"' (6 January 1997) *Modern Healthcare* 39.

Sheils, J. F. and Lewin, L. S., 'An Alternative Estimate: No, Pain, No Gain', (Spring 1994) 13(1) *Health Affairs* 50.

Shonick, W., *Government and Health Services: Government's Role in the Development of US Health Services 1930–1980* (New York: Oxford University Press, 1995).

Shultze, C. L., *The Public Use of Private Interest* (Washington, DC: The Brookings Institution, 1977).

Sisk, J. E. *et al.*, 'Evaluation of Medicaid Managed Care: Satisfactory Access and Use', (1996) 276(1) JAMA 50.

Sloan, F. A. and Becker, E. R., 'Cross-Subsidies and Payment for Hospital Care', (1984) 8 *J. Health Polit. Policy Law* 660.

Sloan, F. A., Blumstein, J. F. and Perrin, J. M. (eds), *Cost, Quality, and Access in Health Care: New Roles for Health Planning in a Competitive Environment* (San Francisco: Jossey–Bass, 1988) 70.

Smith, S. *et al.*, 'The Next Ten Years of Health Spending: What Does the Future Hold?', (1998) 17(5) *Health Affairs* 128.

Starr, P., *The Social Transformation of American Medicine* (New York: Basic Books, 1982).

Steinmo, S. and Watts, J., 'It's the Institutions, Stupid! Why Comprehensive National Health Insurance Always Fails in America', (1995) 20(2) *J. Health Polit. Policy Law* 329.

Swedlow, A., Johnson, G., Smithline, N. and Milstein, A., 'Increased Costs and Rates of Use in the California Workers' Compensation System as a Result of Self-Referral by Physicians', (1992) 327 *New Eng. J. Med.* 1502.

Thomson, R. B., 'Review: Competition among Hospitals in the United States', (1994) 27(3) *Health Policy* 205.

Thorpe, K. E., 'Incremental Approaches to Covering Uninsured Children: Design and Policy Issue', (1997) 16(4) *Health Affairs* 64.

Todd, J. S., 'Reform of the Health Care System and Professional Liability', (1993) 429(13) *New Eng. J. of Med.* 1733.

UK *New NHS: Modern, Dependable*, a White Paper, Cm 3807 (8 December 1997). Online. Available HTTP: http://www.official-documents.co.uk/document/doh/newnhs/newnhs.htm (accessed 15 March 1999) (London: Department of Health).

United States General Accounting Office, 'General Insurance Standards: New Federal Law Creates Challenges for Consumers, Insurers, Regulators' (report to the Chairman, Committee on Labor and Human Resources, US Senate, February, 1998.) Online. Available HTTP: http://hippo.findlaw.com/healthins.html (accessed 28 March 1999).

Wallack, S. S. *et al.*, 'A Plan for Rewarding Efficient HMOs', (1988) 7(3) *Health Affairs* 80.

Weiner, J. P., 'Forecasting the Effects of Health Reform on US Physician Work-Force Requirement: Evidence from HMO Staffing Patterns', (1994) 272 *JAMA* 222.

Weisbrod, B., 'The Health Care Quadrilemma: An Essay on Technological Change, Insurance, Quality of Care, and Cost Containment', (1991) 29(2) *J. of Econ. Lit.* 523.

Welch, W. P., Verrilli, D., Katz, S. J. and Latimer, E., 'A Detailed Comparison of Physician Services for the Elderly in the United States and Canada' (working paper of The Urban Institute, Washington, DC, October 1995).

White, J., *Competing Solutions: American Health Care Prospects and International Experience* (Washington, DC: Brookings Institution, 1995).

—— 'Which "Managed Care" For Medicare?', (1997) 16(5) *Health Affairs* 73.

White House Domestic Policy Council, *The Clinton Blueprint: The President's Health Security Plan, The Complete Draft Report of the White House Domestic Policy Council* (New York: Times Books, 1993).

Wing, K. R., 'American Health Policy in the 1980s', (1985-86) 36(4) *Case Western Reserve Law Review* 608.

Wholey, D., Feldman, R. and Christianson, J. B., 'The Effect of Market Structure on HMO Premiums', (1995) 14(1) *J. of Health Econ.* 81.

Woolhandler, S. and Himmelstein, D. U., 'The Deteriorating Administrative Efficiency of the US Health Care System', (1991) 324(18) *New Eng. J. of Med.* 1253 .

— 'Correction: The Deteriorating Administrative Efficiency of the US Health Care System', (1994) 331(5) *New Eng. J. of Med.* 336.

— 'Annotation: Patients on the Auction Block', (1996) 86(12) *American J. of Public Health* 1699.

Yao, D. A., Rirordan, M. H. and Dahdouh, T. N., 'Antitrust and Managed Competition for Health Care', (1994) 39(2) *Antitrust Bulletin* 301.

Zelman, W. A., 'The Rationale behind the Clinton Health Care Reform Plan', (1994) 1 *Health Affairs* 9.

Zwanziger, J. and Melnick, G. A., 'Can Managed Care Plans Cost?', (1996) 15(2) *Health Affairs* 185.

Index